PUBLIC SPEAKING IN A FREE SOCIETY

PUBLIC SPEAKING IN A FREE SOCIETY

Thomas L. Tedford
The University of North Carolina at Greensboro

McGraw-Hill, Inc.

New York St. Louis San Francisco Auckland Bogotá Caracas Hamburg
Lisbon London Madrid Mexico Milan Montreal New Delhi Paris
San Juan São Paulo Singapore Sydney Tokyo Toronto

This book was set in Times Roman by the College Composition Unit
in cooperation with General Graphic Services, Inc.
The editors were Hilary Jackson and Fred H. Burns;
the interior design was done by Nicholas Krenitsky;
the cover was designed by Leon Bolognese;
the production supervisor was Louise Karam.
Arcata Graphics/Halliday was printer and binder.

Grateful acknowledgment is made for the following materials:

Chapter 3: *SCA Free Speech Credo*—Used with permission of the Speech Communication Assocation.

Chapter 7: ''The Day Care Dilemma'' by Elinor F. Vaughan Bridges; ''Real Estate Salespeople'' by Betsy Brown.

Chapter 11: ''Abolish the Blue Law'' by Douglas Wentz; ''The Equal Rights Amendment'' by Betsy Brown; ''Three Services of the Humane Society of Guilford County'' by Angelia Moon Snypes; ''The Noah Principle and the Public Sector'' by D. Wayne Calloway—Used with permission of Vital Speeches of the Day.

Chapter 12: ''I Have a Dream'' by Martin Luther King, Jr.—Reprinted by permission of Joan Daves. Copyright © 1963 by Martin Luther King, Jr.

Appendix II: ''Now You See It, Now You Don't'' by Rob Craig; Speech on ''Campus Crime'' by Susan Minelli, from *Winning Orations*, 1988, pp. 31–34—Used with the permission of the Interstate Oratorical Association.

Appendix III: ''Donate Blood'' by Chris O'Keefe, from *Winning Orations*, 1987, pp. 110–113—Used with the permission of the interstate Oratorical Association; ''I Have a Dream'' by Martin Luther King, Jr.—Reprinted by permission of Joan Daves. Copyright © 1963 by Martin Luther King, Jr.; ''Democratic Convention Keynote Address'' by Barbara C. Jordan—Used with permission of Vital Speeches of the Day; ''Dust'' by Theresa Beuscher from *1987 Championship Debates and Speeches*, pp. 142–148—Used with permission of the American Forensic Association.

Chapter Opening Photo Credits

Chapter 1: Les Stone/Impact Visuals; **Chapter 2:** Susan Lapides/Design Conceptions; **Chapter 3:** The Bettmann Archive; **Chapter 4:** Jean-Claude Lejeune; **Chapter 5:** Jim Harrison/Stock, Boston; **Chapter 6:** Marilyn Humphries/Impact Visuals; **Chapter 7:** Addison Geary/Stock, Boston; **Chapter 8:** Jean-Claude Lejeune; **Chapter 9:** Jean-Claude Lejeune; **Chapter 10:** Steve Payne; **Chapter 11:** UPI/Bettmann Newsphotos; **Chapter 12:** Janice Fullman/The Picture Cube; **Chapter 13:** UPI/Bettmann Newsphotos; **Chapter 14:** Joel Gordon; **Chapter 15:** UPI/Bettmann Newsphotos; **Chapter 16:** Lionel Delevigne/Stock, Boston; **Chapter 17:** Susan Lapides/Design Conceptions.

Public Speaking in a Free Society

2 3 4 5 6 7 8 9 0 HAL HAL 9 5 4 3 2 1

ISBN 0-07-063388-6

Library of Congress Cataloging-in-Publication Data

Tedford, Thomas L.
    Public speaking in a free society / Thomas L. Tedford.
        p.   cm.
    Includes index.
    ISBN 0-07-063388-6
    1. Public speaking.   I. Title.
PN4121.T39   1991
    808.5'1—dc20   90-45071

About the Author

THOMAS L. TEDFORD is professor of communication and theater at the University of North Carolina at Greensboro where he teaches courses in basic public speaking, advanced public speaking, rhetoric in Western culture, semantics, freedom of speech, and communication ethics. His Ph.D. in speech communication is from Louisiana State University, where his major area of study was rhetoric and public address. Professor Tedford is active in the work of the Speech Communication Association, with special interests in the commissions and interest groups that are concerned with public address, freedom of speech, and communication ethics. He is the author of *Freedom of Speech in the United States* (Random House, 1985), and, with John J. Makay and David L. Jamison, edited *Perspectives on Freedom of Speech: Selected Essays from the Journals of the Speech Communication Association* (Southern Illinois University Press, 1987). In addition, his articles have been published in *Communication Education,* the *Free Speech Yearbook,* and the *English Journal.*

I am pleased to dedicate this book to my teacher—Waldo W. Braden, Emeritus Professor of Speech, Louisiana State University

Contents

Chapter 9
INTRODUCING OUTLINING:
THREE PRACTICAL CONCEPTS 151

Chapter 10
ORGANIZING AND OUTLINING THE BODY
OF THE SPEECH 171

Chapter 11
INTRODUCTIONS, CONCLUSIONS, AND TRANSITIONS   197

PART THREE
Speech Presentation

Chapter 12
LANGUAGE IN PUBLIC SPEAKING   219

Chapter 13
DELIVERING THE SPEECH   235

PART FOUR
Types and Forms of Public Speaking

Chapter 14
SPEAKING TO INFORM   255

Chapter 17
SPECIAL FORMS AND OCCASIONS   321

Appendix I
SPEECH CRITICISM: ANALYZING AND EVALUATING
PUBLIC SPEECHES   335

Appendix II
EXTEMPORANEOUS SPEAKING: MODEL OUTLINES, NOTE
CARDS, AND SPEECHES   349

Appendix III
SPEECHES FOR STUDY AND DISCUSSION   364

Preface

Public Speaking in a Free Society is a text for the college-level course in public speaking. While writing the book I have been guided by three principles that I believe are of vital importance to public speaking in a free society. The first is that the speaker should be a critical thinker who is informed about and holds genuine convictions on the subjects about which he or she speaks. Secondly, both the effectiveness and quality of public speaking are greatly enhanced by a thorough understanding of rhetorical theory. And thirdly, public speakers in a free society should understand and appreciate democratic values, including respect for persons, and should demonstrate their commitment to these values by speaking thoughtfully and honestly. I have tried to help the public speaking student understand and apply these principles by writing a book that urges speakers to think before they speak, to apply sound rhetorical theory to their speech preparation and delivery, and to be sincere and ethical when they speak.

Beginning with the survey of our rhetorical heritage in Chapter 1, the student is urged to think critically before speaking. This theme is sustained throughout the book, for the student is encouraged to choose significant speech topics, to research them well, to apply rigorous logical tests to reasoning and evidence, and to respect the intellectual capacities of the members of the audience. Rhetorical theory is presented as a valuable intellectual discipline worth mastering because it teaches us the art of practical reasoning as well as how to communicate that reasoning effectively to others. Furthermore, the importance of exercising our communication freedoms in a responsible way is presented in specific terms in Chapter 3, and that theme is continued throughout the book. For instance, the student is reminded of relevant issues of communication ethics in the chapters on audience analysis, subject choice, supporting materials, outlining, language, and persuasion. Also, communication ethics is an important part of the essay on speech criticism presented in Appendix I. Let us now look at the special features of the book in more detail.

FEATURES OF THE BOOK

Rhetorical Theory. Chapter 1 consists of a brief history of rhetorical theory in the West. The chapter not only summarizes important developments in the study of rhetoric, but also explains that democracy requires rhetoric for the discussion of public issues. Also, it points out that freedom of expression is needed to permit rhetoric to serve the democratic society. After studying this chapter, the student should have an improved understanding of our rhetorical heritage, as well as an enhanced appreciation for the important place of public speaking in a free society. The principle that rhetorical theory is valuable both to the public speaker and to society at large is emphasized throughout the text.

Communication Freedom and Responsibility. Chapter 3 presents the basic values of a democracy that provide the foundation for free and responsible speaking. The chapter then summarizes the practice of free speech in the United States with a focus on the public speaking situation. Legal limits on free speech are explained and illustrated from landmark decisions of the United States Supreme Court. In addition, the responsible use of free speech is discussed, with specific standards of communication ethics set out for student consideration. Throughout the book, the student is reminded that he or she should think before speaking, believe in what is being said, and support claims with good evidence.

Speech Organization. Chapters 9, 10, and 11 present a detailed discussion of speech organization. Chapter 9 introduces outlining by explaining that a speech is constructed with ''speech units''—that is, with blocks of discourse consisting of a statement and support for that statement. Examples, diagrams, and simple tests show the student how to construct a speech unit in which main points and subpoints are logically related to one another. Chapter 10 applies these principles to outlining the body of the speech. Here, the text explains that one's approach to outlining varies, depending on whether the general purpose of the speech is to inform (in which the points serve to clarify) or to persuade (in which the points serve to prove). This distinction provides the theoretical basis for an explanation of how organizing an informative speech differs from organizing a persuasive one—a distinction often neglected in the literature on *dispositio.* Finally, Chapter 11 concerns the organization of introductions and conclusions. Here, as in Chapter 10, the differences between informative and persuasive speaking are applied. The student is shown how to plan introductions and conclusions for both types of speeches: however, special attention is given to the challenges of effectively opening and closing the speech to persuade.

Persuasion: Theory and Practice. The book includes two unusually thorough chapters on persuasion, both of which combine traditional rhetorical theory with extensive contemporary research. Chapter 15, which focuses on theory, discusses *logos, ethos,* and *pathos* as the ''means of persuasion.'' Unique diagrams in connection with a variety of concrete examples explain forms of reasoning and how they are employed in speechmaking. This is followed by a research-based discussion of *ethos.* Various ways of communicating speaker credibility to the audience are explained. The chapter concludes with an explanation of psychological-emotional appeals, integrating traditional views on *pathos* with the contemporary views of psychologists Abraham Maslow (need theory) and Milton Rokeach (value theory). Chapter 16 applies persuasion theory to the preparation of specific types of persuasive speeches. As in Chapter 15, traditional theory is supplemented with extensive contemporary research.

Both chapters stress the importance of having a logical foundation for persuasive speeches of all types, even those that make considerable use of emotional appeals.

Speech Criticism. An essay on speech criticism is presented in Appendix I. After discussing the basic principles of speech criticism in terms easily grasped by the student, the essay explains how to apply the principles to classroom speeches and to speeches heard in society at large. The essay is designed not only to help the student improve his or her own speaking, but also to become a better consumer of the messages received from others—especially those that are communicated via public speaking.

PLAN OF THE BOOK

The book is organized according to a fairly traditional plan that moves logically from general historical and philosophical considerations to specific points of rhetorical theory and practice. With the possible exception of Chapters 9 and 10 on speech organization and outlining, which should be studied as a unit, each chapter is self-contained, making it easy to adapt the materials to a variety of course plans and syllabuses.

Part One, Speaking and Listening in a Democratic Society, introduces the student to the history of rhetorical theory, emphasizing the relationship of democracy to free speech and public speaking. Chapter 1 surveys rhetorical theory from the Greeks to the present day. Chapter 2 explains the fundamentals of speech preparation and delivery (including attention to stagefright) so that student speechmaking can begin while the remaining introductory chapters are read and discussed. Chapter 3 discusses the application of the First Amendment of the U.S. Constitution to public speaking, and discusses standards of communication ethics. Chapter 4 rounds off Part I of the text by explaining the communication process and the principles of effective listening. The sum of Part I is to present the student with an overview of the public speaking process that provides a unified foundation for the remainder of the text. This unity is grounded in tradition as supplemented by contemporary research, tied to a communication model that stresses speaker–audience interaction and critical thinking and listening, and related to a societal context that stresses speaker responsibility.

Part Two, Speech Preparation, covers the process of invention. Chapter 5 concerns how to analyze the audience and the occasion. Chapter 6 is about how to choose and narrow a subject, and how to determine the speech purpose. Chapter 7 explains and illustrates different types of speech supports (including visual aids), and Chapter 8 is a discussion of how to conduct research for public speaking.

Chapters 9, 10, and 11 are about speech organization. Chapter 9 introduces outlining by explaining the speech unit, the types of relationships points have to each other within the unit (superior, subordinate, and coordinate), and how to check the logic of those relationships. Also, this chapter provides the student with a logical answer to the question, "If I have one subpoint, must I have two?" Chapter 10 explains how to outline the body of the speech, and Chapter 11 discusses the planning of introductions, conclusions, and transitions. Standard form in outlining is presented, and a complete model outline appears at the end of Chapter 10.

Part Three, Speech Presentation, concerns language and delivery. Chapter 12 addresses both the semantic and stylistic functions of language. The material on semantics discusses the communication of meaning, and the material on style explains that language in public speaking should be appropriate, clear, and vivid. Chapter 13 is devoted to delivery. It covers the various types of speech presentation (with an emphasis on extemporaneous delivery), voice and diction, and what contemporary research tells us about nonverbal elements such as visual directness and bodily movement during speechmaking.

Part Four, Types and Forms of Public Speaking, focuses on specific kinds of speeches. Chapter 14 concerns informative speaking, setting out an approach to expository rhetoric that is easy to understand and apply, yet is grounded in modern research. Chapter 15 is a research-based presentation of persuasion theory utilizing Aristotle's three means of persuasion: logical argument, speaker credibility, and psychological appeals. Chapter 16 applies the theory presented earlier in the text, including that from Chapter 15, to specific types of persuasive speeches. Chapter 17, the final chapter, concerns special types and forms of speaking, such as speeches of inspiration, good will, courtesy, and entertainment.

Three appendices complete the book. Appendix I is an essay on speech criticism, Appendix II includes model outlines, note cards, and two student speeches, and Appendix III publishes the complete texts of four great speeches from American history, as well as two additional student speeches.

RESOURCES FOR TEACHING AND LEARNING

To facilitate student understanding, the text is carefully organized, and the content is presented in a clear, readable style. Each chapter begins with an outline of chapter content and concludes with a thorough summary of important points. Internal summaries are provided as needed, and key terms are carefully defined. Important rhetorical principles are generously illustrated with specific examples from student speeches and from great speeches of American history. Also, a number of instructional charts and diagrams are used, including several that are unique to this text.

In addition, there are a number of specific instructional and learning resources available to the teacher and the student. The instructor's manual for *Public Speaking in a Free Society* contains course outlines, suggested speaking assignments, critique sheets, exercises, and readings that will help the instructor in planning and teaching the course. Each chapter of the text concludes with several practical exercises and a list of recommended readings (annotated). The exercises, which can be either assigned by the instructor or done independently by the student, are designed to help the student explore important rhetorical principles.

Appendix II serves as a unified, central source of information on outlines, note cards, and model student speeches for the entire text. Rather than scatter these instructional materials throughout the book, most of the models are brought together in this appendix for ease in location and use. Any time the student wishes to check on outline form or note card preparation, or read a model student speech with commentary, a quick turn to Appendix II will do the job. Here the student will find two model student speeches, one to inform and another to persuade. Each is complete with a sentence outline and a set of note cards such as one might use for extemporaneous speaking.

Appendix III completes the special resources by publishing the complete texts of four great speeches from American history, each of which sets high rhetorical standards for the student speaker. Also, there are two additional model student speeches in this appendix.

ACKNOWLEDGMENTS

I am indebted to many individuals for their encouragement and help with this project. In particular, I am grateful to those who reviewed the manuscript and offered their comments and suggestions along the way. Their ideas and insights were invaluable. These reviewers were: David W. Addington, Georgia Southern College; Phil Backlund, Central Washington University; Bernard K. Duffy, California Polytechnic State University; Susan Duffy, California Polytechnic State University; L. Dean Fadely, University of North Carolina at Greensboro; Janet L. Fallon, Marymount University; Robert H. Fogg, Millersville University; Thurmon Garner, University of Georgia; Kathleen German, Miami University; Nola J. Heidlebaugh, State University of New York at Oswego; Catherine Hischak, State University of New York at Cortland; Sandra W. Holt, Tennessee State University; Richard W. Massa, Missouri Southern State College; Daniel J. O'Neill, Youngstown State University; Robert E. Pruett, Wright State University; and Steven A. Ward, University of Portland. Also, a special word of appreciation goes to Don Smith of the University of New Hampshire for class-testing Chapter 1 on the history of rhetoric, and Chapter 3 on democratic values, free speech, and ethics.

I would also like to express my appreciation to the several public speaking students at the University of North Carolina at Greensboro who gave me permission to quote from their speeches; to Larry Schnoor, Executive Director of the Interstate Oratorical Association, for permission to reprint student speeches from *Winning Orations*; and to James Pratt, Secretary of the American Forensic Association, for permission to reprint a student speech from *Championship Debates and Speeches*.

I am grateful for the encouragement and cooperation of my colleagues in the Division of Communication Studies, Department of Communication and Theatre, University of North Carolina at Greensboro, during the writing of the book. In particular, I want to thank Ethel Glenn, Director of the Division of Communication Studies, for adjusting my teaching schedules so that I would have the time to conduct research and write the manuscript. Also, I am indebted to Nancy Fogarty, Mark Schumacher, and other members of the staff of the Reference Department of the Jackson Library, University of North Carolina at Greensboro, for their assistance in preparing Chapter 8 on research.

I would like to thank Kathleen Domenig, Roth Wilkofsky, Hilary Jackson, and Fred Burns, all of McGraw-Hill, Inc., for their encouragement, advice, and assistance on the many details that attend the publication of a textbook. In particular, I want to express my gratitude to Kathleen Domenig who has worked with me on the project from the beginning. Her talents in manuscript development are marked by both wisdom and patience, and her supervision of the project has been, in a word, *superb*.

Finally, I owe a special debt to my wife, Ann, whose unfailing support for the project, and whose help in protecting my daily "writing time," made the work on the book a pleasant and rewarding activity.

Thomas L. Tedford

PUBLIC SPEAKING IN A FREE SOCIETY

PART I

Speaking and Listening in a Democratic Society

> *...a free republic...bestows*
> *importance upon the powers of*
> *eloquence, to every class and*
> *description of citizens....Our*
> *institutions...are republican. Their*
> *vital principle is liberty. Persuasion, or*
> *the influence of reason and of feeling,*
> *is the great if not the only instrument,*
> *whose operation can affect the acts of*
> *all our corporate bodies; of towns,*
> *cities, counties, states, and of the*
> *whole confederated empire.*

—John Quincy Adams,
Lectures on Rhetoric and Oratory (1810)[1]

Chapter 1

THE STUDY OF PUBLIC SPEAKING IN A DEMOCRACY

*T*his is a book about public speaking—your public speaking. It tells you how to improve your methods of speech preparation, and how to deliver a speech effectively to your public speaking class, a campus organization, a gathering of political activists, or a business or professional group. In addition, this book is about the free society in which you live, and in which you practice the art of public address. It discusses why a democratic society such as ours needs responsible, articulate citizens who are willing—indeed, *anxious*—to express their opinions, and it emphasizes the importance of communication freedom to the process of self-government.

No doubt you come to the course in public speaking with personal goals in mind; perhaps these include the ability to speak with clarity, with conviction, and with confidence. You may want to improve your capacity to think an issue through before you speak on it, and, like most students of public address, you want to learn how to be persuasive. In a free society, however, these personal goals cannot be separated from the broader challenge of participating in the discussions and debates so essential to a democracy.

Let us suppose for a moment that a speaker has an important message to deliver. The speech is well-organized, the reasoning is sound, and the evidence is convincing. However, the country in which this speaker lives has an authoritarian government that refuses to permit delivery of the speech. No auditorium can be rented, no public gathering of listeners can be assembled, and the channels of broadcasting are denied to this would-be communicator—and to other speakers as well—unless the content of each speech is first approved by the government. In addition, the government threatens speakers with punishment if they express opinions at variance with the official view of the state. Obviously, there would be little need for citizens of such a society to become talented communicators, for to speak freely would be dangerous.

On the other hand, our society places a premium upon one's ability to communicate effectively. Our schools offer courses in speaking and writing, and our parents, teachers, and friends encourage us to become articulate in our public statements. Something is present here that is significantly absent from the undemocratic state. Somewhere within the democratic system, and within the values that sustain that system, something creates a need for effective public speech. There are, in other words, some fundamental reasons for the study of public speaking in a free society.

What are those reasons? Why does our society encourage us to improve our speaking skills? Why does your college or university offer courses in the art of effective public speech? In this chapter we will search for answers to these questions by turning to the history of Western democracy. First, we will examine public speaking and its relationship to free speech and self-government in the democratic periods of classical Greece and Rome, then we will look at the relationship of public speaking to the development of democracy in England, and in the United States.

I. Public Speaking in the Classical Democracies

The Greeks, who invented Western-style democracy, also gave us the study of communication (with an emphasis on public speaking), freedom of speech, and a concern for high standards of ethics in public discourse. The Romans, during the time of the democratic Republic, also practiced freedom of speech, refined and improved Greek theories of public speaking, and stressed ethical standards in public communication. This remarkable combination in Athens and Rome was no accident, for democratic systems depend on informative and persuasive expression for the institutions of society to work. The institutions of democracy that depend upon talk include government, of course, but they also include others such as the educational, religious, artistic, and commercial sectors of society. Let us look first at the Greeks.

Greece

The Athenians formulated the first organized system of communication theory in the West. They called this system *rhetoric*, by which they meant the art of practical public communication—persuasive speaking in particular. *By persuasive speaking they meant speeches planned to modify the beliefs and actions of listeners in ways intended by the speaker.* Examples included speeches to members of a jury (''vote for my side of the case''), to an audience of legislators in an assembly (''my proposal is the best solution to the problem''), or to a group of citizens gathered for some event (where any number of topics and viewpoints could be addressed). To the Greeks and Romans, the term ''rhetoric'' was a positive word that described the serious study of how to speak effectively and responsibly on genuine issues of the day. The term certainly did not mean ''hot air'' or ''empty phrases,'' as some contemporary misuses of the word suggest.

The teaching of public speaking originated in the fifth century B.C. in the Greek colony of Syracuse, on the island of Sicily, when a dictatorship was replaced by a democracy. Here, and time and time again in history, *democracy created a demand for free speech, and both democracy and free speech found rhetoric essential.*

Following the overthrow of the tyrant Thrasybulus, the citizens of Sicily turned to the courts to recover property that had been unjustly taken from them. Corax, a Sicilian Greek, observed that some citizens were more effective than others in pleading their cases. To assist those who needed help in speaking before the court (each citizen had to speak for himself, there being no attorneys), Corax wrote a practical manual on persuasive speaking; then he and his pupil Tisias taught the principles of this manual to others.

Corax observed that effective speaking usually consisted of three parts: an introduction, in which the speaker sought to gain attention and a friendly hearing from the judges; a discussion (or ''narrative'') that set out the arguments of the case; and a conclusion that summarized the key arguments, then urged a just verdict. Thus, in a situation similar to that faced by an attorney in a modern courtroom, was born the art of teaching and learning how to speak before an audience.

6

———

*Part I
Speaking
and Listening
in a
Democratic
Society*

Tradition has it that Tisias, the pupil of Corax, journeyed to Athens where he taught public speaking to the citizens. Whether the story of Tisias is accurate or not we cannot be sure; however, we do know that about this time (450–350 B.C.) the study of rhetoric received serious attention in Athens. Having developed a system of democracy that depended on ordinary people to serve as legislators, judges, and public administrators, Athenians learned that they needed to be able to speak in public to make their system work.

One of the most important teachers of public speaking in Athens was Aristotle, whose *Rhetoric*, written about 330 B.C., is the first complete text on public speaking in the West. Because so much of the *Rhetoric* has proved accurate and useful in practice over the centuries, it is without question the single most influential work on public speaking ever written. In it, Aristotle defines rhetoric as "the faculty of discovering in the particular case what are the available means of persuasion."[2] In modern terms, we can say that Aristotle viewed rhetoric as the study of how a speaker can skillfully analyze a specific audience and occasion in order to determine the most effective means of persuasion.

Having put the audience at the center of his theory of communication, Aristotle identified three means of persuasion, or "proofs," that a speaker could employ in preparing and presenting a speech. Note how practical they are, even for today's public communicator.

Logical proof (logos), consisting of reasoning, and evidence in support of that reasoning.

Emotional proof (pathos), consisting of psychological appeals that are not necessarily logical, but that are often essential to the motivation of belief and action in humans. Aristotle said that these include appeals to emotions such as fear, anger, love, hatred, and pity.

Ethical proof (ethos), meaning the credibility of the speaker as perceived by the members of the audience. Aristotle observed, quite correctly, that we are more easily influenced by a person whom we like, respect, and trust than by one who arouses our suspicions or our hostility. He said, therefore, that speakers should demonstrate to the audience that they possess three characteristics (the components of *ethos*): friendliness and sincerity; intelligence and knowledge of the subject; and good moral character.

Aristotle's teachings concerning communication were influential in Rome, and later in England and America. Indeed, the *Rhetoric* is still an important source of ideas for the theory and practice of public speaking, and many of its concepts are included in this text.

Rome

When the Athenian empire came to an end in 404 B.C., the Classical world turned to the growing authority of Rome. Although the Romans were not as democratic as the Athenians, they did develop a form of self-government that demanded a high degree of freedom of speech and education in the art of speaking. During the time of the Roman Republic, senators debated freely and voted on issues of public policy. In addition, Roman citizens serving in the assembly listened to speeches on social and political topics before casting their votes.

Romans who were active in public life worked to improve their oratorical skills by studying handbooks on the art of oratory. Two writers of speech texts during the time of the Republic are of major importance: the unknown author of the *Rhetorica ad Herennium*, and the statesman Cicero, who wrote several books on public speaking. Later, during the formative years of the Empire, a third writer, Quintilian, emerged as an influential teacher of rhetoric to the ruling families of Rome.

The *Rhetorica ad Herennium* (Latin meaning the "handbook on public speaking found at Herennium") was composed about 90 B.C. This brief manual is the earliest known Roman text on rhetoric. Written in practical, undecorated language, it has exerted a strong influence on the study of oral and written communication in the West. The book divides the study of public speaking into five topical areas (sometimes called *canons*), the first four of which continue to be significant to the study of public address in modern times. The five canons are as follows:

Inventio (invention, meaning "discovery"). Invention is the art of finding speech content, especially the proofs that will be effective in persuading an audience to accept your point of view. It is what you do when you research your subject, think it through, find and evaluate evidence, test your reasoning, and adapt to your audience by choosing those proofs that will be effective and omitting those that will not help you achieve your purpose. By invention you decide what to include in a speech, what to leave out, and *why*.

Dispositio (disposition, meaning "organization"). Disposition is the art of organizing the content of the speech so that it will be clear and persuasive to the audience. This process includes not only the general arrangement into introduction, statement of purpose, body, and conclusion, but also the internal ordering of arguments and evidence for maximum effectiveness with the audience.

Elocutio (style, meaning "language"). Style is the art of expressing the ideas of your speech in clear, moving language that is fitting to the speaker, the listeners, and the occasion. Among the characteristics of language that you might consider as you work on a speech, and as you deliver it, are clarity, appropriateness, and impressiveness (moving listeners to belief and action).

Pronuntiatio (pronunciation, meaning "delivery"). Delivery is the art of using the voice and body to present your ideas effectively to the audience. Skillful delivery is of critical importance to effective public speaking, for without it the impact of speech content—no matter how logical—is greatly weakened.

Memoria (memory, meaning "memorization"). The art of *memoria*, which covers memorization of speech materials and the recall of appropriate materials while speaking, is often called the "lost canon of rhetoric" because it has not survived to modern times. However, it was taught to the Romans as a part of the orator's overall mastery of speaking skills. One reason that memory is no longer a significant part of the speech curriculum is that there is simply too much information available today for speakers to commit all or most of it to memory. In ancient times, however, knowledge was limited, making it possible for speakers to memorize most of what they needed to recall while speaking.

The second writer of significance from the Roman Period is Cicero. A famous Roman orator and statesman who lived from 106 to 43 B.C., Cicero wrote

Cicero, a Roman orator and statesman, was a significant writer on public speaking. In De Oratore, *he discussed the relationship between political freedom and the study and practice of public speaking. (Bettmann Archive)*

several books about public speaking, the major one being *De Oratore*, written about 55 B.C. In this book, Cicero recognizes that political freedom and the study and practice of persuasive speaking go together. As he puts it, the art of speaking "has constantly flourished above all others in every free state, and especially in those which have enjoyed peace and tranquility, and has ever exercised great power."[3] In addition to giving good advice on content, organization, and delivery, Cicero taught that honest, enlightened leadership was the underlying purpose of persuasive speaking in a free society, and that thorough knowledge of the liberal arts was the foundation of great speaking.

Quintilian, the third major teacher of rhetoric in Rome, lived from 35 A.D. to about 95 A.D.—during the early years of the Empire Period. In the *Institutes of Oratory*, written during the time of despotic rule by the Emperor Domitian, Quintilian describes a comprehensive plan of liberal education beginning at birth and continuing to maturity. Although freedom of speech no longer existed in Rome following the establishment of the Empire, Quintilian was aware of the freedoms of the past. His idealism fits a free society more than it does an authoritarian one.

Quintilian advocated a curriculum that varied from rhetoric to philosophy to physical education. Like Cicero, he stressed a thorough grounding in the liberal arts, believing that such an education would mold the morally upright citizen-speaker who would lead others by means of persuasion. As a contemporary student of public speaking, you should note the importance that leading teachers of the Classical Period placed upon *informed* communication. We echo these teachers today when we urge you to know your subject in depth before you speak.

When the democratic Republic collapsed and the authoritarian Empire began in 27 B.C., freedom of expression was one of the casualties. As the Caesars proceeded to punish political and social dissent, authentic persuasion faded. For the next fifteen hundred years in the West the danger persisted as voices of dissent in politics, religion, science, literature, and the arts were systematically crushed by the undemocratic regimes of Europe and England. There being little need for persuasion (the authorities had all the answers), the study of rhetorical theory languished until the seventeenth and eighteenth centuries when the Enlightenment generated the philosophical foundation for a new age of political and intellectual freedom.

II. Public Speaking in England

The fall of the Western Roman Empire in 476 A.D. marks the onset of the Middle Ages—also called the Dark Ages, a period generally dated from 476 A.D. to about 1500 A.D. Although there were advances in politics, learning, and the arts during this time, they were less dramatic than during the Renaissance that followed. By the sixteenth century, however, the soft breezes of progress of the Middle Ages were becoming the winds of change in England and on the Continent. Fueled by Johann Gutenberg's invention of movable type and his improvement of the printing press in 1450 A.D., and further stirred by discoveries in science and geography, the currents of innovation of the sixteenth and seventeenth centuries (the Renaissance) became windstorms of radical and permanent change in the eighteenth century (the Enlightenment—also called the Age of Reason).

During the Renaissance and the Enlightenment, numerous ideas concerning individual liberty, political freedom, and democratic government were proposed and debated. As libertarian views on these topics were gradually accepted in England and in the American colonies, the need for persuasive speaking on real issues of government and social policy became evident. Public speaking, that tool of self-government employed so well by the Greeks and the Romans, became important to society once again.

Among the many Englishmen who wrote and lectured about public speaking, three have exerted the strongest influence on modern rhetorical theory and practice. These are Hugh Blair, George Campbell, and Richard Whately.[4] The most popular public speaking book of eighteenth-century England, and one that was widely used in America as well, was Hugh Blair's *Lectures on Rhetoric and Belles Lettres* (1783). Blair, a minister of the Scottish Church and professor of rhetoric at the University of Edinburgh, was both a well-known preacher and an effective teacher of speech. Although he contributed few in-

10

*Part I
Speaking
and Listening
in a
Democratic
Society*

novations to public speaking theory, he was skillful at organizing useful rhetorical concepts from a variety of sources, including the classical rhetorics, and teaching the results to his students. Blair discusses speaking in three contexts—the legislative assembly, the courts, and the pulpit—all important parts of the democratic revolution underway in England at the time. In addition, he taught that speaking and writing should be polished, reflecting a style fitting an educated communicator.

Another important British teacher of rhetoric was George Campbell, a Scottish Presbyterian clergyman whose *Philosophy of Rhetoric* (1776) was used as a text in speaking and writing courses in both England and the United States well into the nineteenth century. Campbell helped to elevate evidence to an important place in the study of public speaking (strange as it might seem, the study of evidence had been neglected over the years). In addition, he made a major contribution to the study of human communication by applying the theories of the psychologists of his time to the practice of persuasion. Let us examine further this second contribution.

Campbell made a connection between the principles of rhetoric developed in the past and modern theories of science and social science. By demonstrating that the insights of social scientists—particularly psychologists—were applicable to persuasion, he became a pioneer in the move to apply science to the study of rhetoric. Indeed, Campbell's writings started a trend that endures to the present, for we base much advice to students in contemporary public speaking courses upon the views of psychologists. For example, audience analysis and attitude theory, a contribution of twentieth-century social psychology, is a vital part of modern public speaking instruction.

Richard Whately, a third influential teacher of public speaking, published his *Elements of Rhetoric* in 1828. In this book, Whately stated that he intended to emphasize *argumentative composition*, which we can define as *speaking and writing that focuses on the use of logical reasoning and evidence to persuade others*. Because of his stress on logical proof, Whately has exerted a strong influence upon the teaching of *logos* in public speaking courses, and upon the theory and practice of argumentation and debate as well.

The works of Blair, Campbell, and Whately gave direction to the teaching of speaking and writing not only in British schools but in American classrooms as well. We now turn our attention to the United States.

III. Public Speaking in the United States

American interest in public speaking is a natural development, given the democratic principles of our society. Charles J. Ingersoll, Philadelphia author and statesman, observed in 1823 that the "talent for effective oratory is...common in America...where laws are made, controversies are settled, and proselytes are gained by it every day." He added: "The legislature, the court house, and the church are thronged with auditors of both sexes, attracted by that talent which was the intense study and great power of the ancient orators."[5]

As Ingersoll noted, public address plays an important role in our society, not only for significant national events such as major political campaigns and presidential addresses, but also for average citizens in rural areas, small towns, and cities across the country. Throughout our history, and without fanfare or major headlines, ordinary people—men and women in business, members of city councils, teachers, attorneys, ministers, and others—have been speaking on issues that concerned them. As in centuries past, this speech activity so essential to a democratic society created the need to study public speaking and to practice freedom of expression.

In Colonial times, American students read from the rhetorics of Aristotle, Cicero, and Quintilian to prepare for classroom exercises involving speaking, as well as for delivering ceremonial addresses and participating in debating societies. Before long, American scholars started to lecture and write on the subject of public speaking. Building upon the classical rhetorics, and upon the works of British rhetoricians such as Blair, Campbell, and Whately, American teachers published texts designed to help young people learn to speak well, and thereby to participate effectively in the rhetorical give and take of a democratic America.

One of the first of these American teachers of public speaking was John Quincy Adams, a professor of rhetoric at Harvard who later became the sixth President of the United States (1825–1829). His *Lectures on Rhetoric and Oratory* was published in 1810. Other communication texts published by Americans during the early part of the nineteenth century included *Lectures on Moral Philosophy and Eloquence*, by John Witherspoon, President of Princeton, and *A Practical System of Rhetoric*, issued in 1827 by Samuel P. Newman.

By the beginning of the twentieth century the teaching of debate and public speaking had become a standard part of the curriculum of numerous schools. Departments of speech were being formed, and some colleges and universities even established special professorships in public address.[6] During 1914–1915, several leading teachers of speech founded the National Association of Academic Teachers of Public Speaking, known today as the Speech Communication Association (SCA is the nation's foremost professional organization for teachers of speech communication).

Like the British communication scholars, many American teachers have employed the views of psychologists to help modernize their theories of persuasive speaking. One of these was James A. Winans, a founder of the National Association of Academic Teachers of Public Speaking, whose 1915 speech text set forth a system based on the psychology of attention. Another was Charles Henry Woolbert, whose 1927 edition of *Fundamentals of Speech* adopted modern behavioral psychology as the foundation of a theory of persuasion.[7]

Since the first two decades of the twentieth century, and the innovative writings of Winans and Woolbert, the study of human communication, including public speaking, has grown tremendously in the United States. The traditional field of rhetorical studies summarized in this chapter has given birth to "communication theory"—the empirical study of human communication using the methods of social science, such as controlled observation and experimentation. Scientific studies in communication have supplemented traditional views, thereby improving our knowledge of how humans communicate; they

12

Part I
Speaking
and Listening
in a
Democratic
Society

have helped us understand not only what is "going on" during public speaking, but also how humans communicate interpersonally, in small groups, and via the mass media. In addition, numerous speech texts have been published since the 1920s for use in the hundreds of public speaking courses taught in America's secondary schools, junior colleges, and senior colleges and universities.[8]

The policy of continuing the best of the past while adding to it the best of today helps to explain the development of public speaking instruction. Whereas public speaking remains an art (not a science), it is a more exact art today than ever before—as the numerous studies cited throughout this book will testify.

This Chapter in Brief

In the history of Western culture, the Greeks are credited with the invention of democracy, rhetorical theory, and freedom of speech. These remarkable contributions should be understood as interacting ingredients of the complex process of self-government. In service to the democracy of Athens, Aristotle wrote the *Rhetoric*, the West's first complete text on public speaking. Aristotle made the audience the center of his theory of communication, observing that effective persuasion required not only the use of logical argument (*logos*), but also an understanding of human motivation (*pathos*). Furthermore, he emphasized that persuasion depended for its effectiveness on the audience's perception of the credibility of the speaker (*ethos*).

The Romans refined and organized the theories of persuasive speaking described by the Greeks, and put those theories to work on behalf of the democratic Republic. Like the Athenians, the Romans learned that skill in public speaking was necessary to self-government, and that freedom of expression was required for the operation of democratic institutions. The unknown author of the *Rhetorica ad Herennium* influenced the study of persuasion in the West by describing the canons of invention (*inventio*), organization (*dispositio*), language (*elocutio*), delivery (*pronuntiatio*), and memory (*memoria*). In addition, both Cicero and Quintilian viewed speech training as essential for providing enlightened, honest leadership to society. Both taught that speakers should have a thorough knowledge of the liberal arts in general, and of the subject of the speech in particular, before an address is delivered.

English and American rhetoricians have added new concepts about public address to those learned from the Greeks and the Romans. In the eighteenth and nineteenth centuries, British teachers of public speaking, such as George Campbell, developed theories based upon emerging principles of social science—psychology, in particular—and thereby helped lead the study of public speaking into a modern age. At about the same time, speech educators in the United States, such as John Quincy Adams and John Witherspoon, were lecturing and writing on the subject, for the establishment of a democratic system of government had made the ability to speak in public a valuable asset for all citizens.

This chapter emphasizes the view that a free society gives birth to both freedom of speech and the study and application of the principles of effective public communication (including public speaking). The three components—a free society, freedom to speak, and public communication—nourish one another. When one is missing, the others are diminished in strength and may wither and die. Furthermore, the principles of democracy that make speaking important to the institutions of government extend to other social groups and institutions as well, including those of education, religion, business, and the professions. The training that you will receive in the speech classroom will help prepare you for the wide range of speaking opportunities that you will encounter in your career and in your lifetime as a citizen of a democracy. To help you start that educational process, we turn our attention in the chapter that follows to the basics of preparing your first classroom speeches.

EXERCISES

1. Aristotle said in the *Rhetoric* that persuasive speaking had four purposes, namely, (1) to uphold truth and justice, (2) to explain complex matters to ordinary people, (3) to help us understand all sides of an issue and all arguments on that issue, and (4) to defend oneself against unjust accusations. Is this list too limited for today's complex world? What other purposes for persuasive speaking can you add to Aristotle's list?

2. Think for a few moments about the groups, organizations, and institutions on your college campus, in your local community, and in the state and nation at large. Make a list of a dozen or so. How many of those on your list could function smoothly and effectively if all informative and persuasive speaking were eliminated? Narrowing to the college campus, consider how much of your education—starting with classroom lectures and discussions—depends on some form of public address.

SELECTED READINGS

Aristotle. *The Rhetoric of Aristotle*. Trans. Lane Cooper. New York: Appleton-Century, 1932. Aristotle's *Rhetoric*, the first complete text on public speaking in the West, was written about 330 B.C. Relatively brief and rich in good advice for public speakers, it is one of the world's best books. You can read it in a weekend.

Benson, Thomas W., ed. *Speech Communication in the Twentieth Century*. Carbondale: Southern Illinois University Press, 1985. Several essays in this collection concern the development of public speaking theory and the practice of free speech. For example, see Chapter 2 on "The History of Rhetoric: The Reconstruction of Progress" by Richard L. Enos; and Chapter 11, "Freedom of Expression and the Study of Communication" by Peter E. Kane.

Benson, Thomas W., and Prosser, Michael H., eds. *Readings in Classical Rhetoric*. Boston: Allyn and Bacon, 1969. (Paperback text reprint, Hermagoras Press, 1988.) Key selections from the works of leading teachers of public speaking of the Classical Period, including Plato, Isocrates, Aristotle, Cicero, and Quintilian.

Golden, James L., and Corbett, Edward P. J., eds. *The Rhetoric of Blair, Campbell, and Whately*. New York: Holt, Rinehart and Winston, 1968. This anthology reprints the most significant portions of the communication texts of the leading English theorists. An introductory essay by the editors provides an excellent overview and summary of the influence of Blair, Campbell, and Whately upon communication educaion.

14

*Part I
Speaking
and Listening
in a
Democratic
Society*

Wallace, Karl R., ed.   *History of Speech Education in America*. New York: Appleton-Century-Crofts, 1954. A collection of essays on the development of speech education in America from the Colonial Period to modern times.

ENDNOTES

1. John Quincy Adams, *Lectures on Rhetoric and Oratory* (New York: Hilliard and Metcalf, 1810), vol. 1, pp. 50 and 71. Published in two volumes. John Quincy Adams, sixth president of the United States (1825–1829), was the son of John Adams, second president of the United States. Prior to his political career, John Quincy Adams was the first lecturer of the Boylston Chair of Rhetoric and Oratory at Harvard.
2. Aristotle, *The Rhetoric*, trans. Lane Cooper (New York: Appleton-Century, 1932), p. 7.
3. Cicero, *On Oratory and Orators*, trans. J. S. Watson, with an introduction by Ralph A. Micken (Carbondale: Southern Illinois University Press, 1970), p. 11.
4. In general, see James L. Golden and Edward P. J. Corbett, eds., *The Rhetoric of Blair, Campbell, and Whately* (New York: Holt, Rinehart and Winston, 1968).
5. Charles J. Ingersoll, "A Discourse Concerning the Influence of America on the Mind," cited in Robert T. Oliver, *History of Public Speaking in America* (Boston: Allyn and Bacon, 1965), p. xx.
6. Giles W. Gray, "Some Teachers and the Transition to Twentieth-Century Speech Education," in Karl R. Wallace, ed., *History of Speech Education in America* (New York: Appleton-Century-Crofts, 1954), p. 423.
7. The Winans reference is to *Public Speaking* (New York: Century Company, 1915). Woolbert's is *The Fundamentals of Speech*, rev. ed. (New York: Harper & Brothers, 1927).
8. For a summary of some recent statistics on the growth of speech instruction in the United States, see Gustav W. Friedrich, "Speech Communication in American Colleges and Universities," in Thomas W. Benson, ed., *Speech Communication in the 20th Century* (Carbondale: Southern Illinois University Press, 1985), pp. 235–252.

" Ad astra per aspera *is a good motto for the class in Speech. Or, 'This place is not dedicated to those who are excellent, but to those who wish to do better.'* **"**

—C. H. Woolbert,
The Fundamentals of Speech, rev. ed. (1927)[1]

Chapter 2

YOUR FIRST SPEECHES

As you begin the course in public speaking, keep in mind that the speakers of the past—the famous and the not-so-famous of Athens, Rome, England, and America—began learning how to talk in public by making a first speech. The same holds true for each member of your class; improving your communication skills for effective participation in our modern democratic society means making a start. As a rule, that start consists of preparing and delivering speeches early in the course, before you have read the entire text, and before the instructor has delivered a full range of lectures. Here are three points to consider at the outset.

First, *you should understand the assignment clearly*. Ask questions of your instructor if necessary so that you will feel confident about the work that you are doing. For example, if the assignment is for a speech on how to make or do something, do not talk about your summer vacation, or on why the members of the class should join a particular political organization. Also, be sure to conform to the time limits set by the instructor for the speech.

Second, *you should take the challenge of speech preparation seriously*. Give the task of preparing a speech the same detailed attention you would give to writing an essay for publication, or to studying for a tough exam. You owe it to your audience to have something worthwhile to say by preparing each speech thoroughly.

Finally, *you should start the process of speech preparation early*. A prompt beginning gives you the opportunity to find good subjects, gather your materials, select the best content, and organize your remarks. As a rule, you should have each speech fully prepared a day or two prior to delivery so that you will have enough time to master the content and rehearse the talk in order to deliver it well.

With these recommendations in mind, we now consider three topics. First, we will examine a systematic approach to speech preparation. Second, we will summarize the essentials of planning a speech of introduction—such as you might deliver to your public speaking class at the beginning of the course. Then, we will conclude with a discussion of public speaking anxiety—often called "stage fright."

I. Preparing Your First Speeches

You can prepare your first speeches according to a systematic, five-step process, as follows: (1) analyze the audience and occasion; (2) determine the subject and goal; (3) find and select supporting materials; (4) outline the speech; and (5) rehearse and deliver the speech. You can then adjust this approach to your specific needs and work habits as the course progresses. Let us look first at the audience and the occasion.

Analyze the Audience and Occasion

Analyzing the audience and the occasion for your speeches in a public speaking class is more convenient than for situations with which you are less familiar. In a speech course you get the "feel" of the situation by being a class member, becoming acquainted with your instructor and classmates, and becoming familiar with the physical details of the room and the general atmosphere of the class. The challenge that remains is that of skillfully analyzing your fellow students, for they compose the audience for your speeches in the course.

There are three essential considerations that you should apply to your classmates as you plan your first speeches, namely, their *interests, knowledge*, and *attitudes*. To begin with, you need to think about the types of subjects that will *interest* those in the class. You can do a general evaluation of class interests by considering such things as major fields, age, and career plans. For example, a subject that would be of immediate interest to an adult education class of part-time students majoring in business might not interest a class of younger, full-time freshmen and sophomores who were still deciding on majors and careers. The adult group might be immediately interested in a talk on "Three Ways to Reduce the Costs of Doing Business," whereas the class of younger freshmen and sophomores might be more interested in "Careers for the Twenty-First Century: What's Hot and What's Not."

In addition to interests, audience *knowledge* of a subject is a critical factor in choosing and developing a speech topic. For example, if your listeners are thoroughly informed on a subject, there is no need for a speech covering what they already know. Instead, pick a topic that allows you to present something new. On the other hand, if your listeners are not knowledgeable on the subject, be sure to include enough background information to help them understand the main ideas you are discussing.

Finally, you will need to consider the *attitude* of your listeners toward your subject. An attitude is the predisposition of a person to respond to your viewpoint in a favorable or unfavorable way. Knowing the attitude of the audience helps you determine whether or not your listeners will be inclined to support or oppose your proposal. This knowledge is particularly important when preparing a persuasive speech (that is, one in which you attempt to modify the beliefs or actions of your listeners), for the degree of opposition to or support for your proposal determines the nature of your arguments and evidence. Specifically, *the stronger the opposition, the stronger should be your logical reasoning and your supporting evidence*. Also, keep in mind that there is no point in trying to persuade an audience to believe what it already believes, or to do what it is already doing. For example, if most class members are involved in a systematic exercise program, there is no point in urging them to start one.

Determine the Subject and Goal

After you have carefully evaluated the interests, knowledge, and attitudes of your classmates, you are ready to work on the next step, which involves choosing and narrowing the subject, then determining the exact goal of the speech.

Choose a Subject

The subjects you select for your first classroom speeches should meet three basic standards, namely, they should be appropriate to *you*, to the *audience*, and to the *specifics of the assignment* as announced by your instructor. To

20

Part I
Speaking
and Listening
in a
Democratic
Society

begin with, choose subjects that you are familiar with, that you understand well (or are willing to research thoroughly), and that are not too complicated. For possible topics, look to your hobbies, job experiences, travels, artistic talents, interesting things in the community (museums, historical sites, manufacturing activities), your major field of study, and so on. For instance, a student whose hobby is skydiving could talk on how to correctly fold a parachute; a worker in a restaurant could explain the procedures followed by restaurants to keep food clean and safe; and a student majoring in communication disorders could explain what is meant by "aphasia."

In addition, your subjects should be appealing to your *audience*. Choose topics that will be worth listening to, that will catch and hold interest, and that will teach your classmates something they do not already know. For example, you will get a better response to a topic such as "Three Secrets to Studying for a Difficult Exam" than to something as obvious (and dull) as "How to Shave," or "How to Wash Your Car."

Finally, select a subject that *fits the assignment, including the time limits* imposed by your instructor. In addition to picking the type of subject your instructor asks for, be sure the subject is not too broad. If it is too big for the time you have, you should narrow it to something specific (that is, to some smaller aspect of the subject) before developing it. For example, the "History of Clocks" is much too broad for a short speech. By narrowing the topic of "clocks," you might talk instead on "Why Quartz Timepieces Are So Accurate." Similarly, the subject of "The American Banking System" is too big for a short speech; instead, speak on "What Happens to Your Checks After You Write Them?"

Here are some additional examples to stimulate your thoughts concerning speech subjects. For speeches to inform, consider topics such as:

How to Save a Drowning Victim

How Our School Honor Code Began

The Services of the University Placement Center

Making Jewelry from Native Stone

The Difference Between VHS and Super-VHS Video

For speeches to persuade, consider topics such as:

Abolish Sexist Language

You Should Register to Vote

Why I Joined a Fraternity

We Need a State Lottery

The University Student Government Association Needs Your Support

Determine the Speech Goal

After you have selected and narrowed your subject, you next need to decide on a realistic speech goal. You can formulate your goal in three steps: determine the *general purpose*, phrase a *specific purpose*, then convert the specific purpose into a *central idea*. The first step, determining the *general purpose*, means to decide whether the speech is "to inform" or "to persuade." Your general purpose is "to inform" if you limit your goal to teaching or explaining something so that the audience understands it. However, if you are trying to get your classmates to change their opinions or actions, your general purpose is "to persuade."

Second, formulate the *specific purpose* means to combine the general purpose (to inform, or to persuade) with the narrowed subject and write the result as an infinitive phrase. For example, if your subject is "the working of the human vocal mechanism," and your general purpose is "to inform," you would write the specific purpose this way: "to inform my audience of how the human vocal mechanism works." Or, if your subject is "the candidacy of John Smith for student body president," and your general purpose is "to persuade," you would write: "to persuade my listeners to vote for John Smith for president of the student body." This specific purpose helps you, the speaker, by stating clearly the goal you have set for yourself in the speech.

Finally, adapt the specific purpose to your audience by phrasing it as a complete sentence such as you might use in the delivered speech. This sentence is called the *central idea*. Because you will actually use it in your speech, it should be worded in language that is diplomatic as well as clear. In a nutshell, the difference between the specific purpose and the central idea is this: the specific purpose tells *you*, the speaker, what your goal is for the speech; the central idea states that goal to the *audience*. For example, if your specific purpose is "to inform my audience of how the Wankel gasoline engine works," your central idea might be phrased this way: "The Wankel gasoline engine works in a radically different way from the standard piston engine."

When you view the overall process of choosing the subject and formulating the purpose of a speech, five steps emerge: (1) determine the broad subject, (2) narrow this broad subject to a subarea that you have time to discuss, (3) decide on the general purpose (whether to inform or to persuade), (4) form the specific purpose (by connecting the general purpose with the narrowed subject), then (5) convert the specific purpose (which is stated as an infinitive phrase) into a clear, appealing central idea (which is stated as a complete sentence). Here is an example of the five steps at work (you will find additional examples in Chapter 6).

1 **Broad Subject:** Physical aspects of the communication process in humans.
2 **Narrowed Subject:** How the human vocal mechanism works.
3 **General Purpose:** To inform.
4 **Specific Purpose** (combine steps 2 and 3): To inform my audience of how the human vocal mechanism works.
5 **Central Idea** (a complete sentence for the audience): Your vocal mechanism creates speech in a four-step process.

Now that you have a concrete subject in mind and you have phrased your specific purpose and an audience-centered central idea, you are ready to proceed to the next step of preparation—collecting speech materials.

Find and Select Supporting Materials

22

*Part I
Speaking
and Listening
in a
Democratic
Society*

The formulation of a specific purpose gives you a clear direction for collecting supporting materials that sustain interest, clarify, and—for persuasive speeches—help prove your case to your audience. The main types of supporting materials are *examples, comparisons and contrasts, statistics*, and *statements from authority*. Let us look more closely at each one.

Specific examples—such as stories, illustrations, and case histories—are a major form of speech support. You use examples anytime you say, ''Let me illustrate,'' and proceed to tell a story or give a concrete instance of what you are talking about. As a rule, you should present the examples in your own words, telling them in a direct, conversational manner. Because audiences like the concrete, and enjoy listening to interesting stories, well-chosen examples are an effective type of speech support.

A second form of support, *comparisons and contrasts*, can be thought of as a variation of the example. With the comparison, for instance, the speaker likens one example to another with an emphasis on similarities (such as comparing one small town to another, or one football team to another). The use of contrast, on the other hand, emphasizes how an example differs from another (such as explaining the key differences between two or more pickup trucks, or word processing programs). You would use comparison if you were speaking on gun control and compared your program to a similar one being used successfully in another country, and you would use contrast if you pointed out the major differences between your proposal for gun control, and that advocated by the National Rifle Association.

Third, you can support a point by the use of *statistics*. Some basic standards for clear communication should be kept in mind when using statistics in your speeches. These include using numbers sparingly (detailed, overdone statistics will confuse and bore your audience), and presenting your figures in simple form (such as by the use of round numbers). Also, be sure that the statistics are recent and accurate. To help your listeners keep up with the figures, consider using visual aids such as the chalkboard or simple charts that you prepare in advance.

Finally, you can support a point by citing *authority*. This means using such material as expert testimony, quotations from history and from literature, and explanations or definitions from encyclopedias, dictionaries, or similar sources. For instance, if you are planning an informative speech explaining how high definition television (HDTV) works, you could support your speech with references to technicians and scientists who have worked on developing the new technology. When speaking, be sure to mention the names and qualifications of your authorities in order to increase your audience's confidence in what you are saying.

If you are basing the speech on personal knowledge and experience, you will not have much, if any, research to do. However, if you are not fully informed on the topic, you need to do adequate research so that you will know what you are talking about. You can gather speech materials by various means, including use of the library, interviews with experts on the subject, and field trips that permit you to observe something directly (such as a manufacturing process, or a historical site). Be sure to use a systematic note-taking system for saving the information that you need for the speech. Let us now look at the process of organizing your ideas and supports into a coherent outline.

Outline the Speech

A written outline provides you with a means of organizing your thoughts in a clear, logical sequence prior to delivery. This helps you think through what is important and what is not, and its use helps the audience to keep up with and remember your remarks. Research confirms, for example, that audiences understand organized speeches better than disorganized ones.[2] In the section below, we will discuss the steps of outlining as follows: first, outline the body of the speech (this is essential and is the "heart" of any talk, and thus deserves your attention at the outset); second, outline the introduction and the conclusion.

Outline the Body

The body of the speech consists of two parts: the *central idea*, and the *points and subpoints* that explain and prove the central idea. After you have stated the central idea in clear language, develop it with the major headings that will form the "main points" of your discussion. You should outline the complete set of main points first before working on the subpoints. In other words, after you have all main points worked out, you can develop each of them, one at a time.

The following three standards are recommended for your main points. First, *use complete sentences* for all points (this facilitates checking the logic of your outline). Second, *avoid overlapping ideas* between headings (that is, cover only one idea per point). Third, *keep the total number of main points small*, preferably in the range of two to five. As a practical matter, consider that in a short speech you do not have the time to develop a large number of points. Even in longer speeches, listeners become restless, and some will "tune out," if the speaker tries to cover too many points in a single talk.

The next consideration is to employ one method of division for all main points. This means that you should follow a single logical design, called a "speech pattern," for your points. Five of the most widely used speech designs are the *chronological pattern*, the *physical components pattern*, the *topical pattern*, the *causal pattern*, and the *problem-solution pattern*.

A *chronological pattern* is one based on a time sequence, such as hours (first hour, second hour, third hour, and so on), days, or years, or one that employs a past-present-future plan. This pattern is useful for tracing a historical development, or for explaining the steps in a process or procedure (such as how to make or do something). For example, the subject of how a bill becomes law lends itself to a chronological division (the first step of the process, the second step, and so on). If your specific purpose is "to inform my audience of how a bill becomes law in our state legislature," your central idea and set of main points could be as follows.

Central Idea: There are five main steps in the process of a bill becoming law in our state.

I.   First, a legislator writes the bill.

II. Second, the bill is placed "in the hopper" for consideration.

III. Third, the bill is studied and voted on by appropriate committees.

IV. Fourth, the bill is debated and voted on in both houses.

V.   Finally, the bill is signed by the governor.

24

*Part I
Speaking
and Listening
in a
Democratic
Society*

The *physical components pattern* is a second method of organizing a speech. This pattern is used when you divide an object, device, mechanism, or geographical area into its physical parts, pieces, or spaces. This pattern is appropriate when your central idea names one physical object or geographical area which you then explain by a verbal "exploded diagram" of physical components. For example, by considering the human ear as a single physical "thing," you can outline an informative talk on how the ear works according to its three physical sections: the external ear, the middle ear, and the inner ear. Or you can organize a talk built around a geographical unit (such as a campus, a county, or a state) by dividing the unit into logical subsections. For instance, an informative speech on earthquake activity in California could be presented according to different areas of that state, as follows.

Central Idea: Earthquake activity varies in different sections of California.

I.   First, let us examine earthquake activity in Southern California.

II. Next, let us examine earthquake activity in Central California.

III. Finally, let us examine earthquake activity in Northern California.

The *topical pattern* is a third method for organizing the main points of a speech. The topical method is used when you organize your subject according to types, traits, qualities, logical groupings, and so forth. For instance, a speech about the aspects of management of the major American automobile companies could be arranged by three topics, each serving as a main point: General Motors, Ford, and Chrysler. Or a speech about careers in public service could be organized by vocational opportunities in each branch of government: executive, legislative, and judicial. Similarly, a speech about the life of a famous person, such as General Robert E. Lee, could be arranged by admirable traits, such as: he was a brilliant general; he was a great educator; he was a generous and kind human being.

A *causal pattern* is a fourth way to organize a speech. The causal pattern is a two-point plan that divides the topic according to cause and effect. The first point would set out the cause of something, and the second point would discuss its effect. For instance, an informative talk on volcanoes could first explain what causes a volcano to erupt; then, point two could explain the effects of an eruption on the surrounding countryside. Or a persuasive speech advocating less use of chemical fertilizers in agriculture could first argue that chemical fertilizers cause environmental damage, then, second, explain the effects of that damage to the land, lakes, and streams.

The *problem-solution pattern* is a fifth method of organization, one that is particularly useful for speeches to persuade. If you use the problem-solution plan, the body of your speech will have only two main points. The first point sets out the problem, and is supported by evidence that the problem should be of serious concern to your audience. The second point details a solution to the problem. For example, for a persuasive speaking assignment, a student could decide on a specific purpose based on a campus issue, such as: "to persuade the members of the class to participate more fully in student government on our campus." Point one of the body should be supported by evidence (such as reports from interviews with members of student government, and statistics about participation in recent elections) to prove that the problem is serious. Point two of the body would set out a workable solution, such as calling upon class members to consider running for office, and urging each one to vote in campus elections.

After you have developed a logical set of main points, you are ready to "flesh out" the outline with subpoints. These subpoints consist of supporting ideas and speech materials (such as examples, comparison and contrast, statistics, and authoritative statements). Starting with the first main heading, develop each by adding the supports that are needed to make the point clear and—for speeches to persuade—persuasive to your audience. This process can be illustrated using point one of the California earthquakes example discussed above.

I. First, let us examine earthquake activity in Southern California.
   A. Specific illustrations and examples.
   B. Statistical data.
   C. Statements from authorities.
   (Continue as needed, until point one is fully developed; do the same for the other main points.)

After you have developed each main point, and have before you a working draft of the outline of the body of your speech, you are ready for the final steps of speech organization—outlining the introduction and conclusion.

Outline the Introduction and Conclusion

The introduction to your first speeches should accomplish at least three things: first, catch the attention of your listeners; second, smoothly lead into the subject and motivate audience interest by explaining why the topic is important; and third, state the central idea of the speech. The outline of your introduction, together with some ideas for accomplishing the three things listed above, would look something like this.

INTRODUCTION

I. Attention material: open with an interesting story, a striking statement, or some unusual statistics; this material should be related to your subject.

26

*Part I
Speaking
and Listening
in a
Democratic
Society*

II. Lead into the subject and motivate interest: define terms as needed; tell why the subject is important to the listeners; tactfully state your qualifications to speak on this subject.

Central Idea: State the central idea clearly and diplomatically. (In the outline, no number is placed before the central idea because it stands alone as the thesis of the entire speech.)

After you have completed the introduction, you are ready to finish the outline by developing the conclusion. Keep at least two goals in mind as you outline the conclusion: first, summarize the important ideas of the body of the speech, and—if the talk is to persuade—appeal for belief and action; second, end the speech with a creative touch that is relevant to the subject, such as a quotation, a story, or a touch of humor that helps to ''wrap up'' the theme of the talk. The outline of your conclusion should look something like the following example.

CONCLUSION

I. Summarize the main points of the body (and, for persuasion, appeal for belief or action).

II. Conclude with a ''creative touch,'' such as a quotation, illustration, or humor that underscores the central idea of the speech.

When you are finished with the conclusion, arrange the outline drafts of the introduction, body, and conclusion in correct order, then revise and polish the overall content of the speech as needed. *For additional help on speech organization, see Appendix II where you will find illustrations of complete outlines, examples of topical note cards (for use during delivery) based on those outlines, and the texts of the speeches as delivered.*

Rehearse, then Deliver the Speech

With your speech outline before you, go through the entire speech aloud once or twice, timing it carefully. If the talk is too long, do the necessary cutting. Once you are satisfied with the timing, *prepare a final draft of the outline.* Next, prepare a ''key word'' notecard for use during delivery. (Check with the instructor to be sure that notecards are permissible for the assignment.) Referring to the complete outline, jot down in correct sequence key words from the outline that will remind you (at a glance) of the point, illustration, or other idea that you intend to discuss. Include direct quotations and exact statistics on the card for ready availability during the speech. You may use more than one notecard if necessary, for the concept here is not how many cards you have, but how well you use them. Keep in mind that, with the exception of direct quotes that you intend to use in the speech, the notecard is not a manuscript to be read. Rather, it should be a ''bare framework'' of topics that help keep you on track during delivery.

Rehearse your speech two or three times using the brief key word outline as recorded on the notecard. The technique to practice is to glance at the notecard to be reminded of the next topic, then explain that topic while looking directly at your audience, using language that comes to you without further reference to the notecard. If you are planning to use visual aids, rehearse putting them up and using them during the speech.

On the day of the speech, plan to arrive at class a few minutes early. Visit with your classmates and generally make an effort to be at ease. When your time comes to speak, walk confidently to the front of the room, and use your body and voice—the tools of delivery—to achieve three things: visual directness, communicative body movement, and vocal variety. Let us briefly examine each of these "elements of delivery."

Visual directness. Look directly into the eyes of your listeners as you speak (not at their chins or foreheads, or at the wall in the back of the room). Maintain visual directness with all parts of your audience by moving your attention from section to section of the room, seeing people in groups or sections as you speak. Avoid favoring any one person or group of persons. By looking at all persons in your audience you help involve each listener in the communication experience.

Communicative body movement. At the outset, there are some common mistakes of bodily communication that you should try to avoid. These include a slumping posture, shifting weight nervously from side to side, fumbling with keys or coins in the pockets, and using mechanical, memorized movements and gestures. On the other hand, some positive principles of bodily communication should be rehearsed, then followed during the speech. These include balancing your weight evenly on both feet as you speak, and maintaining an alert but comfortable posture during the talk. In addition, your movements and gestures should flow naturally from the ideas you are discussing at the moment. This includes such things as holding up fingers to indicate which point you are starting to explain (one finger for point one, two for point two, and so on), pointing to key sections of a visual aid, and stepping to one side, then the other, of the speaker's stand from time to time to get closer to your audience or to emphasize key points of the speech.

Vocal variety. Finally, use your voice to help communicate the ideas of the speech. Speak up so that you can be heard, yet try to keep the voice conversational and expressive. Be sure to project with adequate loudness to those who are sitting in the back of the room. Be careful not to talk too rapidly; rather, pace your speech so that all sounds are clearly formed and all words properly pronounced. Use vocal variety of rate and pitch to "interpret" the ideas of the speech, such as pausing for dramatic effect at appropriate times, or speaking louder or softer, for emphasis.

II. Speeches of Introduction

In many public speaking courses, one of the first assignments is a speech of introduction in which you introduce yourself or one of your fellow students to the class. If your instructor makes such an assignment, here are some suggestions that should prove helpful.

Introducing Yourself to Others

An obvious advantage in preparing an introduction of yourself to the class is that you know the subject matter, so no research is necessary. However, you should take the time to think through and outline your remarks so that you can cover what is important, yet stay within the time limit. You can begin by making notes under topics such as these:

28

Part I
Speaking
and Listening
in a
Democratic
Society

Hometown and family. Interesting information about your home community (historical facts, unusual customs or celebrations, manufacturing of unusual items, etc.), and entertaining facts about your family (unusual business or profession, achievements, hobbies).

Your own hobbies and special recreational activities.

Your college interests. Why you chose this particular college or university, organizational memberships and offices held, and extracurricular activities such as cheerleading, marching band, theater, sports, etc.

Your major field and future plans. Why you chose your major (or, if no decision has been made, the major programs you are thinking about), what you hope to gain from a course in public speaking, what you plan to do after graduation (such as graduate school), and career plans.

After you have made notes on the topics you wish to cover, prepare a brief outline following the suggestions given in the first part of this chapter. Begin by outlining the body of your talk, noting that the speech is an informative one, with a specific purpose "to introduce myself to the members of my public speaking class." Your central idea might be: "Today I would like to tell you something of where I came from, why I'm here, and where I'm going"; or simply: "Today I would like to tell you a little bit about myself." Your main points could be built around three or four topical headings, such as (1) hometown, (2) campus life, and (3) future plans. Fill in each of the main points with interesting facts, stories, and other details.

After you have developed the body of your talk, outline your introduction and conclusion. Put a short version of your overall outline on a notecard, then rehearse your remarks several times, glancing at the notecard occasionally to make sure you stay "on track." On the day of the speech, when your turn comes to speak, walk confidently to the front of the room, stand erect, look directly at your audience, and begin. Maintain a direct, friendly delivery throughout the talk. A final suggestion: when you pronounce your name, do so slowly and distinctly so that everyone will understand it (if your name is unusual, or difficult to pronounce, try writing it on the board and saying it two or three times).

Introducing Other Persons

If, instead of self-introductions, the instructor assigns each person the name of a classmate to introduce, you should make an appointment for an interview with the student assigned to you. (Similarly, the person who will introduce you will need to make an appointment with you.) Plan your questions around headings, such as those listed above (home and family, hobbies, college activities, and future plans—plus any additional topics needed to cover the person's particular interests and achievements). Be sure to get the correct spelling and pronunciation of the student's name.

After you have secured needed information, prepare an outline of your speech. The process of outlining can follow the same steps given above, that is, outline the body first, then plan the introduction and the conclusion. Take your responsibility seriously, for a speech of introduction should present to the audience a *positive* image of the person being introduced. Before delivery, go over the content of your outline with the student you are introducing as a means of double-checking the accuracy of what you are about to say. Then, deliver your speech in a direct, friendly manner.

III. Dealing with Public Speaking Anxiety

Public speaking anxiety—often called "stage fright"—is a natural occurrence similar to the preperformance nervousness reported by many actors, musicians, and others who appear before audiences. Since ancient times speakers have commented on the phenomenon, including such accomplished orators as Demosthenes of ancient Greece and Cicero of classical Rome. Outstanding American speakers who recount experiences with "stage fright" include Abraham Lincoln, Franklin D. Roosevelt, and Ronald Reagan.

If you feel that, on occasion, you have a high degree of tension before and during delivery, be aware that you are not alone. Be assured, however, that for most individuals, this tension can be understood and controlled; in fact, many speakers have managed to all but eliminate it from their list of serious communication problems. To help you do the same, we will look first at an explanation of speech anxiety based upon contemporary studies; then, we will set out a series of practical suggestions to help you manage and control the problem.

An Explanation of Speech Anxiety

Teachers of public speaking have long been familiar with the problem of speech anxiety. In recent years, a number of communication researchers have given serious attention to it, with helpful results.[3] Professor Joe Ayres of Washington State University is one of these researchers who, after a careful examination of the findings of others, and after conducting experiments of his own, set out an explanation of speech anxiety that you should be able to apply to your own speaking.[4] Ayres focuses on two key points:

First, *fear of public speaking "emerges from a personal assessment that one's speaking abilities fall short of audience expectations."* In other words, if you believe that you cannot live up to what your listeners expect of you, you will likely be unduly apprehensive.[5]

Second, *fear of public speaking is intensified when the speaker believes that "important inadequacies will be revealed."* Speakers are especially concerned about revealing weaknesses in mastery of the intellectual content of the speech, in delivery skills, and in their ability to make a general impression of competence as assessed by the audience.[6]

What can be done about these concerns? The research reveals that when speakers discover that they can meet or exceed audience expectations, and

30

Part I
Speaking
and Listening
in a
Democratic
Society

that the audience is "not as difficult to please as they had thought, their fear subsides because they perceive themselves as better able to meet these lower expectations."[7] Stated in positive terms, this suggests that if you believe that you have a problem with public speaking anxiety, you should attack the problem directly with a program to help build confidence in at least four related areas, as follows:

■ Confidence in meeting or exceeding audience expectations
■ Confidence in mastering intellectual content, including knowledge of the subject and the ability to employ sound reasoning and evidence
■ Confidence in the mastery of delivery skills
■ Confidence that you can establish an overall impression of competence and credibility

Let us now examine some specific recommendations based upon these findings.

Practical Methods for Managing Speech Anxiety

As you develop a program for managing public speaking anxiety, keep two kinds of problems separate in your thoughts. First is the problem that is primarily *imaginary*—one that exists in your head, and nowhere else. An example would be for you to believe that you appear awkward and nervous while speaking, when, in fact, you appear relaxed and normal to your audience. Second is the *real* problem that does distract your audience, and that you need to overcome by an intelligent program of study and practice. For instance, some persons are nervous about public speaking because they have a poor vocabulary and substandard pronunciation—and know it. The realistic solution in such a case is a program of vocabulary improvement and professional help with pronunciation (such as a course in voice and diction). The point is this: make a distinction between those roadblocks to speaking confidence that are imaginary, and those that are real, then develop a plan to deal with both concerns.

This is not to say that those matters that are primarily perceptual—that is, "in your head"—are not significant. If a problem seems real to you, it deserves attention. It does say, however, that the way you solve a perceptual barrier differs from the way you approach a barrier based in reality. When addressing a perceptual problem, you need to grasp that it is imaginary, then reason your way to its reduction or elimination. For example, you could say to yourself, "Now that I have learned from my classmates and my instructor that my posture, movement, and gestures appear relaxed and natural, I won't worry further about those things."

Let us now look at the four areas of confidence building that we identified earlier, with a focus on specific recommendations for dealing with both imaginary and real problems of speech anxiety.

1. *Meeting or exceeding audience expectations*. If you think that you cannot live up to audience expectations, recognize that this problem is mainly "in your head." A realistic assessment of the speaking situation will reveal in al-

most every case that the expectations of your listeners are similar to those you have when you are in the audience. Ask yourself, "When I am listening to others, do I expect them to be brilliant in every remark and polished in all aspects of delivery?" Your answer is probably, "No, of course not." In fact, you are more likely to have modest expectations, and to be sympathetic if and when the speaker makes a mistake. And so it is when you are speaking, for your listeners also have a sympathetic attitude and generally modest expectations. Think it through before your next speech, then say to yourself, "I *can* meet or exceed the expectations of my audience!"

2. *Demonstrate a mastery of speech content.* In a broad sense, your total education provides the basic foundation of knowledge which leads to the mastery of speech content, and the confidence such mastery gives you. This includes not only knowledge of specific subjects but also training in critical thinking, the ability to do research, and the ability to organize your thoughts clearly so that audiences will be able to follow you. More immediately, here are three positive steps you can take.

First, carefully choose speech topics that you want to discuss, and about which you are knowledgeable (such knowledge can come through personal experience, or by research). An experimental study supports this recommendation, concluding that a speaker's familiarity with the speech subject is helpful in building self-assurance and reducing anxiety.[8]

Second, prepare the details of speech content thoroughly. Outline clearly, then master the points of your outline so that you can approach the speaking situation knowing that you are "on top" of the main points and subpoints of the speech.

Third, review the reasoning and evidence of the speech before delivery. Ask yourself, "Am I making clear, logical sense?" and "Is my supporting evidence relevant and adequate for developing the points of the speech?" If you are sure of your reasoning and evidence, you will be more self-assured as you speak.

3. *Be confident in your delivery of the speech.* Here are four recommendations for building and maintaining self-confidence in your delivery skills.

First, do not memorize your speeches (fear of a memory lapse causes many people to become nervous before an audience). Instead, use notes as a back-up in case you forget which point comes next in sequence. Knowing that you have the "insurance" of a notecard can help greatly in reducing speech anxiety.

Second, rehearse your talk several times (as recommended earlier in this chapter) so that you have a "feel" for the visual directness, bodily movement, and gestures that fit the content of the speech. At the time of delivery, walk confidently to the front of the room, stand erect, and while looking directly at your audience, begin without apology or hesitation.

Third, speak with deliberation—do not rush. Take the time to articulate your sounds distinctly and to pronounce your words properly.

Finally, if you have any *real* problems of delivery—such as difficulty with articulation, pronunciation, and voice—ask your instructor to advise you about readings, exercises, and even additional courses that will help address the problem. For example, a dull, monotonous voice might be helped by a course in the oral interpretation of literature. Other courses you can consider taking are advanced speaking, persuasion, and argumentation and debate. For practical experience outside of class, take advantage of speaking opportunities on campus and in the community, for the more experience you get, the more you will be "at home" before an audience.

32

*Part I
Speaking
and Listening
in a
Democratic
Society*

4. *Realize that you can appear credible to your audience.* Aristotle observed that speaker credibility (*ethos*) is assigned by the audience when it perceives the speaker to be a person who is trustworthy, knowledgeable, and friendly. You can build trust between you and your listeners by talking on subjects you really want to talk about, and by being intellectually honest in your reasoning and evidence. You can demonstrate that you are an intelligent and well-informed speaker by researching the speech thoroughly and knowing the content well, and by presenting that content in a clear, organized way. And you can demonstrate that you are a friendly, caring person by having a sincere concern for your listeners, and by speaking with a social conscience. In a nutshell, by choosing subjects you believe in, by preparing well, and by presenting your views in a sincere, congenial way, you can establish yourself as a credible communicator.

This Chapter in Brief

You can prepare your first speeches in a systematic way by following a five-step process. First, analyze the audience and occasion, with particular attention to audience interests, knowledge, and attitudes. Second, select a subject that is suitable to you, the audience, and the assignment, then narrow the subject to a concrete speech goal called the specific purpose (for example, "to explain to my audience why the sky looks blue"). Third, from personal experience and research find appropriate supporting materials for your speech, such as examples, comparisons and contrasts, statistics, and authoritative statements. Fourth, outline your speech, starting with the body (because it forms the "heart" of any speech), then outlining the introduction and conclusion. Fifth, rehearse your speech several times before delivery.

If you introduce yourself or another person to the class, follow the five-step process above, adapting it to the nature of the assignment. This includes noting basic biographical and personal facts concerning family, hometown, hobbies, achievements, college activities, and future plans. The speech of introduction should present information in a positive manner that enhances your credibility—or that of the person you are introducing—with your classmates.

An important factor in delivery is how well you control tension, nervousness, and anxiety—sometimes called "stage fright." Public speaking anxiety is a normal occurrence that can be reduced and controlled by an intelligent program of theory and practice. Recent research reveals that speakers experience speech anxiety when they believe that they cannot meet audience expectations, and when they believe they will reveal important inadequacies to others as they speak. A program addressing these concerns includes the following points.

First, audience expectations are, in fact, modest. A speaker who understands this can reason to a reduction of anxiety by realizing that audience expectations of perfection in public speaking are a figment of the speaker's imagination.

Second, the speaker who knows the content of the speech well, and who has it logically organized, can approach the speaking situation with the confidence that comes with thorough preparation.

Third, delivery skills can be improved by practice, and by specific plans to deal with any *real* delivery problems a speaker might have (such as problems of voice and diction).

Finally, overall credibility can be established by a speaker who knows the subject, is well-organized, demonstrates sincerity while speaking, and shows good will toward the audience. Listeners assign credibility when they sense that the speaker is informed, trustworthy, and friendly.

EXERCISES

1. The next time you are a member of the audience in a public speaking situation, analyze your personal expectations for the speech or speeches scheduled. Would you describe your expectations as "reasonable, modest, and sympathetic?" If so, is it not safe to assume that others think similarly about you when you are speaking? Apply these thoughts to yourself prior to your next speech.

2. Identify an effective speaker on your campus or in your community. You might choose a teacher, a business or professional person (such as an attorney), or your minister. Talk with that person about "stage fright." Does he or she agree that some prespeech tension is normal, or that experience in speaking helps reduce tension and nervousness? What recommendations does this person make to help you control public speaking anxiety?

SELECTED READINGS

Bradley, Bert E. *Fundamentals of Speech Communication: The Credibility of Ideas.* 5th ed. Dubuque, Ia.: Wm. C. Brown, 1988. In Chapter 3, "Understanding Performance Apprehension," Bradley analyzes public speaking anxiety, citing extensively from current research. He includes a variety of practical recommendations for controlling what he calls "performance apprehension."

Gregory, Hamilton. *Public Speaking for College and Career.* 2d ed. New York: McGraw-Hill, 1990. In Chapter 3, "Controlling Nervousness," Gregory discusses the reasons for nervousness before and during public speaking, and presents a number of "guidelines" for managing speech anxiety.

Richmond, Virginia P., and McCroskey, James C. *Communication: Apprehension, Avoidance, and Effectiveness.* 2d ed. Scottsdale, Ariz.: Gorsuch Scarisbrick, 1989. This brief paperback discusses not only public speaking anxiety but also shyness and general communication apprehension and avoidance in our daily lives. Chapter 7 discusses methods for overcoming communication apprehension.

34

*Part I
Speaking
and Listening
in a
Democratic
Society*

1. C. H. Woolbert, *The Fundamentals of Speech*, rev. ed. (New York: Harper & Brothers, 1927), p. 64.
2. Ernest C. Thompson, ''An Experimental Investigation of the Relative Effectiveness of Organizational Structure in Oral Communication,'' *Southern Speech Journal* 26 (Fall 1960): 59–69.
3. Theodore Clevenger, Jr., ''A Synthesis of Experimental Research in Stage Fright,'' *Quarterly Journal of Speech* 45 (April 1959): 134–145; and Joe Ayres, ''Perception of Speaking Ability: An Explanation for Stage Fright,'' *Communication Education* 35 (July 1986): 285–287. For a summary of what contemporary public speaking texts report and recommend, see Mary H. Pelias, ''Communication Apprehension in Basic Public Speaking Texts; an Examination of Contemporary Textbooks,'' *Communication Education* 38 (January 1989): 41–53.
4. Ayres, ibid., 275–287.
5. Ibid., 276.
6. Ibid., 278, 281–282.
7. Ibid., 284.
8. John A. Daly et al., ''Pre-Performance Concerns Associated with Public Speaking Anxiety,'' *Communication Quarterly* 37 (Winter 1989): 39–53, at p. 48.

> *In the public philosophy, freedom of speech is conceived as the means to a confrontation of opinion—as in a Socratic dialogue,...in the critiques of scientists..., in a court of law, in a representative assembly, in an open forum....[However] the right to freedom of speech is no license to deceive, and willful misrepresentation is a violation of its principles.*

—Walter Lippmann
The Public Philosophy (1955)[1]

Chapter 3

DEMOCRATIC VALUES, FREE SPEECH, AND SPEAKER ETHICS

W hen you are speaking in public, in class and elsewhere, you are exercising a right that many people take for granted—the right of free speech. A corollary of that right is your responsibility to speak ethically to others. However, neither free speech nor the standards for ethical communication emerge from a social vacuum—both reflect the values of our democratic society. Furthermore, as numerous communication scholars have recognized, those same values provide a rationale for the general enterprise of speech education in United States.[2]

In Chapter 1 we saw that a democratic society requires free and effective public communication in order for self-government to work. We now ask, what are the specific points of democratic theory that create a need for public speaking and the practice of free speech? Also, what do the tenets of democracy say to us about right and wrong in public communication? In the discussion that follows, we seek some answers to these questions, first by examining basic democratic values; second, by looking at some important principles of free speech that apply to public speaking in the United States; and finally, by examining how democratic values guide us in establishing standards for ethics in public speaking.

I. Democratic Values: The Foundation for Free and Responsible Speaking

In order to locate the basic democratic principles upon which free and responsible speaking are built, we will examine two key topics. First, we will discuss the tenet of respect for the individual; and second, we will look at some operational assumptions about democracy that flow from our respect for persons.

The Value of the Individual

Our society believes in the value of each person. This belief is often expanded and supported by three concepts about persons: individual dignity and worth; capacity to reason; and equality. Let us note each of these briefly.

Individual dignity and worth. Because we believe that each person has dignity and worth, we stress that our institutions, including those of government, should serve the people, and not the other way around. It follows from this democratic perspective that public speakers, being persons of worth, should be accorded a courteous hearing, even if we, as members of the audience, disagree with them. Also, it follows that speakers should avoid the ''know-it-all,'' authoritarian harangue that insults listeners, and instead, demonstrate respect for the individuals who compose the audience.

Capacity to reason. We believe that each person of normal intelligence has the capacity for rational thought and intelligent decision making. This tenet of democracy gives us an additional reason for listening courteously when we are an audience member, or as a speaker, approaching our audience with respect, for we accept the view that both speakers and listeners are capable of thinking an issue through and reaching a sensible conclusion about it.

Equality. We also believe in the right of each person to participate equally in society. This includes equal participation in the institutions of self-government. Education in public speaking serves this value, for it enables citizens to take part in democratic discussion and debate on an equal footing. Even though we recognize that abilities vary from person to person, we try to provide the same opportunities to all. This ideal was stated eloquently by Thomas Jefferson in the Declaration of Independence: "We hold these truths to be self-evident, that all men are created equal, that they are endowed by their Creator with certain unalienable Rights, that among these are Life, Liberty, and the pursuit of Happiness."

Assumptions of Democracy

At least four assumptions of democracy flow from our beliefs in individual worth, capacity, and equality. These are a preference for persuasion over force, freedom of speech so that persuasion can take place, decision by majority vote, and respect for minority rights.

Preference for persuasion. Persuasion is a civilized, nonviolent means of achieving political and social change. Even though changes brought about by persuasion are usually evolutionary rather than revolutionary, we prefer it to the alternatives of coercion and force.

Freedom of speech. For persuasion to be effective, individuals must have freedom to communicate and to receive information and opinion communicated by others. As Yale Law Professor Thomas I. Emerson observes in *The System of Freedom of Expression*, "By its very nature a system of free expression involves—in fact is designed to achieve—persuasion....[T]he introduction of coercion destroys the system as a free one."[3] By practicing liberty of speech, we hope to keep viable a "marketplace of ideas" that supplies citizens of a free society with essential information and a variety of points of view.

Decision by majority vote. After the members of a group, or the citizens of a democratic society, are "made wise" by free, vigorous discussion and debate on the issues in question, a vote is taken. The decision of the majority prevails.

Respect for minority rights. Within the context of majority rule, certain fundamental rights are protected for the minority. In the United States, a number of these rights are set forth in the federal Constitution, and include such important matters as freedom to communicate, freedom of religion, protection from arbitrary search and seizure, and the right of an accused person to a fair trial.

We are now ready to apply the basic values and assumptions of democracy to your right of free speech and to the formulation of ethical standards for public communication in a free society.

II. Speaking Freely:
Legal Issues for the Public Speaker

The First Amendment to the U.S. Constitution states:

Congress shall make no law respecting an establishment of religion, or prohibiting the free exercise thereof; or abridging the freedom of speech, or of the press; or the right of the people peaceably to assemble, and to petition the Government for a redress of grievances.

40

Part I
Speaking
and Listening
in a
Democratic
Society

In 1925, the U.S. Supreme Court ruled that the First Amendment is binding on the governments of the states as well as upon the federal government. In other words, neither the federal nor the state governments may deny us freedom of speech or of the press.[4]

Freedom of speech, however, is not an absolute—not in the United States, and not in other democratic societies, ancient or modern. Both Athens and Rome, for example, punished *slander* (that is, spoken accusations that tend to destroy a person's good reputation) and *sedition* (undermining the democracy by extreme forms of criticism). England has for centuries permitted the government to punish speakers for the same two kinds of expression. For many years England also enforced laws against *blasphemy* (the criticism of religion), although they are rarely invoked in modern times.

Furthermore, not all speech that is protected by the Constitution is ethical. Just because speech is permitted does not mean that what results is always based upon sound reasoning, solid evidence, a commitment to truth, and a sense of social responsibility. Public speakers, then, need to be aware of two areas of concern: the legal controls applied to public communication in the United States, and the standards of communication ethics that speakers should follow when addressing their fellow citizens.

In the United States, the language of the Constitution is open to interpretation by the courts, especially the U.S. Supreme Court which has the final word on the judiciary's views of the Constitution. Although the Supreme Court has interpreted the First Amendment to mean that most speech is protected, it has also said that some speech (such as false advertising) is not. College speech students should be familiar with the way the courts have ruled in at least three areas of public communication: controls upon the content of speech; the regulation of expression involving parades, marches, or demonstrations; and freedom of speech on the campus.

Controls Upon Speech Content

There are three major issues of speech content that you should be aware of as you plan your speeches. They concern criticism of the government (sedition), defamation of individuals (slander and libel), and criticism of the majority religion (blasphemy).

Criticism of the Government

One of the purposes of the First Amendment is to permit citizens to criticize the government without fear of punishment. As a nation, we have not always been true to this principle, as illustrated by the passage of the Alien and Sedition Acts of 1798 (at least twenty-four newspaper editors were prosecuted under the Sedition Act for criticizing the administration of President John Adams); the silencing of antislavery dissent in the South prior to and during the Civil War; legal proceedings against over 2000 Americans during World

The United States Supreme Court in Washington, D.C. *While the First Amendment to the United States Constitution protects freedom of speech, it is open to interpretation by the courts.(Michael Mazzaschi/Stock, Boston)*

War I for a variety of forms of antiwar expression; and the prosecution of suspected members of the American Communist Party following World War II.

However, in the 1969 case of *Brandenburg v. Ohio*, the U.S. Supreme Court interpreted the First Amendment so as to provide strong protection for antigovernment expression. This case came to the High Court after Ohio Ku Klux Klan leader Clarence Brandenburg, who had been convicted of making a speech the state considered illegal, appealed his conviction. In his brief talk to fellow Klansmen, Brandenburg had said, "We're not a revengent organization, but if our President, our Congress, our Supreme Court, continues to suppress the white, Caucasian race, it's possible that there might have to be some revengeance taken."[5]

A unanimous Supreme Court reversed Brandenburg's conviction, ruling that the speaker did not present a *real* danger to anyone or to the state. The High Court observed that he had boasted and "blown off steam," but he did not actually incite his audience to violence. Therefore, his speech was protected by the First Amendment. Narrowing the definition of sedition more than ever before, the Supreme Court put into place an "incitement" standard that stated: "the constitutional guarantees of free speech and free press do not permit a State to forbid or proscribe advocacy of the use of force or of law violation *except where such advocacy is directed to inciting or producing imminent lawless action and is likely to incite or produce such action.*" [Emphasis added.] Under this rule, speakers are protected in their criticism of the government except when they attempt to incite an audience to lawless action, *and* the listeners are on the verge of actually taking that advice.

42

Part I
Speaking
and Listening
in a
Democratic
Society

Defamation of Individuals

The law of libel serves to protect the good name of an individual (and, in some instances, the reputation of a company, product, or institution) from false charges that tend to destroy one's position in society. By legal tradition, speech is considered defamatory if it tends to lower a person's standing before others, or cause that person to be shunned or exposed to hatred, contempt, or ridicule.

Although any falsehood that destroys reputation can be considered defamatory, four are of particular concern to the law: assertions that an individual (1) is a criminal, (2) has a contagious or offensive disease, (3) is dishonest in business, trade, or profession, or (4) is immoral—especially in reference to sexual mores. Examples would be false statements made orally or in print that John Doe "is a common thief," "has syphilis," "cheats his customers," or "is guilty of adultery."

Punishment for defamation is usually a civil fine, called "damages," imposed by the jury. This fine can range from a small amount to a large award of hundreds of thousands or even millions of dollars. In theory, a speaker could be ruined financially for life by a jury's decision to grant sizable damages. For this reason, and for ethical reasons as well, public speakers should be cautious about making slanderous accusations (especially if the truth of the accusation is in doubt).

The U.S. Supreme Court has consistently ruled that defamatory falsehoods of private persons are not protected by the First Amendment. The attitude of the Court continues to be in harmony with the view of the late Justice Potter Stewart, who wrote in a 1966 defamation case that the right to protect one's "own reputation from unjustified invasion and wrongful hurt reflects no more than our basic concept of the essential dignity and worth of every human being—a concept at the root of any decent system of ordered liberty."[6]

Criticism of Religion

One of the most emotional free speech issues in the history of Western culture is speaking in opposition to the religious views of those in control of church and state. Americans addressed this matter in the First Amendment by declaring not only that we shall have freedom of speech but also that legislative bodies "shall make no law respecting an establishment of religion, or prohibiting the free exercise thereof." Although some prosecutions for "blasphemy" have occurred in the United States, despite the language of the Constitution, Americans generally have been free from legal action by the government on matters of religious dissent.

The U.S. Supreme Court has never ruled on a case in which the central issue was blasphemy; however, it has indirectly made it clear that speech critical of religion is protected by the Constitution. In the 1952 case of *Burstyn v. Wilson*, New York authorities, at the urging of a number of influential clergymen of the state, had suppressed the Italian film *The Miracle* on the grounds of "sacrilege." *The Miracle*, directed by Roberto Rossellini and starring Anna Magnani, concerns a simple-minded peasant woman who believes, despite the jeering of townspeople, that her pregnancy resulted from a love affair with St.

Joseph, and that her out-of-wedlock baby is a miracle from God. Although many believed the film to be religious (and inspirational), others perceived it as sacrilegious.

By a unanimous vote the judges of the U.S. Supreme Court overturned New York's ban on *The Miracle.* In so doing, the Court said: "from the standpoint of freedom of speech and the press, it is enough to point out that the state has no legitimate interest in protecting any or all religions from views distasteful to them...." The Court then added: *"It is not the business of government in our nation to suppress real or imagined attacks upon a particular religious doctrine, whether they appear in publications, speeches, or motion pictures."* [Emphasis supplied.][7]

In a nutshell, under the First Amendment you have a high degree of freedom to say what you wish in the United States, including the criticism of politicians, government policies, and religion. However, there are constraints upon speech content that the courts have recognized. These constraints include inciting an audience to illegal conduct, and defamatory falsehoods that destroy a person's reputation. Let us now examine another dimension of public communication—expressing our views by staging protest marches and demonstrations.

Parades, Marches, and Demonstrations

In addition to understanding the controls upon speech content, the public speaker should know the basic principles of law that apply to communicating in the context of a mass demonstration, or a march or parade. In the 1939 landmark case of *Hague v. CIO*, the U.S. Supreme Court ruled that public streets, parks, sidewalks, and similar places must be open for the expression of opinion. Such public places may be regulated by cities and states, said the Court, but they may not be closed completely to the exercise of First Amendment rights.[8] In a 1972 case the Supreme Court clarified its basic position as follows: *"The crucial question is whether the manner of expression is basically incompatible with the normal activity of a particular place at a particular time."* [Emphasis added.][9]

In practical terms, the High Court has said that you may march, parade, or demonstrate, but that you must do so sensibly. For example, you should neither expect permission to march on a busy street during rush hour, nor to hold a demonstration near a school, a hospital, or a nursing home. It is legal for a city to require a parade permit, provided that it is issued on a content-neutral basis. In other words, all groups, regardless of what they stand for, should be treated equally under the law. If you are planning a march or demonstration, secure the required permits and follow the rules. If you find the rules arbitrary or otherwise unfair, negotiate. If negotiation does not resolve the dispute you can then consider a legal challenge.

Freedom of Speech on the Campus

Constitutional protection for expression on the college campus is generally the same as for society at large, provided the campus is state-supported. However, the courts have ruled that private schools—those that are not tax-supported or publicly owned or operated—are exempt from the free speech guarantees of state and federal constitutions. For this reason, students and faculty members in private schools must establish their academic freedom by means other than appeals to the First Amendment (such as by terms of a written contract, or by convincing those who govern the school of the desirability of freedom of expression on the campus).[10] The comments that follow, therefore, are applicable to public institutions, but not necessarily to private ones.

44

*Part I
Speaking
and Listening
in a
Democratic
Society*

Academic freedom for teachers and students is an important element of the system of free expression in America. Although the U.S. Supreme Court has never ruled that academic freedom is a fully protected constitutional right, it has come close. In a 1967 academic freedom case, for example, the Court praised campus liberty by saying: "Our Nation is deeply committed to safeguarding academic freedom.... That freedom is...a special concern of the First Amendment, which does not tolerate laws that cast a pall of orthodoxy over the classroom." American schools need a "robust exchange of ideas," added the Court, and thus should guard the right of dissent on the campus.[11]

There are, however, rules of law that govern campus dissent, just as there are for expression off campus. Incitement to riot, or defamation, for example, can be punished whether expressed on or off campus. Also, the courts have held that reasonable campus rules to regulate time, place, and manner of speaking, so as to protect the educational enterprise, are not violations of rights of free speech. For example, you do not have the right to disrupt classes or to disturb the quiet of the library by speechmaking.[12]

Finally, limits placed by your instructor upon topics for classroom speeches do not necessarily violate your constitutional rights. For example, an instructor need not give credit to a student who delivers an informative lecture on "The Life of Cicero" when the assignment is for a persuasive speech on a contemporary community issue. The freedom of a campus forum is not extended to the classroom where specialized assignments are required to meet legitimate educational goals.

As we have seen, speakers in America have a wide degree of freedom to criticize the government and to speak on various issues that concern them. But what about speaker responsibility? Based upon the democratic values derived from our respect for persons, and the various assumptions that flow from those values, what standards of ethics should we apply to our public statements? We conclude this chapter by examining your responsibilities as a speaker in a free society.

III. Speaking Responsibly: Ethical Issues for the Public Speaker

The Greeks gave the West democracy, rhetorical theory, and freedom of speech. They also gave us a concern for the responsible exercise of the art of public speaking. As early as the fourth century B.C., the Athenian philosopher Plato criticized those teachers of persuasion who encouraged their students to win agreement by any means, including dishonest ones. The Romans, too, were concerned with the ethics of the speaker. In the *Institutes of Oratory* (ca.

Freedom of assembly is protected in state-supported schools, much the same as it is in society as a whole. Private institutions, however, are exempt from state and federal guarantees of free speech. (Michael Grecco/Stock, Boston)

95 A.D.), Quintilian sets forth his "good man theory" of rhetoric by asserting that to be a *great* communicator, a person must be both morally upright and eloquent—that is, "a good man, skilled in speaking." Above all, he emphasizes, the speaker should be morally good. It would be tragic, Quintilian adds, if we used "the power of speech to be the accomplice of crime, the foe to innocency, and the enemy of truth."[13] Eighteen-hundred years later, John Stuart Mill, the British author of *On Liberty*, recognizes that freedom to communicate can be abused when he states: "The gravest of [offenses is] to argue sophistically, to suppress facts or arguments, to misstate the elements of the case, or misrepresent the opposite opinion."[14]

Modern teachers of public speaking are also concerned about communication ethics. Reflecting this concern, the Speech Communication Association—the nation's largest professional society for teachers of communication theory and practice—has established both a Commission on Freedom of Expression and a Commission on Communication Ethics. In addition, the SCA has adopted a "Credo for Free and Responsible Communication in a Democratic Society." (See Figure 3.1.)

As we begin our examination of right and wrong in public speaking, we need to remind ourselves that disagreement on issues, and unethical speech,

CREDO FOR FREE AND RESPONSIBLE COMMUNICATION

IN A DEMOCRATIC SOCIETY

Speech Communication Association

Recognizing the essential place of free and responsible communication in a democratic society, and recognizing the distinction between the freedoms our legal system should respect and the responsibilities our educational system should cultivate, we members of the Speech Communication Association endorse the following statement of principles:

We believe that freedom of speech and assembly must hold a central position among American constitutional principles, and we express our determined support for the right of peaceful expression by any communicative means available.

We support the proposition that a free society can absorb with equanimity speech which exceeds the boundaries of generally accepted beliefs and mores; that much good and little harm can ensue if we err on the side of freedom, whereas much harm and little good may follow if we err on the side of suppression.

We criticize as misguided those who believe that the justice of their cause confers license to interfere physically and coercively with the speech of others, and we condemn intimidation, whether by powerful majorities or strident minorities, which attempts to restrict free expression.

We accept the responsibility of cultivating by precept and example, in our classrooms and in our communities, enlightened uses of communication; of developing in our students a respect for precision and accuracy in communication, and for reasoning based upon evidence and a judicious discrimination among values.

We encourage our students to accept the role of well-informed and articulate citizens, to defend the communication rights of those with whom they may disagree, and to expose abuses of the communication process.

We dedicate ourselves fully to these principles, confident in the belief that reason will ultimately prevail in a free marketplace of ideas.

FIGURE 3.1

Credo for Free and Responsible Communication in a Democratic Society by the Speech Communication Association. (Endorsed by the Speech Communication Association, 1972, and reprinted here with the Association's permission.)

are not the same thing. There is a difference between lying, falsifying evidence, and deliberately misrepresenting one's beliefs, and in holding an opinion—a "personal truth"—that others do not accept. For example, in the debate over abortion rights, both those who believe that abortion should be a private decision, and those who want legal abortion ended, can be equally sincere; both sides express the "truth as they see it," yet they disagree on what the "truth" is. In other words, speakers who disagree can practice the art of persuasion ethically while arguing different points of view. Honest disagreement should not be confused with rhetorical irresponsibility.

The democratic perspective set forth at the beginning of this chapter provides the philosophical foundation for this text's approach to responsible public speaking in a free society. As the late Karl R. Wallace, for many years chairman of the Department of Speech of the University of Illinois, observed, "communication inevitably must stand for and must reflect the same ethical values as the political society of which it is a part."[15] These values, which include a respect for persons and a preference for persuasion over coercion for developing social policy, guide us in formulating standards of communication ethics. In the discussion that follows, we will focus on four areas of concern: responsibility to yourself, to your audience, to speech content, and to society at large.

Responsibility to Yourself

You have a personal duty to believe in your subject and be knowledgeable about it. Public speaking, including classroom speaking, is not a game of "let's pretend." Those who approach it without sincerity demean themselves and the art of human communication. In all of your speaking, keep in mind the adage, "Unto thine own self be true." To illustrate, in a public speaking class in a small, liberal arts college several years ago, a leader of a campus religious organization delivered her first persuasive speech on why she believed in social drinking. During the discussion period, the instructor asked the young woman if she really believed in social drinking. Her reply was "no," for she opposed all drinking of alcoholic beverages. Why, then, had she spoken as she did? "I didn't think it mattered what I spoke on," she said, "just so long as it concerned a controversial issue."

At this point the instructor stressed to the entire class that students in public speaking compose a *genuine* audience—not a group gathered to hear unrealistic exercises in voice, diction, and delivery. Therefore, classroom speeches should be derived from the sincere beliefs and knowledge of the speaker, just as they should for speeches delivered elsewhere. The instructor then urged the members of the class to base future speeches on viewpoints about which they had honest convictions. This principle applies to *your* speechmaking as well, both in class and out. Being true to your own beliefs is the first step in being ethical with your audience—our next area of concern.

Responsibility to the Audience

You have a responsibility to respect the members of your audience. Each speech you prepare and deliver should reflect your esteem for those who will listen to you and think about your ideas. Keep asking yourself: am I honoring my audience (and, at the same time, being true to myself) by speaking on subjects in which I sincerely believe, that are derived from knowledge and reason, and that will, if accepted, benefit my listeners? In short, are you recognizing that those to whom you speak are persons of dignity and worth who have the capacity for critical thinking? Remember that this standard should be applied to all of your audiences, including the one composed of fellow students in the speech classroom.

An example of a student speaker who was responsible to her audience occurred several years ago in a university public speaking class. In this instance, the student discussed with the instructor her plans to deliver a persuasive speech stating her opposition to the decision of the U.S. Supreme Court to—as she put it—"take God out of the classroom by banning prayer in school." While agreeing that the topic was a fine choice for a persuasive speech, the instructor did specify that the student must study the opinion of the court on the issue.[16] A few days later the student delivered her speech, passionately

48

*Part I
Speaking
and Listening
in a
Democratic
Society*

defending the Supreme Court's decision. The difference between her initial position and the one she came to support was knowledge, for she had learned that the Supreme Court had not done what she had been led to believe. Furthermore, she agreed with the Court's position once she understood it. The result was a speech in which the speaker was, at once, true to herself and to her audience, for her speech expressed an informed opinion that she believed the audience ought to understand—and accept.

Responsibility to the Content of the Speech

You should be sure that your speech is based on sound inferences and evidence, that your terms are defined, and that the arguments are clearly presented so that your listeners can follow them, comprehend them, and subject them to critical examination. In the area of logical support (*logos*), this means that your reasoning should be of the highest quality, and that your evidence should be factual and honestly used. Put another way, avoid the deliberate use of fallacious reasoning and the falsification, misrepresentation, or distortion of evidence.

Cases developed by logical argument are not always persuasive. In order to move listeners to decision and action, appeals to human emotions, needs, and values (*pathos*) are sometimes required. Also, people often do not respond to a logical view communicated by a speaker whom they dislike or disrespect. Therefore, the speaker needs to include in the speech information that will help establish his or her credibility (*ethos*) with the audience.

The ethics of persuasion derived from *pathos* and *ethos* depends upon how they are used. For example, a speaker who is urging residents to leave a community situated near an active volcano because the volcano is showing signs of erupting, and who develops a rational, scientific case for the recommendation, can employ the appeal of fear—a classic type of *pathos*—to strengthen the persuasiveness of the message. Assuming the speaker sincerely believes that a tragedy will occur if the people do not evacuate immediately, the use of an appeal to fear is certainly ethical. Indeed, the speaker in this instance is morally bound to employ emotional proof if that is the available means of persuasion!

If this same speaker is a volcanologist, he or she is also being ethical to say so. Such knowledge does enhance the speaker in the listeners' minds—that is, it creates credibility—thus adding persuasive force to the message. On the other hand, a speaker who falsely claims to be an authority on volcanoes is being unethical. In your speaking, therefore, you employ *ethos* responsibly when you enhance a message that is sincere and based on logic by letting the audience know those facts about yourself which help build your credibility. This includes information that informs the audience that you know what you are talking about, that you believe in your proposition sincerely, and that you respect the integrity of your listeners.

Responsibility to Society at Large

Finally, you have a responsibility to society at large—a society that assumes that it is desirable to have a variety of voices in the "marketplace of ideas" so that, through the clash of debate, the "best" thoughts emerge and are accepted by a free citizenry. Admittedly, this assumption entails considerable risk; yet, it is a cornerstone of our free society. You support this system of liberty of expression when you become thoroughly informed about your speech subjects, base your speaking upon reason and evidence, use honest information to establish your credibility, and employ appeals to human emotions, needs, and values responsibly. In addition, you demonstrate a constructive concern for a free society when you encourage others—including those with whom you might disagree—to participate in the marketplace of ideas by presenting their opinions for consideration by the citizenry.

This Chapter in Brief

Freedom to speak and responsibility in public speaking work together for the social good in a democratic society. Both are derived from our democratic values, which include respect for the individual as a person of dignity, worth, and critical capacity. The assumptions of democracy that flow from respect for persons include preference for persuasion over force as a means of change, the right of free speech, decision by majority vote, and regard for minority rights.

Although speakers in the United States have almost unlimited liberty to address any subject of concern, some restrictions do apply, as set forth by the courts over the years. First, concerning speech *content*, speaking on political and social issues, including criticism of the government, is permitted until it reaches the point of inciting an audience to illegal conduct in those circumstances the audience is likely to actually carry out that conduct. In addition, defamatory falsehoods (slander and libel) are not protected by the Constitution; such expression invites civil suits for monetary damages, especially when a person falsely accuses another of such things as criminality, disease, dishonesty, or sexual immorality. However, you are protected from government action when you discuss or criticize religion, for the Supreme Court has ruled that the state has no "legitimate interest in protecting any or all religions from views distasteful to them."

Second, reasonable *regulations of time, place, and manner* are permitted, especially as applied to parades, marches, and demonstrations. Rules that require securing a parade permit in advance of an event are allowed by the courts, provided the issuing agency administers the permit system without picking and choosing from among applicants (that is, without "discretion"). In short, permits must be given in a way that is equitable to all.

Third, the U.S. Supreme Court has been supportive of *freedom of speech on the college campus*, including academic freedom, although some restrictions do apply. In general, students and faculty members in public colleges and universities (but not necessarily in private ones) have the same liberty of expression while on campus as they do off the campus. However, this liberty should be exercised on campus so as not to interfere with or disrupt the educational process.

In addition to communication freedom, the speaker in a democracy has at least four key areas of *communication responsibility*: (1) to himself or herself; (2) to the audience; (3) to the content of the speech; and (4) to society at large.

50

*Part I
Speaking
and Listening
in a
Democratic
Society*

The personal responsibility means that the speaker should be prepared, knowledgeable, and sincere. In addition, the audience should be approached with an attitude of respect. Speech content should be founded in reason, and should be supported by sound evidence. Finally, the speaker should be concerned with the social consequences of the message.

In his discussion of the *Ethics of Speech Communication*, Professor Thomas R. Nilsen of the University of Washington summarizes well the theme of this chapter. Writes Nilsen:

> In public discourse the speech that serves our values...is that which strengthens the processes of democracy, fosters freedom of expression, provides information adequate for constructive decisions, engages in significant debate, examines alternatives and objectively appraises evidence and conclusions, and inspires to noble objectives. This includes truth telling.[17]

EXERCISES

1. Keep a "Freedom of Speech and Communication Ethics" scrapbook during the course, saving newspaper and magazine stories on issues and cases of free speech and ethics in public communication. Be sure to record the source, date, and page for your clippings as you enter them in your scrapbook. Near the end of the course arrange with the instructor to show your collection to the class, and to discuss your overall reaction to the problems you have noted.

2. Check with the office of student affairs at your school to see what official regulations, if any, are applicable to student, faculty, and visitor freedom of expression on campus. If the regulations are in print, make copies for your public speaking class. Arrange with the instructor to distribute the material and to discuss the rules in class.

3. Think about your own standards of communication ethics, then write a statement setting out the standards of ethics you should apply to yourself. Date your statement and save it for future reference (and for revision and improvement as additional thoughts occur to you).

SELECTED READINGS

Readings on Freedom of Speech

Brant, Irving. *The Bill of Rights: Its Origin and Meaning.* Indianapolis, Ind.: Bobbs-Merrill, 1965. Brant, biographer of James Madison, traces our civil liberties as embodied in the Bill of Rights to early English law, the Magna Carta, and the evolution of concern for personal liberty in England and in early American history.

Haiman, Franklyn S. *Speech and Law in a Free Society.* Chicago: University of Chicago Press, 1981. Presents the thinking of a leading communication scholar on issues of freedom of speech. Well-written, comprehensive, and recommended.

Hentoff, Nat. *The First Freedom: The Tumultuous History of Free Speech in America.* New York: Delacorte Press, 1980. A popular history of free speech, with an emphasis on the development of freedom for political dissent and for the communication rights of religious minorities.

Levy, Leonard W. *Emergence of a Free Press*. New York: Oxford University Press, 1985. In this update of his 1960 study, *Legacy of Suppression*, Levy uses detailed historical research to uphold his view that many of the founding fathers were not supportive of free speech. He stresses that we must maintain our communication freedoms with *contemporary* arguments rather than relying too heavily on history.

Tedford, Thomas L. *Freedom of Speech in the United States*. New York: Random House, 1985. A survey of the history of freedom of speech in the West, and a summary of major areas of law ranging from defamation and "obscenity" to commercial advertising and broadcasting. Written for the nonlawyer.

Readings on Communication Ethics

Andersen, Kenneth E. *Persuasion: Theory and Practice*. 2d ed. Boston: Allyn and Bacon, 1978. Students of communication ethics should see Chapter 15, "Ethics and Persuasion," and Chapter 16, "Totalitarian Persuasion."

Bradley, Bert E. *Fundamentals of Speech Communication: The Credibility of Ideas*. 5th ed. Dubuque, Ia.: Wm. C. Brown, 1988. Bradley discusses speaker responsibilities in Chapter 4, and the responsibilities of listeners in Chapter 5.

Johannesen, Richard L. *Ethics in Human Communication*. 3d ed. Prospect Heights, Ill.: Waveland Press, 1990. Johannesen's text does an excellent job of introducing the reader to the literature of communication ethics.

Minnick, Wayne C. *The Art of Persuasion*. 2d ed. Boston: Houghton Mifflin, 1968. Chapter 11 sets out Minnick's views on the ethics of persuasion, including the ethical use of emotional proofs.

Nilsen, Thomas R. *Ethics of Speech Communication*. 2d ed. Indianapolis, Ind.: Bobbs-Merrill, 1974. Nilsen, who has written often concerning speech ethics, pulls his views together in this brief volume. Recommended for all public speakers.

Wallace, Karl R. "An Ethical Basis of Communication." *The Speech Teacher* 4 (January 1955): 1–9. Wallace constructs his four moralities of speech communication on the values of a democratic society.

ENDNOTES

1. Walter Lippmann, *The Public Philosophy* (New York: The New American Library, 1955), pp. 98–99.
2. For some typical views on the relationship of public speaking and democracy, see Karl R. Wallace, "An Ethical Basis of Communication," *The Speech Teacher* 4 (January 1955), 5–6; Thomas R. Nilsen, "Free Speech, Persuasion, and the Democratic Process," *Quarterly Journal of Speech* 44 (October 1958), 235–236; Waldo W. Braden and Earnest Brandenburg, *Oral Decision-Making* (Harper & Brothers, 1955), pp. 4–8; and A. Craig Baird, *Rhetoric: A Philosophical Inquiry* (New York: Ronald Press, 1965), pp. 77–115.
3. Thomas I. Emerson, *The System of Freedom of Expression* (New York: Random House, 1970), p. 22.

52

*Part I
Speaking
and Listening
in a
Democratic
Society*

4. The U.S. Supreme Court ruled that the First Amendment applied to the states in the case of *Gitlow v. New York*, 268 U.S. 652 (1925).

5. The U.S. Supreme Court's landmark sedition opinion came in the Ku Klux Klan case of *Brandenburg v. Ohio*, 394 U.S. 444 (1969).

6. Justice Stewart's remark about defamation is from *Rosenblatt v. Baer*, 383 U.S. 75 (1966), at p. 92.

7. *Burstyn v. Wilson*, 343 U.S. 495 (1952).

8. *Hague v. CIO*, 307 U.S. 496 (1939). The case originated in Jersey City, N.J., where the mayor, Frank Hague, refused to permit prolabor groups, such as the CIO, to speak.

9. *Grayned v. Rockford*, 408 U.S. 104 (1972). This case concerned a demonstration near a school.

10. For a discussion of communication rights in private schools, see George E. Stevens, "Contract Law, State Constitutions and Freedom of Expression in Private Schools," *Journalism Quarterly* 58 (Winter 1981): 613–627 ff.

11. The academic freedom case is *Keyishian v. Board of Regents*, 385 U.S. 589 (1967).

12. *Tinker v. Des Moines Independent Community School District*, 393 U.S. 503 (1969).

13. For Plato's remarks on communication ethics see the *Gorgias*, trans. W. C. Helmbold (Indianapolis, Ind.: Bobbs-Merrill, 1952), pp. 22–24. The Quintilian quote comes from *The Institutio Oratoria*, ed. Charles E. Little, vol. 2 (Nashville, Tenn.: George Peabody College for Teachers, 1951), pp. 223–224.

14. John Stuart Mill, *On Liberty*, ed. David Spitz (New York: Norton, 1975), p. 51.

15. Karl R. Wallace, op. cit., (January 1955): 5.

16. The school prayer case that had attracted the interest of the public speaking student is *Engel v. Vitale*, 370 U.S. 421 (1962). For a discussion of this case, see Leo Pfeffer, *Religious Freedom* (Skokie, Ill.: National Textbook Co., 1977), pp. 77–80.

17. Thomas R. Nilsen, *Ethics of Speech Communication*, 2d ed. (Indianapolis, Ind.: Bobbs-Merrill, 1974), p. 41.

> *...the task of the citizen today, to an unprecedented degree, is to distinguish sense from nonsense, confronted as we are by the greatest deluge of words that human beings have ever faced.*

—S. I. Hayakawa,
ETC (1949)[1]

Chapter 4

THE COMMUNICATION PROCESS AND LISTENING

I magine that you have worked hard to prepare a speech for a campus debate on a subject of current concern, that you have researched your content carefully and have made a special effort to develop sound reasoning and evidence to support your opinion. You show up for the meeting to find that you and a speaker for the opposite view are the only people present. Both of you face an empty room. Even if you decide to go ahead with your planned remarks, and speak eloquently to the empty chairs in the room, you are not delivering a genuine speech. Why not? Because a speech requires an audience—*listeners*—in order to be real. Without listeners, your talking is reduced to an exercise.

As this example makes clear, public speaking is not a one-way activity; rather, speaking is part of a complex communication process that includes listening—and other factors as well. To help you better understand what is happening when you make a speech, or when you listen to one, we will examine two key topics. First, we will consider the dynamic relationship between speaking and listening within the context of the communication process. Then we will focus on listening, with specific suggestions for improving listening skills.

I. The Communication Process

The Components of the Communication Process

Communication can be defined as the process by which humans attempt to share thoughts, attitudes, and feelings with one another. Students of human communication have identified at least seven components of the communication process. Briefly stated, they are as follows: (1) a message *source* (2) generates a *message* (3) that is sent over a *channel* (4) to a *receiver* who (5) responds with *feedback*. (6) Those things that distract from this process are called *interference*. All of the above occur within (7) a communication *situation*.[2] This basic model of the process of communication, with an emphasis on how it works during speechmaking, is illustrated in Figure 4.1.

The components of the communication process can be illustrated further. The *source* of a message is the individual, group, or institution that originates the information or viewpoint to be communicated; sources include journalists, speakers, filmmakers, poets, scriptwriters, advertisers, and so on. The *message* consists of the information or opinion to be communicated, and includes such things as speeches, written statements, and the various ideas that can be communicated by other means—such as by music, pictures, film, or video. The *channel* is the means employed for conveying the message to the receivers. It can vary from the soundwaves that carry human speech from one person to another, to media channels such as newspapers, magazines, books, telephone wires, cable, and so forth. The *receiver* is the person or group of persons to whom the message is sent. This includes those in an audience who

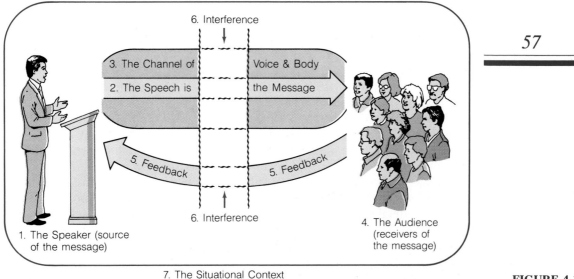

6. Interference

3. The Channel of | Voice & Body

2. The Speech is | the Message

5. Feedback 5. Feedback

6. Interference

57

1. The Speaker (source of the message)

4. The Audience (receivers of the message)

7. The Situational Context

FIGURE 4.1

The Communication Process Applied to Public Speaking. *There are seven elements in the communication process of public speaking: (1) The message* source, *or speaker, prepares a (2)* message (speech), *that is communicated by means of the (3)* channel *of vocal and physical delivery to (4) the* receivers (audience) *who respond with (5)* feedback *to the speaker. (6)* Interference *in various forms affects the clarity of the communication to the audience, as well as the clarity of the feedback to the speaker. The entire process occurs within (7) a* situational context *that includes both the immediate occasion and the circumstances of society at large.*

listen to a speech, a participant in conversation or group discussion (who both speaks and listens), a reader, a person who views a television program or film or who listens to the radio, etc. *Feedback* is the response of the receiver to the source and message. It can vary from the mental response of agreeing or disagreeing with the ideas being communicated, to observable responses such as nodding the head, applause, donating money, joining a cause, or purchasing the product being advertised. *Interference* is anything that distracts from the communication process. It includes such things as static on a phone line, a jet flying overhead, or a baby crying in an auditorium during a speech. Finally, the *situation* is the overall context in which the communication process occurs. It varies from sitting alone while reading a book to viewing a movie in a theater, or talking to fellow students in the dining hall, or listening to a speaker during commencement exercises.

The examples just given should make it obvious that the communication process is at work in numerous ways in our daily lives. You are a message source, for example, when you write a letter home, compose a short story or a poem, order a pizza, or ask a question in class. You are a receiver of a message when you read a textbook, watch television, read a billboard, or listen to a classroom lecture. In either case, whether you are the source or the receiver, the communication includes a message being sent over a channel, your response (or the response of others), the various forms of interference that occur, and the situational context in which it all happens. Let us now look at this process at work in speechmaking.

58

*Part I
Speaking
and Listening
in a
Democratic
Society*

The Communication Process and Your Speaking and Listening

1. *The public speaker is the message source.* Suppose that a speaker stands before the city council and says, "I have just learned that toxic waste has been dumped in a drainage ditch behind my house, and that nothing is being done to clean it up." That speaker is the source of a message, just as you are when you deliver a classroom speech or talk to an organization on campus or in the community. Some message sources have more credibility with their audiences than do others. For example, speakers who reveal a lack of knowledge about the subject under discussion, or who speak in an insincere or offensive manner, soon lose the trust of their listeners. On the other hand, when a speaker displays a sincere belief in the message being communicated, supports that belief with sound reasoning and evidence, and reveals in-depth knowledge of the subject, the credibility of that speaker is enhanced in the minds of the listeners. You can establish your credibility as a message source by demonstrating to your audiences that you are informed on the subject, that you sincerely believe in the message you are communicating, and that you are a person of integrity and good will.

2. *The speech is the message.* The message in public speaking consists of the ideas to be presented, the supporting materials of the speech (examples, statistics, quotations, etc.), the organization of the speech content, and the language used. The message is communicated by both verbal and nonverbal means. By verbal is meant the words the speaker employs, and by nonverbal is meant the tone and quality of the voice, movement and gesture, facial expression, visual directness, and the dress of the speaker.

Speakers should be aware that words are symbols; that is, words stand for objects, actions, and concepts, but are not the same thing as the objects, actions, and concepts for which they stand. If you doubt this, write the word "bicycle" on a piece of paper, then try to ride it around the campus; or, when you wake up tomorrow morning, write "hot coffee" on a piece of paper and try to drink it. Because words function as symbols, they do not literally "inject" the speaker's meaning into the minds of those in the audience. Rather, *words stir up meaning that is already present within each listener.* When you are speaking, therefore, keep in mind that meaning does not exist within the words you use—meaning exists within the individuals in your audience. Your message is clear to the extent that your verbal symbols stimulate in your listeners the meaning that you intend.

Messages phrased in unfamiliar or abstract words can be assigned meaning by the listener that differs from the meaning intended by the speaker. For example, the phrase "he responded in a vacillating manner" would be confusing to some audiences; the speaker would be clearer to simply say "he couldn't make up his mind." Likewise, saying that "Bill has minimal cognitive awareness at 6:00 A.M." is not as clear as saying "Bill finds it difficult to wake up in the morning."

Similarly, vague and abstract terms—such as "justice is served," "humane response," and "subversive activity"—can cause misunderstanding because people interpret these terms in different ways. For example, the assertion, "Joe took part in a subversive activity," might stir a variety of meanings among listeners concerning what Joe had done. On the other hand, stating the point in concrete language, such as "Joe sold a blueprint of a secret airplane to a foreign government," would generate a more exact meaning in the listeners' minds. By using words that are familiar to the audience, and that are specific rather than abstract, speakers can improve the accuracy of the message they are trying to communicate.

3. *Delivery by means of voice and body is the channel.* In the typical public speaking situation where the speaker talks to a group of people in a room or auditorium, the message reaches the listeners by means of soundwaves and lightwaves, there being no cable, wire, or other special channel involved. In other words, as sound and sight travel over the air through the room, the listener hears and sees the speaker, and thus receives the message. Of course, the speaker who converses on the telephone, uses a loudspeaker, talks on radio, or appears on television adds the electronic channels of those media to the process of communication.

4. *The listeners are the receivers of the message.* An audience is essential to the public speaking situation. As was noted at the beginning of this chapter, if you stand before an empty room to deliver your message, you are not making a real speech, for no communication with other persons has occurred. From the viewpoint of the speaker, each audience needs to be carefully analyzed and the speech adapted to its beliefs, values, and attitudes. From the audience's viewpoint, however, it is the other way around—that is, the task of the member of the audience is to listen carefully, and to critically evaluate the speaker and the speech. From this perspective, listeners are not thought of as passive receivers of a message but as active participants in the communication process.

5. *The audience responds with feedback.* Just as a speaker employs both verbal and nonverbal means of communicating with an audience, so do listeners provide feedback that is verbal and nonverbal. Although most immediate feedback in the public speaking situation is nonverbal, it can be verbal if questions are permitted, or if an audience member shouts words of encouragement (or derision) at the speaker. Nonverbal feedback includes how attentive listeners are during the speech, head movement (such as nodding in agreement), facial expression, shifting of the body or shuffling of the feet when bored or restless, and so on. Feedback continues after the speech is finished in many instances, and can consist of such responses as casting a vote, participating in a post-speech discussion, signing a pledge card, or purchasing a product or service.

You are influenced by audience feedback when you are making a speech. If you sense boredom, you might decide to skip over a part of the content and complete the speech sooner than intended; or, if you see that those in the back of the room are straining to hear your remarks, you might speak louder. The overall result is circular communication, from speaker to audience and back to speaker, in a dynamic, unified, two-way process. In particular, note that at the same moment you are talking to your audience, your audience is "talking" to you.

60

Part I
*Speaking
and Listening
in a
Democratic
Society*

6. *Interference detracts from the communication process.* All communicators should be aware that various kinds and degrees of interference can distract both speakers and listeners during the communication process. There are generally three forms of interference in the public speaking situation. First are those distractions related to the facilities being used. The room can be poorly lit, the space can be uncomfortably hot or cold, or a noisy heating or cooling system can make it difficult to hear the speaker.

Second, members of the audience can contribute interference by coughing, yawning, whispering, "studying for the next class," or consuming food and drink during the speech. Finally, outside occurrences such as a thunderstorm, or the sirens of emergency vehicles passing nearby can distract the attention. No doubt you have experienced distractions similar to those suggested above, either as a speaker or as a member of an audience.

If interference occurs while you are speaking, you will need to measure the effect on your audience and deal with the problem in an appropriate way. "Appropriate" action can range from ignoring a passing distraction, such as a plane flying overhead, to stopping the speech to comment on the problem and to make an effort to eliminate it (such as having a noisy fan turned off, or an open door closed in order to block sounds from a busy hallway).

7. *Speaking and listening occur within a specific situation.* Communication does not occur within a vacuum. Rather, for both the public speaker and listener, communication occurs within a given context, or situation, such as a student organization, an academic classroom, a church service, a court of law, or a session of your state legislature. As speaker, an important part of your speech preparation is to gather information about the speaking situation, including the sponsors of the event, the purpose, the place of meeting, the expected size of the audience, and the special interests of those who will attend. When you are a listener, however, other factors emerge—factors that we now examine in some detail.

II. The Skills and Responsibilities of Listening

Although you are taking a public speaking course in order to improve your skills in presenting ideas to others, you actually spend a much larger proportion of your communicating time listening rather than speaking. Research on how we spend our time communicating reveals that about 50 percent is spent in listening, whereas only about 25 percent is used for speaking. The remaining time is used for reading (about 15 percent) and writing (about 10 percent).[3] If you will consider your "communication day"—the time spent listening to classroom lectures, talking with friends, attending meetings, working in the library, and so on—you will, no doubt, confirm that you listen more than you speak, read, or write. It follows that your total communication proficiency should include skill in listening.

In particular, we are concerned with two kinds of listening: informational and critical. By *informational listening* we mean listening to gain knowledge, such as note taking during a lecture, or concentrating on the instructions of a doctor concerning a schedule of medication. By *critical listening* we mean attending to persuasive messages of various types, such as television commercials, sermons, or campaign speeches. Both forms of listening command our attention because they are important to education, business, the professions, and the function of democratic government.

Some Listening Fundamentals

There are at least three areas of significant difference between receiving a message by reading and receiving a message by listening, namely: communicator difference, contextual difference, and content difference. Let us look briefly at each of the three.

First, when the *communicator* is a writer, that individual is not present for you to evaluate "in person" when you are reading. On the other hand, in listening you see and hear the speaker in a living transaction. The face-to-face nature of the speaking situation allows you to take the measure of the individual who is delivering the message. The complexity of your responsibility in listening includes being aware of physical and vocal elements of communication as well as the subjective reaction to the communicator's dress, sincerity, personality, etc. We should consider what we know about a writer as we read, of course; however, in listening we experience challenges of evaluation that are absent when we read.

Second, the *context* for reading is one of quiet solitude, for the reader is not surrounded by an audience and does not face the public speaker. During reading we hear no speaker's voice, see no visual emphasis by means of movement and gesture, experience no face-to-face confrontation with the message source. The opposite is the case when we listen to a speech. Because of the dynamics of the speaking-listening situation, special skills are needed for listening so that we can focus on the ideas being presented and evaluate them wisely. Even when we are listening to a message on television, the visual elements demand skills of perception quite different from our "reading corner" experience.

Third, the *content* of a written message can be carefully—even slowly— read and reread if necessary. If it is complicated, we can study it, look up words in the dictionary, and even resort to an encyclopedia or other reference work for assistance. Not so in listening to a speech. As a rule, we hear it once; we cannot stop the speaker and ask for an instant replay; we must grasp what is being said during the moment of presentation or else miss some of the meaning that the speaker is attempting to communicate. In short, we must put forth the effort to hear, and to think, while listening.

At least five fundamental listening skills should be developed so that you can meet your responsibilities as a consumer of oral discourse.

Prepare yourself to listen, then listen actively. When possible, do some reading and thinking in advance of the speech so that you will be knowledgeable about the subject to be presented. During the speech listen actively by putting forth the mental energy—the concentration—necessary to follow the important points, the reasoning, and the evidence employed by the speaker. This is the application of your freedom to listen that serves as a counterpart to the speaker's freedom to communicate.

Responsible listening requires concentration, critical examination of ideas and arguments, careful thought, and judicious decision making. (Kathleen Foster/Impact Visuals)

Be alert to interference. As noted earlier, interference of various types is a component of the communication process. The skillful listener is prepared for interference and deals with the problem purposefully. Interference can vary from those distractions that occur within yourself—such as letting your mind wander, or even daydreaming—to external ones such as audience activity or the physical features of the room or auditorium in which you are listening. Be prepared for interference in advance, and when it occurs, deal with it by pulling your thoughts back to the ideas of the speaker.

Listen past delivery. The speaker's dress, physical appearance, and use of voice and body influence us when we listen. Being human, we are inclined to pay more attention to a person who speaks directly and confidently than to one who is hesitant, evades eye contact, or speaks in a monotone. Keep in mind, however, that the speaker with the weak delivery might have the best ideas on the subject, whereas the one with strong delivery might have the weaker case. Dynamic delivery is no substitute for solid ideas, sound reasoning, and high-quality evidence. Therefore, make an effort to listen past delivery, whether it be weak or strong, to mentally examine the arguments, the reasoning, and the evidence set forth by the speaker.

Make use of the speech-thought differential. The concept of a speech-thought differential comes from studies that report that listeners can evaluate a speech three to four times faster than a speaker can deliver it.[4] Obviously, this provides you as a listener with a valuable mental tool, for you have the advantage of being able to think rapidly about what is being said without being left behind by the speaker.

Postpone decision making. In most instances of listening you do not have to make an immediate decision concerning the opinions or actions urged by the speaker. Pause to weigh the ideas presented; don't be rushed unless it is imperative because of some unusual circumstance (such as having to cast a vote immediately on the issue being debated). Go over the ideas in your mind. Perhaps you will want to talk to others before deciding, or do some research on the subject. With these concepts in place, we now turn our attention to listening for the purpose of gaining knowledge, and listening critically to persuasive discourse.

Informational Listening

Informational listening means listening to *understand*. It occurs when you attend a speaker who is giving directions, explaining how something works, or lecturing on a subject such as "The Early Life of Abraham Lincoln," or "Leading Economic Theories of the Twentieth Century." It also applies to your evaluation of persuasive messages—those messages that attempt to modify your beliefs or actions—for understanding the ideas of a speech that is aimed at changing your mind is an important responsibility of the listener in a free society. In addition to applying the five fundamental listening skills discussed above, you can improve your informational listening in two other ways: first, develop an organized system for following the content of the speech; and second, learn to take clear, written notes.

Listen to content in a systematic way. You can apply a practical, effective method for comprehending speech content by listening for three key elements of a speech, namely, the purpose, the main points that develop that purpose, and the supporting ideas and evidence that back up each main point. Some speakers will help you by clearly stating a purpose, such as "I want to tell you about the three types of insurance our company offers as fringe benefits," or "Let me explain why I favor a national sales tax." When the speaker doesn't state a purpose, you will need to identify it by noting such cues as the title, the speaker's introductory remarks, or the general nature of the subject matter. Either way, concentrate first on identifying the speaker's purpose as accurately as possible.

Second, follow the development of the purpose by systematically noting the main points of the speech. If the speaker announces a pattern of development, organize your thinking around that pattern. For example, a speaker might say that he or she will first examine "the dimensions of the problem under discussion," then will "set forth proposals for solving the problem." You can immediately identify a problem-solution pattern in such a statement, and be prepared to listen carefully as the two points are discussed.

Here are some additional examples of patterns for main points that you can listen for (in some cases you will need to infer the pattern on your own, for some speakers don't state their plan of organization clearly). A *chronological plan*, such as past-present-future, could be used to organize a promotional talk about a local historical museum. Here the speaker could divide the material by

64

*Part I
Speaking
and Listening
in a
Democratic
Society*

how the museum began, its present exhibits and services, and its future plans. A speaker can organize a discussion around the *geographical sections* of a territory, such as a city, a state, or a nation. This system is illustrated by a talk on the population growth of a state when the information is presented according to population figures from the eastern, central, and western parts of the state. Or, a speaker can use *topical enumeration*, such as explaining careers with the federal government according to the three branches (topics): legislative, executive, and judicial. Once you have recognized a plan or pattern in the discussion, use that knowledge as a tool for systematically focusing on key points of the speech.

Finally, after identifying a main point, mentally file supporting materials under it. In other words, allow the main headings to serve as "mental filing boxes" in which you place significant subpoints, examples, statistics, statements from authority, and the like. In some instances, however, you will need to supplement your recall skills with written notes. Let us, therefore, briefly examine some basic skills of notetaking.

Take written notes systematically. Even efficient, skillful listeners do not always depend on memory to retain the important details of a message. Examples include classroom note taking in preparation for an examination, or covering an important campus or community speech for your student newspaper or for the purpose of making a classroom report. In such cases, accurate written notes are needed.

When taking written notes, you can follow the same three-step system recommended above for "mental note taking." Also, use a standard set of numerals, such as you use when outlining a speech or term paper, to record your notes in a systematic way. Here is an actual example, taken from the notes of a college student in an argumentation and debate class. The instructor had announced that he would discuss "some thoughts concerning the place of debate in a democratic society." The student outlined the instructor's remarks as follows.

Subject of lecture: reasons for debate and conditions necessary for debate in a democracy.

I. Reasons for debate.
   A. When honest differences of opinion occur (inevitable in a complex society).
   B. When group doesn't know how to conduct a problem-solving discussion (or refuses to do so).
   C. When assembly is too large for informal discussion of the issue (discussion difficult when group larger than 15).
   D. When organization needs a quick decision.

II. Conditions necessary for democratic debate.
   A. Need sincere, willing speakers on both sides of issue.
   B. Need balanced presentation of both sides.
   C. Need organized body of listeners (an audience).
   D. Need fair governing rules (such as system of parliamentary procedure).

E. The two sides must agree on issue being debated, and on definition of terms.

F. Finally, decision is by majority vote.

In conclusion, instructor emphasized: debate is a useful tool for making decisions in a democracy; in fact, it is often absolutely essential. It should be conducted according to fair rules (agreed to in advance), and when finished, decision made by majority vote.

When the speaker goes beyond communicating knowledge and attempts to persuade us to change our attitudes or behavior, we need to listen for more than information. This extra challenge includes such matters as evaluating the speaker's reasoning and evidence and the social consequences of the proposal being presented. In other words, during persuasion, we need to listen *critically*.

Critical Listening: A Special Responsibility

When you are a member of an audience rather than the speaker, you have some listener responsibilities that are based on the principles of a free society. These include encouraging debate—the free and open exchange of ideas—and permitting the speaker (or speakers) to be heard. You should avoid intimidating a speaker, or participating in activities that prevent a person from speaking. As the Speech Communication Association's *Credo for Free and Responsible Communication* states: "We criticize as misguided those who believe that the justice of their cause confers license to interfere physically and coercively with the speech of others, and we condemn intimidation, whether by powerful majorities or strident minorities, which attempts to restrict free expression." (The complete text of the *Credo* appears in Chapter 3.)

A special note of concern applies to your public speaking classroom. Just as speakers outside the classroom situation deserve the quiet, courteous attention of the members of the audience, so do you and your classmates deserve the respectful attention of each other when one of you is making a speech. When speeches begin, therefore, you should give the speaker your direct, thoughtful attention. Just as you appreciate an attentive audience, so do your classmates.

In addition to listening courteously, we should listen critically, evaluating carefully what the speaker is saying according to the same four areas of concern that apply to the responsibilities of the speaker: the speaker's duties to himself or herself, to the audience, to the content of the speech, and to society in general. Let us see how you can apply them to listening.

The Speaker. As you listen, make the best judgment you can about the speaker's knowledge and sincerity. As a critical listener you should try to decide whether the speaker has fulfilled a personal responsibility to talk on a subject about which he or she is informed and believes in sincerely.

The Audience. In this second area, listen for evidence that the speaker respects you and the other members of the audience. Be alert to authoritarian attitudes that suggest the speaker is somehow superior to other people and has

66

Part I
Speaking
and Listening
in a
Democratic
Society

the "absolute truth" on the subject. Note whether the speaker respects democratic values by treating you and the others in the audience as persons of dignity and worth, and of thinking ability. For example, the speaker who asserts that persons of differing views are "absolutely wrong" or "intellectually dishonest" shows little respect for contrary opinion. However, the speaker who asserts a sincere belief in the ideas of the speech, while acknowledging that "honest disagreement exists," is showing an awareness of the diversity of opinion in our society.

The Content. The critical evaluation of the ideas of a speech involves how well you apply your listening skills to the speaker's logical and emotional appeals, as well as to how the speaker employs speech content to build his or her credibility with the audience. In the area of logical analysis (*logos*), listen for the speaker's central idea, and the reasoning and evidence used to back up that idea. Focus your thinking on two key questions: is the speech based on sound reasoning, and is that reasoning based on sound evidence? In addition, note whether the speaker identifies and qualifies the sources of the evidence to assist you in evaluating the supporting materials used. For example, the speaker who says "the experts agree with me on this subject," but fails to identify any "experts," is certainly not qualifying sources. On the other hand, the speaker who cites a source as "Dr. John Doe, director of research on communicable disease at State Medical College" provides specific information that helps you assess speech content.

Other supports include appeals to human emotions (*pathos*, or "emotional proof"), as well as the appeals derived from speaker credibility (*ethos*, or "ethical proof"). We cannot completely separate emotional and ethical proofs from logical proofs in any speaking situation; that is, at any given moment in a speech, we are being influenced by a mixture of *logos, pathos*, and *ethos*. As a thoughtful listener, therefore, keep asking whether or not the speech makes logical sense, no matter how emotionally moving it is, and no matter how impressed you are with the personality of the speaker.

The Society. Finally, ask yourself whether the speaker demonstrates a genuine concern for the social consequences of the speech. Be especially alert to evidence that the content is primarily self-serving, furthering the personal goals of the speaker to the detriment of those who listen and of society in general. The key question you should ask is this: *if the ideas of the speech are adopted, whom would they benefit the most*? You are justified in being critical of a speech if you determine that the sole or major beneficiary of its proposals is the speaker, or the group he or she represents, rather than the audience and society. For instance, an executive who pretends patriotic fervor in advocating government approval of a weapons system designed by his or her company, but who is really interested in the financial bonanza that would result from such approval, is being selfish rather than speaking with a social conscience.

This Chapter in Brief

The seven interacting components of the communication process (with special attention to the public speaking situation) can be summarized as follows: (1) a message *source* (or speaker) (2) generates a *message* (or speech) that (3) is sent over a *channel* (the vocal and physical expression of the speaker conducted to the audience by sound and light waves) to a (4) *receiver* (listener) who responds with (5) *feedback*; distractions during the process are called (6) *interference*; all of this occurs within a (7) specific *situation* (such as a classroom lecture, a speech in a campus auditorium, a political rally, etc.). Over the years communication theorists have focused on the source and the message (that is, the speaker and the speech) to the neglect of those who listen. In recent years, however, the theory and practice of effective listening have received serious attention from communication scholars.

Five basic listening skills are identified and explained. In summary form, the five basic skills are as follows: (1) prepare to listen, then listen actively by concentrating on the task at hand; (2) be alert to interference (including daydreaming), and keep your mind focused on the speaker and the message; (3) listen past the delivery of the speaker to carefully understand and evaluate the ideas being presented; (4) take advantage of the speech-thought differential (which reveals that you can listen and evaluate faster than a speaker can talk); and (5) when possible, postpone decision making to provide time for reflection.

Two kinds of listening are of primary importance in the give and take of public communication in a free society: *informational listening*, in which we seek to gain knowledge and understanding; and *critical listening*, in which we thoughtfully evaluate the speaker's motives and the soundness of the ideas being presented. When we are listening for information, we should follow the content in a systematic way, noting the purpose of the speech, the main points, and key supporting materials. When taking written notes, we should employ an organized system for recording the speech purpose and supporting points and materials. A method of outlining while note taking is recommended.

Critical listening, in which you evaluate both the speaker and the message, is a special responsibility of citizenship in a democracy, for it goes beyond the skills of listening to encompass the challenge of being a thoughtful and wise consumer of information and persuasion. As a listener, you should observe four areas responsibility, namely: (1) determine how well the speaker fulfills a personal obligation to be informed on the subject of the speech, and to sincerely believe in the message being presented; (2) note whether or not the speaker shows respect for the members of the audience by approaching them as persons of dignity, worth, and critical capacity; (3) listen carefully to determine whether or not the message is founded upon sound reasoning and evidence; and (4) evaluate the social consequences of the message.

EXERCISES

1. Apply the suggestions of this chapter concerning informational listening to your classes. Use the ideas regarding both mental and written note taking to evaluate and improve your personal listening skills in your courses. Make a special effort to improve your method of taking lecture notes.

2. Attend an event that features a speech on a controversial issue. Using your skills of critical listening, observe whether or not the speaker employs logical reasoning and sound evidence in support of the opinions presented. How influential was the speaker's personality and manner of delivery? Would you classify the speech as "responsible" or "irresponsible?" What are the reasons for your classification?

68

Part I
Speaking
and Listening
in a
Democratic
Society

SELECTED READINGS

Floyd, James J. *Listening: A Practical Approach.* Glenview, Ill.: Scott, Foresman, 1985. Floyd's well-organized introductory text presents the essentials of effective listening in a concise style.

Steil, Lyman K.; Barker, Larry L.; and Watson, Kittie W. *Effective Listening: Key to Your Success.* Reading, Mass.: Addison-Wesley, 1983. The authors, who conduct seminars in listening for business, government, and educational groups, summarize the basic theory and practice of effective listening.

Wolff, Florence I.; Marsnik, Nadine C.; Tacey, William S.; and Nichols, Ralph G. *Perceptive Listening.* New York: Holt, Rinehart and Winston, 1983. This text, written for college courses and classes in adult education, covers the theory of listening, and includes numerous practical suggestions to assist the student in applying the theory to daily living.

Wolvin, Andrew D., and Coakley, Carolyn G. *Listening.* Dubuque, Ia.: Wm. C. Brown, 1985. An excellent college-level text that reports contemporary research in listening as well as explaining the practical applications of that research. Includes suggestions for improving one's system of taking written notes (see pp. 184–190).

ENDNOTES

1. S. I. Hayakawa, "The Task of the Listener," *ETC* 7 (Autumn 1949): 14.
2. See David K. Berlo, *The Process of Communication: An Introduction to Theory and Practice* (New York: Holt, Rinehart and Winston, 1960), pp. 23–38. Also, B. Aubrey Fisher, *Perspectives on Human Communication* (New York: Macmillan, 1978), pp. 98–134. For other models of human communication see Abne M. Eisenberg, *Living Communication* (Englewood Cliffs, N.J.: Prentice-Hall, 1975), pp. 1–21, and Andrew D. Wolvin and Carolyn G. Coakley, *Listening* (Dubuque, Ia.: Wm. C. Brown, 1985), pp. 31–40.
3. For a review of research on how we spend our time communicating, see Wolvin and Coakley, *Listening*, pp. 7–9. Also, see Lyman K. Steil, Larry L. Barker, and Kittie W. Watson, *Effective Listening: Key to Your Success* (Reading, Mass.: Addison-Wesley, 1983), pp. 2–6.
4. Wolvin and Coakley, op. cit., pp. 177–180. Also see Florence I. Wolff et al., *Perceptive Listening* (New York: Holt, Rinehart and Winston, 1983), pp. 154–160.

PART II
Speech Preparation

> *[Y]ou compose your speech for an audience, and the audience is the 'judge.'*

—Aristotle,
The Rhetoric[1]

Chapter 5

ANALYZING THE AUDIENCE AND OCCASION

*S*everal years ago in a university public speaking class, a student speaker began to deliver his first persuasive speech of the semester. Following some brief opening remarks, he announced that the subject of his speech was "Why You Should Attend College." For the next eight to ten minutes the members of the class listened in bewilderment to a talk that urged them to believe what they already believed, and to do what they had already done, namely, to attend college. For some reason it had not occurred to the student speaker that his topic was a poor choice for the audience and occasion he was to address. As you can readily see, his error was avoidable—all he needed to do was to apply some basic audience analysis early in the speech preparation process.

A few years later in another university, another student faced his classmates to deliver his first persuasive speech in a public speaking course. But this student's analysis of the audience and occasion had been done carefully, for he chose to speak on a question of immediate campus concern, namely, should the university permit social fraternities and sororities to organize and be officially recognized? A student vote on the issue was imminent, and the results of that vote were to be an important element in the decision of the university trustees on the issue. In addition to its timeliness, the issue was one in which the members of the audience were involved and interested. Unlike the talk on "Why You Should Attend College," this talk on "Why We Should Permit Fraternities and Sororities at Our School" was a success. Because of his careful analysis of the audience and occasion, this second speaker managed to secure the genuine interest of his listeners, and to get them to seriously think about his point of view.

As the examples above demonstrate, speeches are not delivered in a vacuum; rather, they are delivered to a specific audience, at a specific time, and on a specific occasion. In particular, keep this in mind as you plan your talks for the class in public speaking, for your classmates compose a *real* audience that should be kept uppermost in your thoughts while selecting and developing topics.

I. The Purposes of Audience Analysis

What Audience Analysis Should Not Do

Before summarizing the main purposes of audience analysis, let us look at two things that it is *not* intended to do. To begin with, audience analysis should not cause you, the speaker, to compromise your convictions or to misrepresent your views. Although you probably can recall an instance when you suspected a politician or other person in public life of doing a "flip flop" on an issue following the publication of some public opinion poll, that approach is not recommended here. Rather, your study of public speaking should help you learn how to address others tactfully and effectively concerning your beliefs without compromising those beliefs and without pretending to support a viewpoint in which you do not believe.

Second, the purpose of audience analysis is not to give the speaker some kind of ''secret weapon'' for overwhelming the views of others. It is not a tool for ''brainwashing,'' although some persuaders have looked upon it in that way (the pronouncements of Adolf Hitler on how to persuade crowds come to mind).

What Audience Analysis Should Do

What, then, are the responsible, sensible purposes of audience and situation analysis by a speaker in a free society? Audience analysis is at the heart of the art of public speaking for the obvious reason that *speeches are for audiences.* It follows that a sensible consideration of those for whom you are planning—including your audience of fellow students in a public speaking class—is a natural, inherent part of the speech preparation process. Such an analysis assists you in the choice and refinement of your subject and purpose, helps you decide on appropriate main points and subpoints, and guides you in the selection of supporting materials. Furthermore, it gives you direction in deciding how to say something so that it will be understood; and, in the case of persuasion, it is the basis for determining how to present your views—including controversial ones—so that you gain and maintain an attentive, courteous, and intelligent hearing.

Even the most skillful audience analysis is a mixture of the scientific and the intuitive, the fact-based decision and the one based on ''good judgment'' and the ''educated guess.'' Although we know more today about human psychology than ever before, we still know too little to be able to predict with unfailing precision how a group of individuals will respond to our speeches. Yet, thorough audience analysis can provide us with valuable guidance on what not to do (don't use an excessive amount of technical language when explaining a complex subject to a popular audience) as well as on what is fitting and probably effective (such as quoting Thomas Jefferson on personal freedom when speaking to a group of civil libertarians). Be as scientific as you can, but don't hesitate to make use of informed estimates and ''common sense'' decisions derived from a thoughtful consideration of your audience.

II. What to Look for When Analyzing the Audience

There are at least two important, interacting areas that you should evaluate when analyzing an audience: the mental state of your listeners (interests, knowledge, and attitudes) toward you and your topic, and audience demographics (such as age, sex, education, and occupation). We will now consider both of these areas, beginning with interests, knowledge, and attitudes.

Audience Interests, Knowledge, and Attitudes

As you begin the process of audience analysis, ask yourself three basic questions: how *interested* will my audience be in the speech subject; how much *knowledge* of the subject does the audience have; and what *attitudes* does my audience have toward me and my subject (unfavorable, neutral, favorable)? Each of these questions is now considered in turn.

Interest Information

To begin with, consider which speech topics will attract the attention and interest of your listeners. People find subjects attractive for a variety of reasons, ranging from the natural interest we have in the unique or novel ("The Day the Drug Squad Raided Our House by Mistake") to an intense concern about those things that are vital to our health and safety ("Violent Crime on Our Campus and What You Can Do About It"). Often, you need only use common sense to decide whether a topic will appeal to people. For instance, your classmates in a public speaking course would likely be interested in subjects that concern their college life, those dealing with financial problems while in school, choosing a major field wisely, and making career choices. On the other hand, college graduates who are several years into their careers, who have families, and who are paying for a home and a car, will be interested in different subjects—such as how to prepare financially for a child's college education, types and amounts of insurance to carry, and ways of learning new skills to enhance one's professional standing.

On the other hand, there are some topics that audiences ought to be interested in, but for one reason or another (such as lack of information) are not. In such cases, you believe that the subject is important, that the audience needs to hear about it, and that listeners will become interested once they are aware of the subject's significance to their lives. For this type of speech, you will need to work extra hard on interest materials, especially in the introduction where you catch attention and motivate audience concern for what follows. For example, a classroom speech on healthy eating habits might not "grab" the intense interest of your classmates when announced. However, if you have case histories and statistics of severe health problems in college students because of poor eating habits, including a shocking example or two from your own student body, you can create interest and motivate your audience to listen.

Assuming that the subject you have chosen is either inherently interesting for your audience or one that you can make interesting early in the speech, you should next ask the question, "How much do my listeners know about this topic?" To help answer that question, we now turn our attention to analyzing audience knowledge on a given subject.

Knowledge Information

You need to know the level of knowledge the audience has on your subjects for both informative and persuasive speeches. For informative speeches, knowing the degree of understanding an audience has on a given topic helps you decide whether or not the topic needs further discussion. If the audience is fully informed, you should move on to some other subject. In other words, avoid trying to teach people something they already know. Furthermore, gauging the depth of knowledge helps you determine where to begin in your coverage of the topic. An audience might know about a subject up to a point; at that point you can begin to build upon what is known, and deepen that knowledge. You will then be applying the principle of teaching the unknown on the foundation of the known.

For persuasive speaking, an understanding of audience knowledge on your subject tells you how much background information you need to provide, the kinds of definitions and basic explanations you need to include, and in general, the overall simplicity or complexity of your speech content. Remember that much persuasion is built on information, and that it is futile to try to persuade a group to a point of view that the members of the group do not understand.

Therefore, as a key part of audience analysis, determine as accurately as possible audience knowledge on your intended subject by asking these two questions: *how much knowledge does the audience have on this topic* (is it in-depth and thorough, or shallow and incomplete), and *what is the quality of the knowledge* (is it accurate or inaccurate)?

Part IV of this chapter discusses in considerable detail how you can gather information about your audience. In anticipation of that discussion, it is appropriate here to note that it is fairly easy to gather information from the members of your speech class because you meet them on a regular basis. You can ask questions of your fellow students, or even prepare and administer simple questionnaires to find out what topics they are informed about, and what topics they would like to learn more about. Specifically, a list of ten or twelve suggested subjects can be passed out in class and the students ask to cross out those they are already informed on, and to circle those they would like to hear you discuss. Let us now go a step further in audience analysis by considering what you need to know concerning the attitudes of your listeners toward you and toward your subject.

Attitudinal Information

The study of attitudes has been a central concern of social psychologists during most of this century. Attitudes cannot be seen, touched, tasted, smelled, or otherwise experienced directly by the senses—yet, psychologists tell us that we have them. How do psychologists define "attitude"? Simply stated, the term "attitude" refers to the tendency of a person to respond to the events of life in a predictable manner. More specifically, we will define *attitude* as the *predisposition of an individual or an audience to evaluate an issue, action, object, symbol, person, or situation in an unfavorable or favorable way.* Our attitudes give direction to our behavior.[2]

Attitudes are learned (from our experiences in life, both direct and indirect), and are formulated out of our beliefs and values. They are not the same as our beliefs and values, but interact with and emerge from them, as when our beliefs and values converge on the issue of the moment and determine whether we respond favorably or unfavorably to it. To put it another way, our beliefs and values form our attitudes (our likes and dislikes) and predispose us to behave in ways that are consistent with those attitudes.[3]

Expanding on the concept, we can say that a *belief* is something we accept as correct, or right, or "true." Examples are: "I believe that the earth is round," "I believe that some insects carry disease," or "I believe that blood circulates through the body." On the other hand, a *value* is a behavior (such as being truthful) or a goal (such as happiness) that we find preferable to opposite behaviors or goals (being truthful is preferable to telling falsehoods, and happiness is preferable to misery).[4] Leading values of our society, as identified by

Accomplished speakers consider the beliefs, values, and attitudes of their audiences. (Jim Levitt/Impace Visuals)

a psychologist who specializes in value analysis, include not only truthfulness and happiness, but also honesty, accepting responsibility, ambition, tolerance, peace, family security, freedom, and equality.[5]

Let us look at two examples of how beliefs and values interact to form attitudes. We might believe, for instance, that authoritarian regimes censor the press; and we might value personal and political freedom, including the right to express our opinions and to freely read and hear the opinions of others. Taken together, the belief and the value predispose us to have a favorable attitude toward proposals for a free press, and an unfavorable attitude toward proposals for censorship. To illustrate further, we might believe that smoking is harmful to one's health, and that some persons who do not smoke get headaches and watery eyes when they are in a room where others are smoking. Also, we might value good health, and we might have a respect for life. Therefore, when a no-smoking policy is proposed for our workplace, our beliefs and values related to that proposal blend and emerge to make us respond favorably toward it. In short, we have a favorable attitude toward the banning of smoking on the job. (Perhaps others will have an unfavorable attitude about the suggested change, and some might even be neutral on the issue.) The attitude we hold is not the same as our beliefs, or our values, but results from them. Later, when we are asked to vote on the matter, our attitude shapes and gives direction to our behavior; we vote ''yes'' on the policy to eliminate smoking.

Gathering information on the attitudes of your audience can be a great help to you as a public speaker. Such an approach does not ignore beliefs and values; rather, it uses available knowledge of beliefs and values to better explain and understand attitudes. In turn, attitudinal analysis becomes a practical procedure for helping measure the predisposition of your listeners to respond to you and your speech in a predictable way. Let us look at two characteristics of attitudes that you should consider as you analyze your audience and plan your speech. These characteristics are the *location* of audience attitudes on the unfavorable-neutral-favorable scale, and the *strength* of those attitudes.

Location. As previously mentioned, attitudes are measured on a scale that ranges from "unfavorable, to neutral (or undecided) to favorable"; variations are sometimes seen in language such as "disagree, neutral, agree," "disapprove, neutral, approve," or "oppose, neutral, support." For example, you could measure the attitudes of an audience concerning a state's mandatory seat belt law by asking, "What is your position on the law requiring you to use seat belts when riding in an automobile?" Respondents would then check their attitude on a scale marked "oppose the law," "neutral or undecided," and "favor the law."

Strength. A second characteristic you need to consider is the strength (or intensity) of the attitude you are investigating. Two or more persons can hold a similar attitude, but for different reasons, and at different levels of intensity. For example, Sally might hold a strongly favorable attitude toward seat belt laws because a member of her family who was using a seat belt recently survived an automobile accident, suffering only minor injuries. John, on the other hand, might hold a moderately favorable attitude on the same issue because of an article he read in the newspaper. You can show the variations of intensity between the attitudes of Sally and John by providing additional categories on the attitude scale, such as *strongly unfavorable*, and *strongly favorable*. Your range would now include at least five positions: "strongly unfavorable, unfavorable, neutral or undecided, favorable, strongly favorable." (See Figure 5.1.)

Finally, you will need to consider audience attitudes not only toward your subject, but also toward yourself. What does the audience know about you? Are you well-known (as is a minister to his or her congregation), known only by reputation (as is a national political figure who flies to your city to make a speech, or a writer whose works have been read by those in the audience), or not known very well or at all (in which case the attitude of the audience might be neutral toward you)? Does the audience have information about you that will cause it to think of you in a favorable or unfavorable way prior to the speech? Because speaker credibility is a critical factor in public speaking (an audience is more likely to respond favorably to a speaker whom it likes and

STRONGLY UNFAVORABLE	MODERATELY UNFAVORABLE	NEUTRAL UNDECIDED	MODERATELY FAVORABLE	STRONGLY FAVORABLE
oppose disagree	oppose disagree		support agree	support agree

FIGURE 5.1

A Basic Attitude Scale. *An attitude is the predisposition of a person or group of persons to evaluate an issue, action, object, symbol, individual, or situation in an unfavorable or favorable way. For speech planning, the attitude of the audience on the speech subject can be located, and the strength of that attitude shown, by placing it on a scale like the one above.*

trusts than to a speaker whom it holds in low esteem), you will want to make an informed judgment of audience attitudes toward you. If unfavorable, plan to deal with the attitude and try to modify it in the direction of being favorable; and if favorable, recognize the advantage, support it, and try to move it toward strongly favorable. We are now ready to examine audience demographics, an area that will help you evaluate the interests, knowledge, and attitudes of your listeners.

Audience Demographics

A demographic inventory of your audience should include at least eight areas: age, sex, education, occupation, economic status, ethnic background, geographic (regional) background, and voluntary group associations (political, religious, professional, social, etc.). This information guides you in determining audience interests, knowledge, and attitudes. For instance, professional pollsters routinely report attitudinal data according to national demographics. To cite one example, a 1989 Gallup Poll concerning the attitudes of Americans on gun control includes results according to age, sex, geographic region, ethnic background, education, and household income (economic status).[6]

Note that the demographic information is not an end in itself. Rather, it is a means to better understanding your audience so that you will make sound rhetorical decisions on such matters as choosing interesting and vital subjects, phrasing the central idea to be both clear and diplomatic, and selecting the most persuasive arguments (main points) to support your central idea. Furthermore, it guides you in the choice of evidence (such as examples and statistics that listeners can identify with and understand), and the use of language that is clear and persuasive.

Although demographic elements cannot be neatly separated from one another as they overlap and merge in complex ratios, we will consider them one by one for convenience. When we are finished, be sure to blend them together as you analyze the audience as a whole.

Age. Awareness of the age of those who compose an audience has been recommended to public speakers since the Classical era. For example, age is the first audience characteristic discussed by Aristotle. In *The Rhetoric*, Aristotle tells his students that people can be grouped generally into three ages: youth, "prime of life," and old age.[7] Young people, he says, are "passionate," "fond of honor," and "trustful, for as yet they have not been often deceived." Youth, he continues, "live their lives for the most part in hope, as hope is of the future." Those in the prime of life are "exempt from the excess of either young or old." They are more inclined to "judge each case by the facts," be balanced between honor and expediency, and "combine self-control with valor." As for old age, persons are more cautious, less trusting (having been often deceived), more cynical than youth, for they have witnessed that "more often than not the affairs of men turn out badly." "They aspire to nothing great," Aristotle adds, "but crave the mere necessities and comforts of existence."

You will make your own judgments about the characteristics of each age, of course, but you will certainly want to know as much as possible about the ages of those who will listen to you. This information helps you make a wise choice of subject, purpose, supporting material and language. For example, an audience of high school juniors and seniors would be more interested in a speech on "How to Secure Financial Aid for Attending College" than would an audience of retirees. On the other hand, an audience of retirees would be more interested in a talk on "How to Live Well on a Fixed Retirement Income" than would the students in your public speaking class.

Sex. Advance information on the sexual demographics of your audience is especially important today in view of the sensitivity of many women and men to issues of sexism in the United States. These concerns can range from the vocational and economic (for example, belief in equal opportunity and equal pay in the marketplace) to the linguistic (the use of sexist language, such as referring to all persons as "man"). In addition, you need to know whether your audience is all female, all male, or a mixture of females and males. Such information guides you in the selection of speech subjects and in choosing appropriate supporting materials for those subjects. To illustrate, speaking on sexual bias in the business and professional world might, for an audience of men, emphasize a change of attitude toward women workers and colleagues; for an audience of women the speech might explain and urge the adoption of strategies for overcoming the "old boy" network in a company or profession; and for a mixed audience the speech might emphasize working together to overcome sex bias in business, profession, and society at large.

Education. The educational level of your audience is another factor you need to consider when planning your speeches, for it should be obvious that your central idea, supporting points, and word choice will vary depending on the intellectual-educational sophistication of your listeners. For instance, contemporary research informs us that in persuasive speaking, a two-sided presentation (that is, stating opposing views and answering them) is more appropriate for educated audiences than for uneducated ones (uneducated persons find it easier to follow the presentation of one side only).[8] In addition, intelligent persons do not respond well to persuasion backed by illogical, irrelevant, unsupported arguments; however, they are influenced by arguments that are logically sound and that are supported by strong evidence.[9]

Occupation. One's vocation brings focus to the daily activities of life for many people. Your audiences will often be made up of those from a variety of occupations; however, on occasion, you are likely to speak to a group of persons from a single vocation—such as teachers, librarians, bankers, salespersons, or attorneys. The vocations of those in your audience, be it one vocation or a mixture of several, will be a major factor in analyzing interest in, knowledge of, and attitudes toward your topic. In your public speaking class, try to learn the career plans of those not yet at work in a full-time occupation; this knowledge will help you in the immediate task of audience analysis for classroom speaking.

Economic status. Knowing the approximate economic status of your audience will provide additional insight into the interests and attitudes of those whom you will address. In general, determine whether your listeners are of low income, middle income, or high income, or represent a general mixture of income levels. For example, a talk on investing in the stock or bond markets, while appropriate for some middle- and high-income audiences, would hold little interest for those of low income who struggle to meet the monthly bills.

Ethnic background. This broad and extremely important area includes the cultural and racial background and traditions of the people to whom you speak. Because people are usually very sensitive to matters of culture and race, you will need to gather information on the ethnic factors of your audience, and use the results wisely. Are you speaking to an audience composed of a single ethnic group, or a general mixture? What do you know about the group, including its customs, its concerns, its priorities? If you were planning a talk on racial bias in community housing, to be delivered to an audience composed of racial minorities, you might focus on how to organize and use current laws to combat racial bias in housing; on the other hand, for an audience of middle-class whites, your talk might urge support for new and stronger laws to make discrimination in housing unlawful (concluding with an appeal such as, "write your state representative," or "join our organization, for we are dedicated to making open housing a reality for all citizens").

Geographic background. In some instances, information on the regional background of your auditors will prove helpful. People from southern California, for example, might have an attitude toward your topic that differs considerably from that of persons from the South, or from New England. Similarly, you will find different interests, knowledge, and attitudes depending on whether your audience is composed of city dwellers, or persons from small towns or rural areas. For instance, if you were speaking on some aspect of the nation's agricultural policy to a group of students from rural families in a "farm belt" region of the country, you could assume that your audience had first-hand information concerning farm problems and was generally sympathetic to the grower's side of the issue. On the other hand, a talk on the same subject to a group of students in a large city would need to take into account the view of the grocery consumer. This does not suggest that city dwellers are not sympathetic to farm problems—only that they perceive those problems from a perspective that differs from those who live and work on the farm.

Voluntary group affiliations. Finally, be sure to consider the groups with which the members of your audience voluntarily associate. Students of human motivation have said for many years that knowledge of group affiliations—especially religious, political, and social memberships—is vital to audience analysis.[10] Ask yourself, what is the religious affiliation of those in the audience; is it, among other things, liberal, moderate, or conservative? Also, with what political party or parties do those in your audience identify? And, are your listeners members of community action groups, or social clubs, or other organizations that you need to be aware of when preparing your remarks? If you are planning a speech advocating strict handgun control, for example, and you know that many in your audience are members of a local hunting and sport-shooting club, you could reason that your persuasive effort would be more difficult than if your audience included no hunting club members and was generally neutral on the issue of handgun control.

Now that we have looked at the essentials of a demographic analysis—including the eight areas of age, sex, education, occupation, economic status, ethnic background, geographic background, and voluntary group associations—we are ready to examine the speaking occasion.

III. What to Look for
When Analyzing the Speaking Occasion

If you want to be fully prepared in your speaking, you will need to go beyond analyzing the knowledge, attitudes, and demographics of your audience to look closely at the overall occasion for your speech. This should include gathering information about five interacting situational factors: the occasion's nature and purpose, overall program of events, audience size, meeting facilities, and the use of recording or broadcasting equipment.

Nature and Purpose of the Occasion

At the outset you need to find out who is sponsoring the meeting, and why—that is, what is the purpose of the event? Also, is this a regular or special meeting (and if special, why is it necessary)? With this knowledge in hand, find out why you have been asked to speak (what is expected of you). For example, if you are the only guest speaker for an organization's annual dinner meeting, you might decide to reinforce group goals with an inspirational speech that relies primarily on appeals to emotions and values; however, if you are one of several speakers addressing that same group on a controversial subject in a "working session" of a convention, you would likely be more argumentative (emphasizing logical reasoning and evidence) in order to convince the audience that your views were preferable to the views of others.

If the event is open to public participation with no special invitations (such as a town meeting to debate a proposed tax increase), carefully think through what you wish to accomplish, and plan accordingly. Keep in mind that on occasions of public debate, time limits are usually imposed (and the time allowed is short—five minutes maximum in many cases).

Overall Program

You will need to find out about the degree of formality for the occasion. Is there a set sequence of events (such as at a convention, or a high school or college commencement), or will events occur informally? If the occasion is formal, will the activities appear in a printed program? If so, try to secure a copy in advance in order to evaluate your place in the overall scheme, including attention to what goes before and after your speech. Are you the only major speaker or are there several? Finally, what is the time of day for your speech? A talk scheduled at the end of a long day, after the participants in a meeting have listened to a number of other speakers, presents you with challenges—such as maintaining interest and keeping your remarks brief, while still managing to get your message across—that you do not face so directly if you are the opening speaker of the day and begin speaking at ten in the morning to an alert audience.

Audience Size

Ask the sponsors of the event about the attendance expected so that you can have a realistic "audience picture" in mind as you prepare your speech. This

Analysis of the audience and the speaking occasion are both essential to effective speaking. (Ulrike Welsch)

knowledge is particularly helpful when you begin rehearsing your remarks, for you can imagine your audience more realistically, and rehearse accordingly (for example, you might plan an informal, conversational delivery for a small group, and a more animated delivery with strong voice projection for a large group). If you plan to distribute pamphlets or other materials, a knowledge of anticipated attendance lets you know how many copies to bring along. Finally, knowing audience size guides you in the preparation of visual aids (if any) so that the visuals are large enough to be seen by all present.

Meeting Facilities

Be sure to check on the size and physical features of the room or auditorium in which you will speak. If you need a microphone, is one available? Is the room arranged in a traditional seating pattern, or is the seating nontraditional (such as "conference style," with listeners sitting around tables)? Is there a chalkboard in case you need it? If the meeting is local, you might drop by the facility to get a first-hand look; otherwise, a few good questions asked of the sponsors by phone or by mail will have to do. Arriving early to check out the physical features of the room, and to test the microphone, is a good practice to follow.

Broadcasting of the Event

Will your speech be broadcast on radio or television? If so, you will want to plan carefully to stay within time limits, and to manage your notes or manuscript efficiently. And because some colors show up better on television than others, you will need to give some extra thought to appropriate dress for the occasion.

IV. Gathering and Using Information About the Audience and the Occasion

Now that we have an idea of what you need to know about the audience and the occasion, how do you get this knowledge, and what do you do with it once you have it? First we will examine some practical steps for securing the information you need, and then we will discuss how you can use it to adapt your speech to the audience and the situation.

Gathering Audience and Occasion Information

You can secure information about your audience and the occasion in four ways: general observation, asking questions, library research, and preparing and administering your own questionnaires to prospective listeners.

General observation. It is likely that much of your speaking will be in the community where you live, and to people whom you know or whom you encounter generally as you go about your daily business. Making an estimate of audience interests and attitudes is not difficult to do under these circumstances (especially if you are a member of the group that you will address). Also, keep in mind that gathering knowledge by means of direct observation is a key method to use in your public speaking course, for you will be able to make an educated estimate of audience interests, knowledge, and attitudes after several class meetings and after listening to a round or two of speeches. However, there will be times—even in the local community, or on your college or university campus—when you will need to supplement your general observations with some specific questions about the audience and occasion.

Ask questions. To add to your knowledge of audience and occasion based upon observation, and to secure as much information as possible about audiences you are not directly acquainted with, ask the sponsors of the event some specific questions. Ask about the purpose and goals of the sponsoring organization, the nature of the audience and occasion, the anticipated size of the audience, and their expectations of you as a speaker. If the engagement is out of town, you can inquire by phone or by mail concerning these details in order to plan wisely. The combination of general observation and the asking of key questions will enable you to secure the necessary information for wise audience and situation evaluation for many of your speeches.

Library research. Another source of information about audiences is the library, where you will find published opinion polls concerning a variety of contemporary political and social issues. Of course, the polls reported in various library sources will not, as a rule, focus on the specific audience to which you will speak. However, you can find information on national, regional, and state opinions and attitudes that will help you estimate audience views on subjects such as the death penalty, arms control, civil rights, censorship, prison reform, and the like. Use the newspaper indexes, such as those for the *New York Times* or the *Washington Post* (both report poll results on a regular basis), or use the *Readers' Guide to Periodical Literature* to locate a variety of polls in other sources—including those from weekly newsmagazines such as *Newsweek, Time,* or *U.S. News and World Report.* Also, the monthly *Gallup Report* publishes the results of the latest Gallup surveys on a variety of current issues.

Questionnaires. If you are planning to speak to an audience of persons who meet regularly, you can design a simple questionnaire to secure information concerning how much your prospective listeners know about your subject as well as their attitudes toward it. Because this method fits well with the format for most public speaking courses, let us examine it with the thought that you might use it in your speech class.

As a general rule, three types of questions will serve your purposes in preparing questionnaires for checking audience knowledge of and attitudes on a speech subject. These are the open-ended question, the close-ended question, and the scaled question. First, the *open-ended question* does not structure an answer, but permits the individual to fill in the answer in his or her own words. For example, ''What should be the law of our state concerning capital punishment for persons found guilty of first degree murder?'' You then provide space on the questionnaire for the individual to write in a brief response. Although you will find out something from open-ended questions, the responses will not be uniform, and in some cases will not even address the issue in a way that is useful to you in your effort to analyze audience views on the subject. You might, therefore, consider a structured question or series of questions that are close-ended in nature. (See Figure 5.2.)

A *close-ended question* is one for which structured answers are provided, and the respondent checks the one that most accurately reflects his or her knowledge or opinion. For example, ''Do you think that capital punishment is ever justified? ____Yes; ____No; ____Undecided.'' The definite responses listed make the question a closed rather than an open-ended one. This technique permits you to focus on securing information that you think you need in order to plan wisely, leaving less room for irrelevant responses. However, one problem with the structured (closed) question is that it is highly restrictive in its options, and therefore does not tell you much about the range of attitudes present in your audience. For a more thorough evaluation, you can use a scaled response form.

The *scaled question*, which is of particular value in gathering information on audience attitudes, permits the respondent to mark his or her view on a continuum, going from strongly disapprove/disagree to strongly approve/agree. For example, you might ask: ''What is your opinion of the proposal to abolish capital punishment by substituting a sentence of life imprisonment without parole for those convicted of premeditated murder? ____Strongly disagree; ____Disagree; ____Neutral or undecided; ____Agree; ____Strongly Agree.'' For planning persuasive speeches, the knowledge you get from scaled questions is especially helpful because the answers reveal not only what attitude your audience holds on the subject but also the strength of that attitude. This information guides you in setting a realistic specific purpose, and in planning your arguments and choosing supporting materials to back up that purpose.[11]

Two additional comments concerning questionnaires are appropriate at this point. First, you should be careful to word your questions in objective,

QUESTIONNAIRE ON CAPITAL PUNISHMENT

1. Have you ever visited "death row" in the state penitentiary?

   ( ) yes ( ) no

2. What number would you guess comes closest to the number of prisoners now awaiting execution in our state prison system?

   ( ) 5 ( ) 10 ( ) 15 ( ) 25 ( ) 50 ( ) 100

3. What number would you guess comes closest to the number of prisoners now awaiting execution nationwide, in all prisons combined?

   ( ) 25 ( ) 50 ( ) 100 ( ) 250 ( ) 500 ( ) 1,000

4. Which answer best reflects your opinion concerning the statement, "Capital punishment should be abolished"?

   ( ) strongly ( ) disagree ( ) neutral, or ( ) agree ( ) strongly
        disagree   undecided   agree

5. Briefly explain why you believe as you do concerning question 4:

6. Which answer best reflects your opinion concerning the statement, "If capital punishment were abolished (for whatever reason), a sentence of life imprisonment without parole should be substituted for persons convicted of violent crimes such as first degree murder"?

   ( ) strongly ( ) disagree ( ) neutral, or ( ) agree ( ) strongly
        disagree   undecided   agree

FIGURE 5.2

The questionnaire above (or one similar to it) could easily be administered to your speech class, or to some other audience, in preparation for a talk urging the abolition of capital punishment. Notice that questions 1, 2, and 3 are close-ended, question 5 is open-ended, and questions 4 and 6 are scaled to secure a range of attitudes.

nonemotional language. Avoid questions such as, "What do you think of the *horrible, cruel,* and *sickening* executions carried out by our state?" or "Do you favor letting the state *murder* people who have been found guilty of killing other people?" Such wording will so slant the question toward a predetermined response that the results probably will not represent the real attitudes of respondents on the subject.

Second, be aware of the possibility of constructing a questionnaire that makes use of different kinds of questions, ranging from open-ended to scaled. (A combination of all three types is illustrated in Figure 5.2.) With careful planning that includes attention to choice of words, you can prepare and administer questionnaires to your fellow students in public speaking—or to some other audience that you plan to address and to which you have access.

We have now examined four ways of gathering information about your audience, these being by general observation, asking questions, library research, and the administration of custom-designed questionnaires. The next logical step in the process is how to use the knowledge gained by audience and occasion analysis in preparing your speeches.

Using Audience and Occasion Information

Although audience and occasion analysis is prerequisite or supplementary to almost everything else that is presented in this text, you should not wait until you have studied all of the chapters before putting the principles to work. You can begin immediately to use information about your audience and the speaking situation in at least three ways: to guide your choice of subject and purpose, to establish common ground, to adapt speech content and language.

Choose subjects and purposes wisely. Audience analysis is the key to choosing an appropriate subject and purpose for each speech you prepare. Connecting your own interests and areas of expertise to the interests and knowledge of your audience can be accomplished by making wise use of the informational, attitudinal, and demographic elements of audience analysis discussed in this chapter. For informative speaking, use audience analysis to choose realistic goals on topics about which your listeners are not fully informed. Similarly, for persuasion, use audience analysis to choose goals that you believe you can reach in the time allowed, and that move the audience to think in fresh directions. There is no point in teaching audiences what they already know, or persuading them to believe or do what they already accept.

Your speech class is a good place to begin. What are the interests and vocational goals of your fellow students? What knowledge and attitudes do they have on a given topic? How will a persuasive purpose relate to their lives? These and similar questions should be asked early in the course as you develop subjects for classroom speeches. For example, in a college public speaking class the instructor assigned an informative speech early in the course, requiring that the subject be useful to the members of the audience. One student who was a major in speech communication decided to talk on ''The Speech Preparation of President Franklin D. Roosevelt,'' one of the most effective public communicators in American history. The student reasoned that the subject would be of interest to her fellow public speaking students, for it would give them some practical ideas for their own speech preparation. She was correct, for her carefully researched remarks emphasized down-to-earth steps that President Roosevelt followed in planning speeches (such as rehearsing each speech several times in order to master the content). Audience response to the presentation was positive, for the listeners were able to see a connection between the ideas of the speech and the curriculum in which they were enrolled. You can apply this principle in your public speaking class, and before student and community groups while you are in college, by keeping audience analysis in mind when you ask yourself, ''What am I going to talk about?''

Establish common ground. In the introductions of your speeches you need to build a bridge of shared interests and values to your audience by establishing common ground—and, once established, common ground needs to be maintained throughout the speech. Employ illustrations, examples, and points of view that cause your listeners to identify with you, and to perceive you as one who understands them, likes them, and shares important concerns with them. For instance, in your public speaking classroom, you can use your knowledge of campus life to establish common ground. This knowledge includes the experiences of dormitory living (or commuting to school), eating in the campus dining facilities, and taking many of the same courses. From these areas of commonality you can get a feel for everyday occurrences and mutual concerns. Your speeches can make references to favorite professors, stories from the student newspaper, campus events, and shared problems of student life.

If your analysis reveals that your audience is strongly opposed or hostile to your speech goal, you can use points of common ground, in conjunction with strong speaker credibility (*ethos*), to help win a fair and friendly hearing for your remarks. Herbert Simons, a researcher in the field of persuasion, recommends the following procedures to help overcome audience hostility toward you or your speech purpose.

> *Work extra hard to establish rapport and good will.* Establish common ground at the beginning, and sustain good feelings with the audience throughout the speech. Among other things, a direct, friendly delivery, and the skillful use of humor, help win an audience over. Also, reveal your qualifications to speak on the subject, and emphasize shared experiences, interests, and values.
>
> *Begin with areas of agreement before moving to areas of disagreement.* In other words, get listeners on your side at the beginning of the speech, and try to keep them there by moving slowly and tactfully to the points of disagreement.
>
> *Use evidence and sources that the audience can identify with and accept.* While preparing the speech, you make choices about what sources you will research, and what items of supporting evidence you will use (and not use). Give preference to sources and materials that your audience will readily accept as contrasted with those that might provoke further hostility. For instance, for a speech opposing censorship of sexual materials planned for delivery to an audience of religious conservatives, it is better to use pro-freedom statements from religious authorities *respected by the audience* than to base the speech upon articles published in an unacceptable source—such as *Playboy* magazine.[12]

Adapt content and language. In addition to helping you establish common ground, audience analysis is generally useful in adapting the content and language of your speech to the specific audience and occasion, even when listeners are friendly from the outset. In other words, employ audience analysis to help select the most appropriate speech content—including the clearest and most persuasive main points, supporting points, and items of evidence—no matter what type of audience or occasion you will face.

For instance, in your public speaking class you can make intelligent choices based on your observations and acquired knowledge about your fellow students. If most are in the eighteen to twenty-five-year-old age group, examples concerning romantic relationships, dating, courtship, and marriage would be appealing. Or if most of the students come from a single professional school, such as business administration, supporting materials relative to business, the economy, and the politics of economic policy might fit. By selecting content materials that are "close to the listener," and not so removed from the lives of your classmates as to be irrelevant, you will be practicing adaptation wisely.

Another important consideration in planning for a speech is the use of language that is appropriate to your listeners. In particular, your choice of words should be adjusted to the level of audience knowledge of your topic, and to demographic factors such as age and education, so that you can avoid talking "over the heads" of your listeners. Also, use information about audience beliefs, values, and attitudes to help choose language that is acceptable and persuasive, avoiding language that your listeners might find offensive, embarrassing, or otherwise detracting.

This Chapter in Brief

Audience analysis is at the heart of speech preparation, for it guides you from the outset in the choice of subject, and in adapting speech content so that you win an intelligent and friendly hearing. When evaluating the mental state of your audience, include the three areas of listener interests, knowledge, and attitudes. In practical terms this means speaking on a subject that your audience is interested in, being clear (avoid speaking "over the heads" of your listeners), and knowing whether your audience is opposed, neutral, or in favor of the viewpoint you plan to present. Demographic data (such as age, sex, educational, occupation, economic status, ethnic and geographical background, and group affiliations) are useful in helping you determine audience interests, knowledge, and attitudes. Also, secure information concerning the speaking occasion. This should include the nature and purpose of the event, complete program details, anticipated size of the audience, the type and arrangement of meeting facilities, and whether or not the speech will be recorded for radio or television.

You can gather audience data in four ways: by general observation, by asking specific questions, by library research, and by the use of custom questionnaires (such as those you prepare yourself). After you have secured the data, and have evaluated audience interests, knowledge, and attitudes, you can use the information for guidance in choosing subjects and purposes, for establishing common ground with your listeners (including overcoming listener opposition), and for adapting the overall content and language to your listeners.

With this background on audience analysis in mind, let us now turn to its first major application, namely, as a basis for wisely determining the subject and purpose of your speech. This critical process is the focus of the chapter that follows.

EXERCISES

1. Prior to your next informative speech, prepare and distribute to the class a brief questionnaire designed to find out how much knowledge your classmates have on the subject you plan to discuss. Use the results as a guide in speech preparation (and, if you discover that the audience is generally well-informed on the topic, consider changing to another topic about which the audience is less well-informed).

2. Before your next persuasive speech, prepare and distribute to the class an attitudes questionnaire concerning the central idea you plan to support. Use the suggestions in this chapter as a guide to designing a questionnaire that secures information concerning audience attitudes ranging from strong agreement to strong disagreement on your subject.

SELECTED READINGS

Andersen, Kenneth E. *Persuasion: Theory and Practice.* 2d ed. Boston: Allyn and Bacon, 1978. For Andersen's ideas on audience analysis, see Chapter 3, "Motivation, Attitudes, and Behavior," and Chapter 4, "Receiver and Situation Analysis."

Bettinghaus, Erwin P., and Cody, Michael J. *Persuasive Communication.* 4th ed. New York: Holt, Rinehart and Winston, 1987. The authors discuss basic areas of audience analysis in Chapters 2, 3, and 4, covering attitude theory, personality theory, and the influence of group affiliations on listener beliefs, values, and attitudes.

Bostrum, Robert N. *Persuasion.* Englewood Cliffs, N.J.: Prentice-Hall, 1983. In particular, see Chapter 3 in which Bostrum discusses "Attitudes, Attitude Change, and Behavior."

McCroskey, James C. *An Introduction to Rhetorical Communication.* 4th ed. Englewood Cliffs, N.J.: Prentice-Hall, 1982. For McCroskey's thoughtful discussion of audience analysis, see Chapter 3, "The Nature of the Receiver: Attitude Formation and Change."

Simons, Herbert W. *Persuasion: Understanding, Practice, and Analysis.* 2d ed. New York: Random House, 1986. Simons discusses the audience in Chapter 4, "Behavioral Theories of Attitude Change," and Chapter 8, "Audience Analysis and Adaptation."

Zimbardo, Philip G.; Ebbesen, Ebbe B.; and Maslach, Christina. *Influencing Attitudes and Changing Behavior.* 2d ed. Reading, Mass.: Addison-Wesley, 1977. This handbook, which can easily be comprehended by the layperson, explains attitude theory, types of attitudes scales, and the practical application of attitude theory to persuasion. A recommended source for students of public speaking.

ENDNOTES

1. Aristotle, *The Rhetoric*, trans. Lane Cooper (New York: Appleton-Century, 1932), p. 141.
2. For an overview of the development of attitude theory in the twentieth century, see Richard E. Petty, Thomas M. Ostrom, and Timothy C. Brock, eds., *Cognitive Responses in Persuasion* (Hillsdale, N.J.: Lawrence Erlbaum Associates, 1981), pp. 1–29. For more on the definition of attitude, see pp. 31–32.
3. The position that attitudes are formed from a combination of our beliefs and values is derived from a number of theorists, including: Edward E. Jones and Harold B. Gerard, *Foundations of Social Psychology* (New York: Wiley, 1967), pp. 157–159; and Ronald Fernandez, *The I, the Me, and You: An Introduction to Social Psychology* (New York: Praeger, 1977), pp. 283–284. Also, see generally Herbert W. Simons, *Persuasion: Understanding, Practice, and Analysis*, 2d ed. (New York: Random House, 1986).

4. Milton Rokeach, *The Nature of Human Values* (New York: The Free Press, 1973), p. 5; also, see generally pp. 1–25.

5. Milton Rokeach, "Change and Stability in American Value Systems, 1968–1971," *Public Opinion Quarterly* 38 (Summer 1974): 222–238. For more on how an understanding of values helps the public speaker, see the discussion of the Rokeach value system in Chapter 15 of this text.

6. "Gun Control," *The Gallup Report* (January 1989): pp. 25–26. Note: Gallup's national results on gun control reveal that 67 percent favor registration, 84 percent favor licensing, and 91 percent favor a seven-day waiting period before purchasing a handgun.

7. Aristotle, op. cit., pp. 132–137.

8. Carl I. Hovland, Irving L. Janis, and Harold H. Kelley, *Communication and Persuasion: Psychological Studies of Opinion Change* (New Haven, Conn.: Yale University Press, 1953), pp. 105–111.

9. Hovland, Janis, and Kelley, *Communication and Persuasion* (New Haven, Conn.: Yale University Press, 1961), p. 183.

10. For an excellent summary of how groups of various types influence us, see Erwin P. Bettinghaus and Michael J. Cody, *Persuasive Communication*, 4th ed. (New York: Holt, Rinehart and Winston, 1987), pp. 62–82.

11. For more on attitude scales, including types not discussed in this chapter, see Philip G. Zimbardo, Ebbe B. Ebbesen, and Christina Maslach, *Influencing Attitudes and Changing Behavior*, 2d ed. (Reading, Mass.: Addison-Wesley, 1977), pp. 213–220. This source is recommended because it is easily comprehended by the layperson.

12. Herbert W. Simons, op. cit., pp. 153–154.

> *In speaking there is always some end proposed, or some effect which the speaker intends to produce on the hearer. The word* eloquence *in its greatest latitude denotes, 'That art or talent by which the discourse is adapted to its end.'*

—George Campbell,
The Philosophy of Rhetoric (1776)[1]

Chapter 6

DETERMINING THE SUBJECT AND PURPOSE

*A*ll of us, in one way or another, set goals in our lives. These goals can range from the simple (to satisfy one's hunger, causing us to visit the coffee shop for a bite to eat) to the complex (to prepare for a profession, such as law or medicine, causing us to spend several years of our lives attending institutions of higher learning). A musician might set a goal of composing a beautiful melody, an architect of designing a quality home, or a cook of baking a delicious cake. Likewise, a public speaker should have a goal, namely, that of planning and delivering an effective speech.

But there is more to it than that. "An effective speech" on what subject? And is it intended to communicate information only, or does it go beyond informing to try to persuade those in the audience to change their attitudes or actions concerning the subject being discussed? In other words, what is the precise objective of the speech?

The purpose of this chapter is to help you answer these and related questions concerning speech subjects and specific rhetorical goals. To accomplish this, the discussion that follows is presented according to three main steps: find, choose, and narrow the subject; determine the purpose (both general and specific); and based upon the first two steps, formulate the central idea of the speech.

I. Find, Choose, and Narrow the Subject

For some speaking situations, your subject is determined by the nature of the event itself. In some instances, the invitation even includes a topic assigned by the hosting organization. Examples would be a student government debate on a specific issue, such as the budget for the school year, or a political meeting where you have been asked to speak on behalf of a certain cause or candidate. At other times, however, deciding on a subject is not so easy. This is sometimes true in public speaking classes when the instructor provides general instructions (such as "a speech to inform in which you make a complex theory, idea, or operation clear to the audience"), but leaves the choice of a specific subject up to you. Let us first look at the problem of finding speech subjects, then examine how to narrow a broad subject to something specific that suits you, the audience, and the occasion.

Finding Subjects for Speeches

In Chapter 2 we discussed how you could start a list of subjects for your classroom speeches by calling upon personal experience and interests, and jotting down on note cards as many possible subjects as you could think of. We are now ready to go beyond that list to consider a larger body of knowledge and opinion that will help you generate additional interesting and worthwhile subjects for your speeches. As with the earlier list, the use of note cards is recommended for ease in adding to, revising, and organizing the headings. We will look at two lines of approach to finding speech subjects: first, the topical approach, and second, the problem-centered approach.

Subjects Derived from Topics

One convenient starting place for discovering speech subjects is an inventory of topics based upon general areas of knowledge. Such an inventory is provided below. Note that there is some overlap between certain topics (such as "freedom of speech" and "law"). This is done deliberately in order to emphasize the potential of certain headings. You can expand or consolidate the topics based on your own knowledge and interests, and on what you believe your audience would like to hear. The topical inventory is followed by some examples of how you can use the list to formulate speech subjects.

You might wish to write each of the following headings at the top of a note card; later, go through the cards, writing down under each heading the relevant subtopics that occur to you, and that you think might be appropriate for a speech. If no ideas come to mind for a given heading, skip it for the time being—you might be inspired on that topic later. Also, feel free to add headings that are not mentioned, but that you think of as you work on the list. Keep the cards handy during the semester for reference when deciding on subjects for classroom speeches.

Agriculture

Anthropology

Architecture (housing, interior design)

Business (economics, industry, labor)

Careers and professions

Computer technology

Education

Engineering (automotive, space, electronic, military, agricultural)

Fine arts (music, dance, sculpture, painting, theater)

Folklore

Freedom of expression (history, issues, and cases)

Geography, earth science, and the environment

History and biography

Home economics (child development and family studies)

Journalism and the mass media

Law (history, principles, definitions, specific laws)

Literature (history, movements, writers, works)

Medicine and health

Philosophy, ethics, and religion

Politics (campaigns, candidates; local, state, and national issues; foreign policy issues)

Psychology

Recreation (games, entertainment)

Science (biology, chemistry, physics, astronomy, etc.)

To illustrate how you can use the inventory above to generate subjects for both informative and persuasive talks, let us choose two topics that are quite different from each other: "freedom of expression" and "geography." Here are some specific speech subjects derived from these headings.

Freedom of expression
a. Informative topics:
  1. The trial of John Peter Zenger (New York, 1735) and its impact on freedom of the press in America.
  2. A short history of the law of defamation.
  3. What is meant by the "bad tendency test" as applied to freedom of speech?
b. Persuasive topics:
  1. Libel laws should be abolished.
  2. Commercial advertising should be fully protected by the First Amendment.
  3. Why I support (or oppose) government censorship of broadcasting.

Geography, earth science, and the environment
a. Informative topics:
  1. America's earthquake zones: where and why.
  2. What is geothermal energy?
  3. What cloud formations tell you about predicting the weather.
b. Persuasive topics:
  1. Stop destroying the ozone!
  2. We need a national policy to stop the pollution that causes acid rain.
  3. You should plan to install a solar energy system in your home.

Let us now examine a slightly different approach to discovering good subjects for public speeches: focusing on contemporary problems.

Subjects Derived from Problems

In a democratic society, much of the speaking that takes place is concerned with problems and their solutions. This is so in a wide variety of institutions, ranging from student and faculty organizations on your campus to the state legislatures and the national Congress. For instance, the treasurer of a university club might speak about the problem of inadequate funds, and suggest ways of raising money so that the club will be in sound fiscal condition. Or a member of the Congress might speak in support of a bill providing for more AIDS research, emphasizing the seriousness of the problem, and the pressing need to find a medical solution. You can begin your search for subjects using this approach by jotting down as many important problems as you think of concerning your school, the local community, your state, the nation, and the international scene.

Although there is some overlap between the topic-centered and problem-centered approaches (a topic often points to a problem, as when the topic of "education" suggests a problem such as "illiteracy in America"), the difference in emphasis is great enough to make both approaches useful. In a nutshell, by shifting your emphasis from topics to problems, you will likely identify some excellent speech subjects that did not occur to you earlier. Here is a starter list of problems; add to it, based upon your knowledge of other current issues that concern you.[2]

Health care (high costs; care of the poor and elderly; catastrophic illness)

The environment (air and water pollution; garbage disposal; what to do with toxic wastes)

Ethics in society (in government, business, and the professions)

Gun control (handguns; assault weapons; registration of guns; permits)

Racial and sexual discrimination (segregation in housing; sexual harassment of women; issues of equal pay)

Poverty (homelessness; undernourished children)

Economic issues (national debt; fair taxation; minimum wage; military spending versus spending on social problems)

Energy needs (nuclear power; solar energy; substitutes for gasoline; fossil fuels and the environment)

Drugs (see examples of subjects below)

Crime (see examples of subjects below)

Here are some examples of how you can use problems to develop subjects for both informative and persuasive speeches. We will use the last two problems named above: *drugs*, and *crime*.

Drugs
a. Informative topics:
   1. What cocaine does to the human body (a scientific report).
   2. The medical uses of marijuana.
   3. How a professional drug treatment program works.
b. Persuasive topics:
   1. Why I oppose (or favor) drug tests as a condition of employment.
   2. Why I oppose (or favor) the legalization of drugs.
   3. Drug addicts need medical care, not jail.

Crime
a. Informative topics:
   1. INTERPOL: how the international police information system works.
   2. What FBI crime statistics show about crime in America during the last decade.
   3. The story of the "bullet-proof vest."

b. Persuasive topics:
   1. The death penalty should be (or should not be) abolished.
   2. The problem of theft on our campus, and what we can do about it.
   3. Gambling should be (or should not be) legalized.

Now that we have considered the use of general topics and of contemporary problems to generate a subject file, let us examine the way to choose a subject for a given speaking situation, and how to narrow it once it is chosen.

Choosing and Narrowing the Subject

In the preceding discussion you were reminded that at times you will be able to move directly to a specific subject (and purpose), whereas at other times you will begin with a general subject and work by steps to something more concrete. For example, the broad subject of "business and economics" can be narrowed to a specific topic such as "The Work of the Federal Trade Commission." Here are two additional examples—one informative and the other persuasive—that demonstrate the contrast between a broad and a narrowed subject.

Informative:
a. **Broad Subject:** Legal terms all citizens should know.
b. **Narrowed Subject:** The meaning of the term "common law."

Persuasive:
a. **Broad Subject:** Education in America.
b. **Narrowed Subject:** Improving the federal financial aid program for America's college students.

Throughout the process of choosing a subject, keep three "tests" in mind. These are that the subject should be appropriate to the speaker, the audience, and the occasion.

Appropriate to the Speaker

First, choose subjects that are appropriate to your own interests, knowledge, and beliefs. The discussion of communication ethics earlier in the text emphasized that public speaking is not a game of "let's pretend," but a serious activity that helps to keep a free society functioning. This means that you should not only be genuinely interested in the subjects you choose to speak about but also that you should be knowledgeable on those subjects and, when persuading, you should sincerely believe in the opinions you express. In other words, your speeches to inform should be based on in-depth understanding of the topic, and your speeches to persuade should be based on knowledge and conviction arrived at by study and sound reasoning.

Therefore, ask yourself at least three key questions when choosing a speech subject:

Am I genuinely interested in the subject?

Do I know enough about the subject (if not, am I willing to become knowledgeable through research)?

Speech topics should be appropriate to the speaker, the audience, and the occasion. (Paul Conklin/Monkmeyer Press)

For persuasive speaking, is the viewpoint that I am proposing not only based on knowledge and sound reasoning but also one in which I sincerely believe?

Appropriate to the Audience

Second, keep your audience foremost in your thinking, paying particular attention to the interests, knowledge, and attitudes of your listeners. When evaluating audience knowledge, for example, keep in mind that there is no need to inform an audience on a topic about which it is already informed (a common mistake, by the way, in student speeches).

When persuading, pick subjects that are of genuine concern to your listeners, and that take into consideration their beliefs, values, and attitudes. For example, if your audience already believes as you do on a topic, there is no need to make a speech on that particular point of agreement; rather, choose a subject that challenges the audience to move in new directions.

Finally, apply an ethical standard to audience analysis when choosing a speech subject. Keep in mind that your listeners are persons of dignity and worth, and have the capacity for critical thought. In practical terms, respect for the individuals in your audience means that what you choose to talk about should be for the benefit of your listeners, and of society in general.

In sum, when choosing a speech subject ask yourself these four audience-centered questions:

Does this subject fit audience interests?

Does the audience need to be informed on this subject (avoid explaining what an audience already knows)?

For persuasion, does the subject (and purpose) attempt to move the audience in fresh directions of belief or action (avoid trying to persuade others to believe or do what they *already* believe or do)?

Is my speech goal ethical; that is, is it for the benefit of the audience and of society in general?

Appropriate to the Occasion

Third, choose subjects that fit the speaking situation. Consider such matters as the nature and purpose of the occasion, what organization is sponsoring the event, what goals the organization has, what is expected of you as a speaker, and what other events are a part of the program. In informal settings, such as a business meeting or a public debate on some local controversy, there might be no set sequence of speakers; however, there is a purpose to the event which suggests what is appropriate and what is not. For example, an open debate on the annual budget of a student club calls forth speeches concerning that particular budget; it is certainly not the time or place for a talk on the drug problem, or the nation's foreign policy. The point is that you should be thoroughly informed about the occasion, and use common sense to select and adjust your subject accordingly.

In addition, keep in mind that the occasion determines the time limit of your speech. In a public speaking class, for example, the instructor will usually announce a specific speech length—something required by the instructional occasion (obviously, classroom time must be budgeted to allow several students to speak during a class period). Similarly, other occasions have time constraints; you should know about them and abide by them. Be aware that the first step of staying within the time limit set by the occasion is to choose and narrow your subject well.

Finally, for your public speaking class, be sure that your choice of subject fits the assignment made by the instructor. Read (or take notes on) the assignment carefully, and if you have any questions about it, discuss your concerns with the instructor. If the assignment is to inform, don't make a persuasive speech—and vice versa. And if the assignment is for a short talk, as is true for many classroom speeches, don't choose a complex subject that cannot possibly be covered in a brief period.

Concerning the occasion, then, ask yourself these questions about the choice of subject:

Does the subject fit the nature and purpose of the scheduled event, and does it fit into the overall program?

Have I narrowed the subject adequately so that it can be covered in the time limit?

For my public speaking class, does the subject fit the assignment made by the instructor?

Having carefully selected a subject that fits your interests, knowledge, and convictions, and one that is appropriate to the audience and occasion, you are now ready to focus upon the purpose of the speech.

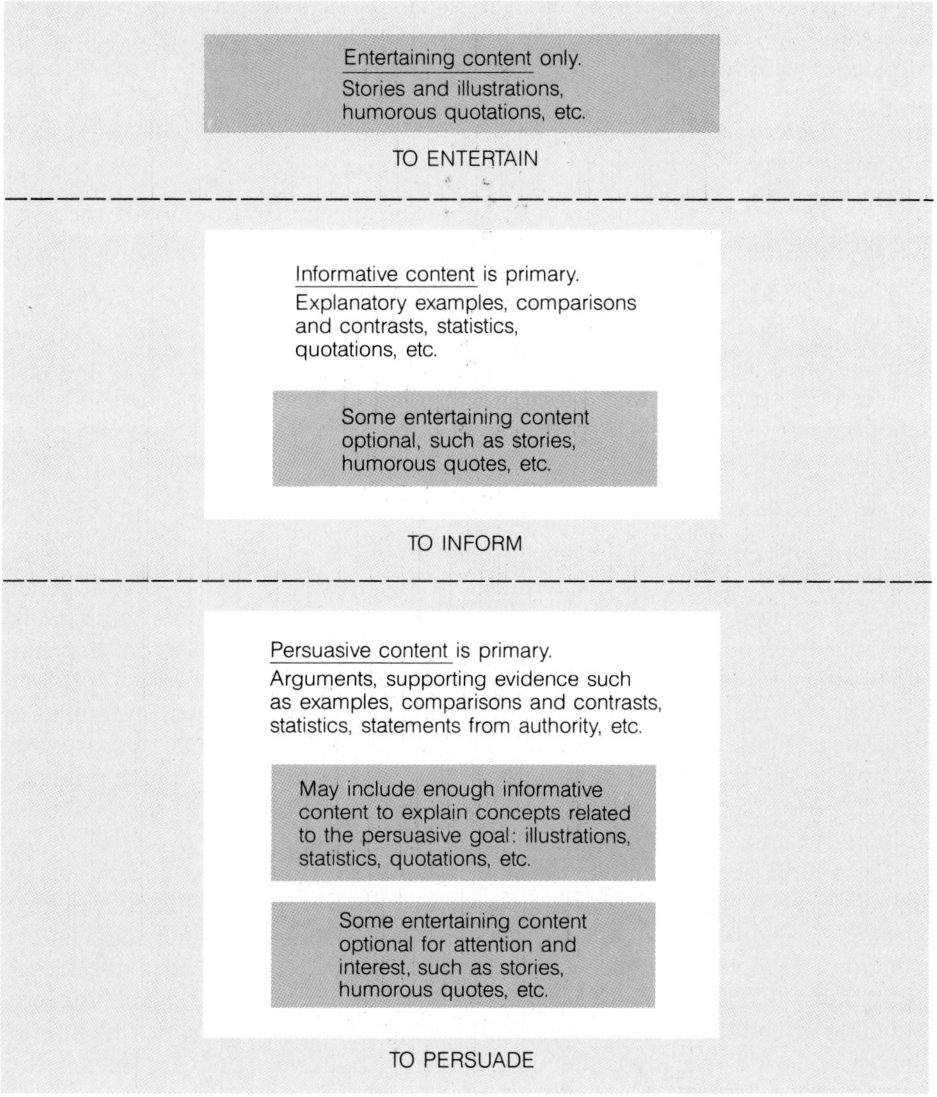

Entertaining content only.
Stories and illustrations,
humorous quotations, etc.

TO ENTERTAIN

Informative content is primary.
Explanatory examples, comparisons
and contrasts, statistics,
quotations, etc.

Some entertaining content
optional, such as stories,
humorous quotes, etc.

TO INFORM

Persuasive content is primary.
Arguments, supporting evidence such
as examples, comparisons and contrasts,
statistics, statements from authority, etc.

May include enough informative
content to explain concepts related
to the persuasive goal: illustrations,
statistics, quotations, etc.

Some entertaining content
optional for attention and
interest, such as stories,
humorous quotes, etc.

TO PERSUADE

FIGURE 6.1

Content Limits of General Purposes. *The content of the speech* to entertain *is limited to that which amuses. The speech* to inform, *however, may include some entertaining content (to hold audience attention); note that informative speeches do not intentially include persuasion. The speech* to persuade *is the broadest of the three, for it may include materials of both an informative and an entertaining nature in support of the goal of influencing attitudes and behavior.*

II. Determine the Purpose

After you have selected the subject of your speech, you next need to make an informed decision concerning the purpose of your speech. While it is true that some thought about purpose goes into the matter of selecting and narrowing a subject, the time comes when you need to make a firm decision about that purpose and "pin it down" in the form of a short, clear statement. This is done in two steps, as follows:

Step 1: Determine the *general purpose* (choose one: to entertain, to inform, or to persuade).

Step 2: Determine the *specific purpose* of the speech (by combining the general purpose with the narrowed subject).

Determine the General Purpose

As mentioned earlier, there are three general purposes for speeches; namely, to entertain, to inform, and to persuade. Each of these is explained in more detail below.

To Entertain

The speech to entertain is designed to delight and to please. Although it might unintentionally touch on some elements of information or persuasion, it is not intended primarily to teach or to change belief or action. The entertaining talk can range from one that is hilariously funny to one that depends upon suspense and mystery for its effectiveness (for instance, an exciting but true adventure tale). If you deliver such a speech, and your audience pays attention, is amused, and enjoys what you have said, you have fulfilled your purpose. An example would be an after-dinner talk by a retired football coach with this specific purpose: "to entertain the audience with humorous but true sports stories from my years as a coach."

Be careful not to confuse a highly entertaining speech to inform, or an amusing speech to persuade, with the more limited purpose of the entertaining speech. As Figure 6.1 illustrates, speeches to inform may include some entertaining material, as may speeches to persuade; however, this does not necessarily mean that the general purpose is to entertain or to persuade. Indeed, including attention materials and entertaining content in speeches to inform and to persuade are recommended, for such materials help to sustain the interest of the listener. The distinction is in how far you go. To entertain, and no more, is to limit content to that which diverts and pleases, and you should be aware of that limitation as you make a decision about a general purpose.

Students interested in preparing an entertaining speech are referred at this point to Chapter 17, on special forms and occasions, where the speech to entertain is discussed further. Meanwhile, our emphasis in the intervening chapters will be on speeches to inform and to persuade. Entertaining is not ignored in these chapters; however, it is discussed mainly as a means of gaining and holding audience attention and interest in informative and persuasive speaking.

To Inform

The speech to inform is for the purpose of communicating knowledge. The informative speech—also called expository speaking, lecturing, explaining, and giving instructions—teaches an audience, but does not focus upon trying to change attitudes or behavior as does the speech to persuade. It is used to give directions, to explain processes or procedures and the working of institutions and organizations, to describe objects, formations, or structures, and to narrate history or present biographical information. No doubt there are other variations of this very common form of discourse. To illustrate, a lecture early in a course on basic computing could have this goal: "to inform the class about how computer 'floppy disks' are manufactured."

Although the speech to inform is not for the purpose of persuading, it—like the speech to entertain—might at times have an unintended persuasive effect upon a listener. For example, you might describe how a product works, restricting your "lecture" to factual information; yet, someone who hears you, and who likes the product you describe, might decide to buy it. In this case, your limited goal of communicating knowledge had the unintended effect of persuading a listener to action. The concept that you should keep clear in your planning is this: if your general purpose is exposition—that is, the communication of knowledge—and the speech is not intended to try to change attitudes or actions, your purpose is "to inform." As with the speech to entertain, informing is a matter of intent and emphasis.[3]

To Persuade

This text defines *persuasive speaking* as *spoken discourse that is planned so as to modify the beliefs, values, attitudes, and behavior of others in directions intended by the speaker.* As Figure 6.1 illustrates, persuasion may include both entertaining and informative materials; however, it goes beyond entertaining and informing by attempting to change the thinking or conduct of the audience. For example, a speech favoring or opposing strict government regulation of banks and savings and loans would be a persuasive speech concerning audience thinking—that is, the listeners' mental position—on the subject. Such speeches need not call for specific action. On the other hand, a speech urging the students of your school to "vote for John Jones for student body president" would be a persuasive speech to actuate because it urges a specific behavior, namely, casting a vote for Jones.

We have now discussed the general purposes of entertaining, informing, and persuading. Let us now turn our thoughts to the process of making those general purposes specific.

Formulate the Specific Purpose

The specific purpose is formed by combining your *narrowed subject* with your *general purpose.* It is stated as an infinitive phrase, beginning with infinitives such as "to inform," or "to persuade." The specific purpose is your personal statement of the key objective of your speech. You should phrase it carefully, for it sets the exact direction of the speech, influencing all of the preparation that follows. (The speaker who does not have a clear specific purpose often rambles, omits important information, and fails to persuade the audience to change its thinking in any concrete way.)

Keep in mind that the specific purpose is for your use; it is not announced to your audience (for the audience, you phrase a *central idea,* as discussed below). Also, the specific purpose places limits on the content of your speech, thereby giving you guidance on what belongs and what does not. In a nutshell, if subideas and materials are covered by the specific purpose, it is logical to consider including them. However, if some subideas and materials you are considering are not within the boundary defined by your specific purpose, you probably should leave them out.

Here are three examples of specific purposes illustrating how you can proceed from subject to general purpose to the specific wording of your goal. First, the purpose of an expository speech could be made concrete as follows:

Narrowed Subject: The work of the Federal Trade Commission in policing false advertising.
General Purpose: To inform.
Specific Purpose: To inform my audience of the major programs of the Federal Trade Commission in policing false advertising.

Second, a persuasive speech based upon the same subject might be focused as follows:

Narrowed Subject: The work of the Federal Trade Commission in policing false advertising.
General Purpose: To persuade.
Specific Purpose: To persuade my audience to support the work of the FTC in the area of policing false advertising.

In summary, after you have selected and narrowed your subject, there are two steps to determining your purpose. First, decide upon the *general purpose* of your speech. The general purposes from which you can choose are ''to entertain,'' ''to inform,'' or ''to persuade.'' Second, combine the general purpose with your narrowed subject to form a *specific purpose*. For example, if your narrowed subject is ''the legislative process of the city council,'' and your general purpose is ''to inform,'' your specific purpose could be as follows: ''to inform my audience about how a proposed ordinance becomes law in the city council of our town.'' Let us now examine the final step in the process of choosing a subject and formulating a speech purpose, namely, wording the central idea.

III. Phrase the Central Idea

The *central idea* can be defined as *the sentence that announces the purpose of your speech to the audience*. It serves two important functions. First, it adapts the specific purpose to your audience. Second, whereas the specific purpose/central idea combination establishes a goal for the speech, it also sets limits on what content fits and what does not. Each of these two functions of the central idea is discussed further below.

Adapt the Specific Purpose to the Audience

The central idea does not change the theme stated by your specific purpose; rather, it simply rewords it in language that you believe is appropriate to your

The Specific Purpose Is Retained "Inside" the Central Idea. *The Central Idea restates the Specific Purpose in sentence form, and phrases it in tactful language for the audience. However, the speech goal set out by the Specific Purpose is retained within the Central Idea.*

audience. As Figure 6.2 illustrates, the goal you set in the specific purpose is retained "inside" the central idea. Remember, however, that the specific purpose is not announced to the audience, for it is an infinitive phrase designed to help the *speaker*, and, therefore, it need not be diplomatically worded. On the other hand, the central idea adapts your specific purpose to the *audience* by wording it as a complete sentence and in language that is diplomatic (when tact is needed, as with controversial or sensitive topics).

If your subject is not sensitive or controversial, you will not need to be greatly concerned about politeness in the wording of the central idea. For example, if your specific purpose is "to actuate my audience to make a pledge of financial support to the local soup kitchen," you can word the central idea in similar language because soup kitchens are not, as a rule, the subjects of controversy. The resulting central idea might be: "The downtown soup kitchen is in desperate need of your financial support."

However, if your subject is controversial, or if it deals with a matter that requires sensitive treatment, you will want to word the central idea carefully so as not to create unnecessary opposition or to needlessly offend the audience. The principle at work here is that you need to get a friendly hearing for your views if the information or arguments of the body of the speech are to be heeded. For example, if you are speaking to a church group on why you believe Sunday closing laws should be repealed, your specific purpose might be: "to persuade my audience that Sunday closing laws should be abolished in our community." In adapting this frank statement to your audience, you could phrase the central idea this way: "Today I would like to tell you how I came to believe that Sunday closing laws are a form of religious discrimination."

In summary form, therefore, we can compare and contrast three factors that apply to both the specific purpose and the central idea, as follows.

Your goal stated as a specific purpose:

1 To be used by the speaker (that is, not announced to the audience)
2 Worded as an infinitive phrase
3 Need not be in diplomatic language

Your goal stated as a central idea:

1 Intended to be spoken to the audience
2 Worded as a complete sentence
3 Should be phrased in diplomatic language

*The formulation of the specific purpose and central idea helps focus the speech
for the speaker and the audience. (Peter Vandermark/Stock, Boston)*

Let us illustrate further with two examples, one informative and the other persuasive. First, an informative purpose adapted for audience use.

Specific Purpose: To inform my audience about the two standard library book classification systems, namely, the Dewey Decimal System and the Library of Congress System.
Central Idea: I would like to explain the differences between the Dewey Decimal System and the Library of Congress System for cataloguing library books.

Second, let us see how a persuasive purpose is adapted to the audience.

Specific Purpose: To persuade my audience to develop the habit of listening to the campus radio station.
Central Idea: For music and talk shows designed with your interests and enjoyment in mind, listen regularly to our campus radio station.

In addition to rephrasing the specific purpose in diplomatic language for audience consumption, the central idea also serves to focus and limit the content of the speech. Let us look briefly at that important function.

Focus and Limit the Content of the Speech

The specific purpose/central idea formulation says to you, and to your audience, *this is what I intend to talk about*. At the same time, it is important to realize that the formulation also defines what you are *not* going to discuss, for the boundary set by the central idea excludes more than it includes.

The practical value of thinking in terms of both inclusion and exclusion of materials is that it gives you guidance on what to leave out, namely, everything that is not a part of meeting the goal set by the specific purpose. This means that irrelevant points and supporting materials—such as examples, statistics, and quotations—should be eliminated from the speech outline. For example, a speaker whose specific purpose is "to inform my classmates of the services of the student health clinic on campus" should focus on the health clinic, and not discuss in lengthy detail other student services such as recreation programs, career placement, or financial aid.

This Chapter in Brief

Determining the subject and purpose of your speech is a critical phase of preparation, for your decisions on these matters establishes both the goal of the speech and the limits on what is suitable in achieving that goal. To determine your subject and purpose, follow three major steps (the first two of which consist of two substeps each):

Step I.   Choose and narrow the subject.
A. Choose a broad subject area.
B. Narrow to a specific topic within the broad subject area; this topic should be suitable to the speaker, the audience, and the occasion.

Step II.   Determine your purpose.
A. Determine your *general purpose* (to entertain, to inform; or, to persuade).
B. Determine your *specific purpose* (by combining your general purpose with the narrowed subject).

Step III.   Finally, formulate your *central idea*.
A. Reword the specific purpose in diplomatic language such as you might use in the delivered speech.
B. Keep the content within the limits established by the central idea.

An example of the steps in this procedure is given below. Recall that the first two steps come under "choosing and narrowing the subject," and the next two steps come under "determining the purpose." The final step—the central idea—stands alone, for it is the end result of the four steps above it.

Broad Subject: The American Revolutionary War.
Narrowed Subject: George Washington's military strategy in choosing Valley Forge for the encampment of the winter of 1777–1778.
General Purpose: To inform.
Specific Purpose (combine the general purpose with the narrowed subject):   To inform my audience of why Washington chose Valley Forge for the winter encampment of Revolutionary troops in the winter of 1777–1778.
Central Idea (restates the specific purpose as a sentence for use in the delivered speech):   I would like to explain the military considerations that

caused George Washington to pick Valley Forge for the encampment of Revolutionary troops during the winter of 1777–1778.

After you have chosen a subject for your speech and have narrowed it to a central idea, you are ready to begin thinking about what types of specific supporting materials you will need in order to explain and otherwise "back up" the points you will make. Therefore, we turn our attention in the chapter that follows to "Supporting Materials for Public Speeches."

EXERCISES

1. During the next round of speeches in your public speaking class, listen carefully for the statement of a central idea by each speaker. Write down the central ideas and note how clear and tactful each was. Could you "improve" upon the way in which certain central ideas were announced? If so, how? Why do you think a change in wording might help?

2. Make a list of several controversial subjects suitable for speeches. Phrase a specific purpose appropriate to each subject, then, with a familiar audience in mind (such as a club of which you are a member, or your speech class) reformulate each as a diplomatic central idea such as you might employ in announcing your purpose to that audience.

3. Find the central idea for each of the model outlines and speeches in the appendices to this book. Are any difficult to find? Are any unclear, or undiplomatic in the way they are stated? If so, what changes would you recommend, and why?

SELECTED READINGS

Dickens, Milton. *Speech: Dynamic Communication.* 3d ed. New York: Harcourt Brace Jovanovich, 1974. In Chapter 4, "Speech Purposes," Dickens outlines some excellent ideas on choosing a speech goal, including how to avoid the "common mistakes" in making the choice.

Ehninger, Douglas; Gronbeck, Bruce E.; McKerrow, Ray E.; and Monroe, Alan H. *Principles and Types of Speech Communication.* 10th ed. Glenview, Ill.: Scott, Foresman, 1986. A number of suggestions for finding speech subjects is provided in Chapter 4. The "subject categories" at the conclusion of this chapter should be especially useful to the student in need of ideas for speeches.

Hooker, Zebulon Vance, II. *An Index of Ideas for Writers and Speakers.* Chicago: Scott, Foresman, 1965. Though long out of print, this collection of topics for speeches and essays might be available in your library. It consists entirely of hundreds of speech/essay topics on a wide range of subjects. Helps break "mental blocks" on subject choice.

Mills, Glen E. *Message Preparation: Analysis and Structure.* Indianapolis, Ind.: Bobbs-Merrill, 1966. This brief text focuses on finding speech subjects, determining purposes, and adapting both to the audience.

Walter, Otis M., and Scott, Robert L. *Thinking and Speaking: A Guide to Intelligent Oral Communication.* 5th ed. New York: Macmillan, 1984. This text is an excellent source of ideas for speech topics concerning problems, including their causes and solutions (see Chapters 6, 7, and 8 in particular). In addition, Chapter 9 discusses speaking about definitions, and Chapter 10 discusses speaking about values.

ENDNOTES

1. From George Campbell, *The Philosophy of Rhetoric*, Book I, Chap. 1; in James L. Golden and Edward P. J. Corbett, eds., *The Rhetoric of Blair, Campbell, and Whately* (New York: Holt, Rinehart and Winston, 1968), p. 145.
2. The starter list of problem-centered subjects was derived by scanning the issues that concern Americans as presented in *The Gallup Report* for 1988 and 1989. *The Gallup Report* is a monthly summary of Gallup Polls that has been published since 1965.
3. The view that the distinction between informing and persuading is, to a large degree, one of intent and emphasis, is held by a number of writers in the field of rhetoric. See, for example, Donald C. Bryant and Karl R. Wallace, *Fundamentals of Public Speaking*, 5th ed. (Englewood Cliffs, N.J.: Prentice-Hall, 1976), pp. 169–173; Wayne C. Minnick, *Public Speaking* (Boston: Houghton Mifflin, 1979), p. 178; and James C. McCroskey, *An Introduction to Rhetorical Communication*, 4th ed. (Englewood Cliffs, N.J.: Prentice-Hall, 1982), pp. 131–137.

> *Rhetoric initially is the discovery and selection of essential materials to be incorporated in the development of the discourse—whether the aim is chiefly to explain, persuade, or impress.*

—A. Craig Baird,
Rhetoric: A Philosophical Inquiry (1965)[1]

Chapter 7

SUPPORTING MATERIALS FOR PUBLIC SPEECHES

*S*everal years ago, in a college public speaking class, a student spoke on the need for improved day care facilities for the small children of working parents. Assume for a moment that the student had started the speech with the following statement: "Many mothers have found that their children have not been taken care of very well in various day care centers around the state." Does that statement "grab you," and rivet your attention on the subject? Probably not. And, to the speaker's credit, it is not the opener that was used. Instead, Elinor Vaughan, the speaker, began with a true story, as follows.

> A Raleigh woman told a reporter for the *Raleigh News and Observer* what happened recently when she went by her daughter's day care center a little earlier than she was expected. She found her three-month-old daughter lying in the same diaper, at four o'clock in the afternoon, that she had put on the child at 7:30 in the morning. The baby was removed from the center immediately.[2]

As you can see, the story that Vaughan actually used (one that she found while researching the subject) is much more interesting than was the hypothetical opening sentence given earlier. And it was effective, for the audience listened attentively and sympathetically as the speaker gave additional examples, as well as statistics, and statements from authorities, to back up her claims.

Supporting your central idea and the various main headings with specific details—as speaker Vaughan did so well—is essential if you want your presentations to be interesting, clear, and persuasive. Each time you speak, your listeners will be silently thinking, "summarize a case," "illustrate your idea," "state the exact numbers," and "give me the views of some experts." In other words, listeners demand specifics, and giving the audience those specifics is what this chapter is about.

In order to examine the use of supporting materials in public speaking, the chapter is organized around three important topics: the functions and standards of supporting materials; types of supporting materials; and supporting a speech with visual aids.

I. Functions and Standards of Supporting Materials

Supporting materials can be defined as the *specific details used to make the general points of a speech interesting, clear, and persuasive*. These details include *examples* (specific instances or stories employed to illustrate a speech point), *comparisons and contrasts* (comparing the similarities or contrasting the dissimilarities of two or more examples), *statistics* (specific instances that have been organized and reported numerically), and *statements from authority* (such as quoting from experts on a given subject). To illustrate, the general statement "automobile seat belts save lives" needs some concrete support to gain audience assent. The support might include examples of persons who survived a serious automobile accident because they wore seat belts, comparisons and contrasts of crash survival of those who wore seat belts and those who did not, national statistics showing the validity of the general statement "seat belts save lives," and statements from safety authorities on the matter.

Functions of Supporting Materials

The three functions of supporting materials in public speaking are to help make the speech interesting, clear, and persuasive. The *interest function* refers to the use of speech materials to help the speaker gain and hold the attention of the audience. In informative and persuasive speaking, these materials often do double duty, for they not only hold attention but also help explain something, or help motivate the listener to agree with the speaker's point of view. For example, an informative speech on how to administer artificial respiration to a drowning victim could include a true story of a college student who saved the life of a friend by employing the procedure being explained (with that procedure being restated, step by step, as the story is told). Such an account would not only help summarize important information but also would add dramatic interest to the speech.

The *clarification function* refers to supporting materials that help explain something to the audience. These materials include such things as examples, statistics, and visual aids (charts, maps, graphs, and so forth) that aid listener understanding. For example, when a speaker uses a diagram (poster) of a device in order to explain how that device works, that speaker is employing supporting material that clarifies.

The *persuasive function* refers to those supporting materials that help the speaker change or strengthen audience attitudes on the subject of the speech. For example, a speaker whose central idea is, "We should prohibit all smoking in the work place," might support this view by quoting from an authoritative medical study that reports that the breathing of smoke-filled air endangers the health of all in the room, including nonsmokers. Such material (also called evidence) provides the audience with the type of concrete support that helps make the central idea of the speech persuasive.

Furthermore, research supports the assumption that the use of evidence in persuasion strengthens the effectiveness of the speech. As one study concludes, "Including good evidence may significantly increase sustained audience attitude change regardless of the source's initial credibility [or] the quality of the delivery of the message."[3] Another study finds that the use of high-quality evidence enhances the communicator's credibility with the audience,[4] whereas a third study reports that evidence helps to strengthen listener attitudes against counter-persuasion.[5]

Standards of Supporting Materials

The three basic standards that all evidence should meet are those of accuracy, clarity, and relevance. Later in the chapter we will consider those standards that help you evaluate specific types of support. But first, let us examine those that apply to supporting material in general.

To begin, you should check all support materials for *accuracy*. In addition, be sure to interpret and report your examples, comparisons and contracts, statistics, and authoritative statements so that you do not mislead the audience as to their meaning.

Second, use speech supports that will be *clear* to your audience. Based on an evaluation of such factors as age, education, and general knowledge of your listeners, select supports that will be readily understood. In particular, be alert to complex statistics and technical testimony that will muddle rather than illuminate the subject in the minds of your listeners.

Finally, choose supporting materials that are *relevant* to your topic. In other words, don't chase "rhetorical rabbits" by spending valuable time talking about things that have little or nothing to do with your speech. Review all supports to see that they back up your purpose by adding interest, clarity, and proof. In this way you can help keep your speech marching steadily toward its goal, without distracting "side trips" and diversions.

II. Types of Supporting Materials

As noted above, supporting materials can be classified according to four basic types: examples, comparisons and contrasts, statistics, and statements from authority. Each of these is explained in more detail below.

Examples

Examples are the specific instances (also described as stories, anecdotes, and illustrations) that you use to support the general statements in your speech. They vary in length from short, to medium, to long, and they can be *real* (that is, factual), or *hypothetical* (that is, fictional, having been made up by the speaker in order to illustrate a point).

One of the most effective forms of support for speeches is the use of examples. The reason for this is simple, namely, audiences like the concrete, the specific; and they enjoy listening to stories. Perhaps you can recall times in your own experience when your mind wandered during a lecture, sermon, or other public speech, only to be brought back to attention and focus when the speaker cited a specific instance or a story to illustrate a point. You should do the same thing in your speaking.

Let us look at how some speakers have used examples effectively. In a persuasive speech planned to help create good will toward the real estate profession, former Realtor Betsy Brown used a series of *specific instances* (that is, short examples) to support the point that realtors do more than help home buyers sign papers.[6]

The service that a Realtor gives a customer is more than showing the house and preparing papers for signing. I've arranged for phones to be installed and for utilities to be turned on. I've met the movers, and supervised the unloading of furniture. I've taken the wife shopping, and even brought my daughter along to babysit! In addition, I always try to supply customers with a list of emergency telephone numbers, covering everything from pediatricians to plumbers.

National leaders, too, often make use of examples to add interest and persuasive impact to their speeches. On March 15, 1965, President Lyndon B. Johnson addressed a joint session of Congress on behalf of a national voting rights bill, and in support of his argument that the federal government should assure all citizens the right to register and vote, he told this story.[7]

My first job after college was as a teacher in Cotulla, Texas, in a small Mexican-American school. Few of them could speak English, and I couldn't speak much Spanish. My students were poor and they often came to class without breakfast, hungry. They knew even in their youth the pain of prejudice. They never seemed to know why people disliked them. But they knew it was so, because I saw it in their eyes. I often walked home late in the afternoon, after the classes were finished, wishing there was more that I could do. But all I knew was to teach them the little that I knew, hoping that it might help them against the hardships that lay ahead.

Somehow you never forget what poverty, and hatred can do when you see its scars on the hopeful face of a young child.

I never thought then, in 1928, that I would be standing here in 1965. It never even occurred to me in my fondest dreams that I might have the chance to help the sons and daughters of those students and to help people like them all over this country.

But now I do have that chance—and I'll let you in on a secret—I mean to use it. And I hope that you will use it with me.

Testing Your Examples

The examples you use in your speeches should meet the following three standards.

Use examples that are typical. When employed as evidence in support of a point of view, examples should be representative of their class. Stated another way, they should be the rule, and not the exception to the rule. To illustrate, if a speaker charges that "the entire campus police force should be dismissed for brutal conduct toward students," and cites one instance of the misconduct of only one officer from a force of twelve campus police, then the speaker is using evidence that is not representative of the group of officers as a whole.

Use enough examples to support your reasoning. Generally speaking, an example or two, without further support, would be inadequate to prove a point. (A single example might gain interest, or make a point clearer, but standing alone, it would likely not "clinch your case" in a persuasive speech.) When you are planning a speech to convince or to actuate, therefore, check to see that you have enough evidence to back up your point. In particular, don't depend on a single example to do the job.

Use real rather than hypothetical examples when you are persuading. Whereas hypothetical examples might serve to attract attention, or to explain something, they are less useful when you are trying to prove a point in persuasion. Apply this test to your own thinking. If you were listening to a speech urging humane standards for the use of laboratory animals, would you be impressed more by fictional accounts made up by the speaker, or by true stories of painful experiments upon animals? The answer should be obvious.

Comparison and Contrast

Comparison and contrast should be thought of as a variation of the example. In *comparison* (sometimes called analogy), the speaker compares one example to another with an emphasis on existing similarities (such as comparing one small, private college to another small, private college). When using *contrast*, the speaker emphasizes the differences between two examples (such as explaining the key differences between two life insurance policies).

Comparisons, or analogies, are of two types: figurative and literal. *Figurative comparisons* are those that compare two things that are not literally alike, but that can be presented in the form of a "figure of speech" in order to add interest or explain something. Speakers do this when they compare life to a baseball game in which the "players" sometimes "strike out," and at other times "make home runs." Likewise, if a speaker compares the federal government to a three-legged stool as a means of adding vividness to the concept of three branches of government, that speaker is making a figurative comparison. While useful, such comparisons are not very logical and therefore should be used with care. In persuasive speaking it is a good idea to back up figurative analogies with other forms of support that have a strong logical base (such as solid statistics, and testimony from experts).

Literal comparison (or literal analogy) occurs when a speaker compares two things that are alike or similar, such as two athletic teams, two states, or two word processing programs. Obviously, literal comparisons are more logical than figurative ones, for the examples being compared are actually alike in some aspects (the more the two are similar, the stronger the analogy). To illustrate, a speaker could urge the board of commissioners to reorganize the county ambulance service by presenting a plan based on one that improved ambulance efficiency in an adjoining county. "It worked for them," the speaker might say, "and, therefore, it will work for us."

Finally, a speaker can do the opposite by emphasizing *contrasting details* between two or more instances or situations. For example, a speaker could explain the advantages and disadvantages of two word processing programs by comparing what both can do, then contrasting them by explaining what one can do that the other cannot, and vice versa. To illustrate further, a fraternity member in a college public speaking class employed contrast in his persuasive speech in support of fraternities. His account went like this.

Many people think of fraternities as a form of "Animal House," with loud noises, excessive partying, and rude pranks played on fraternity brothers and on the members of other Greek organizations. I joined a fraternity because I found out that the "Animal House" image did not fit. What I discovered before joining, and have confirmed since becoming a fraternity member, is that the fraternities on our campus encourage academic achievement and support campus and community service projects by helping raise funds for causes that range from university scholarships to the

Muscular Dystrophy Association. Life in my fraternity is in sharp contrast to anything resembling ''Animal House.''

Testing Your Comparisons and Contrasts

Your literal comparisons and contrasts should meet these two basic standards.

Use comparisons and contrasts that are based upon facts. Your comparisons and contrasts will not stand scrutiny if the details you are discussing turn out not to be true. For instance, if a speaker urges hospital ''A'' to develop a surgical unit like that in hospital ''B'' because both hospitals operate on similar budgets, when in fact hospital ''B'' has twice the income as hospital ''A,'' the factual discrepancy would make the comparison invalid.

Use comparisons that are alike in essential details. Literal analogies are strengthened when the elements of similarity outweigh the elements of difference. For instance, when comparing the repair records of automobiles built by two companies, it makes more sense to compare two comparably equipped economy cars than to compare an economy model of the first manufacturer with a heavy, ''fully equipped'' luxury sedan of the second. Obviously, the larger car will require more upkeep and repair because there is more to ''go wrong'' in its numerous mechanical and electronic parts. Because such upkeep is normal for more complex cars, it is not logical to compare the repair record of the larger car to that of the smaller one.

Statistics

Statistics can be defined as a collection of specific instances that have been organized and classified, then reported in numerical form. Presented poorly, they can be confusing and dull; but presented wisely—that is, according to sound rhetorical principles—statistics can add interest, clarity, and persuasiveness to a communication effort. Let us look at some types of statistics commonly employed by speakers, some tests you should give them before using them, and some suggestions for presenting statistics in a clear, meaningful way to your auditors.

Public speakers can make use of a variety of types of statistics, ranging from simple numbers (''our town currently has a population of 80,000'') to more complex figures derived from statistical methods. Rhetorically useful figures reached by statistical methods include percentages, arithmetic means, and medians.

Percentages

Percentages are often used by public communicators, both to inform and to help persuade listeners and readers. Typical examples include learning that a certain percentage of Americans can neither read nor write, that a certain percentage of Americans graduate from college, or that a certain percentage of our tax dollar goes for interest on the national debt.

Percentages can be misleading, however, and you should be careful to interpret and use them honestly. To illustrate, you might be impressed to read in your student newspaper that ''fifty percent of the students'' in a certain course have a grade of "A." However, if you learned that there are only four students in the class, the significance of the percentage is greatly diminished, for, in this case, "fifty percent" means exactly *two*.

The Arithmetic Mean

The arithmetic mean is a second type of statistic that public speakers use regularly. The mean should be understood as one of three variations of central tendency employed by statisticians. Because all three are sometimes called an "average," you need to understand each type so that you can interpret and report them accurately in your speaking. For an overview of the three, see Figure 7.1.

The mean, often described as the "simple average," is the most useful of the three variations of central tendency. It is reached by adding a group of scores, then dividing the sum by the number of scores in the group. This is what most people have in mind when they report "the average." For example, the weights of seven persons are recorded as follows: 210, 298, 172, 160, 158, 150, and 145. By adding these numbers and dividing by seven, you reach the arithmetical mean (or simple average) of 184.7. However, 184.7 pounds is not the *median* for this group.

The Median

The median is a second form of "average," or central tendency; however, it represents the midpoint of a set of numbers arranged according to magnitude. When the median is given, you know that half of the numbers are above it and half of the numbers are below it. In the weights of seven people given above, the median is 160 pounds. When you contrast the *mean of 184.7* with the *median of 160*, you can readily see the importance of knowing how to interpret and report "averages" correctly. (The *mode*, a third type of "average," is the score that occurs most often in a group of scores. It is of little use to public speakers because it does not reveal much useful information; however, it is included in Figure 7.1. in order to "complete the picture" of the three "averages.")

Testing Your Statistics

You should apply at least three basic standards to your statistics.

Use statistics accurately. Accuracy in the use of statistics includes not only getting the numbers right but also interpreting them honestly and intelligently. To illustrate, a percentage based upon interviews with six persons is certainly not as significant as a percentage based upon the extension of these interviews to six hundred persons. And, you should accurately explain your "average" by making clear whether it is the mean or the median.

Use statistics from a reliable source. In general, statistical information from objective research studies, such as those done by university researchers or other impartial persons or groups, is more reliable—and more persuasive with your audience—than is information from sources that have a vested interest in achieving a certain result. For example, a report of the average miles

A. The <u>mean</u>

The mean (also called the "arithmetic mean," or "simple average") is obtained by adding up a group of scores, then dividing the result by the number of scores in that group. For example, if five students take an exam, and their scores are 65%, 75%, 83%, 88%, and 94%, the <u>mean for that exam is 81%</u> (obtained by adding the five grades, and dividing the result by five).

B. The <u>median</u>

The median is the score that falls exactly in the middle of a group of scores that are arranged by size. When scores are arranged in this manner, half are above the median and half are below it. To illustrate, in the following list of "annual incomes," the median (or midpoint) is $25,000.00.

$18,000.00
$20,000.00
$25,000.00 ◄——— median
$32,000.00
$50,000.00

(The <u>arithmetic mean</u> for these salaries is $29,000.00, thus illustrating that it <u>does</u> matter which "average" is reported.)

C. The <u>mode</u>

The mode is the score that occurs most often in a group of scores. For example, the mode for the test reported below is 80%.

Twenty-three students took an exam, with these results:

Three received 90%
Five received 88%
Ten received 80% ◄——— mode
Four received 75%
One received 60%

FIGURE 7.1

Measures of Central Tendency: Mean, Median, and Mode. *Of the three methods of determining "central tendency," the* mean *is ordinarily the most useful because it provides an average of the* value *of the scores in a group, something that the median and the mode do not do. The* median, *on the other hand, does reveal the middle position on a scale, and is, therefore, of limited use. Generally, the* mode *is of little use, for it reveals no average value, and no midpoint; rather, it shows only the score that occurs most often.*

per gallon of fuel for a certain automobile is more believable if it comes from an independent test done by a consumers' laboratory than if it is from a test performed by the manufacturer of that automobile.

Use recent statistics. Because statistics in many areas of life change regularly, you should secure the most recent numbers available. The prices of houses, for example, change over time; the mean cost of a house in a given locale five years ago would likely not be the same as the mean of today. Speakers who support their points with dated statistics risk misleading the audience, and in the process, losing credibility with that audience because the supporting materials are not current.

Using Statistics Effectively

Because statistics are sometimes complex and difficult for the audience to follow, you should pay special attention to how you use them. Here are three suggestions. First, *use statistics sparingly*. Remember that you are communicating the information orally, and that your listeners need to comprehend the statistics quickly and easily as you continue to speak. If you employ numerous complex figures, your speech might be "tuned out" by auditors who become overloaded with information. If some statistical complexity is required, both common sense and research support the view that it should be simplified as much as possible, then supplemented with visual aids, such as presenting the information in chart form on posters, with an overhead projector, by writing on the blackboard, or with an information sheet that you give to *each* person in the audience (see Figure 7.3).[8]

Second, *present the statistics in a form that facilitates understanding*. One method for doing this is to convert complex figures to simple, round numbers. For instance, instead of saying that a replacement part costs $102.32, say that "replacement parts are about one hundred dollars each." A second method is to interpret the significance of the statistics for your listeners. In a speech urging support for scholarship and loan programs for college students, the speaker might state that "one-fourth of all students on our campus have some form of scholarship or loan." Then, rather than moving immediately to the next point, the speaker could dramatize the significance of this number by saying, "According to a recent report of the Chancellor, if the scholarship and loan programs on our campus were canceled, and the students currently using them were to drop out of school, we would have to dismiss one hundred teachers, close two dormitories, and delete about 20 percent of the current course offerings from the catalog. That's how important scholarships and loans are to the future of this university!"

Finally, *supplement your statistics with other forms of support*. Don't count on statistics alone to make your point, for numbers are often perceived by listeners as dry, uninteresting, and lacking in persuasive impact. After citing the statistics, therefore, add rhetorical strength to the point by illustrating it with an interesting example, or backing it with an attention-getting quote from an authority on the subject.

Statement from Authority

Another form of support that is employed by public speakers is the statement from authority. Such statements include reports of laypersons who, although not authorities in the usual sense, are informed on a matter they have seen or otherwise experienced directly. An example would be a dormitory student speaking in support of improved campus security after testifying that he had, on two occasions, encountered a strange man in the dormitory, and that, each time, the man was carrying a gun. Such first-hand testimony makes that student an "authority" in a limited sense, for he has had relevant experience on the subject being discussed.

However, public speakers make more use of expert testimony than statements of lay witnesses. For example, a speaker opposed to nuclear power might quote from a study done by a group of nuclear scientists, or a speaker concerned about equal pay for women might cite a national salary survey done by a university economist. Variations include statements from scholarly essays and books, definitions from authoritative dictionaries, and court opinions.

You can present your statements from authority either by paraphrasing them (that is, putting them in your own words), or by quoting directly. You can avoid long, detailed quotations by presenting the ideas from authority in your own language. However, you should use the direct quote from time to time when it serves the purpose of dramatizing what a person, a study group, a dictionary, or a court opinion actually said.

To illustrate, let us assume that the student speaker concerned with improving campus security has a transcript of the testimony of the chief of the campus police force as presented recently to the board of trustees. Combining paraphrase and direct quotation, and including a statement of the qualifications of the testifier, the speaker could employ statement from authority in the following manner.

> Just three months ago, Chief of Campus Police Frank Jones testified before our trustees about the growing problem of security on the campus. Chief Jones, who has been with the college police for over ten years, and who has been chief for the past four years, told the trustees that despite a 25 percent increase in enrollment and the addition of two dormitories and a large classroom building during the last five years, not a single new officer has been added to the campus police during that time. To quote Chief Jones, "Add to these factors an increase in violent crime of about 10 percent a year, and you can understand why we must have help. Quite frankly, ladies and gentlemen of the board, we cannot protect this campus with the current force."

Testing Your Statements from Authority

Supporting materials derived from authority should meet the following three standards.

Use authoritative statements from qualified sources. In other words, make sure that the source is prepared by education, experience, or position to serve as an "authority" on the statement you are using. Once you have determined that the source is qualified, decide how to work that information into your speech smoothly and briefly. Research shows that persuasive speakers in particular should do more than simply mention the source of authoritative statements; to add credibility to the reference, the speaker should also explain to the audience *why that source is qualified.*[9] In the example above, the speaker mentioned the qualifications of the Chief of Campus Police. To illustrate further, a speaker who used a quotation about the harmful effects to nonsmokers of breathing smoke-filled air, might add: "That statement came from Dr. John Smith, head researcher on lung diseases at State Medical School, following over ten years of research into the problem."

Use authoritative statements that are fair and objective, having a minimum of speaker bias. Although some degree of bias will be present in all sources, you should make an effort to avoid statements that are biased to the point of distortion. The partisan and the propagandist are usually less objective than is the person trained in research who "seeks the truth" wherever the search might lead. Admittedly, some of your decisions on this standard will be intuitive; nevertheless, you should make the judgment to the best of your ability.

Use authoritative statements that are supported by other authorities, and by other forms of evidence. Try to avoid depending too heavily on one authority. Check to see if others agree, then mention some additional authorities to back up your key reference. Also, consider using a variety of types of supporting materials to supplement the statement from authority.

Having examined the four basic types of speech support—examples, statistics, comparison and contrast, and authoritative statement—we are now ready to consider a special means of presentation: visual aids.

III. Supporting Your Speech with Visual Aids

Visual aids serve the same three purposes in public speaking as do supporting materials in general, namely, to help make the speech interesting, clear, and persuasive. Of these three, the primary purposes are *to clarify* and, in some persuasive talks, to add *persuasive impact* to the point you are making. Not all speeches call for visual support (for instance, you could present a pep talk before a football game, or a convincing speech on "Why I Oppose Capital Punishment" without visuals). On the other hand, here are four examples of speech situations that do call for visual supports.

When you are trying to simplify and clarify a complex topic. This concept would apply in explaining such matters as statistical data, the working of a complicated device, or a detailed plan or procedure. To illustrate, an informative speech on "How a Diesel Engine Works" would be clearer if the speaker employed a diagram of a diesel engine.

When you need to help the audience visualize a plan, design, or relationship. Examples include explaining such things as battle plans, vacation itineraries, artistic concepts, and comparisons of size. To illustrate, a talk on an architectural plan for a new student union building would be helped by a diagram of the basic plan.

When it is important for the audience to remember a list of points. A typical example is a lecture during which the instructor writes a series of topics on the board and hints that the list "might prove useful on the next exam."

When visuals are needed to make a persuasive argument vivid and impelling. For instance, a person speaking on "Smoking and Health" could make effective use of a chart showing the annual deaths of heavy smokers from lung cancer over a period of years; or a person talking about air pollution could use photographs of a forest in which the vegetation had been killed by acid rain.

Types of Visual Materials

The types of visual materials most often used by public speakers are: three-dimensional models or objects; two-dimensional charts, maps, diagrams, or pictures (including those that are projected on a screen); and films and videotapes. Let us examine each of these briefly.

THE FOUR FORMS OF "AUTOMATIC" LIBEL
(Libel per se)

False charges of . . .

1. Criminality

2. Offensive Disease

3. Sexual Immorality

4. Attack Upon Reputation in
   Business or Profession

FIGURE 7.2

A Chart of Topical Headings. *A list of key topics, placed on a poster-type chart, or projected from a transparency, helps the listener follow the main points of the speech—and later to remember those points.*

Models or Objects

Three-dimensional models are useful when you are explaining such things as how a device works, the parts of an object or organism, or the steps in a process or procedure. For example, a plastic "see-through" working model of a piston engine would help explain a machine; a 3-D model of the human ear would help explain a part of the body; and a series of pottery models, showing the shaping of a bowl from its beginning as a ball of clay to the finished product, would help make a process clear. You could even use another person, such as a classmate, to serve as a visual aid for certain types of demonstrations, such as how to apply stage makeup, or how to administer artificial respiration.

Charts, Maps, Diagrams, or Pictures

This static, pictorial type of visual aid is used frequently by public speakers because it is fairly easy to prepare, and it can be readily "customized" to fit the precise demands of a given subject. Two-dimensional "poster" type visuals are appropriate for presenting topical headings (see Figure 7.2), statistical charts and graphs (see Figure 7.3), geographical relationships (such as the map illustrated by Figure 7.4), and similar representations that can range from a simple sketch to a photograph.

Films and Videotapes

Motion pictures presented to an audience by means of film or videotape can be effective in some circumstances. However, they should be reserved for those occasions when there is enough time to use them well, when the equipment is readily available, and when the content addresses the subject in a precise way. For example, a two-minute videotaped segment prepared by the speaker specifically for a given speech could vividly illustrate a problem the speaker is discussing (such as community slums, or homeless persons on the streets). Keep in mind that "showing a film" is not a substitute for making a speech. The visual should serve as support, not as the speech itself.

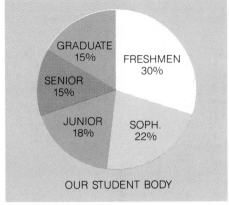

A. Pie Chart

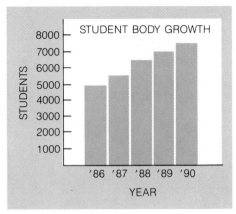

B. Bar Graph

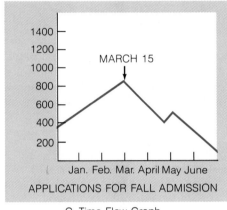

C. Time Flow Graph

FIGURE 7.3

Visuals Help Make Statistics Clear. *Three common forms of charts are: (A.) the* Pie Chart; *(B.) the* Bar Graph; *and (C.) the* Time Flow Graph.

Media for Displaying Visual Aids

The three most common media for displaying your visual aids are: the three-dimensional objects themselves; two-dimensional posters, handouts, or the chalkboard; and static or moving pictures that are projected or shown on a video screen. Let us look at each briefly.

Objects

Objects useful to public speakers range from professionally constructed models (such as a model of the human heart, or a plastic dummy used to teach life-saving techniques), to those assembled by the speaker specifically for a given speech (such as the use of cans and plastic flowers to demonstrate the basic steps of flower arranging). Also, speakers who make things or collect things can use the items they make or collect for visual aids.

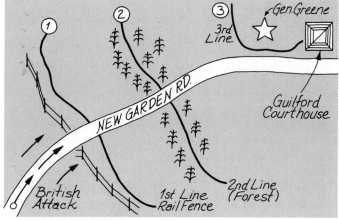

THE BATTLE OF GUILFORD COURTHOUSE (1781)
1st Line: North Carolina Militia
2nd Line: Virginia Militia
3rd Line: Regular Continentals

FIGURE 7.4

A Simple Map. *When using a map as your visual aid, sketch it yourself (or have it done according to your instructions) with only the essential details shown. This type of "visual simplicity" is easier for your audience to comprehend than a regular map that is cluttered with details not relevant to your subject.*

Posters, Handouts, and the Chalkboard

Posters are popular as visual aids because they are inexpensive, relatively easy to prepare, and can be "customized" by the speaker to fit the point being discussed. Variations of the poster include the strip chart, and the flip chart. A *strip chart* covers key words or pictured areas with removable strips of cardboard (fasten the strips with small pieces of tape, or push them into slots cut into the cardboard) that are "stripped" away at an appropriate moment in the speech to reveal the "next point" to be discussed. The *flip chart* is made up of several charts or diagrams sketched on sheets of heavy paper or cardstock, connected at the top, and mounted on a tripod or similar holding device. The speaker discusses the first chart, then flips it over to reveal the second, and so forth.

The *handout* is another medium for getting your visual aids before an audience. Modern photocopying has made this medium practical and inexpensive. If you use it, prepare enough copies for everyone in your audience. Also, to keep the handout from distracting your auditors, don't distribute it until you reach the point in the speech when it is needed. For large audiences, arrange for several people to help you give the material out quickly and efficiently at the appropriate moment.

Although often overlooked, the *chalkboard* is a highly useful medium for visual support in speechmaking. Because most college classrooms are equipped with this aid, you should consider using it for simple diagrams (those you can sketch hurriedly while continuing to speak), the listing of points, or for placing a set of statistics before the audience. The key is to plan in advance so that you will know what you are going to put on the board. While writing or sketching, *keep talking to your audience*—not to the chalkboard.

Projectors and Video

You can project two-dimensional charts, graphs, sketches, maps, and pictures with an *overhead projector*, or with a *slide or filmstrip projector*. By preparing transparencies for overhead projection (many schools have an audiovisual department that offers this service), or by using a 35mm camera to prepare color slides, you can make visuals for projection that are designed for your specific speech.

The *movie projector* has its place as a medium for speech support; however, because of its operational complexity, noise, and the difficulty and expense of preparing customized film, it has been generally replaced by the videotape. If you have access to dependable equipment, and if a needed segment is available on film, you can consider the use of the movie projector. Be sure to arrive early and to set up your equipment prior to the speech.

Videotapes have become the medium of choice for many speakers who need to show motion pictures in support of key points in a speech. The ready availability of videocameras along with the ease of use allow a speaker to prepare quickly and inexpensively "custom designed" video visuals. If your classroom or other speaking facility is equipped with a monitor and a VCR, the videotape is worth considering.

Suggestions for Preparing and Using Visual Aids

At the outset, make sure that you have decided upon visuals that are genuinely important to the content of your speech. In other words, the visuals should help explain significant ideas, and not be artificially "tacked on" to some minor point. With this standard in mind, let us look briefly at some suggestions for preparing your visuals, rehearsing with your visuals, and setting up and using visual aids on the day of the speech.

Preparing Visual Aids

Some visuals are professionally made (such as a large, printed poster), whereas others are made by the speaker, or by persons working under the speaker's supervision. In your public speaking class you might find that preparing a chart, sketch, or diagram yourself is the most practical method for illustrating the points that require visual support. In either case, secure or prepare visuals that are large enough to be seen by all in your audience (for posters, be sure all lettering is clear and easy to read from a distance). Also, prepare visuals that are not cluttered with excessive details. For example, an outline map that *you* prepare, showing only those points that are essential to your speech, is preferred to a regular map that includes more detail than is needed (see Figure 7.4).

Rehearsing with Visual Aids

After your speech has been outlined and your visual aids prepared, go over your talk several times, using the visuals as you intend to do at the time of actual delivery. Your practice should include putting up and taking down models or poster-type materials, working with flip charts or strip charts, and "hands on" manipulation of any projectors or video playback equipment that you intend to use. Be sure to practice pointing to the section of your visual aid that is relevant to the idea you are discussing. In addition, remember to practice talking to your audience—not to the visual aid.

Speaking with Visual Aids

On the day of the speech, arrive early so that you can prepare your visuals for use. In order not to distract from other persons' speeches, or from the introduction of your own speech, keep objects or posters covered and out of view until you are ready to use them. For example, you can bring a cloth cover for large objects, or keep them in a box until they are needed. Posters can be kept face down on a table, then taped to the board, or otherwise mounted, at the time they are actually needed in the speech.

While speaking, be sure to stand to one side so that the audience can see the visual aid. Also, make use of the visual by pointing as appropriate and referring to its content (in other words, don't ignore the visual aid after you put it up). While discussing the content of the visual, keep talking directly to the audience. Finally, when the speech is finished, take down the visual, or cover it and move it aside, so that it will not interfere with other speeches or activities.

This Chapter in Brief

In order to make the general statements of a speech interesting, clear, and persuasive, you should employ specific supporting materials that are accurate, easy for your audience to understand, and relevant to the purpose of your speech. The four basic types of support, together with a brief explanation of each, are as follows.

1 *Examples* are the specific instances and stories that you use to illustrate the general points of a speech.

2 *Comparison and contrast* occur when you compare the similarities of two or more examples (such as comparing the public relations department of one company to that of another), or when you contrast the differences between two or more examples (such as how automobile A differs from automobile B).

3 *Statistics* are specific instances that have been organized, classified, and reported numerically. Common forms of statistics used by public speakers include percentages and averages. As a conscientious public speaker, you need to understand the three types of "average"—namely, the mean average, the median average, and the mode average (as explained by Figure 7.1)—so that you can use them accurately and honestly.

4 *Statements from authority* consist of those materials you secure from expert testimony, books and articles written by knowledgeable persons, public speeches, dictionaries, court opinions, and the like.

Visual aids are a special form of speech support that should be considered when you are trying to explain a complex topic, present a visual plan or design, help the audience remember a list of points, or "drive home" a key point in a persuasive speech. Common types of visual aids for public speaking include three-dimensional objects or models, poster-type or projected charts, maps, and diagrams (see Figures 7.2, 7.3, and 7.4), and moving pictures (shown via film or video). When you use visual aids, be sure that they are large enough to be seen by all in your audience (including the lettering on poster-type visuals). Also, get acquainted with your visual aids by rehearsing with them prior to the speech. At the time of delivery, stand to one side of the visuals so your audience can see the aid, point to and use the visuals (don't ignore them), but keep talking directly to your audience. The logical question to be asked at this point is: "How does the speaker locate the specific materials needed to support the points of the speech?" In answer, we turn our attention to the matter of "Research: Finding Speech Materials," which is the subject of the next chapter.

EXERCISES

1. Read two or more of the model speeches in the appendices. On a piece of paper, note how many of the major types of support—examples, comparison and contrast, statistics, and authoritative statements—you find in each speech. Which types of support appear most often? Which types "grab your attention" most effectively?

2. Listen to several lectures or speeches while focusing on the specific examples, comparisons and contrasts, statistics, and statements from authority employed by the speaker. Which type of support did you find most interesting? Are general statements clearer and more persuasive when backed up by concrete supports?

3. During the term of your public speaking course, pay particular attention to how your classmates, your professors (in all courses), and other speakers you hear on and off campus make use of *visual aids*. Make a note of both effective and ineffective uses of visual aids. Based on your observations, compose a list of those things you should do, and those you should avoid doing when supporting a speech with visuals.

SELECTED READINGS

Borden, Richard D. *Public Speaking—As Listeners Like It!* New York: Harper & Brothers, 1935. This little classic is rich in ideas for making your speeches appealing to your audience. Chapter 2, "Listeners' Laws for Speech Substance," discusses the use of concrete speech supports, the "for instances" that listeners expect and enjoy.

Hanna, Michael S., and Gibson, James W. *Public Speaking for Personal Success.* 2d ed. Dubuque, Ia.: Wm. C. Brown, 1989. Chapter 10 includes a variety of illustrations of visual aids, ranging from pie charts to photographs.

Huff, Darrell. *How to Lie with Statistics.* New York: Norton, 1954. Huff employs numerous examples along with a sense of humor to explain the fallacies of certain uses of statistics. Enlightening—and fun to read.

Lucas, Stephen E. *The Art of Public Speaking.* 3d ed. New York: Random House, 1989. See Chapter 6 for a discussion of speech supports, and Chapter 12 for good advice on the preparation and use of visual aids. Chapter 12 includes numerous illustrations of types of visual aids.

Walter, Otis M. *Speaking to Inform and Persuade.* 2d ed. New York: Macmillan, 1982. The importance of strong supporting materials for public speaking is discussed in Chapter 6, "Persuasive Logic: The Tactics of Persuasion."

Williams, Frederick. *Reasoning with Statistics: How to Read Quantitative Research.* 3d ed. New York: Holt, Rinehart and Winston, 1986. Williams wrote this book for those with little or no technical background in statistics. The book is useful not only for public speakers but also for any student interested in learning how to interpret the statistics in research studies.

ENDNOTES

1. A. Craig Baird, *Rhetoric: A Philosophical Inquiry* (New York: Ronald Press, 1965), p. 36.
2. Elinor Vaughan, "The Day Care Dilemma," a persuasive speech to actuate delivered in the advanced public speaking course, University of North Carolina at Greensboro, December, 1984.
3. The quotation on evidence is from James C. McCroskey, "A Summary of Experimental Research on the Effects of Evidence in Persuasive Communication, *Quarterly Journal of Speech* 55 (April 1969): 169–176, at p. 175.
4. John A. Kline, "Interaction of Evidence and Readers' Intelligence on the Effects of Short Messages," *Quarterly Journal of Speech* 55 (December 1969): 407–412.
5. James C. McCroskey, "The Effects of Evidence as an Inhibitor of Counter-Persuasion," *Speech Monographs* 37 (August 1970): 188–194.
6. Betsy Brown, "Real Estate Salespeople," a persuasive speech to convince (create good will) delivered to the advanced public speaking class, University of North Carolina at Greensboro, March, 1982.
7. Lyndon B. Johnson, "Special Message to the Congress: The American Promise," March 15, 1965, in *Public Papers of the Presidents: Lyndon B. Johnson, 1965*, vol. 1 (Washington, D.C.: U.S. Government Printing Office, 1965), pp. 281–287, at p. 286.
8. Gloria D. Feliciano, Richard D. Powers, and Bryant E. Kearl, "The Presentation of Statistical Information," *AV Communication Review* 11 (May–June, 1963): 32–39.
9. Robert N. Bostrom and Raymond K. Tucker, "Evidence, Personality, and Attitude Change," *Speech Monographs* 36 (March 1969): 22–27.

> "
> *...for it is well that in all activities,*
>
> *and most of all in the art of speaking,*
>
> *credit is won, not by gifts of fortune,*
>
> *but by efforts of study.*
> "

—Isocrates,
Antidosis (354 B.C.)[1]

Chapter 8

RESEARCH: FINDING SPEECH MATERIALS

I. *Resources for Speech Materials*
  A. The Library
  B. Interviews
  C. Other Resources

II. *Organizing Your Search for Speech Materials*
  A. Start Early with Basic Questions
  B. Talk to Knowledgeable People
  C. Use the Library Efficiently
  D. Record Materials Carefully

*S*amuel Johnson, the famous eighteenth-century poet and literary critic, once said, "Knowledge is of two kinds. We know a subject ourselves, or we know where we can find information upon it."[2] Dr. Johnson's division of knowledge into what a person knows, and what a person needs to study further, provides a practical way for looking at your own needs in preparing speech content. For some subjects, such as a speech about a personal experience or hobby, you already have enough knowledge to plan your remarks. In other cases, however, you need to know where to find facts and opinions that will help you understand and support your subject.

The purpose of this chapter is to give you some practical guidelines on how to find materials needed to supplement what you already know about your speech topic. We will do this in two steps, first by examining the research resources you have available, and second, by looking at some suggestions for organizing your research efforts.

I. Resources for Speech Materials

Research for your speeches can include the library, personal interviews, and miscellaneous resources such as field trips and writing directly to organizations. Let us begin with the library.

The Library

The library is your most valuable resource for finding speech materials. To begin with, visit your school's library and ask a librarian about published guides to use of the facility. Also, sign up for any orientation tours and lectures that are offered by the library staff. Be sure to inquire about the *interlibrary loan program* that enables students to secure from nearby libraries materials that are not available locally.

As a supplement to the information given you by your library staff, we will examine some basic research tools and procedures that should help you in speech preparation. We will do this according to the following six "resource areas": books, magazines and journals, newspapers, reference works, government documents, and computer searches.

Books

Each book in the library is listed in the card catalog, or, if the library is computerized, in the online public access catalog (OPAC)—usually referred to simply as the "online catalog." A book is entered alphabetically in the catalog in three ways: according to the last name of the *author*, according to *title* (ignoring any initial articles, such as "A," "An," or "The"), and according to *subject*. (For an example of a typical book listing, see Figure 8.1.) Thus, if you know the author or the title of a book, you can find it by a straightforward alphabetical search. Or, you can search according to subject. Each entry will

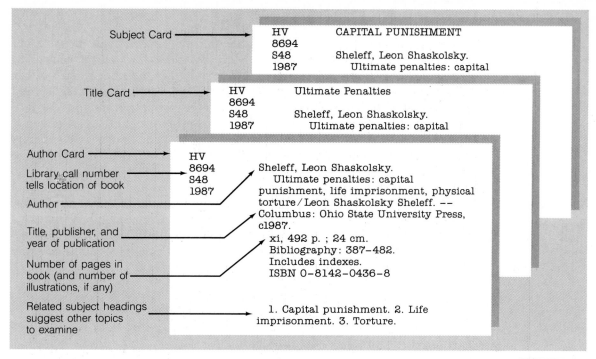

Subject Card →
HV
8694
S48
1987

CAPITAL PUNISHMENT

Sheleff, Leon Shaskolsky.
Ultimate penalties: capital

Title Card →
HV
8694
S48
1987

Ultimate Penalties

Sheleff, Leon Shaskolsky.
Ultimate penalties: capital

Author Card →

Library call number
tells location of book

Author →

Title, publisher, and
year of publication

Number of pages in
book (and number of
illustrations, if any)

Related subject headings
suggest other topics
to examine

HV
8694
S48
1987

Sheleff, Leon Shaskolsky.
Ultimate penalties: capital
punishment, life imprisonment, physical
torture / Leon Shaskolsky Sheleff. --
Columbus: Ohio State University Press,
c1987.
xi, 492 p. ; 24 cm.
Bibliography: 387–482.
Includes indexes.
ISBN 0-8142-0436-8

1. Capital punishment. 2. Life
imprisonment. 3. Torture.

FIGURE 8.1

Sample Bibliographical Content of Card Catalog or Online Catalog. *As a general rule, a library book is listed in the catalog at least three times—by author, by book title, and by subject. Title and subject cards or monitor displays contain the same basic information as does the author card or display. The online catalog also tells you the* location *of the book (stacks, reference, special collection, branch library, etc.), and its* status *(whether it is currently available for you to check out or use).*

provide you with a call number that will guide you to the book's location on the shelves (most libraries post a chart near the catalog that shows the physical location of books by call number groupings).

If you have a speech topic in mind when you begin your research, you will find that the subject headings in the catalog are valuable aids in finding books you can use. *The secret is to find what subject heading is used by the catalog to cover your speech topic.* For example, a person planning a speech about the death penalty will discover that books on the subject are not listed under "death penalty." Instead, the student will be referred to the proper catalog heading, "capital punishment," under which books about the death penalty are located.

A systematic way of discovering how a subject is catalogued is to check the *Library of Congress Subject Headings* (LCSH), a multivolume work that is usually located in the library's catalog area. Look up the topic of your speech, and you will be referred to the major subject heading (or headings) for research in the catalog. In addition, you will find lists of related subjects to consider. For instance, if you look under "death penalty," the LCSH will not only refer you to "capital punishment" but also will state under "capital punishment" a number of related topics such as "death row," "electrocution," "executions and executioners," and "criminal law."

In addition to the standard author, title, and subject searches, many online systems also provide for searches by *key words*. A key word search means that you can locate books that have a specific key word in their titles, even if that word is not recognized as a subject heading by the *Library of Congress Subject Headings* system. For example, a key word search would permit you to locate all books in the library that have in their titles words such as "censorship," "fraternity," "euthanasia," or "Hemingway." If your library is computerized, consult the online user's guide for instructions on how to execute a key word search.

Collections of essays (anthologies) are listed in the catalog by author or editor, and general subject. However, the catalog does not tell you the specific authors or titles of the essays in those anthologies. To find individual essays by author or title, use the *Essay and General Literature Index* in the reference department of the library. This index, which covers materials published since 1900, will guide you to the volumes in which essays about your speech subject are published.

Magazines and Journals

Although the catalog will tell you the names of the magazines and journals (periodicals) in the library, it will not tell you their contents. To locate specific articles concerning your speech topics, you will need to consult the various periodical indexes located in the reference department of the library. In general, these indexes list articles by author and subject, but not by title. Let us first examine leading indexes of popular magazines, then look at those for specialized fields.

The basic index to articles in popular magazines is the *Readers' Guide to Periodical Literature*. Published since 1900 by the H. W. Wilson Company, the *Readers' Guide* indexes approximately 180 periodicals according to an easy-to-use author and subject format (see Figure 8.2). Its monthly and quarterly updates are cumulated annually. In it you will find such magazines as *The Atlantic, Business Week, Consumer Reports, Harper's, Newsweek, Psychology Today, Scientific American*, and *U.S. News & World Report*. Complete instructions for use appear at the front of each volume.

The Magazine Index, available in a self-contained microfilm reader, is a second tool for researching periodicals. This index covers over 400 magazines, including all of those in the *Readers' Guide*. It is cumulated for the previous five years, and is updated monthly. *The Magazine Index*'s "Hot Topics" looseleaf notebook, a printed monthly supplement of subjects of current interest, should be near the microfilm reader.

Thorough research on a speech topic usually requires the student to look beyond the *Readers' Guide to Periodical Literature*, or *The Magazine Index*, to specialized indexes that more narrowly focus on the subject under consideration. For example, the H. W. Wilson Company compiles a number of specialized indexes that employ an author and subject format similar to that for their *Readers' Guide to Periodical Literature* (see Figure 8.2). Therefore, once

Subject heading "See also" suggests other headings to look under

Each entry states title of article, author, name of magazine, volume, page and date.

Subheading identifies specific subtopics on the main subject

Capital punishment
 See also
Executions and executioners
Capital punishment: just or cruel? [interview with D Popco and H. Schwarzchild] A. Kenny. pors *Sch Update* 119:13 F 9 '87
Death row clerk [death penalty work in the Supreme Court] C. Sloan. *New Repub* 196:18+ F 16 '87
Decide on the death penalty. D. Pawelek. il *Sch Update* 119:12+ F 9 '87
Group cities racism in death penalty sentence [views of Amnesty International] *Jet* 72:38 Ap 13 '87
Canada
Capital punishment: the death vote [special section: with editorial comment by Kevin Doyle] il *Macleans* 100:2 8–12+ Mr 16 '87
A return to the gallows? P. Gessell. il *Macleans* 100:10 F 23 '87

FIGURE 8.2

Sample Listing from the Readers' Guide to Periodical Literature. *The H. W. Wilson Company, publisher of the* Readers' Guide, *also publishes a number of other indexes that you might find useful. All of the Wilson indexes follow the same basic system illustrated above.*

you master the simple instructions to the *Readers' Guide*, you should be able to use the other Wilson indexes, such as the following, with ease:

Applied Science and Technology Index

Art Index

Biography Index

Biological and Agricultural Index

Business Periodicals Index

Education Index

General Science Index

Humanities Index

Index to Legal Periodicals

Social Sciences Index

There are three special *key word* indexes available: *Arts and Humanities Citation Index, Science Citation Index*, and *Social Sciences Citation Index*. These permit you to go directly to articles that have words in their titles that concern your speech topic—words such as "homelessness," "abortion," "gambling," "alcoholism," or "feminism"—without going through the usual search by author or general subject heading. There are numerous other specialized indexes—such as *Index Medicus, Psychological Abstracts, Commu-*

nication Abstracts, and *Current Law Index*—to assist you in your speech preparation. Consult the reference librarian for a list of those available in your library.

Newspapers

Research in newspapers is particularly useful when your speech subject concerns newsworthy events of recent years. Examples include topics such as deceptive advertising, federal aid to education, drug abuse, race relations, acid rain, gun control, water pollution, and public opinion polls. As a general rule, the library's newspaper holdings are on microfilm. Most libraries have the *New York Times* (it is indexed from 1851, although not all libraries have holdings going back that far). Check with your librarian to find out which newspapers are available.

Not all newspapers are indexed, and those that are (other than the *New York Times*) have been indexed only recently. The *Wall Street Journal*, for example, is indexed from 1958, and the *Christian Science Monitor* since 1960. Most other newspaper indexes were started in the early 1970s or later, including those for the *Los Angeles Times*, the *Washington Post*, the *Chicago Tribune*, the *New Orleans Times-Picayune*, and the *Atlanta Journal/Atlanta Constitution*.

The *National Newspaper Index* cumulates several newspapers for the preceding three years. It comes in a self-contained microfilm reader, lists contents by author and subject, and covers the *New York Times*, the *Wall Street Journal*, the *Christian Science Monitor*, the *Los Angeles Times*, and the *Washington Post*. An obvious advantage of the *National Newspaper Index* is that you can search five newspapers at once, thereby saving the time of consulting several individual indexes.

Newspaper indexes are a convenient tool for locating public opinion polls. The Gallup poll, for example, is published monthly by the American Institute of Public Opinion as the *Gallup Report*. Unfortunately, the publisher does not provide an up-to-date index. You can use the newspaper indexes, however, to locate these polls by subject, for summaries of the findings appear regularly in the nation's newspapers (alternatively, you can browse through recent issues of the *Gallup Report* to see what is available). Newspaper indexes are also useful in finding other public opinion polls, such as the Harris poll (reported by Louis Harris and Associates), and those done by television networks and major newspapers. In addition to searching under the names of the polling organizations (such as "Gallup," or "Harris"), look under the headings of "public opinion," and "public opinion polls."

Reference Works

In addition to indexes, the reference department of the library contains numerous other aids for the public speaker. These include encyclopedias, dictionaries, biographical materials, almanacs and yearbooks, atlases and gazetteers, and collections of quotations and humor.

Encyclopedias

Encyclopedias are good places to begin research on many speech topics, for they provide an overview that helps the speaker plan additional work on the subject. Also, articles in encyclopedias usually include a basic bibliography that can be used for locating additional information.

Encyclopedias (sometimes described as "dictionaries" by their publishers) are of two types—general and specialized. General encyclopedias have articles on a wide variety of subjects, and include such familiar works as the *New Encyclopaedia Britannica*, and the *Encyclopedia Americana*. Specialized encyclopedias focus on one topical area, such as science or music. Here are some typical specialized works that you might find useful.

Dictionary of American History

Encyclopedia of Bioethics

Encyclopedia of Crime and Justice

Encyclopedia of Philosophy

Encyclopedia of Psychology

Encyclopedia of Religion

Encyclopedia of World Art

Guide to American Law: Everyone's Legal Encyclopedia

International Encyclopedia of the Social Sciences

McGraw-Hill Encyclopedia of Science and Technology

The New Grove Dictionary of Music and Musicians

Dictionaries

Like encyclopedias, dictionaries can be either general or specialized. General dictionaries include *Webster's Third New International Dictionary*, the *Random House Dictionary*, and the *American Heritage Dictionary*. The *Oxford English Dictionary* is recommended if you are looking for the history of a word. Specialized dictionaries include *Black's Law Dictionary*, the *Dictionary of American Slang*, the *Dictionary of Scientific and Technical Terms*, the *American Political Dictionary*, and *Sports Lingo: A Dictionary of the Language of Sports*.

Biographical Materials

The reference department should have a number of works that will provide summaries of the lives and contributions of famous persons. For articles of people in the news, see *Current Biography*. Famous Americans are covered in the *Dictionary of American Biography, National Cyclopedia of American Biography, Who's Who in America, Notable American Women*, and *Who's Who of American Women*. For British persons, see *Who's Who*, or the *Dictionary of National Biography*. And for the world scene, consult such works as *International Who's Who*, or *McGraw-Hill Encyclopedia of World Biography*.

Almanacs and Yearbooks

Almanacs and yearbooks are published annually, and provide up-to-date facts and statistics on a wide range of topics, such as population growth, crime, academy awards, important news stories of the year, names of members of Congress, national income, and so forth. The most widely used include the *Statistical Abstract of the United States*, the *World Almanac and Book of Facts, Information Please Almanac*, and *Readers' Digest Almanac and Yearbook*. In addition, *Facts on File* is a weekly summary of current events that is cumulated and indexed annually as the *Facts on File Yearbook*.

Atlases and Gazetteers

You can find maps and geographical data in atlases and gazetteers. An atlas consists mainly of maps. Leading atlases include *Rand McNally Atlas of the United States, Rand McNally Cosmopolitan World Atlas, National Geographic Atlas of North America, National Geographic Atlas of the World*, and *Times Atlas of the World*. A gazetteer arranges geographical information according to alphabetical headings, similar to a standard dictionary. Popular gazetteers include *Webster's New Geographical Dictionary* and the *Longman Dictionary of Geography*. The *New Rand McNally College World Atlas* includes both an atlas and a world gazetteer.

Collections of Illustrations, Quotations, and Humor

Many libraries arrange anthologies of anecdotes, quotations, and humor together in the reference department. Using the list of books below for starters, you can locate this section and browse through it to find jokes, stories, and famous lines to add zest to your speeches. For quotations, maxims, and proverbs, look at Bartlett's *Familiar Quotations, Dictionary of Quotations*, the *Quotable Woman, Hoyt's New Cyclopedia of Practical Quotations, Oxford Dictionary of Quotations*, Stevenson's *Home Book of Quotations*, and the *Macmillan Book of Proverbs, Maxims, and Famous Phrases*. For humorous materials, examine collections such as Braude's *Handbook of Stories for Toastmasters and Speakers*, Doan's *Sourcebook for Speakers*, Prochnow's *Public Speaker's Treasure Chest, Dictionary of Wit, Wisdom, and Satire*, and *Home Book of Humorous Quotations*.

Government Publications

The U.S. government publishes thousands of pamphlets, booklets, and reports each year. Libraries that receive large numbers of government documents usually keep them in a separate section called the documents department. Ask a reference librarian where these materials are kept in your school's library. Typical of the variety of subjects discussed are acid rain, nuclear power safety, state laws on marijuana use, planning a family budget, how solar hot water systems work, teaching opportunities abroad, consumer guide on funeral expenses, and climate changes to the year 2000.

The standard index to government documents is the *Monthly Catalog of U.S. Government Publications*, which is also published in annual and five-year cumulations. For a ten-year cumulation, see the *Federal Government Publications Catalog*, a self-contained microfilm reader that lists publications by author, title, subject, and name of government agency issuing the material. Also, ask the documents librarian about the availability of a compact disc public access catalog (such as Brodart's *Le Pac: Government Documents Option*) that permits an in-house, computerized search of government publications.

Computer Searches

A computer search is a quick and convenient method of securing a bibliography of articles and reports concerning your speech topic. Most computer searches result in a straightforward reading list (you still must locate the materials in the library, and study them as usual); however, some include summaries (called "abstracts"), and others can even retrieve complete texts of the listed articles. Full text retrieval is particularly helpful if the material is not available in your library.

As a rule, computer searches are done for you by a reference librarian using the commercial computer services to which the library subscribes. These commercial services, called *vendors*, subscribe in turn to numerous collections of information known as *databases*. In other words, the vendor serves as an intermediary between your library and the hundreds of available databases. Most of the databases are similar to the published indexes and abstracting services that you use manually in the library, such as *Psychological Abstracts* or *Resources in Education*.

One of the most widely used vendor services for research libraries is called DIALOG (from Dialog Information Services, a subsidiary of the Lockheed Corporation). Others include ORBIT (from System Development Corporation), and BRS (from Bibliographic Retrieval Services). Your reference librarian can tell you which vendors are available locally. If your library does not have this needed service, try nearby public or school libraries.

Let us look briefly at the widely used DIALOG system to get a general idea of the range of resources available. DIALOG classifies its many databases by headings such as business and industry, science and medicine, law and government, news, energy and environment, education and reference, humanities, social sciences, and people. Typical of specific DIALOG databases available under these headings are *Harvard Business Review, Heilbron* (a complete chemical dictionary), *Biosis Previews* (biological abstracts), *Medline* (medical literature), *Congressional Record Abstracts, Criminal Justice Periodical Index, Food Science and Technology Abstracts, UPI News, Magazine Index, National Newspaper Index, ERIC* (educational research), *Historical Abstracts*, and *Marquis Who's Who* (biographies of about 75,000 famous people).

A computer search should be thought of as a supplement to—not a substitute for—more traditional forms of research. You should first use the printed indexes, articles, reports, and books available in the library until you have a clear idea of what topics you need to pursue in order to complete your project. The computer search is particularly useful at this point, for it can often help you locate materials that you might not find otherwise.

If, after a preliminary study of your speech topic, you think a computer search might be useful, contact the reference librarian in charge of this service to discuss the advisability of a search. *Be sure to ask about costs, for in most instances you will be expected to pay a modest fee for the search.* Also, check on the amount of time it will take to complete the search and secure a printout (this ranges from one to three days for local printing, to a week if the results are to be mailed). The final step will be for you to work with the librarian on determining the strategy of the search, including the key words to be used in looking for materials.

Interviews

Interviews are another source of facts and opinions concerning the subject of your speech. Two types of persons are especially helpful: those who are experts on the content of your topic (such as a professor who is a specialist in the field), and those whose direct experience with a topic is worth recounting (such as a recovered drug addict who is agreeable to discussing the matter).

You should be able to find knowledgeable persons to interview, both on campus and off. Here are some examples. On campus: for a talk on "How to Purchase Life Insurance Wisely," talk to the insurance specialist in business and economics; and a speech on "Support Your Student Government" might be based on a series of interviews with past and present officers of your school's student government association. Off-campus interviews would be appropriate in these instances: a speech on "Job Opportunities in Journalism" could include information from an interview with the personnel director of the local newspaper; or a talk critical of cruelty to animals in laboratory research could cover the views of the president of the local chapter of the Humane Society.

Don't hesitate to ask knowledgeable persons for interviews for fear of being turned down. Many people enjoy being interviewed, and will gladly make an appointment with you. If their answer is "no," you can always ask them to suggest some other person or persons with whom you can talk. If you decide that interviewing is appropriate for your speech, you can plan it according to three simple steps: prepare for the interview, conduct the interview, and evaluate and summarize the interview. Let us look further at each.

Preparing for the Interview

Interview preparation includes doing preliminary research on your speech subject, selecting the interviewee, deciding how you will record the answers to your questions, then preparing essential questions according to an organized plan.

Conduct Preliminary Research

To begin, do some preliminary reading on your subject so that you can decide on a tentative specific purpose for the speech. Use this statement of purpose to formulate the goals of the interview. For example, if the specific purpose of the speech is "to inform the class of contemporary job opportunities in print journalism," and the interviewee is the personnel director of the local newspaper, the goals of the interview could be to secure several specific job descriptions based upon the paper's hiring practices, to find out the salary ranges for these jobs, and to learn what opportunities exist for promotion and advancement.

Select the Interviewee

Next, determine the person (or persons) whom you need to interview in order to secure the desired information. Make an appointment, either in person or by telephone. While arranging the appointment, make your purpose clear, and check to see if the individual is willing to discuss it with you. If the individual declines, ask for advice on whom to see to get the needed information.

Decide How to Record the Results

You should determine how you will record the responses to your questions. Your choices include: written notes only; using a tape recorder without writing anything down (and making notes later from the recording); or simultaneously taking notes and taping the interview (the tape can serve as a backup source for checking your written record). If you use *written notes only*, you will not need to worry about setting up equipment and the possibility of it malfunctioning, or changing tapes during the interview. However, getting everything of importance written down accurately is often difficult to do. A recording does give you some insurance.

If you use a *tape recorder only*, you can be more direct and informal with your interviewee, for you do not have to listen and write at the same time. Later you can prepare your written notes from a playback of the session. On the other hand, the recorder can be clumsy to set up; you might have to interrupt the discussion to insert a fresh tape; and the machine might malfunction, leaving you with a blank. Also, you should always secure the permission of the interviewee before using a tape recorder. (Never record an interview secretly, for such a practice is not only unethical but it is illegal as well in about one-fourth of the states).[3] Some persons prefer not to be taped, although they are agreeable to note taking. If the interviewee objects to being recorded, courteously express your respect for that decision, and proceed to keep a written record.

If you are not sure which method is best, try the *combination of taking notes and using a recorder* (assuming your interviewee agrees to this). Eventually you can decide on what works best for you.[4]

Organize the Interview and Plan Key Questions

An interview, like a speech, should have three parts: an opening, a body, and an ending.[5] In the *opening* of your interview, you should plan a minute or two of informal discussion to "break the ice," then explain your speech plans and the reason for the interview. Also, this is a good time to request biographical data on the interviewee so that later, when delivering the speech, you can qualify your source.

The *body* of the interview is the place to ask the key questions you have prepared. As a rule, your questions will be of two types: broad, or "open questions" that permit the interviewee to answer in general terms; and narrow, or "closed questions" that seek specific information. Here are some examples that would fit an interview with a newspaper's personnel director concerning job opportunities in journalism:

Open questions. Generally speaking, what are the prospects for employment today in newspaper journalism? What job trends do you see in the

Library research is often a vital part of researching a speech. Even if you choose to do research through interviews, the card catalog may help you prepare for the interviews. (Joel Gordon)

future? What type of education and professional skills are you looking for? What advice would you give to a college student who is planning a career in newspaper journalism?

Closed questions. What specific jobs are currently available with your newspaper? Could you give me a copy of a job description for a beginning reporter? What salary do you pay to a beginning reporter? In addition to news reporter, what other positions in journalism does your paper have?

Of course, you should anticipate asking spontaneous questions that clarify and otherwise pursue and develop the answers you will get. In other words, your preparation should include a mental note to "follow through" on responses in order to secure information that your written questions do not address.

To *end* the interview, plan to cover at least two things. First, ask "clearinghouse questions," such as "what have I overlooked that I need to know?" or "what would you like to add to complete the picture?" Second, ask for relevant printed material (including reading lists) that might be available.

Conducting the Interview

Plan to dress neatly and appropriately for the interview, and to arrive on time. Introduce yourself and go over your purpose and the general areas of questioning that you want to pursue. If you intend to use a tape recorder, confirm that it is permissible, then set up the equipment. Remember that interviewing, like public speaking, is a communication activity and should make use of good communication skills, including a friendly attitude, visual directness, distinct articulation, intelligent "follow through" questions, keeping on the subject, and so forth. Finally, be sure to end the interview on time, and to express appropriate thanks to the interviewee as you leave.

Evaluating and Summarizing the Interview

You should promptly evaluate and summarize the results of the interview while the discussion is still fresh in your mind. Go over each question and answer, checking for accuracy and adding those details that you recall but did not have time to record. If you recorded the session on tape, prepare a good set of written notes from the recording. As you evaluate your notes, mark those parts that stand out as potentially useful, and place them on note cards with topical headings. By doing these things soon after the interview, you will greatly facilitate your use of the results when you begin to outline the speech.

Other Resources

Other resources for speech materials include personal investigations and writing to organizations for information.

Personal Investigations

An "on-the-spot" look at a facility or situation related to your speech can be a highly effective means of gathering materials. In some instances, taking photographs for use as visual aids can be a supplement to the investigation. Here are some examples: a talk on hunger in the local community could include the results of a visit to the local Salvation Army headquarters, or a similar social service group that helps feed the poor; a speech concerning crowded conditions in jails and prisons could include a tour of a local jail or nearby prison (and, perhaps, an interview with a jailer or warden); or you could prepare for a speech on a product that is manufactured locally by touring the plant where the product is made.

Writing to Organizations

Another source of information is to write to those organizations that are involved in your topic. For example, if you are working on an informative speech about the work of the American Automobile Association (AAA), you could write to the national headquarters for help. Or, if you are planning a persuasive speech taking a position on the subject of church-state separation, you could request materials from such groups as the American Civil Liberties Union, or Americans United for Separation of Church and State.

You can locate the addresses of these and numerous other organizations in the reference department of the library. The primary source of assistance is the multivolumed *Encyclopedia of Associations*, which lists the names and addresses of approximately 25,000 national and international trade and professional groups. Included are organizations in areas such as business, law, science, education, health, public affairs, religion, hobbies, sports, and labor. A second publication, *National Trade and Professional Associations of the United States*, provides the names and addresses of over 6,000 organizations. Its subject index is helpful in finding groups under specific headings, such as writers, advertising, labor unions, manufacturers, radio-TV, women's groups, and film.

When writing for materials, keep the following points in mind. First, some organizations are slow to respond (occasionally you will get no response at all); therefore, you should write several weeks in advance of delivery of the speech. A self-addressed, stamped envelope (SASE) is requested by some organizations for a reply. Second, the material you receive is sometimes so biased, or so brief, that you will find it of little help. You would be wise, therefore, to think of writing away for material as a *supplement only* to more dependable forms of research, such as use of the library and conducting interviews.

Now that you have an idea of the research resources available, let us consider some practical suggestions for using them.

II. Organizing Your Search for Speech Materials

You can save time and effort by developing a systematic approach to locating and recording speech materials. As a rule, an organized approach to research should include these four steps: start early by asking basic questions; talk with knowledgeable people; use the library efficiently; and record materials carefully.

Start Early with Basic Questions

You should start your research early, allowing enough time for locating, reading, and recording information before beginning work on the outline. With your choice of subject in mind, formulate a tentative specific purpose, then write down several basic questions that emerge from that purpose. You can use these questions to give direction to your early research. For instance, if your specific purpose is "to convince my audience that an honor code should be established in our college," your basic questions might include: What is generally meant by the term "honor code"? What nearby colleges have an honor code, and how well do they work? What are the advantages and disadvantages of honor codes, according to those who use them? What specific local problems create a need for an honor code?

Talk to Knowledgeable People

Often you can get some useful ideas concerning directions for research by talking with people who know something about your speech subject. In these conversations be sure to ask about definitive books or essays on the topic, as well as for the names of other people who should be interviewed. To illustrate, for a speech on how to prepare a set of credentials before looking for a job, begin by talking with the director of your school's career placement office. Or for the topic of adopting an honor code, visit a nearby college that has such a system and talk with those who administer it.

Use the Library Efficiently

As recommended at the beginning of this chapter, library efficiency is enhanced by attending lectures on library use, taking library tours, and studying the printed materials made available by the library staff. You will find that the more you use library facilities, the more you will feel ''at home'' doing your research. In addition, here are two specific techniques that can save you time and effort.

First, *begin your research by reading an "overview" article concerning your subject in a good encyclopedia.* For example, look up your topic in the *New Encyclopaedia Britannica*, or the *Encyclopedia Americana*. For more in-depth coverage, go to one of the specialized encyclopedias. For example, an essay on a scientific subject might be found in the *McGraw-Hill Encyclopedia of Science and Technology*. You should not, however, think of the encyclopedia as the main source of information; rather, view it only as an ''idea-generator''—a starting place—from which you secure suggestions for further study.

Second, *develop the art of systematic browsing in the stacks of the library.* As one authority on library techniques puts it, systematic browsing is not a ''haphazard and inefficient'' method of research; rather, it ''is a very useful method of subject retrieval, and in some cases it is the most efficient method of all.''[6] This is so because the books on a given subject are grouped together by subject matter on the library shelves. Therefore, by using the card catalog to identify one or two books on a given subject, you can often locate a complete shelf—or several shelves—of additional books concerning that subject. By examining the titles, tables of contents, and indexes in the section you have ''discovered,'' you can quickly check numerous volumes for information that might be useful in your speech.

Record Materials Carefully

Recording speech materials involves keeping two types of notes: bibliographical and content. *Bibliographical notes* consist of index cards (use either 3 by 5, or 4 by 6 cards for this purpose) on which you have recorded complete source information. *Content notes* consist of the quotations and paraphrased statements you record from your sources. Content notes can be in the form of index cards on which you have written useful information, or photocopied materials (selected pages or entire articles). For those you write yourself, use a 4

White, Welsh S., <u>The Death Penalty in the Eighties</u>. Ann Arbor: Univ. of Michigan Press, 1987.

call no.: KF
9227
C2W44
1987

Bibliography Card for a Book

DISCRIMINATION (Racial) in Administration of Death Penalty

The data of the extensive study done by Baldus, Woodworth, and Pulaski (1983) reveal "strong evidence of discrimination against killers of white victims. Overall, it appeared that the killer of a white victim was 4.3 times more likely to receive the death penalty than the killer of a black victim."

From W. S. White, <u>Death Penalty in the Eighties</u>, p. 129.

Note Card with Content Information

FIGURE 8.3

Sample Bibliography Card and Content Card.

by 6 (or larger) index card so that you will have space to record a considerable amount of information. Both a bibliography card and a content card are illustrated by Figure 8.3.

You should begin work on the bibliography cards early in your research. For efficiency, use one size card for all entries, write only one source per card, and record each source completely and accurately according to standard bibliographical style. For books, standard style includes the author, title, city of publication, publisher, and year of publication. For articles, standard style includes the author, title of essay, name of magazine, date, and page numbers.

For photocopied materials, be sure to record complete bibliographical information, including page numbers at the top of the first page while you have the original source in hand. For content notes kept on index cards, begin with a topical heading, record the source and page, then jot down the information you wish to keep. Limit each card to one source, and one significant topic from that source.

By following these suggestions, you can easily delete unneeded bibliographical citations and alphabetize those that you plan to use. Also, you can group content cards by topical headings, thereby facilitating speech organization.

This Chapter in Brief

Resources for speech materials include what you already know, and what you learn by various types of research. Mastering the art of research means knowing how to use the library, being able to interview knowledgeable people skillfully, and the use of other resources such as personal investigations and writing away for information. Finding speech materials will be more effective if you develop an organized approach that includes at least four points: start early by formulating basic questions on your topic; ask informed people for ideas; use time-saving techniques in the library, such as getting an overview of your subject from an encyclopedia article, or browsing systematically in the book collection; and record relevant materials carefully.

After you have become adequately informed on your subject and have collected and organized your materials, you are ready for the next step of speech preparation: organizing and outlining the speech. It is to this challenging process of *dispositio* that we now turn our attention.

EXERCISES

1. Visit your library and ask for copies of published guides to library usage. Inquire about lectures and guided tours that explain basic research techniques. Sign up for a lecture and tour. Prior to the lecture, study the published guides and prepare a list of questions of things you would like to know more about. Keep all information on file for future reference.

2. In preparing your next speech requiring library research, try the two efficiency techniques recommended in this chapter, namely: reading an overview article in an encyclopedia, and systematically browsing through books on your subject as they are grouped together on the shelves. Apply the same techniques to other research projects (such as term papers) until you develop a personal approach to efficient use of the techniques.

SELECTED READINGS

Mann, Thomas. *A Guide to Library Research Methods*. New York: Oxford University Press, 1987. Based upon his experience both as student researcher and reference librarian, Mann has written a brief, readable guide to library research. In addition to explaining basic tools and giving practical advice, the author includes a discussion of "Hidden Treasures"—sources not accessible through conventional means.

Skopec, Eric W. *Situational Interviewing*. New York: Harper & Row, 1986. In particular, see Chapter 1 for suggestions on planning and executing an interview, and Chapter 2 for pointers on informational interviewing.

Stewart, Charles J., and Cash, William B., Jr. *Interviewing: Principles and Practices*. 5th ed. Dubuque, Ia.: Wm. C. Brown, 1988. Chapters 1 through 4 discuss various types of interviews and preinterview planning, including how to prepare good questions. Chapter 5 on "The Probing Interview" is particularly helpful because of its emphasis on securing information.

ENDNOTES

1. Isocrates (436–338 B.C.) was a leading teacher of public speaking in Athens. The quotation from *Antidosis* is in Thomas W. Benson and Michael H. Prosser, eds., *Readings in Classical Rhetoric* (Boston: Allyn and Bacon, 1969), p. 51.

2. George B. Hill, ed., *Boswell's Life of Johnson* (New York: Harper & Brothers, 1891), vol. 2, p. 418.

3. Harold L. Nelson, Dwight L. Teeter, and Don R. Le Duc, *Law of Mass Communications*, 6th ed. (Mineola, N.Y.: Foundation Press, 1989), pp. 258–259.

4. For more on note taking vs. the tape recorder in interviewing, see Charles J. Stewart and William B. Cash, Jr., *Interviewing: Principles and Practices*, 5th ed. (Dubuque, Ia.: Wm. C. Brown, 1988), pp. 89–91.

5. Ibid., pp. 39–55. Also, Eric W. Skopec, *Situational Interviewing* (New York: Harper & Row, 1986), pp. 31–35.

6. Thomas Mann, *A Guide to Library Research Methods* (New York: Oxford University Press, 1987), p. 27.

> *It is possible to learn the skills of exposition and persuasion, difficult though they are, because discourses, whether expository or persuasive, are built out of certain simple units.*

—Otis M. Walter,
Speaking to Inform and Persuade (1982)[1]

Chapter 9

INTRODUCING OUTLINING: THREE PRACTICAL CONCEPTS

*T*he subject of speech organization has attracted the attention of public communicators since ancient times. In the fifth century B.C., Corax—the Sicilian Greek who is the earliest known speech instructor in the West—noted that the most successful speakers he had observed presented their ideas in three main parts: first, an introduction in which the speaker sought a friendly hearing from the audience; second, a body that set out the central idea and the main points of the speech; and finally, a conclusion that summarized the main points and urged the audience to accept them. Because this three-part arrangement is both logically and psychologically sound, we continue to teach it (and most speakers practice it) to the present day.

However, there is more to speech organization (called *dispositio* by the Romans) than dividing a speech into three parts. Recall from Chapter 1 that *dispositio* is defined as "the art of organizing the content of the speech so that it will be clear and persuasive to the audience." This means *all* of the content, including the internal arrangement of ideas and supporting materials within *each* major section—introduction, body, and conclusion.

Because each of the three sections has a unique function in the overall scheme of a speech, special attention should be paid to the organizational principles that apply to each section. In keeping with this concept, the purpose of this chapter is to prepare you for the tasks of planning the introduction, body, and conclusion by explaining some fundamental principles that apply to organization in general. This basic information is followed by Chapter 10 on the specifics of outlining the body of the speech, and Chapter 11 on the specifics of outlining introductions and conclusions. Obviously, the three chapters should be studied together, for they combine to form this text's major body of theory on *dispositio*.

At the outset we will look briefly at three topics that help set the stage for what follows, namely: the importance of effective organization; how *dispositio* is intertwined with the other steps of speech preparation, such as audience analysis, and the search for speech materials; and the rules of wording and sentence structure in outlining.

First, effective organization of your speeches is important for at least two reasons. Briefly put, these are that logical organization helps you, the speaker, and it helps the audience as well. Thorough planning puts you, the speaker, "in charge" of the speech, for it gives you an in-depth familiarity with what you are going to say, including the order of presentation of ideas and supporting materials. This knowledge should strengthen your self-confidence as you approach the speaking situation, for you will know that you are well-prepared, and that you are ready to present your ideas according to a logical plan.

Furthermore, clear organization helps the audience follow your line of reasoning. You are able to get more significant information into the short time allowed, and to focus the thinking of your listeners on important points. It follows logically—and research supports this conclusion—that audiences comprehend organized speeches better than disorganized ones.[2] Also, research reveals that a disorganized speech lowers the credibility of the speaker in the minds of the listeners, and reduces the likelihood that listeners will change their attitudes in directions urged by the speaker.[3]

Second, organizing the speech should be thought of as a logical continuation of the overall process of speech preparation—a process that includes audience analysis, choice of subject and purpose, and the search for ideas and evidence to support the goals of the speech. After all, outlines do not exist in and of themselves; rather, they are developed to help you present your specific purpose to the audience in a clear and convincing way. In other words, without content you have nothing to outline; and without a given audience, you have no basis for planning the arrangement of ideas. *Dispositio*, therefore, is not so much a separate task as it is a continuation of the unified process of speech preparation that begins with audience analysis and choice of a subject for the speech.

Third, the outline should follow three standard rules of wording and sentence structure. Let us look at these rules, together with examples taken from the outline on copyright law used throughout this chapter, beginning with Figure 9.1.

1. *Each point should be stated as one short, complete sentence.* In other words, do not use incomplete sentences (such as brief topics), and do not use two or more sentences to state the point.

Incorrect (incomplete sentences)

I.   Purpose and character of use.
    A.   Commercial
    B.   Nonprofit

Also incorrect (more than one sentence)

I.   The first principle concerns the purpose of use. It also concerns the character of use. Let us now take a close look at purpose and character.

Correct (short, complete sentences)

I.   The first principle concerns the purpose and character of use.
    A.   Strict limits apply to commercial, "for profit" use.
    B.   Fewer restrictions apply to educational, "nonprofit" use.

2. *Each point should state one, and only one, key idea.* In other words, avoid long, complicated sentences that crowd two or three ideas into one point.

Incorrect (complicated sentence contains too much)

A.   Some works, such as references, dictionaries, and encyclopedias, invite a high degree of use, and so do collections of speeches, papers, and public documents, as well as many other works I don't have time to mention.

Correct (short sentences, one concept per sentence)

A.   Some works invite a high degree of use.
    1.   Reference works, such as dictionaries and encyclopedias, invite use.
    2.   Collected speeches, papers, and public documents, invite use.

3. *Sets of supporting points should be worded in parallel sentence structure.* Main points in particular should be phrased in parallel form. The concept of parallel sentence structure, which greatly facilitates your testing of the logic of the outline, is best explained by examples. Note that the "incorrect" ver-

sion below employs different kinds of sentences, lacking in parallel construction from point to point. Also note the parallel structure of the wording "the first principle concerns," "the second principle concerns," and so on, in the correct version.

Incorrect (sentences are not in parallel form)

I. First, consider the purpose and character of use.

II. Then, what about the nature of the work?

III. Percentage used is next!

IV. The effect of use upon the market value is the final principle that I want to discuss.

Correct (each sentence follows same plan of wording)

I. The first principle concerns the purpose and character of use.

II. The second principle concerns the nature of the copyrighted work.

III. The third principle concerns the percentage of the work used.

IV. The fourth principle concerns the effect of use upon the market value of the copyrighted work.

We are now ready to examine three practical concepts of speech organization that apply to both informative and persuasive speeches. The concepts should help you by demonstrating how to develop a speech, one manageable section at a time, how to identify and delete illogical and irrelevant points from the outline, and how to decide how much support is needed under each key point. The three concepts are: speech units as "building blocks" of discourse; the relationships of ideas to each other within a speech unit; and how much support is needed to make key ideas clear and convincing.

I. The Speech Unit

A speech unit is a "block of discourse" that consists of two parts: (1) a general statement (usually called a "point"), and (2) support for that general statement (or "point").[4] Here is an example from the outline on copyright law (see Figure 9.1).

> *General statement*: When considering the "fair use" of copyrighted material, note that some works invite a high degree of use.
> *Support for the general statement*: (1) Reference works, such as dictionaries and encyclopedias, invite use. (2) In addition, collected materials, such as speeches, papers, and public documents, invite use.

When this speech unit is placed on the page in outline form, it looks like this:

A. Some works invite a high degree of use.
    1. Reference works, such as dictionaries and encyclopedias, invite use.
    2. Collected speeches, papers, and public documents invite use.

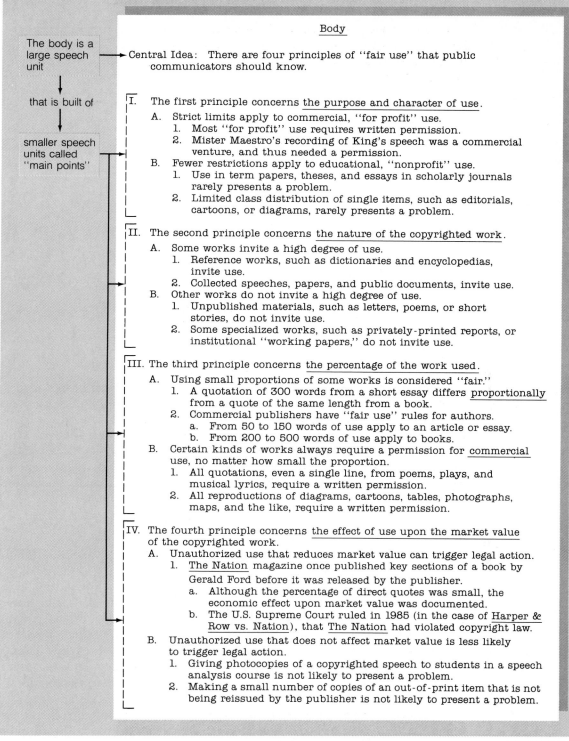

Body

Central Idea: There are four principles of "fair use" that public communicators should know.

I. The first principle concerns the purpose and character of use.
   A. Strict limits apply to commercial, "for profit" use.
      1. Most "for profit" use requires written permission.
      2. Mister Maestro's recording of King's speech was a commercial venture, and thus needed a permission.
   B. Fewer restrictions apply to educational, "nonprofit" use.
      1. Use in term papers, theses, and essays in scholarly journals rarely presents a problem.
      2. Limited class distribution of single items, such as editorials, cartoons, or diagrams, rarely presents a problem.

II. The second principle concerns the nature of the copyrighted work.
   A. Some works invite a high degree of use.
      1. Reference works, such as dictionaries and encyclopedias, invite use.
      2. Collected speeches, papers, and public documents, invite use.
   B. Other works do not invite a high degree of use.
      1. Unpublished materials, such as letters, poems, or short stories, do not invite use.
      2. Some specialized works, such as privately-printed reports, or institutional "working papers," do not invite use.

III. The third principle concerns the percentage of the work used.
   A. Using small proportions of some works is considered "fair."
      1. A quotation of 300 words from a short essay differs proportionally from a quote of the same length from a book.
      2. Commercial publishers have "fair use" rules for authors.
         a. From 50 to 150 words of use apply to an article or essay.
         b. From 200 to 500 words of use apply to books.
   B. Certain kinds of works always require a permission for commercial use, no matter how small the proportion.
      1. All quotations, even a single line, from poems, plays, and musical lyrics, require a written permission.
      2. All reproductions of diagrams, cartoons, tables, photographs, maps, and the like, require a written permission.

IV. The fourth principle concerns the effect of use upon the market value of the copyrighted work.
   A. Unauthorized use that reduces market value can trigger legal action.
      1. The Nation magazine once published key sections of a book by Gerald Ford before it was released by the publisher.
         a. Although the percentage of direct quotes was small, the economic effect upon market value was documented.
         b. The U.S. Supreme Court ruled in 1985 (in the case of Harper & Row vs. Nation), that The Nation had violated copyright law.
   B. Unauthorized use that does not affect market value is less likely to trigger legal action.
      1. Giving photocopies of a copyrighted speech to students in a speech analysis course is not likely to present a problem.
      2. Making a small number of copies of an out-of-print item that is not being reissued by the publisher is not likely to present a problem.

The body is a large speech unit

that is built of

smaller speech units called "main points"

FIGURE 9.1

The Body Is the Largest Speech Unit. *The body, composed of (1) the Central Idea and (2) supporting main points, is the largest, most complete speech unit. The smaller speech units—main headings I-IV—are the building blocks of the body. In turn, as Figure 9.2 shows, each main building block is itself constructed of even smaller speech units. The complete outline, including introduction and conclusion, can be found in Chapter 10.*

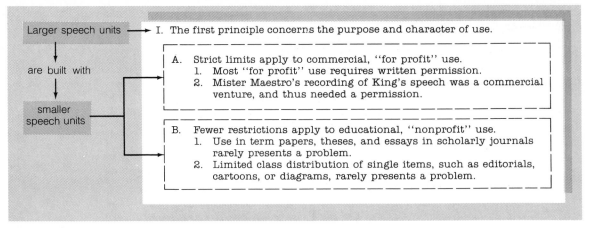

FIGURE 9.2

The Building Blocks of Speech: Large and Small Speech Units. *The largest speech unit above, composed of point I and supporting points A and B, is boxed with a solid line. Everything inside this solid line is part of the speech unit that would, as a rule, be called "main point one." The two smaller units that make up the larger one are marked with dotted lines. As this example shows, larger blocks of discourse are "constructed" of smaller blocks of discourse.*

Speech units vary in size and scope from large, complete blocks of discourse—such as the body of a speech—to smaller, supporting units within the larger unit. This principle of size and scope is illustrated by Figures 9.1 and 9.2. Figure 9.1, for example, shows the body as the major speech unit, and the main headings of the body as subunits that function as building blocks of the body, whereas Figure 9.2 illustrates how a major building block (that is, a main heading) is formed of even smaller speech units. Let us examine further the concept of building the body of a speech with units of discourse.

The Body as a Complete Speech Unit

The body is the major unit of discourse in a speech; it is, in a sense, "complete," for it is the sum of the supporting units. In other words, there are no points or units that are larger than, or superior to, the body. (The introduction and conclusion are special types of speech units, neither of which is logically superior to the body.) The two key components of the body are, (1) the general statement, which we call the central idea, and (2) the headings and subheadings of support under that general statement. A logical analysis of the relationship of the central idea and supporting headings to each other reveals that what we usually call "main points" of the body are actually *subpoints* that clarify or prove the central idea.

To state this concept another way, *a speech has one, and only one, main point, and that is the central idea.* Everything else in the speech is a form of support for the central idea. We pull a semantic trick on ourselves when we call the primary headings of the body "main points," and put Roman numerals in front of them to show their high rank. In fact, the primary headings are not main points at all, but the first order of subpoints under the central idea. If we were to use a Roman numeral to designate the highest point of the speech (namely, the central idea), the logical relationship of the central idea to the main headings of the body would look like this:

I.   **Central Idea:** There are four principles of "fair use" that public communicators should know.
   A.   The first principle concerns the purpose and character of use.
   B.   The second principle concerns the nature of the copyrighted work.
   C.   The third principle concerns the percentage of the work used.
   D.   The fourth principle concerns the effect of use upon the market value of the copyrighted work.

As the designations A, B, C, and D above illustrate, the "main" points are really subpoints A through D in support of the central idea. Tradition decrees, however, that we call these subpoints "main points," and that we mark them with Roman numerals. Based upon this tradition, our outline takes on this standard appearance:

Central Idea: There are four principles of "fair use" that public communicators should know.

I.   The first principle...

II.   The second principle...

III.   The third principle...

IV.   The fourth principle...

There is nothing wrong, necessarily, with this traditional way of showing the central idea and major supporting points, *as long as you know that "main points" are logically the first level of subpoints under the central idea.* Also, observe that no number or letter is placed before the central idea, for it is not "just another heading" in a speech outline; rather, it is the thesis of the entire speech. For this reason the central idea is always shown in the model outlines of this text without a number or letter designation in order to visually recognize its superior rank in the rhetorical scheme. In short, because the central idea stands alone (no other points are above it or equal to it), do not mark it with a letter or number, regardless of where you locate it in the outline.

When organizing the body of your next speech, you might temporarily label the central idea with a Roman numeral I, and show the main headings of the body as subpoints A, B, C, etc., before changing them back to the traditional system. This technique will help you grasp and apply the concept just explained. The logic of your outlining should improve, therefore, if you keep the following two thoughts in mind as you organize:

A speech has only one main point—the central idea. The "main points" of the body are actually the subpoints that directly support the central idea.

Smaller Speech Units as Building Blocks

The speech units that serve as "building blocks" of the body are of two types: main points that directly support the central idea, and subpoints that support the main points. Any point that is developed by one or more subpoints should be thought of as a speech unit. However, a statement with no subpoints does not qualify as a speech unit; instead, think of such statements as components of larger units rather than units within themselves. For an illustration of how main points are constructed of small speech units, see Figure 9.2.

The Speech Unit in Summary

A speech unit is a "block of discourse" made up of two parts, namely, (1) a statement, and (2) support for that statement. The body of the speech, for example, is a large speech unit composed of a statement (the central idea) and supporting headings called "main points." Although the headings that directly support the central idea are, by tradition, called "main points," they are actually *subpoints* of the central idea. Each main point, in turn, is constructed of smaller speech units. These concepts are illustrated by Figures 9.1 and 9.2. Obviously, the overall logic, clarity, and persuasiveness of the body of the speech depends upon the quality of the parts—that is, the speech units—from which the body is built. We are now ready to examine the three types of relationships that ideas (points) have to each other within the speech units.

II. The Relationships of Points to Each Other

Speech organization is the process of arranging the ideas of the speech in a sequence that you believe will be effective in making your thoughts *clear*, and—in the case of persuasion—*convincing* to your listeners. As you arrange the units, you locate ideas in relationship to other ideas. Some ideas are superior to others, some support others, and some are equal to others. Let us examine these relationships further, including how two simple tests help us keep things straight.

Three Types of Relationships

In the logical organization of discourse, ideas are related to each other in three ways: they can be *superior* to other ideas, *subordinate* to other ideas, or *coordinate* (equal) to other ideas. Let us define the three in more detail, keeping in mind that when ideas are located in an outline they are usually described as "points." In other words, for our purposes in the study of *dispositio*, the terms "ideas" and "points" are interchangeable.

Superior Point

An idea (or point) that is more comprehensive or more important than another idea (or point) is *superior* to the smaller ideas that flow from it and support it. In a logical outline, for example, the central idea is superior to the main points of the body. Each main point, in turn, is superior to its subpoints, and so on down the line. The concept of logical superiority is further illustrated by a discussion of subordinate points.

Subordinate Point

An idea (or point) that is a component part of a superior point, or that directly supports a superior idea with reasoning and evidence, is *subordinate* to the point above it. In other words, subpoints are subordinate to superior points.

The "for" test and the "also" test can be useful in testing the logic of the relationship among points in a speech. (Judy Gelles/Stock, Boston)

To illustrate, a speech explaining the three branches of the federal government should show the "federal government" as a superior term in relationship to each subordinate branch. The relationship in outline form would look like this:

SUPERIOR POINT

Central Idea: There are three branches to the federal government of the United States.

SUBORDINATE POINTS

I.   One is the legislative branch.

II. Another is the executive branch.

III. The third is the judicial branch.

Coordinate Point

An idea (or point) that is equal to another is called a *coordinate* point. Any set of two or more subpoints are coordinate to each other if they support the same superior point (see Figure 9.3.). In the example concerning the federal government, the three branches of government are equal to each other, and are, therefore, coordinate points. An outline about automobile manufacturing in the United States, organized around the three major firms, illustrates further the concept of coordinate points:

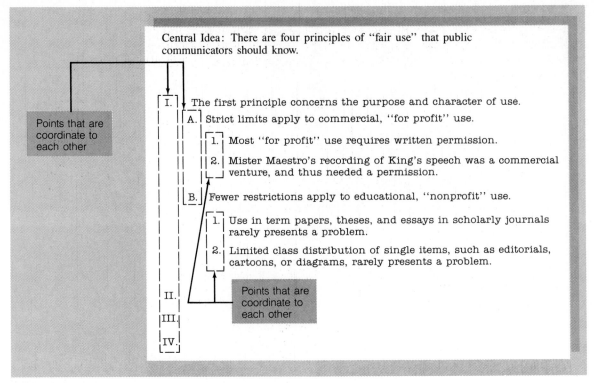

FIGURE 9.3

Coordinate Points in an Outline. *In this example, there are four sets of coordinate points, each set being "blocked" together with dotted lines. Whereas coordinate points are logically equal to each other, they are at the same time logically subordinate to the point that is immediately superior to them. To illustrate, main headings I-IV are each subordinate to the central idea; and points A and B are subordinate to main heading I.*

SUPERIOR POINT

Central Idea: There are three major American automobile manufacturing companies in the United States.

THESE POINTS ARE SUBORDINATE TO THE CENTRAL IDEA,
BUT THEY ARE COORDINATE TO EACH OTHER

I.   First is General Motors Corporation.

II.   Second is Ford Motor Company.

III.   Third is Chrysler Corporation.

Testing the Logic of Relationships

We are now ready to examine a simple system for testing the points of a speech outline to determine whether or not the logic of relationships among superior, subordinate, and coordinate points has been maintained. For the tests to work smoothly, the points have to be worded according to the three rules stated earlier, namely: they are limited to a single, complete sentence; they contain one key idea only; and they employ parallel sentence structure in sets of coordinate points.

Checking Subordinate Relationships: The "For" Test

The "for" test enables you to quickly check the logical relationship between a superior point and each of its subordinate points within the speech unit. The purpose of the test is twofold: it helps you find *irrelevant* points so that you can delete them, or move them to a better location in the outline, and it helps you locate *poorly worded* points so that you can rephrase them for clarity and persuasiveness.

The test, which can be done mentally, aloud, or in writing as part of the outline, is applied in three connected steps. (1) Begin by reading the superior point of the speech unit, then (2) say "for" (as a transition term); (3) third, read the subpoint you are testing. By connecting the superior point to the subordinate point with the transition word "for," you get a sense of whether or not the points work logically together. Here is an example.

LOGICAL RELATIONSHIP CONFIRMED BY THE "FOR" TEST

Central Idea: There are three branches to the federal government of the United States. **(for...)**

I.   One is the legislative branch.

Because the two statements make sense when joined together with "for," you have helped confirm that main point I is logically subordinate to its superior point, the superior point in this case being the central idea. On the other hand, what does the "for" test tell you concerning the example below?

ILLOGICAL RELATIONSHIP REVEALED BY THE "FOR" TEST

Central Idea: There are three branches to the federal government of the United States. **(for...)**

I.   The Russians have a different system.

Obviously, in this second example, the idea of point I doesn't fit when checked against its superior point with the "for" test. In a similar fashion you can check each supporting point of the speech units of your outlines to help maintain solid logical relationships between the ideas of the outlines. The lesson here is crucial to good outlining, namely, it is the *content* of a point—not its arbitrary location in an outline—that makes that point logical in relationship to the other points of the speech unit.

The "for" test is further refined and clarified when administered in conjunction with a second test—the "also" test for evaluating coordinate ideas.

Checking Coordinate Relationships: The "Also" Test

Coordinate relationships in a speech unit can be checked easily by employing the "also" test. In this procedure, you insert the transition word "also" between each of the coordinate points in a set (for an example of coordinate sets, see Figure 9.3). As with the previous test, you can read the sentences aloud, or mentally. To illustrate, the three branches of the federal government conform to the "also" test below.

I. One is the legislative branch. (**also...**)

II. Another is the executive branch. (**also...**)

III. The third is the judicial branch.

When this test for logical coordination is combined with the "for" test for subpoints, the result looks like this.

Central Idea: There are three branches to the federal government of the United States. (**for...**)

I. One is the legislative branch. (**also...**)

II. Another is the executive branch. (**also...**)

III. The third is the judicial branch.

By combining the "for" and "also" tests, you can check the relationships of ideas in each speech unit of the outline, starting with the largest unit (the central idea and main points) down to the smallest subunit. To illustrate, the first main point and its support in the outline on "fair use" of copyrighted material (Figure 9.1) would be tested as follows.

I. The first principle concerns the purpose and character of use. (**for...**)
   A. Strict limits apply to commercial, "for profit" use. (**also...**)
   B. Fewer restrictions apply to educational, "nonprofit" use.

Following through, both A and B above are subunits, and should be tested next. Using A as an illustration, the smaller unit looks like this when checked.

A. Strict limits apply to commercial, "for profit" use. (**for...**)
   1. Most "for profit" use requires written permission. (**also...**)
   2. Mister Maestro's recording of King's speech was a commercial venture, and thus needed a permission.

If a point you have outlined as coordinate really is not equal to the other points of a set, the "also" test will help you spot the error. What problem do you detect in the example below?

ILLOGICAL RELATIONSHIP REVEALED BY THE "ALSO" TEST

Central Idea: There are three branches to the federal government of the United States. (**for...**)

I. One is the legislative branch. (**also...**)

II.   Another is the executive branch. (**also...**)

III.   England has a parliamentary system of government.

As you no doubt realize, when reading from point to point above, main heading III, as worded, does not meet the "also" test. After sensing that something is wrong with the content of the third point, you should remove it and redo point III so that it is coordinate to points I and II in supporting the central idea.

The Relationships of Points in Summary

The points of a speech unit are related to each other in three ways: they can be superior to others; they can be subordinate to others; or they can be coordinate to others. Just as a whole pie is larger than its pieces, a *superior* idea/point is more comprehensive or more important than the smaller, subordinate points that support it. In a logical outline, for example, the central idea is superior to the main headings of the body.

A *subordinate* idea, or subpoint, is a smaller, component part of a superior point, or one that directly supports a superior idea with reasoning and evidence. Just as each piece of a pie is a subpart of the pie as a whole, so are the subpoints of a speech unit subordinate to the superior idea of that unit. In an outline, for example, the main headings of the body are subordinate to the central idea.

A *coordinate* idea is one that is equal to another. Any set of two or more subpoints that support the same superior point have a coordinate relationship to each other (see Figure 9.3), just as the pieces of a pie are coequal—or coordinate—to each other. In an outline, for example, the main points of the body are coordinate, for they all support the same superior point, namely, the central idea. The relationship of subordinate points to superior points can be checked with the "for" test, and the relationship of coordinate points can be checked with the "also" test.

III. The Adequacy of Supporting Points

Recall that *a speech unit is defined as a statement and its support*. As you develop each unit, you must decide on the amount of support necessary to achieve the purpose of the unit—whether the purpose is to explain a statement or to persuade an audience to accept a statement.

Because each speaking situation is varied and complex, there is no precise, scientific answer to the question of how much support is enough. The kind of support needed, and the amount of it, depends upon such factors as the speech subject, audience knowledge and attitudes on the subject, audience attitudes toward the speaker (*ethos*), and the nature of the occasion (including time limits). When planning each speech unit, you will need to make an intuitive decision on whether or not the support you have included is sufficient to make the superior statement of that unit clear and convincing.

In almost every case, you will find that two or more subordinate points are necessary for the unit to be adequately developed. There are, however, at least two exceptions to this general rule. A look at both types of situations should help you "take charge" of your speech outline so that it serves your communication purposes well.

The General Rule: Two or More Subpoints Are Needed

Two or more subordinate points are required to develop the key idea of a speech unit (1) when you divide an idea into its logical subparts in order to explain it, (2) when you present a persuasive statement that requires two or more arguments to be effective, and (3) when you need two or more items of supporting evidence (such as examples, statistics, and quotations) to be clear and convincing. First, you cannot subdivide a topic into one point any more than you can cut an apple into one piece, or break a stone into one chunk. The very nature of subdivision is that two or more subparts are the result of the process of dividing. Examples in speech outlining include subdividing a process or procedure into its main steps (step one, step two, step three, and so on), breaking a geographical area into its sections (such as east, central, and west), or describing an organization according to its major subordinate units (such as the three branches of the federal government). The rule of thumb is that *speech units that are constructed of the subdivisions of the key idea of the unit will always have two or more subordinate points.*

Second, convincing an audience to change its attitude on a topic, or moving an audience to action in a persuasive speech to actuate, is always challenging, and often quite difficult to accomplish. To be persuasive, building a thorough case usually requires several good arguments, complete with subarguments and strong evidence. This view is supported both by common sense and by research. For example, after surveying the literature on the issue, one researcher reports that "messages with more arguments are more effective" in changing attitudes than "those with fewer arguments."[5] In planning a persuasive speech, therefore, you are well advised to assume that *two or more points of support are called for in most units because that is what it takes to make that unit convincing.*

Finally, just as a persuasive point is made stronger by two or more supporting arguments, so are points requiring evidential support made clearer and more convincing by a variety of evidence. In other words, for most speech units, two or more examples, sets of statistics, or quotations from authority are better than one.

In sum, logic decrees that any time you subdivide a superior point into its parts, you must have two or more subpoints. On the other hand, the principle of communication effectiveness decrees that for most persuasive speeches you need two or more arguments to be effective; and, for most speech units, several items of supporting evidence are needed to make the superior point of the unit clear and convincing. There are, however, sensible exceptions to these general principles.

Two Exceptions to the Rule: When One Subpoint Will Do

The "One Good Reason" Exception

In persuasive speaking the main points, and many of the subpoints, consist of *reasons* why the audience should agree with the speaker's views on the subject of the speech. "Let me give you three reasons why I believe that you should

IV. The fourth principle concerns the effect of use upon the market value
of the copyrighted work.
  A. Unauthorized use that reduces market value can trigger legal action.
    1. The Nation magazine once published key sections of a book by
       Gerald Ford before it was released by the publisher.
       a. Although the percentage of direct quotes was small, the
          economic effect upon market value was documented.
       b. The U.S. Supreme Court ruled in 1985 (in the case of Harper &
          Row vs. Nation), that The Nation had violated copyright law.
  B. Unauthorized use that does not affect market value is less likely
     to trigger legal action.
    1. Giving photocopies of a copyrighted speech to students in a speech
       analysis course is not likely to present a problem.
    2. Making a small number of copies of an out-of-print item that is not
       being reissued by the publisher is not likely to present a problem.

FIGURE 9.4

When One Point Will Do. *The example above is point IV of the body of the outline on
"fair use" in copyright law; as you can see, subpoint A is supported by* one
example—the case of The Nation's *unauthorized use of materials from a book by former
President Gerald Ford. In this instance, one example is adequate to illustrate the point.*

vote for John Doe for class president,'' or ''There are two key reasons for supporting the honor system on our campus'' are typical of central ideas for persuasive speaking. For most speaking, two or more sound reasons are given by
the speaker who wants to develop a case fully.

There are two situations, however, when a one-point development is justified, namely: when time is short (''I have only three minutes, so let me tell you
the single, best reason I know for voting for John Doe for class president'');
and when one strong reason is all that is needed to make a convincing case to
the audience.[6] Although it is unlikely that you will deliver one-point speeches
very often (and perhaps never), you should know that such speeches are not
automatically illogical. The decision on the matter should be based on what is
needed to be effective.

Here is an example of a one-point speech in outline form. Note that the
single reason given is a very important human need—the preservation of one's
life—which could be adequate by itself (that is, without additional main points)
to persuade some audiences to agree to the central idea.

Central Idea: You should always ''buckle up'' with your seat belt when
driving, or riding as a passenger in a car. **(for...)**

I. [*One good reason*] Wearing your seat belt can save your life. **(for...)**
  A. Examples and illustrations. **(also...)**
  B. Statements from authority. **(also...)**
  C. Statistics.

The "One Good Item of Evidence" Exception

The second exception to the need for two or more subpoints concerns the use
of evidence—examples, comparisons and contrasts, statistics, quotations,

etc.—in support of a superior point in the outline. There are times when you will sense that one good example, one key set of statistics, or one strong quotation is adequate to make an idea clear or convincing. Also, there will be occasions when your outline is too long and complex, and you will want to shorten and simplify it by deleting some nonessential items of evidence here and there in the outline. To employ only one point of evidence in these situations can be both logically and rhetorically sound. (For an example of the common sense use of one point of evidence, see Figure 9.4.)

The key question you should always ask when considering the use of one point of evidence is, "Does this single item of evidence adequately clarify the point, or make the point convincing?" If your best judgment is "yes, it does," then you have made a sensible rhetorical choice.

This Chapter in Brief

Three basic principles that should help you in organizing your speeches are explained in this chapter, namely: the "speech unit" concept of speech outlining; the relationships that points have to each other in a speech outline; and the number of points needed to develop the thesis statement of a speech unit.

The *speech unit* is the basic building block of speech organization. A speech unit consists of two parts: (1) a statement, and (2) support for that statement. The units may be large or small. For example, the body of the speech is a large speech unit consisting of a thesis statement (the central idea) and a number of smaller units (main points) that support this statement. A small speech unit is any subpoint in the speech that is itself supported by one or more subordinate ideas or pieces of evidence. Both large and small units are illustrated in the chapter by Figures 9.1 and 9.2. The formidable task of organizing a speech is made much more manageable by the speech unit approach, for this method of looking at outlining provides the speaker with a system for constructing a speech one small piece at a time.

The ideas, or points, of a speech unit are related to each other in three ways: superior, subordinate, and coordinate. A *superior point* is one that is above another in the outline because it is a comprehensive or significant statement that requires support (that is, it has subpoints). For example, the central idea of the body is a superior point to the main headings that support it; in turn, each main heading is superior to the subpoints that support it. *Subordinate points* are those that directly support a superior point by stating its subdivisions, or by giving reasons and evidence as forms of proof. A *coordinate point* is one that is equal to another. Any set of two or more subpoints are coordinate to each other if they support the same superior point. For example, the main points of the body of speech outline should be logically coordinate to each other. The principle of logical coordination is illustrated in the chapter by Figure 9.3.

Finally, the matter of how much support is needed to develop the superior statement of any speech unit depends upon the subject, audience, and occasion (time limits in particular). Be guided by the following three principles:

1. In order to effectively clarify and prove the key statements of a speech, you will usually need two or more subordinate points of support for each important statement.

2. Any time a superior point is *subdivided*, two or more points will result. This is logical, for just as you cannot cut an apple into one piece, you cannot divide an idea into one part.

3. One subpoint of support is logically permissible, and sometimes rhetorically sound, when you are not subdividing a topic, but are doing one of the following: (a) stating one good reason in support of a superior point in a persuasive speech, or (b) citing one piece of evidence to clarify or prove a superior point (such as using one example to illustrate a point).

The rule of thumb that emerges can be stated this way: when you subdivide a statement into substatements, you must have two or more subordinate points; however, when you are not subdividing, but are stating reasons or evidence, the decision on the number of subpoints should be made according to what is required to be effective.

We are now ready to apply the concepts of this chapter to the important task of planning the heart of any speech—the body. Outlining the body of the speech, therefore, is the subject of the chapter that follows.

EXERCISES

1. Pay special attention to the organization of the classroom lectures and speeches you hear in each of your courses over the next several weeks. Are some teachers more organized than others? Does clear, logical organization in a lecture help you to understand the content and to take a good set of notes? What do your conclusions say about what you should do in organizing your own speeches?

2. Select a model speech from the examples at the end of this book. Locate several speech units in the speech, and outline each unit in rough draft form. For variety, outline at least one large unit and one small unit. You can use Figure 9.2 as a model for your outlines.

3. Write down two or three topics about which you have strong opinions, then formulate each topic into a specific purpose and central idea for a speech. For each central idea, state the *one* reason that you believe would be most persuasive in convincing your speech class (or other specific audience) to agree with you. The result, of course, is the basic plan for a one-point speech. Could you make a convincing case for any of the topics by developing one, and only one, argument?

SELECTED READINGS

Aristotle. *The Rhetoric of Aristotle*. Trans. Lane Cooper, New York: Appleton-Century, 1932. Aristotle's discussion of speech organization is in Book 3, Sections 13–19. His concept of the basic speech unit is similar to that presented in this chapter. He states, for example, that a "speech has two parts. Necessarily, you state your case, and you prove it" (p. 220).

Gray, Giles W., and Braden, Waldo W. *Public Speaking: Principles and Practice*. 2d ed. New York: Harper & Row, 1963. Chapter 2, "Planning Your First Speeches" includes useful insights into the relationship of ideas to each other in the outline, and a brief mention of the one-point speech.

Mills, Glen E. *Message Preparation: Analysis and Structure.* Indianapolis, Ind.: Bobbs-Merrill, 1966. Chapter 5, "Outlining and Patterns of Arrangement" includes a discussion of subordinate and coordinate relationships of the points of an outline.

Walter, Otis M. *Speaking to Inform and Persuade.* 2d ed. New York: Macmillan, 1982. Walter discusses the concept of the speech unit (which he describes as a "unit of discourse") in Chapter 2, "Exposition: An Overview," and Chapter 6, "Persuasive Logic: The Tactics of Persuasion."

ENDNOTES

1. Otis M. Walter, *Speaking to Inform and Persuade*, 2d ed. (New York: Macmillan, 1982), p. 9.
2. For example, see Ernest C. Thompson, "An Experimental Investigation of the Relative Effectiveness of Organizational Structure in Oral Communication," *Southern Speech Journal* 26 (Fall 1960): 59–69; also, J. E. Baird, Jr., "The Effects of Speech Summaries Upon Audience Comprehension of Expository Speeches of Varying Quality and Complexity," *Central States Speech Journal* 25 (Summer 1974): 119–127.
3. Harry Sharp, Jr., and Thomas McClung, "Effect of Organization on the Speaker's Ethos," *Speech Monographs* 33 (June 1966): 182–183. Also, James C. McCroskey and R. Samuel Mehrley, "The Effects of Disorganization and Nonfluency on Attitude Change and Source Credibility," *Speech Monographs* 36 (March 1969): 13–21.
4. For additional information on the units of discourse, see Otis M. Walter, op. cit., pp. 9–15, 52–58.
5. William L. Benoit, "Argumentation and Credibility Appeals in Persuasion," *Southern Speech Communication Journal* 52 (Winter 1987): 185.
6. The author was first introduced to the concept of the one-point speech by Waldo W. Braden, Professor of Speech at Louisiana State University, in an advanced public speaking course. The concept is mentioned briefly in Giles W. Gray and Waldo W. Braden, *Public Speaking: Principles and Practice*, 2d ed. (New York: Harper & Row, 1963), p. 23.

> *[The] arrangement of topics in speaking, like the arraying of soldiers in battle, can readily bring victory.*

—*Rhetorica ad Herennium*, Book III[1] (ca. 90 B.C.)

Chapter 10

ORGANIZING AND OUTLINING THE BODY OF THE SPEECH

*I*magine for a moment that two architects are sketching blueprints for homes. One begins work on the project several weeks before construction starts, measures the spaces accurately, draws the lines carefully, and checks each detail before completing the final design. The other waits until the last minute, draws hastily, takes shortcuts, and neglects to measure each dimension carefully. Although both architects produce a blueprint, the first plans a house that will be solid, functional, and attractive; the second, on the other hand, has produced a crude design that barely meets the building code, is inefficient in its use of space, and is a visual "eyesore." If you were in the market for a home, which of the two houses would you prefer?

Organizing and outlining a speech is a bit like drawing a blueprint for a house. You are, in other words, the "architect" of your speech, and the outline is your "blueprint." The potential consumers for your design are the individual listeners who compose the audience. What type of speech do you believe will "sell" to your audience? Will your auditors be attracted to a hastily designed talk that rambles from generality to generality and that goes overtime without ever making its point? Or will your listeners prefer to "buy" the ideas that are presented in an easily followed sequence that is clear, interesting, and convincing? The answer is obvious—and this chapter (together with Chapters 9 and 11) is intended to help you design and deliver an organized speech that will appeal to the potential consumers of the ideas of the speech—your audience.

You should study the recommendations of this chapter as a continuation of the three basic concepts discussed in Chapter 9, namely, (1) the concept of speech units forming the building blocks of the outline, (2) understanding the ways in which points are logically related to each other (that is, superior, subordinate, and coordinate relationships), and (3) supporting key points with enough points to be clear and convincing. If you have not yet studied Chapter 9, now is a good time to do so.

In addition, this chapter and the next are arranged so as to present a sequence of outline preparation that works well for many speakers; namely, planning and outlining the body of the speech before working on the introduction (and, of course, the conclusion). The reason for this recommendation is that you can plan the introduction with greater certainty if you have developed the body *first*. An application of this recommendation means that you would organize the speech according to these three steps: first, outline the body (the "essential heart" of any speech); second, outline the introduction; finally, outline the conclusion.

An outline is not a word-by-word-manuscript of what a speaker intends to say. Rather, the outline presents a brief statement of each point that the speaker plans to make; these points are "fleshed out" verbally by the speaker at the time of delivery. In keeping with this concept, we can define *an outline as a "verbal blueprint" of the ideas and supporting materials of a speech that presents those ideas and materials in the order in which the speaker plans to deliver them, and that shows the logical relationships (superior, subordinate, and coordinate) of those ideas and supporting materials to each other.*

The purpose of this chapter is to explain how to outline the body of both informative and persuasive speeches. In order to do this in an organized way, the chapter is divided into three sections, as follows: standard form in outlining; outlining the main points; and supporting the main points with subpoints.

173

Chapter 10
*Organizing
and Outlining
the Body
of the
Speech*

I. Standard Form in Outlining

Your speech outlines should follow a consistent system of labeling points (with numbers and letters), spacing, and indentions, in order to show superior, subordinate, and coordinate relationships. The following markings are standard, and are used throughout this text:

I.
  A.
    1.
      a.
        (1)
          (a)

An application of this standard system is shown in Figure 10.1. Also, for examples of how the markings are applied, see the complete outline based on this standard form on "The 'Fair Use' of Copyrighted Material" near the end of this chapter (pp. 190–193), as well as the model outlines in Appendix II. When looking at the examples, notice that the introduction, body, and conclusion of each outline are numbered separately, and that *no number or letter is placed before the central idea in order to confirm its superior status in the outline as a whole*.

When putting the outline together in standard form, be sure to apply the following three rules of wording and sentence structure: state each point as a single, complete sentence; let each point state one, and only one, key idea; and phrase sets of coordinate points in parallel sentence structure. We are now ready to examine the critical step of organizing the main points of the body of the speech.

II. Outlining the Body: Main Points

The body of the speech can be outlined in a systematic way by following this two-step procedure: (1) support the central idea with main points; then (2) support each main point with subpoints (consisting of subideas and speech materials to clarify, reinforce, or prove the main points). In this section we will focus on developing the main points of the body. Later, in the section that follows, we will discuss the organization of support for each of the main points you have developed.

Main Points: Three Preliminary Considerations

As we begin our consideration of selecting and arranging the main points of a speech, three preliminary concepts need to be mentioned. These concern (1)

Standard Outline Form

Title: _____

Specific Purpose: _____

Pattern for Main Points of Body: _____

Introduction

I. _____
    A. _____
    B. _____
II. _____
    A. _____
    B. _____

Central Idea: _____

Body

I. _____
    A. _____
        1. _____
            a. _____
            b. _____
        2. _____
    B. _____
        1. _____
        2. _____
        3. _____

II. _____
    A. _____
    B. _____
    C. _____

III. _____
    A. _____
    B. _____

Conclusion

I. _____
    A. _____
    B. _____
    C. _____

II. _____
    A. _____
    B. _____

FIGURE 10.1

Skeleton Outline Showing Standard Form. *In the example above, only the first point of the body is developed in detail (the other points are briefer in order to conserve space). While the "Pattern for Main Points of Body" is not a traditional feature of an outline, it is useful to include it in order to confirm that you have followed a speech pattern.*

the number of main points you should have, (2) maintaining a balance in the development of each main point, and (3) following a pattern, or design, for the main points of the speech.

175

Chapter 10
*Organizing
and Outlining
the Body
of the
Speech*

Number of Main Points

Be careful to avoid complicating the speech for your listeners by trying to present too many points. *A total of from two to five points is about right*; when you exceed five main points you begin to exceed the retention and recall ability of the audience and thereby risk losing some of the effectiveness of the speech.

Also, because of time limits that are an inherent factor in all speechmaking, the more main points you have the less time you have to develop each one. For example, a ten-minute speech with two main points, subtracting a minute each for the introduction and conclusion, permits four minutes of discussion on each of the two points. If you have four points instead of two, you cut the discussion time to only two minutes per point.

When you begin a speech outline, therefore, make an effort to construct the basic framework of the body around two, three, four, or five main points. The ideas presented in this chapter fit this recommendation.

Balanced Development of Main Points

Each main point should be of approximately equal importance to the elaboration of the central idea. Therefore, you should balance the points so that each receives about the same degree of support (subideas and speech materials). In terms of delivery, this translates into the following principle: *spend approximately the same amount of time on each of the main points of your speech.*

Note that the term "approximately" is used to set out this principle of balanced treatment. The idea is not to mechanically place exactly the same number of subideas, examples, quotations, etc., in support of each point, and not to be rigid in budgeting the time spent on each point. Rather, you should avoid the problem of an imbalanced presentation by the sensible application of a rule of "roughly equal" development. For example, a three-point speech in which point one is discussed for *five* minutes, point two for *four* minutes, and the third point for *only one minute*, is out of balance. A better budgeting of time would be: point one, *four* minutes; point two, *three* minutes; and point three, *three* minutes.

Choosing Patterns for Main Points

The central idea of your speech should be subdivided into main points according to a systematic method or design, called a *speech pattern*. For example, if your purpose is to explain how to do something, you would probably cover the first step, the second step, the third step, and so forth. This would mean following a "chronological pattern," for the steps of a process fall logically into such a sequence. Or, if you were discussing a campus problem, then proposing action to solve that problem, you would probably cover the problem first and the proposed solution second. This could be done by following a "problem-solution pattern." Speech patterns help the speaker cover the subject logically and thoroughly, while avoiding pointless repetition; furthermore, patterns make it easier for those in the audience to follow the development of speech content.

Much of what follows in this chapter is designed to guide you in choosing the pattern that is most appropriate for your subject and your audience. One factor in making a wise decision is to know which patterns are most useful for communicating information, and which are most useful for persuasion. To facilitate learning the patterns that best fit each type of discourse, we will first look at ideas for arranging the main points of informative speeches, then examine some ideas for arranging the main points of persuasive speeches. (Note that each sample outline in the sections that follow includes the "for" test for logical subordination and the "also" test for logical coordination as explained in Chapter 9.)

Patterns for Informative Speeches

The goal of the informative speech is to communicate information in order to achieve *understanding*. The speech to inform does not intentionally attempt to persuade the audience; rather, the underlying approach is to present information objectively.

The basic method for informing in public speaking is to break the subject into small, digestible pieces of discourse (these pieces can be described as "informative speech units"), and to explain each piece, or part, according to a logical sequence that helps the audience follow the development. After the parts are explained, the listener should be able to fit things together, thus grasping the subject as a whole. In other words, *the central idea of an informative speech names the subject as a whole, and the main points present—one at a time—the parts of the whole.* An example would be a speech explaining a college theater program that is presented according to its three key parts: (1) childrens' theater productions; (2) laboratory productions; and (3) main stage productions. When "added up," the three parts total the program as a whole.

There are three major patterns for informative speeches: chronological, physical components, and topical. We will discuss and illustrate each of these patterns, then look at some additional designs that are used occasionally for organizing key points in informative speaking.

Chronological Pattern

The chronological pattern for dividing an informative subject is based on a *time sequence*. A time sequence lists developments according to the clock or the calendar (including arrangements by minutes, hours, days, weeks, months, years, etc.), or according to the steps of doing something. It is especially useful in organizing the main points of historical subjects (such as the life of a person, or a series of historical events) and for presenting the steps in a process or procedure (such as baking a cake, or manufacturing a product).

For example, an informative speech on the Battle of Gettysburg, fought on July 1, 2, and 3, 1863, fits the chronological pattern well, for the main points could be organized according to days, namely: the first day of battle, the second day of battle, and the third day of battle. In this case, the term "Battle of

Gettysburg'' states the subject as a whole, and each of the three days is a part of that whole. In effect, the three-point arrangement by days can be called a ''chronological parts-of-the-whole pattern.''

To illustrate further the idea of chronological parts of the whole, the outline below presents the steps in a process. The ''whole'' is represented by the term ''five major steps in the process.'' The main points develop this whole, chronologically, one part at a time.

177

*Chapter 10
Organizing
and Outlining
the Body
of the
Speech*

Specific Purpose: To inform my audience of the five steps of securing a license to broadcast in the United States.

Central Idea: There are five major steps in the process of securing a license to operate a radio or television station in the United States. (**for...**)

I. The first step is to locate an unused frequency or channel in the area to be served. (**also...**)

II. The second step (not required for radio) is an ''ascertainment study'' of community needs. (**also...**)

III. The third step is to apply to the Federal Communications Commission (FCC) for a construction permit and a license. (**also...**)

IV. The fourth step is to meet any challenges that might arise from potential competitors. (**also...**)

V. The fifth step is for the FCC to award the construction permit and a license.

Physical Components Pattern

The physical components pattern is used when you subdivide a *single physical unit* (such as a device, a building, or a block of territory) into its major pieces, spaces, or geographical sections. You can think of it as organizing a speech according to the ''physical components of one whole.'' It is reserved for physical things, and does not work for subjects based on abstract concepts, beliefs, classifications, etc. Also, it is reserved for explanations of only *one* physical thing, structure, or geographical area; that one thing, structure, or area is named in both the specific purpose and the central idea.

For example, you could use the physical components pattern for a lecture on the major parts of a computer; however, you could not use this pattern for a talk on the political beliefs of Daniel Webster (because ''political beliefs'' are not physical things). Also, you could employ the physical components pattern for a talk orienting visitors to your campus by explaining the campus according to sections, such as north campus, central campus, and south campus. However, a biographical sketch of the founder of your school, delivered to that same group of visitors, does not qualify for the physical components pattern, for the events in a person's life are not physical pieces, spaces, or geographical areas.

Here is an example of an outline using the physical components pattern to explain the parts of one thing, namely, the human ear. The ''whole'' is stated by the term ''human ear''; the points are the physical parts of that whole.

Specific Purpose: To inform the audience of the parts of the human ear.
Central Idea: The human ear has three main sections. (**for...**)

I.   The first section is the outer ear. (**also...**)

II.   The second section is the middle ear. (**also...**)

III.   The third section is the inner ear.

Another example illustrates how the physical components pattern can be used to organize a talk according to geographical subparts. In the outline below, the term "our state" is the geographical "whole," and the points are the subordinate geographical parts of that whole.

Specific Purpose: To inform my audience of the park system of our state.
Central Idea: No matter where you live in our state, you are close to a state park. (**for...**)

I.   The eastern region of our state has three parks. (**also...**)

II.   The central region of our state has three parks. (**also...**)

III.   The western region of our state has four parks.

Topical Pattern

If your central idea cannot be sensibly subdivided according to a chronological pattern or a physical components pattern, then a topical pattern will likely work for you. The term "topic" means a *heading based upon subject matter*; therefore, a topical pattern is one in which each point names one unit of subject matter that is subordinate to the superior (or whole) subject as stated by the central idea. In other words, the central idea states a subject, and the main points present the topics that flow logically from that subject. Thus, the points represent the topical parts of the whole.

Topical patterns can be classified as either *inherent* or *created*. An inherent pattern is one based upon the "natural" parts of the whole as revealed by the subject itself. For example, the three branches of the federal government—legislative, executive, and judicial—are inherent in the term "federal government." Similarly, the official goals of a group, the existing departments of an organization, or traditional classifications applied to persons (such as male and female), are all inherent, or "natural" topics that one finds already present within a subject.

On the other hand, individual speakers can make up headings based on their own direct experience or research, and shape those headings into a creative topical pattern that is useful in presenting information. We call such topical patterns "creative" because they are not inherent in the subject but are invented by the speaker and applied to the subject. Examples would be a talk on "My Three Favorite Techniques of Word Processing," or "What We Can Learn About Effective Speaking by Studying Great Speeches" (a lecture in which the speaker, after thorough research, decided upon the topics to be discussed).

Here is an example of an outline based on a topical pattern that emerges from headings that are *inherent* in the subject (the four types of schools already exist, and the names are official under state law). The term "public institutions of higher education" represents the whole, and the types of schools are the topical parts of the whole.

179

Chapter 10
*Organizing
and Outlining
the Body
of the
Speech*

> **Specific Purpose:** To inform the audience about how the public institutions of higher education are organized in our state.
> **Central Idea:** The Legislature has established four types of public institutions of higher education in our state. **(for...)**

I. The first is the technical college. **(also...)**

II. The second is the community college. **(also...)**

III. The third is the senior college. **(also...)**

IV. The fourth is the university.

An example of the use of a topical pattern based on the *creative* thinking of a speaker, rather than on headings inherent in a subject, could be a lecture by an experienced parliamentarian concerning the mistakes he or she most often encountered when teaching or practicing parliamentary procedure. The term "three most common mistakes" states the whole, and the main points represent the topical parts of that whole. The parts, which are stated as topical phrases rather than single words, are as follows: "required to use *Robert's*," "secretary must write down everything," and "'call for the question' automatically stops debate."

> **Specific Purpose:** To inform the audience of the three most common mistakes concerning parliamentary procedure that I have observed over the years.
> **Central Idea:** There are three mistakes that occur most often in the practice of parliamentary procedure. **(for...)**

I. First is the mistaken assumption that a group is required to use *Robert's Rules of Order*. **(also...)**

II. Second is the mistaken assumption that the recording secretary must write down everything that occurs in a business meeting. **(also...)**

III. Third is the mistaken assumption that a "call for the question" automatically stops debate without a vote.

Additional Patterns and Combinations

Additional patterns can be based upon relationships, such as from smallest to largest, from simple to complex, or from economical to expensive. Also, patterns can be based upon stock methods of analysis or division (all of which can be considered specialized forms of topical arrangement), such as theory-practice, physical-mental, heredity-environment, problem-solution, or cause-effect.

When using a stock method of division for informative discourse, be sure to keep the content objective (that is, do not permit the speech to become persuasive). The cause-effect pattern, for example, can be used in either informative or persuasive speeches. When used in informative outlining, be sure that the content remains expository, as with a two-point lecture on (1) the causes and (2) effects of earthquakes.

Furthermore, some patterns can be used in combination with others. For example, a speech on the academic achievements of the undergraduates at your school, grouped according to freshman, sophomore, junior, and senior, follows a pattern that combines topical with chronological ("freshman" through "senior" are topics inherent in the term "undergraduates," and the classes are arranged chronologically). The guiding principle of combining two or more patterns is that *the combination you start out with must be maintained throughout the set of coordinate points to which it is applied.*

Finally, it is important to note that the pattern (or combination of patterns) you use for the main points does not automatically "carry over" to the various sets of supporting points throughout the entire outline. In other words, once you finish organizing a set of coordinate points and indent to the next level of support, you may change patterns to meet the demands of that next set of points. For example, main points I, II, and III can follow one pattern (such as topical), and supporting points A, B, and C can follow a different pattern (such as chronological).

Having examined the use of standard patterns for organizing informative speeches, let us now look at how some of the same patterns can be adapted to persuasive speeches. (In addition, we will examine some specialized patterns that are used primarily for persuasion.)

Patterns for Persuasive Speeches

As Chapter 6 on subjects and purposes emphasizes, the goal of a speech to inform is different from the goal of a speech to persuade. The informative speech stresses the communication of knowledge; its goal is understanding. The persuasive speech, on the other hand, goes beyond the communication of knowledge; its goal is to modify attitudes and behavior in directions intended by the speaker.

Although the speech to modify attitudes and behavior does include information where it is needed, it is distinguished from exposition by its larger and more complex persuasive function. It follows that the main points must serve this persuasive function. They do this by going beyond subdividing a subject into its parts for ease in explanation, as in expository speaking, to stating reasons (also called arguments) why the central idea should be accepted by the listeners. In other words, *the unique purpose of main points in persuasion is to state your key reasons to the audience.* Consequently, patterns are employed in persuasive speeches to help you organize your main reasons so that the audience can follow them easily, understand and remember them, and be persuaded by them.

It is appropriate that we describe the patterns below according to their purpose in persuasion, namely, *providing reasons* that support the central idea. Therefore, the major patterns we will examine are labeled as follows: (1) main reasons arranged chronologically; (2) main reasons arranged by physical components; (3) main reasons arranged topically; (4) main reasons arranged by problem-solution; (5) main reasons arranged by cause-effect; and (6) additional patterns and combinations.

Main Reasons Arranged Chronologically

Even though you are likely to employ the chronological pattern of organization more often in expository speaking than in persuasion, nevertheless the sequence is sometimes useful for ordering the main points of a persuasive speech. For example, argument from historical occurrence fits this plan well. To illustrate, a persuasive speech urging a change in the basic plan for taking the national census might be constructed around a chronological plan, with each main point stressing the problems according to this sequence of events: the system was a mess (1) in 1970, (2) in 1980, and (3) again in 1990 (and therefore should be changed in a significant way).

In addition, the chronological sequence of past-present-future is sometimes appropriate for a persuasive speech. For example, a speaker could argue that the federal social security program deserves our continued support for these three reasons: (1) The program has worked well in the *past*; (2) The program is working well at the *present* time; and (3) The program, with minor revisions, will continue to work in the *future*.

181

*Chapter 10
Organizing
and Outlining
the Body
of the
Speech*

Main Reasons Arranged by Physical Components

As with chronological order, the physical components pattern is used more often for informative speaking than for persuasion. However, it does have uses in persuasive speaking. For example, an engineer could urge a major redesign in a machine by discussing the weaknesses of the current design, component by component, with each major component being used as the basis for developing a main reason or argument.

Or a series of main points could be organized according to the geographical areas of a city, county, state, or other unified physical area. To illustrate, a speaker might try to persuade an audience to support a special city tax for parks and recreation by arguing that the tax would benefit all parts of the city: (1) The proposal benefits the *northern* section, (2) the *eastern* section, (3) the *western* section, and (4) the *southern* section of our town.

Main Reasons Arranged Topically

Topical patterns are highly useful in organizing both informative and persuasive speeches. As was pointed out earlier, topics are of two major types: those *inherent* in a subject, and those *created* by the speaker. This classification applies equally well to persuasion, for you can build a set of arguments around topics inherent in a subject, or you can—after careful research and thought—develop main reasons according to topics that you creatively formulate based upon your knowledge.

Here is an outline based on topics inherent in the subject. The key term in the specific purpose and central idea is "student body"; the subdivisions of this term—commuters, town students, and dormitory residents—around which reasons are constructed, are already in existence (that is, are inherent), and thus do not have to be invented by the speaker.

Specific Purpose: To actuate my student audience to vote for John Jones for president of the student body.

Central Idea: John Jones, candidate for student body president, has a platform that meets your needs, no matter where you live. (**for...**)

I.   He has a program to meet the needs of commuters. (**also...**)

II. He has a program to meet the needs of town students. (**also...**)

III. He has a program to meet the needs of dormitory residents.

One of the most commonly used plans for the main points of persuasive speeches is that of *creative main reasons* in which you organize the body of the speech according to the best reasons you can think of as to why the audience should accept your central idea. The main reasons are, in effect, topical arguments that emerge from your reasoning about subject and audience (as contrasted with those that are inherent in the subject). For example, a student speech with the goal of actuating class members to attend the Arts and Lecture Series of the college could be outlined around three creative topical reasons: the series is (1) educationally fulfilling, (2) entertaining, and (3) free to students.

Main Reasons Arranged by Problem-Solution and Monroe's Motivated Sequence

The problem-solution pattern of organization for the main points of a speech is one that is used regularly by persuasive speakers. The pattern is appropriate any time you are pointing out a need to your audience and are suggesting a plan to meet that need. Furthermore, this pattern reflects a natural sequence of thought as applied to problem solving. As early as 1910, John Dewey, American philosopher and educator, observed in *How We Think*, that humans proceed through a series of steps when trying to address a felt need in a rational way. A summary of Dewey's steps is as follows: (1) after becoming aware of a need or problem, we define and analyze it; (2) next, we examine possible solutions; then (3) we weigh the advantages and disadvantages of the various solutions; (4) finally, a solution is chosen and put into effect.[2] When adapted to persuasive speaking, Dewey's analysis looks like this:

1 The speaker defines, describes, and analyzes the problem for the audience.

2 The speaker recommends the solution he or she thinks best.

3 The speaker explains the benefits (or advantages) of the solution offered as compared to other proposals.

4 The speaker urges the adoption and implementation of the solution offered.

This systematic approach is the basis for three variations of the problem-solution pattern in persuasive speaking, namely, (1) a basic two-point plan consisting of the problem and a proposed solution, (2) a more fully developed analysis covering the three points of problem-solution-benefits, and (3) the most elaborate variation, called the "motivated sequence," that includes not only problem, solution, and benefits but also an introductory attention step and a closing appeal for action. Let us look at these three plans further.

The points of your speech should be organized according to a systematic design or speech pattern. (McGraw-Hill photo by Elyse Rieder)

Basic Problem-Solution Plan

The basic problem-solution pattern is used when the body of the speech states two main reasons, the first being the problem, and the second being a proposed solution to that problem. An example would be a student speech in which the speaker tried to convince the members of the class that an honor code policy is needed in the college they attend. The first point would state the problem (dishonesty on exams and in research projects), and the second point would recommend the solution (adoption of a campus-wide honor code).

Problem-Solution-Benefits Plan

A more complete approach adds a third element of analysis—namely, benefits—to the pattern, resulting in a three-point plan that covers the problem, the solution, and the benefits (or advantages) that will result if the proposed solution is adopted. In both the two-point and the three-point plans, the speaker would probably appeal for belief and action in the conclusion of the speech. Using the subject of an honor code, mentioned above in relation to the two-point pattern, here is an illustration of the problem-solution-benefits plan.

Specific Purpose: To convince the class that our college needs a comprehensive honor code policy.

Central Idea: Our school needs a comprehensive honor code. **(for...)**

I.   We have a serious problem of dishonesty on exams and research assignments at our school. **(also...)**

II. A comprehensive honor code policy would help solve the problem. (**also...**)

III. There are several major benefits that would result from adopting an honor code.

Monroe's Motivated Sequence

The third and most elaborate variation of the problem-solution plan was developed by the late Alan H. Monroe, Professor of Communication at Purdue University.[3] Called the "motivated sequence," this plan is so named because it is built around a series of motivational principles based upon human psychology. Reflecting John Dewey's analysis of reflective problem solving, Monroe's motivated sequence is, at base, a problem-solution-benefits pattern. The motivational factors inherent in the sequence include gaining audience attention at the beginning, relating the problem and the solution to audience needs and desires, and making the benefits vivid and impelling to the listeners. Monroe presents the motivated sequence in five steps: (1) *attention*; (2) *need* (problem); (3) *satisfaction* (solution); (4) *visualization* (benefits); and (5) *action*. Let us look at each step in more detail.

1. *Attention*. Your first responsibility as a public speaker is to get the audience to listen to your ideas. You catch attention at the beginning of the speech with appealing and relevant content (such as an entertaining illustration, a shocking statistic, or an unusual quotation) and by direct, confident delivery. You keep the audience listening by supporting the points of your speech with specific examples, interesting comparisons and contrasts, clear statistics, and with statements from authority.

2. *Need*. In this essential step, you make the problem clear, and convincingly demonstrate how it affects those in your audience. If your listeners understand the issue, and are persuaded that it does relate to their lives, they will be motivated to listen and to do something about it. You can make the problem vivid and relevant with interesting and appropriate supporting materials. Dramatic illustrations are especially effective. For example, a speech calling for around-the-clock monitoring of entrances to dormitory living areas as a crime-prevention measure could be made relevant to a student audience with two or three true accounts of recent crimes, such as theft or sexual assault, in campus dorms.

3. *Satisfaction*. The next step is to propose a solution to the problem presented in step two. The solution should be explained in a clear and persuasive way so that the audience is convinced that the proposal can solve (or help to solve) the problem under discussion, thereby "satisfying" the concern of the listeners. In addition, the speaker should demonstrate that the proposed solution is practical, and that it conforms to audience values and attitudes. Continuing our illustration on the topic of crime in the dorms, the speaker would need to explain how the proposed monitoring system would work, and how it would make things safer. A strong form of support would be examples of how such systems work at other schools, including statistics proving that in-dorm crime was greatly reduced by the plan.

4. *Visualization*. In this step, the speaker presents the benefits that will result from the proposed solution. This is done by asking the audience to men-

tally "visualize" how things will be in the future after the solution is put into effect. An option available to the speaker is to first describe how the problem will get worse if it is not solved—in other words, "negative visualization." The speaker could say, for instance, "If you think theft and assault in the dorms is bad now, imagine what it will be like next year, or the next, as would-be thieves, rapists, and drug dealers learn how easy it is to victimize you and your friends while you are studying or sleeping in your own room."

185

*Chapter 10
Organizing
and Outlining
the Body
of the
Speech*

The essential part of this step, however, is to present a "positive visualization" of the future, with a description of how things will be with the solution in place. The speaker could say something like this: "With a guard at the entrances to the living areas of your dorm—one who is acquainted with you and the others who live in the building—you will be much safer. No strangers would be allowed past the lounge area until they are properly identified. No longer would you be confronted in your living quarters with would-be criminals, such as those who have recently robbed, beat up, and even raped students in their rooms on our campus."

5. *Action*. The final step is to appeal for decision and action. In other words, ask for support in implementing the solution that you have proposed. Explain clearly what each person can do to help. For example, the speaker who favors a dormitory monitoring system could have a petition ready for signing. In the conclusion, the speaker would urge each member of the audience to sign the petition supporting guards, adding: "I plan to make copies of this petition and send one to the president of our school, one to the dean of students, and one to the faculty committee on campus security. In addition, I plan to take the original petition to the student legislature at its next meeting and request support for dormitory monitoring."

In order to test the logical relationship of points and supports in an outline based on the motivated sequence, place step one (*attention*) in the introduction of a speech, and step five (*appeal for action*) in the conclusion. After you have done this, you can see the body of the speech consists of steps two, three, and four—that is, the problem (*need*), the solution (*satisfaction*), and the benefits (*visualization*). You then check the points as usual, using the "for" and "also" tests. The relationship of the motivated sequence to a standard speech outline can be illustrated as follows.

Specific Purpose: To actuate the students in my speech class to sign a petition in favor of keeping the library open twenty-four hours a day, seven days a week, while school is in session.

	Introduction
(1) **Attention**	(Create interest with an example or two of students who have had difficulty in using the library.)
	Central Idea: Our library needs to be open around the clock, seven days a week, when school is in session. (**for...**)
	Body
(2) **Need**	I. The limited schedule of operation of our library creates problems for working and commuting students. (**also...**)

(3) **Satisfaction**   II. Keeping the library open all week, around the clock, would solve the problem. (**also...**)

(4) **Visualization**   III. Imagine what a convenience a round-the-clock schedule would be to commuters, working students— and, in emergencies, to *you* as well.

Conclusion

(5) **Action**   (In the conclusion, urge agreement, and ask students to sign a petition that the speaker will present to the administration and the faculty, including the library staff.)

Main Reasons Arranged by Causal Relation

This pattern is useful for outlining persuasive speeches in which the main reasons are based on causal reasoning. Sometimes the reasoning proceeds from cause to effect, and at other times it begins with the effect and reasons "back" to the cause. Both are classified as "causal," and both forms can be employed as speech patterns.

A plan based upon cause-to-effect would state and develop the cause in main reason one, and present the effect in main reason two. A causal plan based upon effect-to-cause would present the effect in the first point, and the cause in the second point. Here is an example of main reasons arranged by a cause-to-effect pattern.

> **Specific Purpose:** To convince my audience that the government should enforce strict standards of emission control in America's "smokestack industries."
>
> **Central Idea:** Strict emission control standards for the "smokestack industries" of the nation should be developed and enforced by the government as soon as possible. (**for...**)
>
> I. Emissions from our country's "smokestack industries" are a form of poison. (**also...**)
>
> II. The effect of "smokestack poisoning" is the death of vegetation and wildlife in many areas of North America.

Additional Patterns and Combinations

Additional plans that can be used for outlining the main reasons of persuasive speeches include patterns such as theory-practice, mental-physical, and local-state-national. No doubt you will think of others, for the list provided in this chapter is not exhaustive (although the most commonly used patterns are covered).

In addition, you can arrange your main reasons according to a climax order (save your strongest and most dramatic argument to the end of the body) or an anticlimax order (begin the body with your strongest argument). Both climax and anticlimax plans are worth considering. Either plan, skillfully employed, can be effective in persuasion. Research is inconclusive as to whether one is more effective than the other. At least one study concludes that, in persuasive speeches in which only one side of an argument is presented, *climax order is superior* to anticlimax order in producing a positive audience response to the speaker's point of view.[4]

Finally, as is true of informative outlining, the pattern used for the main points of the body of a persuasive speech is not necessarily carried over to the subpoints. When you indent and move to a set of points that support a main heading, you may apply a different pattern to those subpoints if logic so decrees. For example, the main points of an outline might employ a problem-solution plan, whereas the subordinate points might be chronological or topical in nature.

187

Chapter 10
*Organizing
and Outlining
the Body
of the
Speech*

Outlining the Main Points in Summary

The function of main points in an *informative speech* is to divide the central idea, or "whole," into small parts of discourse that can be easily comprehended by the audience, one part at a time. Patterns suitable for presenting the parts of the whole include chronological, physical components, and topical. On the other hand, the function of main points in a *persuasive speech* is to help prove the central idea by presenting arguments, or main reasons, why the audience should agree to the speaker's point of view. Patterns suitable for presenting main reasons include chronological, physical components, topical, problem-solution, and cause-effect. A summary and comparison of the relationships of main points to the central idea in speeches to inform and to persuade is presented by Figure 10.2.

We are now ready to complete our discussion of outlining the body by looking at the matter of organizing the subpoints that serve to clarify, reinforce, and prove the main points of the speech.

III. Outlining the Body: Supporting the Main Points

Each main heading that you formulate according to the foregoing suggestions should be considered the first step in constructing a speech unit that directly supports the central idea of the speech. Recall that a speech unit consists of two parts: (1) a statement, and (2) support for that statement. (For more on speech units, see Chapter 9.) Therefore, the number of main points determines the number of major speech units that you need to construct in order to complete the body. In other words, if you have two main points, you need to build two speech units, one around each point; and if you have three main points, you need to build three speech units, one around each point; and so forth.

The speech units are constructed using two types of building materials: *substatements* by which a main point is broken into subideas prior to the use of speech materials, and *speech materials (evidence)*, such as examples, comparisons and contrasts, statistics, and statements from authority, that you have gathered by research, and that provide the concrete details essential to clarification and proof.

Many, though not all, main points require subdivision prior to the use of speech materials in the outline. In these cases, you first subdivide the main point, being sure that the substatements are logically subordinate to the main point they support (give them the "for" test to be certain). Keep in mind that

	SPEECH TO INFORM	SPEECH TO PERSUADE
The speech in general: primary functions and goals	In the speech to inform: 1. The central idea states the subject the speaker plans <u>to explain</u>. 2. The function of the main points (and subpoints) is <u>to clarify</u> the central idea. 3. The goal of the speech is <u>understanding</u>.	In the speech to persuade: 1. The central idea states the viewpoint the speaker wants the audience <u>to accept</u>. 2. The function of the main points (and subpoints) is <u>to prove</u> the central idea. 3. The goal of the speech is <u>to change</u> attitudes and behavior.
RELATIONSHIP OF MAIN POINTS TO CENTRAL IDEA	Parts-of-the Whole Relationship (The central idea states "the whole," and the main points represent the "parts of the whole." The main points—or "parts"—should be arranged according to a logical pattern, such as one of those given below.)	Main Reasons Relationship (The central idea states a viewpoint, and the main points give <u>reasons</u> in support of that viewpoint. The main points—or reasons—should be arranged according to a logical pattern, such as one of those given below.)
Frequently used patterns of organization for main points	Patterns for parts-of-the-whole relationships; divide the central idea by... 1. Chronological parts of the whole. 2. Physical components or geographical parts of the whole. 3. Topical parts of the whole. 4. Additional parts-of-the-whole patterns.	Patterns for main reasons relationships; support the central idea by... 1. Main reasons arranged chronologically. 2. Main reasons arranged by physical components or geographical areas. 3. Main reasons arranged topically. 4. Main reasons arranged according to a problem-solution plan. 5. Main reasons arranged according to a causal (such as cause-effect) plan. 6. Additional main reasons patterns.

FIGURE 10.2

Different Relationships of Main Points to Central Idea in Informative and Persuasive Speeches.

in an informative outline, substatements function to clarify the main point under which they fall, and thus have a parts-of-the-whole relationship to that main point. On the other hand, *if the outline is persuasive, the substatements function to prove the main point under which they fall*, thus having a subreasons relationship to that main point. Just as you did when wording the main points, use complete sentences, and limit each subpoint to only one key idea per point. You then support each subpoint with concrete speech materials, as illustrated below.

MAIN POINT SUPPORTED BY BOTH SUBSTATEMENTS AND
SPEECH MATERIALS

I.   Statement of the main point.
    A.   First subdivision of main point.
        1.   Speech materials/evidence.
        2.   Speech materials/evidence.

B. Second subdivision of main point.
    1. Speech materials/evidence.
    2. Speech materials/evidence.

189

Chapter 10
*Organizing
and Outlining
the Body
of the
Speech*

In some cases, however, main points do not need to be broken into substatements before speech materials are used. Here is a skeleton outline showing how a main point is directly supported by speech materials without intervening subdivisions.

MAIN POINT DIRECTLY SUPPORTED BY SPEECH MATERIALS

I. Statement of the main point.
    A. Speech materials/evidence.
    B. Speech materials/evidence.
    C. Speech materials/evidence.

A more detailed example of how to outline the support for your main points is the outline on "The 'Fair Use' of Copyrighted Material" that was employed throughout Chapter 9, the complete version of which appears at the end of this chapter. The body of the outline, showing main points only, is as follows.

Specific Purpose: To inform the audience of the four principles of fair use in American copyright law.
Central Idea: There are four principles of "fair use" that public communicators should know. **(for...)**

I.   The first principle concerns the purpose and character of use. **(also...)**

II. The second principle concerns the nature of the copyrighted work. **(also...)**

III. The third principle concerns the percentage of the work used. **(also...)**

IV. The fourth principle concerns the effect of use upon the market value of the copyrighted work.

Let us use the first point above as an example of how a main heading is subdivided and supported with specific details. To begin with, point one (which is the *superior* point of this specific speech unit) is subdivided using a *topical pattern*, revealing two subideas: (A) commercial use, and (B) educational (i.e., noncommercial) use. Following this division, both of the subtopics are supported with specific details gathered by research. The result is shown in Figure 10.3.

The outline on "fair use" follows below, complete with introduction, conclusion, and a bibliography of key sources. You can use it as a model for your own speech outlines. In Appendix II you will find other model outlines, including complete manuscripts of the speeches as delivered, examples of note cards, and practical suggestions for delivering a speech from note cards.

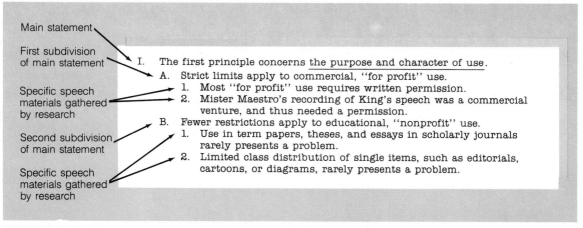

Main statement

First subdivision of main statement

Specific speech materials gathered by research

Second subdivision of main statement

Specific speech materials gathered by research

I. The first principle concerns <u>the purpose and character of use.</u>
  A. Strict limits apply to commercial, "for profit" use.
    1. Most "for profit" use requires written permission.
    2. Mister Maestro's recording of King's speech was a commercial venture, and thus needed a permission.
  B. Fewer restrictions apply to educational, "nonprofit" use.
    1. Use in term papers, theses, and essays in scholarly journals rarely presents a problem.
    2. Limited class distribution of single items, such as editorials, cartoons, or diagrams, rarely presents a problem.

FIGURE 10.3

Supporting a Main Point. In the outline on "fair use," the first main point of the body is subdivided into two subideas, namely, commercial and educational use. In turn, each of these subideas ideas is backed up with specific information and examples gathered by research. Observe in the example above how logical outlines move from the general to the specific—that is, from general statements (such as a main point) to concrete forms of support.

Model Outline

Title: The "Fair Use" of Copyrighted Material: What Every Communicator Should Know

Specific Purpose: To inform the audience of the four principles of fair use in American copyright law.

Pattern for Main Points of Body: Topical

INTRODUCTION

I. Soon after Dr. Martin Luther King delivered his "I Have a Dream" speech in August, 1963, the Mister Maestro record company began to sell phonograph recordings of the speech.
  A. The company had not secured permission from King to use the speech.
  B. The Southern Christian Leadership Conference, which was having the speech copyrighted, asked the courts to stop Mister Maestro from further sale of the recording.
  C. A federal court ruled that Mister Maestro's record was a violation of copyright law, and stopped further sale of the recording.

II. Copyright rules are determined by act of Congress, the latest version being the Copyright Act of 1976.
  A. The 1976 law sets the period of protection as the life of the author or creator, plus fifty years—the standard followed by most nations.
  B. The law protects original works of authorship that are fixed in a tangible form.

1. It protects the usual creative efforts, such as books, magazines, plays, music, photographs, films, and various forms of recordings.
2. It also protects such things as speeches, choreography, blueprints, computer programs, and even video game formats.
- C. The 1976 law provides for the "fair use" of copyrighted materials.
    1. In a 1985 copyright case, *Harper & Row v. Nation*, the U.S. Supreme Court cites with approval this brief definition of "fair use": "a privilege in others than the owner of copyright to use the copyrighted material in a reasonable manner without his consent."

Central Idea: There are four principles of "fair use" that public communicators should know.

III. In preview, the four principles can be summarized:
- A. The first concerns *the purpose and character of use*.
- B. The second concerns *the nature of the copyrighted work*.
- C. The third concerns *the percentage of the work used*.
- D. The fourth concerns *the effect of use on the work's market value*.

191

Chapter 10
Organizing
and Outlining
the Body
of the
Speech

BODY

I. The first principle concerns *the purpose and character of use*.
- A. Strict limits apply to commercial, "for profit" use.
    1. Most "for profit" use requires written permission.
    2. Mister Maestro's recording of King's speech was a commercial venture, and thus needed a permission.
- B. Fewer restrictions apply to educational, "nonprofit" use.
    1. Use in term papers, theses, and essays in scholarly journals rarely presents a problem.
    2. Limited class distribution of single items, such as editorials, cartoons, or diagrams, rarely presents a problem.

II. The second principle concerns *the nature of the copyrighted work*.
- A. Some works invite a high degree of use.
    1. Reference works, such as dictionaries and encyclopedias, invite use.
    2. Collected speeches, papers, and public documents invite use.
- B. Other works do not invite a high degree of use.
    1. Unpublished materials, such as letters, poems, or short stories, do not invite use.
    2. Some specialized works, such as privately printed reports, or institutional "working papers," do not invite use.

III. The third principle concerns *the percentage of the work used*.
- A. Using small proportions of some works is considered "fair."
    1. A quotation of 300 words from a short essay differs *proportionally* from a quote of the same length from a book.
    2. Commercial publishers have "fair use" rules for authors.
        a. From 50 to 150 words of use apply to an article or essay.
        b. From 200 to 500 words of use apply to books.

B. Certain kinds of works always require a permission for *commercial* use, no matter how small the proportion.
1. All quotations, even a single line, from poems, plays, and musical lyrics, require a written permission.
2. All reproductions of diagrams, cartoons, tables, photographs, maps, and the like require a written permission.

IV. The fourth principle concerns *the effect of use upon the market value of the copyrighted work.*
A. Unauthorized use that reduces market value can trigger legal action.
1. *The Nation* magazine once published key sections of a book by Gerald Ford before it was released by the publisher.
a. Although the percentage of direct quotes was small, the economic effect upon market value was documented.
b. The U.S. Supreme Court ruled in 1985 (in the case of *Harper & Row vs. Nation*), that *The Nation* had violated copyright law.
B. Unauthorized use that does not affect market value is less likely to trigger legal action.
1. Giving photocopies of a copyrighted speech to students in a speech analysis course is not likely to present a problem.
2. Making a small number of copies of an out-of-print item that is not being reissued by the publisher is not likely to present a problem.

CONCLUSION

I. The next time you make use of the copyrighted work of another person, recall the four principles of fair use recognized by American law.
A. First, consider the *purpose and character* of use—especially the matter of commercial vs. noncommercial use.
B. Second, consider the *nature of the copyrighted work*—especially the matter of works that invite use (such as dictionaries).
C. Third, consider the *percentage* of the work used.
D. Finally, consider the *effect of use upon the market value* of the copyrighted work.

II. Courts look at the four principles as interacting elements of one big picture.
A. A court can consider only one principle if that is the only issue contested.
B. In some cases, two, three, or even all four principles are considered in deciding the overall question of fair use.

III. You might save yourself a good deal of trouble by applying the "Golden Rule" of fair use: "Take not from others to such an extent and in such a manner that you would be resentful if they so took from you." (Cited by the U.S. Supreme Court in *Harper & Row v. Nation*, footnote 3 of the majority opinion, 53 *Law Week* 4565, 1985).

BIBLIOGRAPHY

Auer, J. Jeffery. "The Rules of Copyright for Students, Writers, and Teachers." *Communication Education* 30 (**July 1981**): 245–255.

Johnson, Donald F. *Copyright Handbook.* 2d ed. New York: Bowker, 1982.

U.S. Copyright Office. *The Nuts and Bolts of Copyright.* Circular R-1. Washington, D.C.: U.S. Government Printing Office, 1980.

193

Chapter 10
*Organizing
and Outlining
the Body
of the
Speech*

This Chapter in Brief

You are, in a sense, the architect of your speech, and the outline is your blueprint. In preparing this "rhetorical blueprint," you should follow standard outline form, as illustrated by Figure 10.1, and by the model outline above.

The main points of the body of your outline are the key ideas that support the central idea. They should be developed with these three considerations in mind: (1) avoid having too many main points (two to five are about right); (2) develop each main point fully (that is, keep the points in balance, spending about the same time discussing each one); and (3) choose the organizational pattern for the main points carefully (pick the pattern that is best suited for a given subject and audience).

The function of main points in an *informative* speech is to break the subject into small units of discourse that the audience can easily digest by being fed one "bite" at a time. After all of the main points are explained, the audience should comprehend the subject as a whole. In other words, *in informative outlining, the central idea states the whole to be explained, and the main points present the parts of that whole.* Patterns useful for organizing the parts of the whole include chronological, physical components, and topical.

The function of main points in a *persuasive* speech differs from that of an informative speech, for persuasion goes beyond the communication of knowledge to state key arguments, or reasons, why the speaker's opinion should be accepted. In other words, *in persuasion the central idea asserts a point of view, and the main points state the primary reasons why the audience should adopt that point of view.* Patterns useful for organizing the main reasons of a persuasive speech include chronological, physical components, topical, problem-solution, and cause-effect. The function of main points in both informative and persuasive speeches is summarized by Figure 10.2.

Once the main headings are determined, each becomes the superior statement of a speech unit. The speech units are then built around the main headings, using subideas and speech materials (evidence) as the raw materials of construction. The supporting materials of informative speeches serve to clarify, and the supporting materials of persuasive speeches serve to prove. An example of how a main point is "constructed" is shown by Figure 10.3, as well as by the model outlines in Appendix II of this text.

To complete the outline, you need to develop the introduction and the conclusion, and to plan the transitions from point to point throughout the speech. It is to these tasks that we now turn in the chapter that follows.

EXERCISES

1. Attend a campus or community program that features a speaker. Listen closely to the speaker's organization, paying special attention to the body of the speech. Can you identify the central idea? Are the main points of the body clearly stated? Is a consistent pattern of organization discernible? What, if anything, could the speaker do to improve the organization of the speech?

2. Browse through a recent issue of *Vital Speeches of the Day* in your school library. Select a speech that attracts your attention and read it through with a focus on organization. Does the speaker make the central idea clear? Are main points and a pattern of organization obvious to you, or must you reread the speech to locate important headings? Looking further through the issue, do you find that some speeches are better organized than others? Are those with clear organization easier to read and comprehend? What lessons concerning the organization of your own speeches do you get by examining the speeches of others?

3. The next time you make a persuasive speech outside of class, employ Monroe's "motivated sequence" as the basic plan for the speech. Study the motivated sequence before doing this by reading in your library from one of the editions of Monroe's *Principles and Types of Speech* (or see Ehninger et al. in the reading list below). Does the sequence "work well" for you? Do your listeners seem to follow the movement of your ideas easily? Was your speech effective?

SELECTED READINGS

Andersen, Kenneth E. *Persuasion: Theory and Practice*. 2d ed. Boston: Allyn and Bacon, 1978. Andersen discusses the organization of persuasive speeches in Chapter 8, including tips on planning organizational strategy depending upon the attitude of listeners toward your subject.

Braden, Waldo W., and Gehring, Mary Louise. *Speech Practices: A Resource Book for the Student of Public Speaking*. New York: Harper & Brothers, 1958. Chapter 3, "How Speakers Organize Their Speeches," includes several manuscripts of actual speeches for you to evaluate. On pages 33–34, for example, you will find a speech that uses the motivated sequence.

Campbell, Karlyn Kohrs. *The Rhetorical Act*. Belmont, Calif.: Wadsworth, 1982. Chapter 10, "The Resources of Organization," includes forms of organization, plus ideas for adapting the organization to the audience. Discusses the climax order of presentation.

Ehninger, Douglas; Gronbeck, Bruce E.; McKerrow, Ray E.; and Monroe, Alan H. *Principles and Types of Speech Communication*. 10th ed. Glenview, Ill.: Scott, Foresman, 1986. For a discussion of the motivated sequence, see Chapters 8, 9, and 17.

ENDNOTES

1. *Rhetorica ad Herennium*, in Thomas W. Benson and Michael H. Prosser, eds., *Readings in Classical Rhetoric* (Boston: Allyn and Bacon, 1969), p. 195.

2. John Dewey, *How We Think* (Boston: D. C. Heath, 1910), p. 72. Also in the 1933 edition, p. 107.

3. The motivated sequence was introduced by Alan H. Monroe in *Principles and Types of Speech*, first published in 1935. Coauthors have been added over the years, and the text now appears as D. Ehninger, B. Gronbeck, R. McKerrow, and A. Monroe, *Principles and Types of Speech Communication*, 10th ed. (Glenview, Ill.: Scott, Foresman, 1986).

4. For a review and discussion of a number of research reports on climax vs. anticlimax order, see Glen E. Mills, *Message Preparation: Analysis and Structure* (Indianapolis, Ind.: Bobbs-Merrill, 1966), pp. 62–69. Also, Kenneth E. Andersen, *Persuasion: Theory and Practice*, 2d ed. (Boston: Allyn and Bacon, 1978), pp. 171–172. For the research finding climax order more effective than anticlimax order, see Anthony J. Clark, "An Exploratory Study of Order Effect in Persuasive Communication," *Southern Speech Communication Journal* 39 (Summer 1974): 322–332.

195

Chapter 10
Organizing
and Outlining
the Body
of the
Speech

> *...An exordium [introduction] is a passage which brings the mind of the auditor into a proper condition to receive the rest of the speech. This will be accomplished if he becomes well-disposed, attentive, and receptive....The peroration is the end and conclusion of the whole speech; [here]...it will be proper...to touch on each single point and so to run briefly over all the arguments.*

—Cicero
De Inventione[1] (ca. 86 B.C.)

Chapter 11

INTRODUCTIONS, CONCLUSIONS, AND TRANSITIONS

W hen Doug Wentz, a student in a college public speaking class, decided to make a persuasive speech on why college students should be opposed to "blue laws" (Sunday closing laws), he first developed the body of the talk, outlined it carefully, then turned his attention to planning the introduction and the conclusion. After thinking it over, he decided to open the speech with an illustration based upon a personal experience, and to conclude with an example that led logically to his appeal for belief.[2] On the day of the speech, Wentz, the son of a minister, walked confidently to the front of the room, looked directly at his fellow classmates and, without apology or distracting comment, began his speech as follows:

> One Sunday a friend and I wanted to take a load of furniture to my home in Raleigh. After we loaded the car, on an unusually hot morning in late April, we began our journey. As soon as we left the campus we noticed that the gas gauge was pointing to "empty"—and the adventure began. We drove to the nearest gas station, but it was closed. We then drove to several other stations before being reminded that all stations within the city limits must stay closed on Sunday until one o'clock in the afternoon. That is Greensboro's "blue law." At this point we became very concerned, and decided to take a chance on finding something open on the interstate. Eventually, on I-85, we found an open gas station. This "wild goose chase" delayed our trip by almost an hour.

Wentz then presented the two main reasons why he opposed the Sunday closing law, namely, (1) the law was applied in an unequal and irrational manner, and (2) the law violated the U.S. Constitution in that it favored one religion over others. After presenting these points, and developing each one with specific speech materials, such as examples and statements from authority, Wentz concluded the speech with an account of how Sam Friedman, an orthodox Jewish merchant in another state, closed his store on Saturday—the Jewish Sabbath—but was arrested and fined for opening his store on Sunday. Moving from this true story, which Wentz had run across while researching his topic, the speaker ended with an appeal for belief.

> Now is the time for us to remember the first amendment of our Constitution, and to support the abolition of blue laws here, and throughout the United States. Let's face it. Is it fair to force a Jewish merchant, who observes Saturday as the Sabbath, to close on Sunday? Furthermore, is it rational in Greensboro to permit the sale of nonessentials, such as tobacco, before one o'clock on Sunday, but to deny travelers a necessity such as gasoline? Think about it.

In the discussion that followed, there was general agreement among the students in the class that the opening story used by Wentz had caught the attention of the audience and focused it upon the subject of the speech. Also, the members of the audience complimented the use of the example of the Jewish merchant in the conclusion, noting that it led logically to the final appeal for belief. At a minimum, the members of the audience expressed a willingness to "think about" what Wentz had said—a first step toward attitude change.

The experience of student speaker Wentz reminds us that our speech planning is not complete until we decide how we are going to begin and end our remarks. Even when the body of the speech is carefully organized and backed with details that are clear, persuasive, and interesting, the way we introduce that content to our listeners, and the way we focus upon key points at the end, are essential components of the rhetorical blueprint we call a speech outline. In addition, we need to pay attention to how we will move smoothly from point to point within the speech—that is, to our transitions—as we complete the preparation process. In order to examine these topics systematically, the discussion that follows is organized in three parts: planning introductions, planning conclusions, and planning transitions.

199

Chapter 11
Introductions,
Conclusions,
and
Transitions

I. Planning Introductions

The proverb that "a good beginning makes a good ending" is certainly applicable to public speaking, for the way in which you introduce your subject helps determine whether your audience responds in a positive or a negative way to you and to the content of the speech. As you prepare your introductions, however, keep in mind that they should not be too lengthy, or you will not have enough time remaining to develop the body of the speech adequately. How long should an introduction be? One study of fifty speeches reported an average of about 10 percent of the total length of a speech is given to the introduction.[3] Although the length will vary, depending on how much preparation is needed to secure a friendly and intelligent hearing, in general terms the 10 percent figure seems about right. This means that a classroom speech eight to ten minutes long should have an introduction of about one minute, a fifteen-minute speech should have an introduction between one and two minutes in length, and so forth.

Let us now examine speech introductions from three perspectives: the goals of introductions in general; the special problems of introductions to persuasive speeches; and procedures for outlining the introduction.

Goals of Introductions in General

As the quotation from Cicero states at the beginning of this chapter, the introduction is "a passage which brings the mind of the auditor into a proper condition to receive the rest of the speech." For both informative and persuasive speeches, this "proper condition" includes achieving at least three goals: catching the attention and interest of the audience; establishing speaker credibility; and winning an intelligent hearing. Let us examine these goals, together with some suggestions for achieving them.

Catch Attention and Interest

You would be wise to assume that your auditors will have a kind of "ho hum" attitude toward your topic at first, and that it is your responsibility to "wake them up'' and to motivate their interest in the subject. In doing this, keep these basic standards in mind:

The opening material should be *relevant* (that is, it should relate to the subject of your speech).

The opening material should be *fresh* (avoid stale stories, overused quotations, and trite remarks).

The opening material should be *appropriate* to the audience and occasion (among other things, it should not be offensive or embarrassing to your listeners).

Let us now examine some specific techniques you can use to gain attention and interest at the beginning of a speech.

Tell a Story

Audiences enjoy listening to interesting stories, examples, and illustrations. Your stories can come from your own experience or from the experiences of others that you learn about through research. Keep the stories brief, and tell them with directness and a friendly, animated delivery. For a good example of how to open a speech with a story, review the introductory remarks of Doug Wentz at the beginning of this chapter.

Use a Quotation

You can begin your speech with a direct quotation, such as words spoken by a great speaker or other person from American or world history, or a quote from a famous historical document, a work of literature, and so forth. This was the way Betsy Brown began her classroom speech in support of equal rights for women:

> "We hold these truths to be self-evident, that all men are created equal, that they are endowed by their Creator with certain unalienable Rights, that among these are Life, Liberty, and the pursuit of Happiness. That to secure these rights, Governments are instituted among Men, deriving their just powers from the consent of the governed." These words from the Declaration of Independence are very familiar to all of us. We know that it states that "all men are created equal." But I am not a *man*. I am a *woman*, and throughout history, women have been governed without giving their consent.[4]

Make a Dramatic or Startling Statement

You can "grab" attention with an opening that is dramatic or startling to your listeners. This does not mean that you should embarrass or upset the audience. Rather, it suggests that unusual statistics, examples, or statements concerning your topic can be effective in gaining immediate audience interest in what you have to say.

Robert H. Malott, chief executive officer of the FMC Corporation, used this technique in addressing a gathering of corporate and law firm attorneys on the subject, "America's Liability Explosion: Can We Afford the Cost?"[5] He focused listener concerns at the outset by noting that the United States has more lawsuits than any other society in the world. "Last year," he observed, "one out of fifteen Americans filed a private civil lawsuit of some kind. In all, over 13 million private civil lawsuits were filed in state and federal courts." Then, before presenting his problem-solution analysis of the situation, Malott startled his audience further with an actual case of a man with a history of coronary disease having a heart attack while trying to start a Sears lawnmower. The man sued Sears, arguing that it took too much effort to start the mower, and the jury awarded him over one million dollars in damages.

201

Chapter 11
*Introductions,
Conclusions,
and
Transitions*

Ask a Question

You can begin by asking a question, or series of questions, that pertain to your subject. For example, a speaker addressing the rising costs of automobile insurance might ask: "How many of you own a car, or plan to buy one as soon as you can afford it?" After a show of hands, the speaker could focus the attention of the audience on the expense of car ownership, including insurance costs. When employing this type of direct questioning, avoid asking about things that are private and personal. For instance, as a general rule you should not ask questions such as, "How many of you use drugs?" or "How many of you are atheists?"

A variation of this technique is the *rhetorical question*—that is, one to which the answer is obvious, and that listeners answer within their minds (such as, "If you won a million-dollar sweepstakes, would you accept the money?"). For example, a speaker could begin a talk on an effective health program involving diet and exercise by asking, "If a doctor offered you a pill that would make you feel healthy and happy for the rest of your life, would you consider taking it?" The speaker could then move to the central idea: "Today, I am offering you such a 'pill,' for I am going to explain a simple program of diet and exercise that will help you stay healthy."

Additional Ways of Beginning a Speech

There are many ways of starting a speech in addition to those explained above. Here are several suggestions; perhaps you will think of others.

Arouse curiosity. For example, a speech on ventriloquism could begin with the statement, "I have often wondered how ventriloquism works. Perhaps you, too, have wondered about this interesting art. Recently I interviewed two professional ventriloquists, and I want to tell you the 'secrets' they revealed."

Issue a challenge. A speech explaining techniques for improving one's study habits might open with a true story of a "C" student who became an "A" student after learning and using the plan to be explained. The speaker could then challenge the audience to listen closely and then apply the ideas of the speech...so that "You, too, can improve your overall grade point average."

Inject humor. Open with a humorous story, or joke, that is fitting to the subject, audience, and occasion. Research shows that humor, wisely used, not only catches attention, but also enhances *ethos* by showing the speaker to be a warm and friendly person.[6]

Refer to a current event. Use something "in the news."

Use a visual aid. Make use of objects, pictures, posters, etc.

Refer to sponsors of the event, to the special nature of the occasion, or to something said by an earlier speaker on the program.

Establish Speaker Credibility

Teachers of public speaking have known for more than 2000 years that audiences are influenced more by speakers whom they like and respect than by speakers who fail to win their good will and trust. As Chapter 1 explains, as early as 330 B.C., the Greek teacher Aristotle noted in the *Rhetoric* that speaker credibility, which he called *ethos*, was important to communication effectiveness. A speaker establishes *ethos*, Aristotle observed, by being perceived as a person of good will, intelligence, and trustworthiness. Contemporary studies in *ethos* confirm that Aristotle was correct. In fact, modern research concludes that it is more than ''important''—it is *crucial* to effectiveness in public speaking that the speaker's *ethos* be established with the audience.[7]

In the immediate speaking situation, at least three important factors interact to establish your credibility with your audience, namely: the attitude you display; the content of the introduction; and the way in which you deliver your opening remarks. Let us examine each briefly.

First, the presence of a *positive attitude* in speaking comes from selecting a subject that you are genuinely interested in, and one that you want to talk about. You then need to communicate your enthusiasm for the subject and your concern for the audience by introducing the speech in a sincere and friendly manner. At the outset, your auditors should feel that you have something worthwhile to say, and that you really want to say it.

Second, the *content of the introduction* should do more than catch attention and interest; it should also establish your qualifications to speak on the topic. In other words, you need to tactfully reveal your personal experience with the subject as well as highlights of the research you have done, so that your auditors will perceive that you know what you are talking about. For example, a speaker who is informing an audience on ''The Care and Cleaning of a Video Cassette Recorder,'' and who is trained as a television and VCR technician, should mention his or her qualifications in a friendly, casual way. On the other hand, a speech that is based primarily upon research—such as an informative talk on ''The Speech Preparation of John F. Kennedy''—could include the following as a part of the introduction:

> In studying how President John F. Kennedy prepared his speeches, I consulted several books in our library, including the biography *Kennedy*, by Theodore Sorensen, who was both an adviser and a speech writer to President Kennedy. In addition, I read two essays on Kennedy's speaking from the *Quarterly Journal of Speech*, and I interviewed a communication professor who teaches American Public Address, a course that includes a unit on Kennedy.

Finally, your *delivery*, including all physical and vocal elements (dress, visual directness, facial expression, gesture, tone of voice, etc.), plays a significant role in forming your image with the auditors. You can begin to establish a positive image by being neatly and appropriately dressed, walking confidently to the platform, looking directly at the audience, and beginning your speech in an assured and friendly manner. Do not apologize, hem and haw, or speak too rapidly. In a firm, clear voice that can be easily heard by all in the room, begin with the opening material that you have planned.

The effective communication of the three factors discussed here—positive attitude, appropriate content, and direct, confident delivery—will help you establish yourself with the audience as a person of good will, knowledge, and trustworthiness. Now let us examine the third goal that an introduction should meet.

203

Chapter 11
*Introductions,
Conclusions,
and
Transitions*

Win an Intelligent Hearing

Gaining attention and interest, and establishing your credibility, should lead naturally to the third goal of an introduction—securing an intelligent hearing. There are at least three things that you should consider doing to prepare your audience to listen wisely to the body of your speech: communicate the subject and purpose; explain terms and provide historical background as needed; and preview the main points to facilitate organized listening. You will not need to do all three of these in the introduction of every speech, nor will you always cover the points in the same sequence. Consider the possibilities, then make intelligent decisions based upon the specific situation.

First, an informed audience needs to know the *subject and central idea* of the speech. Typically, this is done by announcing the subject at the beginning of the introduction, and stating the central idea at the end of the introduction before presenting the body. To illustrate, Doug Wentz, whose speech on "blue laws" is discussed earlier in the chapter, let his audience know in his opening words that the general subject of his speech was Sunday closing laws. However, he did not state his central idea until near the end of the introduction when he announced, "Today I want to tell you why I believe that Sunday closing laws should be abolished."

Second, give your audience the *definitions and historical background* needed to understand the body of the speech. Not all speeches call for this assistance to the audience, but some do. For example, a talk by a communication teacher on "What Television Has Done to Political Rhetoric" might be helped by a definition of what the speaker means by "rhetoric" (recall from Chapter 1 the discussion of the use and abuse of the term). Or, an informative speech on "The Battle of Guilford Courthouse," the Revolutionary War clash fought in 1781 between British and American troops, might require in the introduction a short history of events leading up to the battle.

Finally, consider giving your audience a *preview of the main points* that you intend to develop in the body of the speech. The preview is particularly helpful in informative speaking, for it alerts the listener to the main points to come, and thereby aids retention of key ideas. Research supports the practice. For example, one study of the effects of speech summaries in informative speeches concludes that the inclusion in the introduction of a preview of main points of the body, and inclusion of a review of main points in the conclusion, "produced significantly greater amounts of comprehension" than did speeches that had no such summaries.[8] As a general rule, the preview goes at the end of the introduction after you have stated your central idea.

In summary, we have examined three goals of introductions in general, whether for informative or persuasive speeches. These are: gaining listener attention and interest; establishing speaker credibility; and winning an intelligent hearing. In persuasive speaking, however, special problems sometimes arise when the speaker is planning to discuss a controversial point of view. Let us look at how controversial subjects influence the planning of speech introductions.

Special Problems of Introductions to Persuasive Speeches

You face a special challenge when you prepare the introduction to a persuasive speech on a controversial subject—that is, one that has a specific purpose with which your audience disagrees. Common sense should alert you to the need for diplomacy if you are to "open the minds" of your auditors so that they will at least consider your proposal. Research confirms what common sense tells us.

For example, one study found that listeners who are told at the first that the speech is contrary to their point of view will reject the speaker as biased and change their opinions less than listeners given a more indirect, tactful introduction.[9] A second study reported similar results, concluding that "warning the subject about the intent of a communication has the effect of nullifying the persuasive influence of the communication." However, this second study found that revealing the purpose at the end does *not* nullify the persuasive influence of the communication.[10]

The rule of thumb that emerges is this: *in persuasive speaking, especially when the audience disagrees with you to a significant degree, you should exercise wisdom and tact in announcing your purpose.* Your strategy in complying with this rule should include attention to how you phrase the central idea, and where you locate the central idea in the speech. Let us consider each briefly.

Phrasing the Central Idea

In all persuasive speeches, and especially in controversial ones, avoid using blunt language such as "Today I intend to *persuade* you...," or "I am going to *prove to you that you are wrong*." Such language arouses listener opposition unnecessarily, thereby making effective persuasion much more difficult. Instead, reveal your purpose in a more diplomatic way. For example, a central idea urging smokers to quit smoking invites rejection if announced this way: "I want to remind you of how nasty and dangerous the smoking habit is, and actuate you to stop smoking." A more conciliatory phrasing might be: "Today let's look over some of the latest medical findings concerning the effect of smoking on our health."

Locating the Central Idea in the Outline

Another choice available to you in planning a persuasive speech is the location of the central idea in the overall outline. Most of the time the central idea goes in the introduction, just as it does for informative speaking. However, if stating the central idea in the introduction, no matter how diplomatically you phrase it, is going to arouse listener hostility, consider delaying the statement of purpose until later in the speech—such as placing it between main points in the body, or putting it in the conclusion. Also, consider omitting the preview of main points in order to permit a more gradual development of your case, and thereby win a more open-minded consideration of the main reasons that support your central idea.

To illustrate, in a three-point problem-solution-benefits outline, the central idea can be stated either between the problem and solution, or between the solution and benefits (as in the outline below). The *specific purpose* of the example that follows is "to actuate the members of my audience to stop smoking."

205

*Chapter 11
Introductions,
Conclusions,
and
Transitions*

BODY

I.   Smoking has become a major health *problem* in United States.

II. A *plan* has been developed by medical experts to help smokers break the habit.

Central Idea: You can reap the benefits of a smoke-free life by following the plan I have just explained.

III. Living "smoke-free" produces a number of health *benefits*.

The second alternative is to carefully construct your case in the body of the speech, then announce your central idea in the conclusion. In the outline above, for example, you could wait until the conclusion to state the central idea, reminding your listeners that the sensible thing to do, after considering the problem, a workable solution, and the health benefits that would result, is to *put the plan into effect* (that is, stop smoking). Similarly, you can follow a climax order of arrangement for the main points of the body (that is, building your case step by step, with your strongest argument at the end), then present your central idea at an appropriate place in the conclusion.

In a nutshell, for persuasive speeches, announce your central idea in the introduction, as usual, unless you have good reasons to delay revealing your goal. As a rule, these reasons include the need to provide an opportunity to build speaker *ethos* (especially to gain a friendly hearing) prior to announcing a controversial purpose, and to prepare your listeners to consider your purpose with a more open mind than they might if confronted with a frank statement of that purpose at the outset of the speech.

Outlining Introductions

Generally speaking, introductions are outlined according to the same rules of form and style that apply to the body. These rules, explained in detail in Chapters 9 and 10, include the use of complete sentences, stating only one key idea per point, and following a standard system of labeling (numbers and letters), spacing, and indenting. For an example, see Figure 11.1. Additional examples are found in the model outlines in Appendix II.

Introduction

I. Soon after Dr. Martin Luther King delivered his "I have a Dream" speech in August of 1963, the Mister Maestro record company began to sell phonograph recordings of the speech.
   A. The company had not secured permission from King to use the speech.
   B. The Southern Christian Leadership Conference, which was having the speech copyrighted, asked the courts to stop Mister Maestro from further sale of the recording.
   C. A federal court ruled that Mister Maestro's record was a violation of copyright law, and stopped further sale of the recording.

II. Copyright rules are determined by act of Congress, the latest version being the Copyright Act of 1976.
   A. The 1976 law sets the period of protection as the life of the author or creator, plus fifty years—the standard followed by most nations.
   B. The law protects original works of authorship that are fixed in a tangible form.
      1. It protects the usual creative efforts, such as books, magazines, plays, music, photographs, films, and various forms of recordings.
      2. It also protects such things as speeches, choreography, blueprints, computer programs, and even video game formats.
   C. The 1976 law provides for the "fair use" of copyrighted materials.
      1. In a 1985 copyright case, Harper & Row v. Nation, the U.S. Supreme Court cites with approval this brief definition of "fair use": "a privilege in others than the owner of copyright to use the copyrighted material in a reasonable manner without his consent."

Central Idea: There are four principles of "fair use" that public communicators should know.

III. In preview, the four principles can be summarized.
   A. The first concerns the purpose and character of use.
   B. The second concerns the nature of the copyrighted work.
   C. The third concerns the percentage of the work used.
   D. The fourth concerns the effect of use on the work's market value.

FIGURE 11.1

Outlining the Introduction. *The illustration above shows form and style for outlining an introduction. (The complete outline on "fair use" is in Chapter 10.) Notice that the central idea is clearly marked, but without the use of a label (that is, without a number or a letter); this permits the central idea to stand out visually, thereby reminding you that it is* the *superior point of the speech.*

Planning Introductions in Summary

You should plan your introductions so as to achieve the following three goals: (1) catch attention and interest with material that is relevant, fresh, and appropriate to the subject and audience; (2) establish your credibility by demonstrating that you are a trustworthy, knowledgeable person of good will; and (3) win an intelligent hearing by revealing your subject, defining terms and giving historical context when needed, announcing your central idea, and previewing the main points of the body. For persuasive speeches on subjects that might arouse listener hostility, pay special attention to planning a diplomatic intro-

Careful planning of the introduction and conclusion are essential to an effective speech. (Patrick Watson)

duction that will gain a fair hearing from your audience. Among other things, your strategy for opening a speech on a controversial subject should include wording the central idea in tactful language, and even delaying the announcement of your central idea until near the end of the speech.

II. Planning Conclusions

The conclusion is a special speech unit that should provide a "rhetorical rounding off" of the key ideas of the speech so that the audience is left with a sense of unity and completeness concerning your remarks. As with the introduction, the materials in the conclusion should be relevant to the topic, fresh, and appropriate to the audience and occasion. Also, the content of this "rounding off" should be both clear and interesting. You meet these standards by planning this unit carefully, just as you did when developing the introduction and the body of your speech. To leave matters to chance is to risk having an undesirable, ineffective ending.

Undesirable conclusions include those that are too abrupt as well as those that are too long. The abrupt conclusion leaves the audience with a feeling of incompleteness because the content of the speech has not been "tied together" well. And the long, rambling conclusion that leads nowhere causes the speaker to lose audience interest at a critical point in the speech. How long should a conclusion be? Earlier, we cited a study of fifty speeches that showed introductions to be about 10 percent of the length of a speech; this same study reported that conclusions averaged between 5 and 6 percent of the total length of a speech.[11] This seems about right, although a range of 5 to 10 percent might be more realistic, especially for summarizing complex topics or for developing appropriate appeals that end a persuasive speech on a controversial issue. Using the formula of 5 to 10 percent, the conclusion of a ten-minute speech would be thirty seconds to one minute long; the conclusion of a twenty-minute speech would be one to two minutes long; and so forth.

Let us now look at some specific suggestions for planning speech conclusions. We will discuss these suggestions according to the following three topics: the goals of conclusions in general; special problems of conclusions to persuasive speeches; and the outlining of the conclusion.

Goals of Conclusions in General

As you move from the body to the concluding unit, let your audience know that you are approaching the end of the speech. You can do this with your delivery (for example, slowing the speaking rate, pausing briefly, changing the tone of voice), with a transition comment (such as ''in finishing my remarks, let me stress three points''), or with a combination of the two. Having signaled your listeners that you are preparing to conclude the speech, you should try to achieve at least two goals, namely: lead the audience to focus upon, and to remember, the important points of the speech; and wrap things up with a creative ''finishing touch'' that is relevant to the subject of the speech.

Reinforce and Focus on Important Points

The concluding unit is not the place to develop new points; rather, it is the place to restate and reinforce the points that you have already covered and that you want the audience to remember. This can be done by either a general review of the central idea or by a more specific summary of your central idea and main points.

Some speeches do not call for a thorough summary in the conclusion. For example, a pep talk delivered at a school rally, a patriotic speech delivered on the Fourth of July, or a speech praising the life of some great person could be concluded effectively with a general statement that emphasized the theme of the speech without going into detail. This is what student speaker David Cox did to end his speech on the life of Benjamin Franklin:

> Benjamin Franklin's life symbolizes many things to Americans. He is a symbol of the universal genius who succeeded in science, in business, and as a statesman. There have, of course, been a number of Americans who have excelled in *one* field; few have been as successful in *many* fields as was the remarkable Ben Franklin.[12]

Often, a more specific summary is needed, especially for informative speeches that cover a number of points that the speaker wants the audience to retain. This form of conclusion in a speech to inform is illustrated by Figure 11.2.

In addition, specific summaries are useful when concluding persuasive speeches that have presented key arguments the speaker hopes to impress upon the audience. An example of this is in a persuasive speech delivered by student Angelia Moon to her public speaking class. Moon's purpose was to

Conclusion

I. The next time you make use of the copyrighted work of another person, recall the four principles of fair use recognized by American law.
   A. First, consider the <u>purpose and character</u> of use—especially the matter of commercial vs. noncommercial use.
   B. Second, consider the <u>nature of the copyrighted work</u>—especially the matter of works that invite use (such as dictionaries).
   C. Third, consider the <u>percentage</u> of the work used.
   D. Finally, consider the <u>effect of use upon the market value</u> of the copyrighted work.

II. Courts look at the four principles as interacting elements of one big picture.
   A. A court can consider only one principle if that is the only issue contested.
   B. In some cases, two, three, or even all four principles are considered in deciding the overall question of fair use.

III. You might save yourself a good deal of trouble by applying the "Golden Rule" of fair use: "Take not from others to such an extent and in such a manner that you would be resentful if they so took from you." (Cited by the U.S. Supreme Court in <u>Harper & Row v. Nation</u>, footnote 3 of the majority opinion, 53 <u>Law Week</u> 4565, 1985).

FIGURE 11.2

Outlining the Conclusion. *This illustration shows form and style for outlining a conclusion. It is from the same outline on "fair use" employed in Figure 11.1 to illustrate an introduction. (The complete outline is in Chapter 10.)*

create support for the Guilford County (North Carolina) Humane Society. Observe that she uses the transition phrase, "in summary," to let the audience know that she is concluding the speech (also note her "finishing touch" concerning the adoption of a puppy).

> In summary, please remember three services that the Humane Society of Guilford County offers. The first service is investigative work, the second is providing financial aid, and the third is providing education and information services to the public.
>
> I hope this talk has helped you appreciate the work of the Humane Society of Guilford County. I know it has for me, because when I chose this project I did not know the wide range of services offered. Not only have I become more aware of the Society's work—but also, I have become directly involved...by adopting a Siberian Husky puppy![13]

End with a Creative "Finishing Touch"

Early in the nineteenth century, English rhetorician Richard Whately warned his students against permitting their speeches to end "in a feeble and spiritless manner, like a half-extinguished candle going out in smoke."[14] Whately's warning is timeless, for one of the major weaknesses of student speeches (and many other speeches as well) is the "feeble" and "spiritless" ending. To avoid the conclusion that is a "let down" to the audience, take a few extra moments of preparation time to develop a finishing touch that supports the theme of the speech. Here are some suggestions.

Tell a Story

Because people enjoy listening to interesting stories, you will find narratives to be effective rhetorical devices, whether for opening a speech, for illustrating a point in the body, or for concluding a speech. For example, a speech that has explained a life-saving technique could conclude with a true story of how a person who had just learned the technique saved the life of a friend. Or a persuasive speech in support of fraternities and sororities could end with an account of how a timid, shy underachiever was motivated to succeed by his fraternity brothers (or her sorority sisters), and is now a success in his or her profession.

Use a Quotation

An appropriate quotation can be an effective way of ending a speech. Note that this is the method used to conclude the informative speech on "fair use" in copyright law (see Figure 11.2). Also, it was the way that student speaker Elinor Vaughan ended her inspirational talk on the life of Eleanor Roosevelt:

> In her centennial year, [Mrs. Roosevelt] was remembered by Fredrica Goodman, director of the Eleanor Roosevelt Centennial Commission, in these words: "She is a personal heroine to me. She was a role model for the future—so ahead of her time. And she did it despite every possible roadblock."

Employ Humor

Using relevant humor to emphasize or illustrate your central idea, a major point, or your appeal for belief or action, is another useful technique for concluding a speech. This is what D. Wayne Calloway, Chairman of the Board of PepsiCo, Inc., did to end his speech to the Better Business Bureau of Winston-Salem, North Carolina. Entitled "The Noah Principle and the Public Sector," Calloway's central idea was that business people should become more actively involved in helping solve the problems of society, especially the problems of local communities. After urging the members of his audience to "start—and start now" in helping solve social problems, Calloway concluded as follows.

> Some years after World War II, Winston Churchill was speaking to a group of people seated in a room much like this one. The person who introduced him made a good-natured reference to Churchill's well-known fondness for alcoholic beverages.
> He said: "If all the spirits Sir Winston has consumed were poured into this room, they'd reach to up here"—and he drew an imaginary line on the wall some six or seven feet from the floor.
> When Sir Winston reached the podium, he looked at the imaginary line and glanced up to the ceiling. He then sighed and said, "Ah—so much to be done and so little time in which to do it."
> Well, ladies and gentlemen, there is so much to be done and *so little time* in which to do it. But *we* are results-oriented people. If we keep that

same orientation when dealing with public issues—if we recognize the unique talents that we can bring to bear on these problems and opportunities—if we're firm—if we're focussed—if we're committed—then we really can make a better world.[15]

211

Chapter 11
Introductions,
Conclusions,
and
Transitions

Additional Ways of Concluding a Speech

There are numerous additional ways to end a speech, other than those mentioned above. Here are some of them.

Employ a dramatic or striking statement or statistic.

Use a personal reference or experience.

Use a historical illustration or allusion.

Relate the conclusion to the content of the introduction.

Show how a challenge issued earlier in the speech can be met.

Appeal for belief, or action, or both.

Special Problems of Conclusions to Persuasive Speeches

The conclusion to a persuasive speech differs from that of an informative speech in a significant way, namely, in its goal of trying to change attitudes, behavior, or both. The conclusion is where you make your proposed change specific and appeal for its acceptance.

If your speech is one to convince, you need to emphasize, in a tactful way, the viewpoint you wish your listeners to accept; if your speech is one to actuate, your conclusion should make the recommended action clear and specific. For example, if you want the members of your audience to write a letter of support or protest, tell them exactly where to write (give out papers with the address listed, or put the information on the board; you can even supply addressed envelopes if the audience is not too large). If you want them to join an organization, bring a supply of membership applications. The point is that you should not leave appeals to belief or action in a state of vagueness and uncertainty.

Outlining Conclusions

As with introductions, conclusions are outlined according to standard rules of form and style. These rules include the use of complete sentences for all points, stating only one key idea per point, and following a standard system of labeling, spacing, and indenting. For an example, see Figure 11.2. Additional examples are found in the model outlines in Appendix II.

Planning Conclusions in Summary

You should plan your conclusions with the goals of focusing upon and reinforcing the central idea and important points of the speech, and rounding off the speech smoothly with a "finishing touch" (such as a relevant and interesting story, quotation, or bit of humor). For conclusions to persuasive speeches you need to include an effective appeal for belief or action. In particular, for the speech to actuate, give your listeners some specific recommendations concerning the action they need to take.

Now that you have prepared and outlined the entire speech—introduction, body, and conclusion—you are almost ready to begin rehearsals prior to delivery. Only one step remains, namely, planning your transitions.

III. Planning Transitions

After outlining your speech thoroughly, *you* know where the introduction ends and the body begins, which points are main points and which are supporting points, where the body ends and the conclusion begins, and so forth. However, this does not mean that your listeners will comprehend these steps as you do. After all, they do not have your outline before them, and they have not thought the issues through exactly as you have when preparing the speech. Therefore, it is up to you to help your listeners *orally* by using transitions that tie ideas together smoothly, and that emphasize the points you want them to focus upon.

Transitions can be defined as *the words, phrases, and sentences you employ in the delivered speech (1) to move smoothly and coherently from point to point and from section to section, and (2) to call attention to important points in the speech.* Let us look at some practical ideas for using both types of transitions.

Transitions That Smooth the Way

The skillful use of transitions during delivery provides your audience with a sense of coherent, logical movement from idea to idea within the speech. Examples of words and short phrases that can help you "smooth the way" verbally include: *meanwhile, however, therefore, accordingly, consequently, as a result, for example, furthermore, in addition to, for instance, to illustrate*, and *finally*. Longer transitions include phrases and sentences such as the following: *let me explain; there is one final point to consider; let me define that term; with these facts in mind; now, we turn our attention to the history of the problem; the time has come to ask, what can you do to help?*

The use of transitions can be shown by writing them down. Let us do this with point one from the introduction of the outline on "fair use" as it might be spoken from the outline (see Figure 11.1). The transitions below are in parentheses and in boldface type.

In 1963, soon after Dr. Martin Luther King delivered his eloquent "I Have a Dream" speech, a record company known as Mister Maestro decided to manufacture and sell recordings of the speech. (**Unfortunately...**) the officials of that company had failed to secure a permission from Dr. King to sell these recordings. (**As a consequence...**) the Southern Christian Leadership Conference, which was having the speech copyrighted, went to court to stop Mister Maestro from further sale of the records. (**Because of this legal action**...) Mister Maestro had to stop selling the records, (**for**...) the federal court ruled that the recording was protected by U.S. copyright law.

213

*Chapter 11
Introductions,
Conclusions,
and
Transitions*

As this example shows, transitions help the audience think "smoothly" from point to point. Here are two suggestions for employing speech transitions.

Use a variety of words and phrases. A speaker who uses the same transition (or a limited number of transitions) over and over again will distract the listener from the content of the speech. An example is the speaker who ends each point with "Okay" or "Now," or "So much for that."

Cultivate the practice of thinking and saying transitions "automatically." Many speakers find that they can employ transitions in a natural manner as they speak simply by being mentally aware of the need for them (in other words, they do not have to write them down as the speech is being outlined). This habitual "automatic" use of transitions is the goal you should work to achieve.

Transitions That Identify Key Points

The second type of transitions are the ones that orally call attention to important points, such as the main headings of the body. Sometimes described as "verbal signposts," these transitions include such obvious statements as "The first point is," "The second point is," "The third point is," and so forth. More elaborate forms of verbal signposts include: "First, let us consider the seriousness of the problem," "Second, let us examine a plan that would solve the problem," and "Finally, here are two major benefits that will result if this solution is put into effect."

As you can see, this technique is easy to follow. However, *you do need to remember to do it.* For a start, practice using "verbal signposts" when rehearsing your speech; also, if you use notes, you can underline in red (or employ a similar visual cue) such signpost words as "first," "second," "third," on the note card to remind you to say them aloud. However you do it, keep in mind that *oral organization* helps your audience follow your points, keep up with your content, and identify and retain important ideas.

To see how the introduction and conclusion of the outline on "fair use" fit with the body of the speech, review the complete outline in Chapter 10. (Additional speech outlines that illustrate how to organize introductions and conclusions can be found in Appendix II.)

This Chapter in Brief

In summary, this chapter has explained the basics of how to introduce and conclude a speech effectively, and how to use transition terms in your speaking. *Introductions* in general should be planned to achieve three basic goals: (1) catch listener attention and interest with relevant, fresh, and appropriate opening material (such as a story, a quotation, or a startling statement); (2)

establish speaker credibility by revealing yourself to the audience as a person of intelligence, integrity, and good will (this is done by the attitude you display, the content of your remarks, and the way you deliver those remarks); and (3) win an intelligent hearing by revealing your subject and purpose, by providing appropriate explanations, definitions, and historical background on your topic, and by presenting a preview of the main points of the body of the speech. Special problems of introducing persuasive speeches include phrasing the central idea in diplomatic language, and deciding when to announce the central idea in the speech (whether in the introduction, somewhere in the body, or at the end) so that it will have the maximum persuasive effect.

The *conclusion* provides a rounding off of the speech. In general, conclusions should achieve two goals: (1) focus upon and reinforce important points (such as by restatement of the central idea and a summary of the main points of the body); and (2) provide a creative ending that is both relevant to the topic and interesting to the listener (for example, an appropriate story, quotation, or touch of humor). Persuasive speeches have the added challenge of appealing for belief, or action, or both.

Finally, *transitions* should be employed for two main purposes: (1) to smooth the movement from point to point in the speech, and (2) as verbal signposts that identify and emphasize key points in the speech.

We are now ready to turn our attention to the delivery of the speech. This is done in the two chapters that follow where we consider language in public speaking, and the vocal and physical elements of delivery.

EXERCISES

1. During the next round or two of classroom speeches, take notes on the methods used by your classmates to introduce and conclude their speeches. What types of introductions and conclusions were used most often? In your opinion, what types of introductions and conclusions were most effective in achieving their respective goals? What do your findings suggest about how you can improve the planning of introductions and conclusions for your own speeches?

2. Secure a recent issue of *Vital Speeches of the Day* from your school library. Note the method of introduction and the method of conclusion for each speech in the issue. What type of introduction catches your attention and interest best? Were the conclusions well-developed with summaries and clear appeals for belief or action?

3. Carefully read two or three complete speeches in *Vital Speeches of the Day* or from the appendices in this textbook, paying close attention to the transitions used by the speakers. Select the best speech, photocopy it, and underline each transition word, phrase, and sentence. Notice how "rough" the connection between and among ideas would be if these transitions were deleted.

SELECTED READINGS

Golden, James L., Berquist, Goodwin, F., and Coleman, William E. *The Rhetoric of Western Thought.* 4th ed. Dubuque, Ia.: Kendall/Hunt, 1989. See the essay on "The

Persuasive Power of Ethos and Image,'' pp. 523–534, for an excellent summary of contemporary research on the importance of establishing and maintaining your credibility when speaking.

Lucas, Stephen E. *The Art of Public Speaking.* 3d ed. New York: Random House, 1989. Lucas explains transitions on pp. 158–162, and gives examples of a number of ways to introduce and conclude a speech in Chapter 8, ''Beginning and Ending the Speech.''

McCroskey, James C. *An Introduction to Rhetorical Communication.* 4th ed. Englewood Cliffs, N.J.: Prentice-Hall, 1982. In Chapter 12, ''Introducing and Concluding Messages in Rhetorical Communication,'' McCroskey provides good advice, much of it based upon modern research, on strategies for beginning and ending a speech.

Mills, Glen E. *Message Preparation: Analysis and Structure.* Indianapolis, Ind.: Bobbs-Merrill, 1966. See Chapter 8, ''Introductions, Conclusions, and Transitions,'' for a discussion of various types of speech introductions and conclusions, together with examples of each.

215

*Chapter 11
Introductions,
Conclusions,
and
Transitions*

ENDNOTES

1. The quotations from Cicero's *De Inventione* are from Thomas W. Benson and Michael H. Prosser, *Readings in Classical Rhetoric* (Boston: Allyn and Bacon, 1969), pp. 197 and 204.
2. Doug Wentz, ''Abolish the Blue Law,'' delivered in the advanced public speaking course, University of North Carolina at Greensboro, April 1987. (Note: A few months following the delivery of this speech, the Greensboro City Council repealed the blue law. Obviously, Wentz was not the only person in the community unhappy with the ordinance.)
3. Edd Miller, ''Speech Introductions and Conclusions,'' *Quarterly Journal of Speech* 32 (April 1946): 181–183. Miller found that length of introductions varied from 1 percent to 38 percent of the entire speech, with an average of 9.8 percent.
4. Betsy Brown, ''The Equal Rights Amendment,'' delivered in the advanced public speaking course, University of North Carolina at Greensboro, April 1982.
5. Robert H. Malott, ''America's Liability Explosion: Can We Afford the Cost?'' Delivered in Chicago on October 10, 1985. In *Representative American Speeches: 1985–1986*, Owen Peterson, ed. (New York: H. W. Wilson, 1986), p. 135.
6. Charles R. Gruner, ''Advice to the Beginning Speaker on Using Humor—What the Research Tells Us,'' *Communication Education* 34 (April 1985): 142–147.
7. For a summary of research on *ethos* that includes practical suggestions for the modern speaker, see James L. Golden, Goodwin F. Berquist, and William E. Coleman, *The Rhetoric of Western Thought*, 4th ed. (Dubuque, Iowa: Kendall/Hunt, 1989), pp. 523–534.
8. John E. Baird, Jr., ''The Effects of Speech Summaries upon Audience Comprehension of Expository Speeches of Varying Quality and Complexity,'' *Central States Speech Journal* 25 (Summer 1974): 119–127, at 124.
9. Jane Allyn and Leon Festinger, ''The Effectiveness of Unanticipated Persuasive Communications,'' *Journal of Abnormal and Social Psychology* 62 (January 1961): 35–40.
10. C. A. Kiesler and S. B. Kiesler, ''Role of Forewarning in Persuasive Communications,'' *Journal of Abnormal and Social Psychology* 68 (May 1964): 547–549.
11. Miller, op. cit., p. 182.
12. David G. Cox, ''Benjamin Franklin,'' conclusion adapted from an outline of the

speech, delivered in the advanced public speaking course, University of North Carolina at Greensboro, May 1969.

13. Angelia Moon, "Three Services of the Humane Society of Guilford County," delivered in the advanced public speaking course, University of North Carolina at Greensboro, October 1984.

14. Richard Whately, *Elements of Rhetoric* (James Monroe and Company, 1858), pp. 207–208.

15. D. Wayne Calloway, "The Noah Principle and the Public Sector," delivered in Winston-Salem, N.C., on January 29, 1987. In *Vital Speeches of the Day* 53 (April 1, 1987): 359–360.

PART III

Speech Presentation

But yet what helpeth it though we can find good reasons, and know how to place them, if we have not apt words and picked sentences, to commend the whole matter.

—Thomas Wilson,
The Art of Rhetorique (1553)[1]

Chapter 12

LANGUAGE IN PUBLIC SPEAKING

*I*n the preceding chapters we examined the process of speech preparation, beginning with audience analysis and subject choice, continuing through research and the refinement of your ideas, to the final stage of developing a clear, logical outline of what you plan to say. We are now ready to discuss the culmination of your efforts—the presentation of the speech to your audience. Speech presentation depends upon two things: your use of language and your use of voice and body to deliver your message to others. In this chapter we focus on the language component; we will discuss delivery in the chapter that follows.

In speechmaking, language serves two key functions: the *semantic function*, concerning the communication of meaning; and the *stylistic function*, concerning the clarity, freshness, and impressiveness of the words you use. Stated another way, semantics explains how words work, and style explains how words are used to enhance the message (that is, to increase clarity and persuasiveness). Let us look first at the semantic function.

I. Semantics: Language and the Communication of Meaning

As we examine language and the communication of meaning, at least two important topics deserve our attention. First, we need to understand basic semantic principles of how words work, including what language does and does not do. Second, we need to apply those semantic principles to the overall process of speech preparation and delivery. Let us begin by considering how words work.

The Function of Words

Recall that some basic semantic principles were introduced during the discussion of the communication process in Chapter 4. For instance, Chapter 4 points out that words are *symbols*, and should not be confused with what they symbolize. A symbol can be explained as a "substitute stimulus," thus emphasizing that it is not the same as what it stands for. To illustrate, the word "pencil" is not the same as an actual pencil, and the word "dollar" is not the same as a dollar bill. We now need to expand upon the earlier discussion by examining more fully the difference between symbols and what they stand for, and by applying semantic principles to the public speaking situation.

To begin with, the thing that a word stands for is called the *referent*. A referent can be an object, an action, concept, or a feeling that we have inside ourselves. For example, the referent for the word "cat" is an object (a real cat), the referent for "changing a tire" is an action (the process of changing a tire), the referent for a verbal description of a plan for redecorating a room is the concept in the decorator's head, and the referent for the words "stomach ache" is a feeling (the nausea and pain you feel inside yourself). Semanticists sometimes distinguish between symbol and referent by comparing words to maps and referents to the territories that maps represent. This comparison helps us to understand that just a map is not the same as the territory it depicts, a word is not the same as its referent.[2]

Furthermore, there is no necessary connection between a word and its referent. The labels we assign to things, processes, concepts, and feelings are arbitrary, for they are based on custom and social agreement, not on some universal law. A pig is called a "pig" not because it is required, but because we agree to a particular label so that we can talk about the creature. In fact, we can even utter words that have no referent ("I saw a fire-eating dragon yesterday"), and we can use words so as to distort the referent (such as "I saw John with Mary at the dance last night" when, in fact, you saw John with Susan). In brief, there is no requirement that a referent be symbolized with a certain word, and there is no automatic mechanism in language use that requires words to be based on facts.[3]

In addition, each human user of language is different from every other, for no two people are exactly the same in mental and physical characteristics, life experiences, educational background, and so on. Because of our differences, no two of us respond to stimuli—including words—in exactly the same way. For example, "I have a new dog" means something different to the child who speaks of his new pet, the parent who worries about taking care of the creature, and the neighbor who moans as he begins to think of fencing in his vegetable garden. To illustrate further, the statement "We are having liver for lunch today" evokes a positive response from those who find liver delicious, and a negative response from those who find liver unappetizing.

Keeping the above concepts in mind, we can now state a basic semantic principle concerning the function of words, namely: *words do not literally transfer meaning from one person to another; rather, words are symbols, and their function is to stir up meaning already present in the mind of the listener.* Put another way, the words that you use when speaking do not "inject" meaning into the heads of your listeners. Instead, the words you use stimulate listeners who, in turn, assign meaning from within themselves. This is why semanticists emphasize that meaning does not exist within words, but within people.[4] When we consider that no two people are exactly the same, we can conclude that no two members of any audience will assign exactly the same meaning to what you say.

In summary, we have noted the following principles of semantics:

1 Words are symbols that are supposed to stand for something. The "something" that words stand for is called the referent, and can consist of objects, actions, concepts, and feelings.

2 There is no necessary connection between words and referents. In fact, we can use words that have no referent, or that distort or falsify the referent.

3 Each person who uses words is different from every other person; thus, no two people will respond to a word in exactly the same way.

4 Words cannot transfer meaning from one mind to another; instead, words stir up meaning already present in the mind of the listener. Because of this, semanticists emphasize that meaning does not exist within words, but within people.

Let us now examine some implications of these principles of semantics for your use of language in public speaking.

One of the most important applications of semantic principles to public speaking concerns how carefully you base the content of the speech on factual information. Semanticists underscore this concern for fact-based speaking by saying that just as a map should fit the territory, the words we use should fit reality. The maker of accurate maps checks the territory first, and sketches the map second; similarly, the responsible speaker gets the facts first, and speaks second.[5] Semantics, then, provides additional support for the view emphasized throughout this text that your speaking should be founded upon sound evidence and reasoning.

Second, semantics helps us understand and improve the clarity of our communication with the audience. It does this by explaining how words work during the communication process. In Chapter 4, *communication* is defined as *the process by which humans attempt to share thoughts, attitudes, and feelings with one another*. The tools for communicating your thoughts, attitudes, and feelings are voice, bodily movement, and language. Using these tools, you stir up meaning within the listener. If this meaning is similar to your own, you have communicated successfully; if it is not, misunderstanding occurs. For example, "Meet me in the lobby at noon" sounds clear. However, if the building that is agreed upon has two or more lobbies, the word "lobby" can stir up different mental images in the minds of the persons involved. Consequently, one group might wait in "Lobby A" while another group waits in "Lobby B."

Keeping the principles of semantics in mind, let us now examine some recommendations for using language in your speaking, not only to be clear, but also to be more persuasive.

II. Style: Using Language Effectively

An outstanding teacher of public address has defined style as the speaker's "characteristic way of using the resources of the English language."[6] Put another way, your speaking style refers to how you use language to express your ideas to your audience. Your language can be simple or complex, clear or obscure, concrete or abstract, dull or colorful, and so forth. For example, a person who says, "I prefer gregariousness to monastic isolation," is using an awkward and complex style; the same idea can be expressed in a clear, simple style by saying, "I enjoy being with people." Three elements of style that are of particular concern to public speakers are *appropriateness, clarity*, and *vividness*. Let us consider each of them.

Appropriateness

Throughout this text we have emphasized that speech subjects, purposes, and content should be suitable to three things: the speaker, the audience, and the occasion. These same three areas of appropriateness should also be applied to your speaking style. To begin with, your language should be suitable to you, the speaker. That is, you should speak in a style that is natural for you, and not pretend to be someone you are not. This does not mean that a speaker should excuse a poor vocabulary or incorrect grammar by claiming that they are "natural" to him or her. To the contrary, speakers should cultivate a natural style based upon an adequate vocabulary and correct use of grammar. Work to develop a style of speaking that is suitable to an educated person yet is neither substandard in vocabulary and correctness nor highly complex and difficult to follow.

Also, your language should be appropriate to your audience. As the chapter on audience analysis emphasizes, your speech planning should be centered on audience knowledge and attitudes. After considering how much an audience knows about a subject and key demographic factors such as age and educational level, you should phrase your ideas in a vocabulary that the audience will understand. For example, a scientist speaking to fellow scientists at a professional meeting might say that "as a result of a series of empirical tests, the hypothesis is confirmed." However, when explaining the same research to a civic club, the scientist might say, "We tested the procedure several times, and each time it worked."

In addition to using a vocabulary that your listeners can understand, choose words that the audience will accept as appropriate for public discussion. In practical terms, this means avoid language that the audience will perceive as vulgar, embarrassing, racist, sexist, or otherwise offensive. You can, for instance, eliminate sexist language from your thinking and speaking by combining awareness of the problem with practice in substituting nonsexist terms. Here are some examples: instead of "mankind" say "humankind," or "the human race"; instead of "workman" say "worker"; instead of "policeman" say "police officer"; instead of "chairman," say "chairperson" or "moderator"; and instead of "man-hours," say "work-hours."[7]

Third, you should use a speaking style that is appropriate to the occasion. When the occasion calls for an informative speech, such as a classroom lecture or a technical presentation to a group of new employees, use a clear, plain style. On the other hand, for persuasive speeches you have more flexibility in the use of words that stir the imagination and motivate attitude change. For example, when Winston Churchill first addressed the British Parliament as prime minister upon England's entry into World War II, it was appropriate for him to challenge his countrymen by saying, "I have nothing to offer but blood, toil, tears and sweat." However, such vivid language would be out of place for a teacher of automobile mechanics trying to challenge a class of beginning students. A more fitting choice of words for such a class would be, "Students, learning to be a good mechanic requires hard work—but you can do it!"

Clarity

In the *Rhetoric*, Aristotle comments that "a good style is, first of all, clear. The proof is that language which does not convey a clear meaning fails to perform the very function of language."[8] This advice, while ancient, is not out-of-date, for clarity remains a basic requirement of effective communication. Furthermore, a modern study of speaker credibility found that "messages of high credibility reflected a clearer oral style than did messages of low credibility sources."[9] In other words, audiences have a higher respect for speakers who are clear than for those who are not.

Winston Churchill, former British prime minister, was a master of vivid language. In this speech in the United States House of Representatives, he told Congress, "I have come here not for gold, but for steel; not for favors, but for equipment." (UPI/Bettmann Newsphotos)

In order to be clear on a subject, you should first understand it thoroughly yourself. After you have mastered the material, make your plans to communicate it by using language that meets the standards of *simplicity, familiarity,* and *concreteness.* Let us examine these standards more fully.

Use Simple Language

Speaking in simple language does not mean that you should use a vocabulary suitable only for small children. Rather, it means that, for most audiences, the simple term is preferable to the complex one. For instance, instead of saying "they were involved in an altercation," the speaker could say, "they had a fight." Similarly, instead of saying "she was bedecked in dazzling attire," the speaker could say, "she wore a beautiful dress."

Many outstanding speakers, such as Abraham Lincoln and Franklin Roosevelt, used plain words for powerful effect. For instance, Lincoln's conclusion to the "Gettysburg Address" is well known for its simple eloquence: "...that this nation, under God, shall have a new birth of freedom—and that government of the people, by the people, for the people shall not perish from the earth." Likewise, in January, 1937, in his Second Inaugural Address, President Franklin Roosevelt expressed in simple language the need for Americans to continue to struggle against the great depression: "I see one-third of a nation ill-housed, ill-clad, ill-nourished." Continuing in this plain style: "It is not in despair that I paint you that picture. I paint it for you in hope—because the

Nation, seeing and understanding the injustice in it, proposes to paint it out.''[10]

Use Familiar Language

The use of familiar words means that you "talk the language of your listeners." By using words familiar to your audience, you can stir up the meanings that you intend, thus facilitating communication, clarity, and accuracy. As you know from your own listening experience, unfamiliar words and technical jargon can leave an audience confused. For example, "to oxidize" means "to rust." Because "oxidize" is not a familiar term to many people, the speaker who says "the metal was heavily oxidized" is not as clear as the one who says, "the metal was covered with rust."

When preparing a speech, therefore, be sure to consider the complexity of the subject matter and the level of audience acquaintance with it. Based on this information, employ a vocabulary that the audience will understand. For instance, a public speaking teacher delivering a lecture on speech organization could use the unfamiliar, classical terms "exordium" and "proem" to discuss the beginning and ending of a speech. Obviously, the more familiar terms "introduction" and "conclusion" would be much clearer. Or, the minister who discusses religious unity by saying "I support ecumenism rather than schism" would be clearer if he or she said, "I support harmony and unity rather than division among religious groups."

Use Concrete Language

In addition to using words that are simple and familiar, you can use concrete language to help make your speeches clear. This means to be specific whenever possible, avoiding language that is abstract and vague. For instance, "I spent a bundle on my car" is not as specific—and therefore is not as clear—as "I spent three hundred dollars on a new set of tires for my car." Concrete language strengthens your communication by stirring up specific meaning in the minds of your listeners, thereby helping them visualize the referent that you have in mind. The result is a more precise and more complete shared meaning between you and the listener. Ask yourself, while reading the examples below, which ones stir the more precise meaning in your head.

Abstract: "He handed her the doohickey."
Concrete: "He handed her the tape measure."

Abstract: "She is in business."
Concrete: "She owns and manages the Southside Furniture Company."

Abstract: "I urge you to do something to help the homeless."
Concrete: "Join with me by volunteering at least one Saturday each month to help Habitat for Humanity construct low-cost housing in our town."

Concrete language does more than make a message clear—it can also make the message more honest by cutting through the linguistic fog used deliberately by some speakers to mislead the audience. Language of this type is sometimes called "gobbledegook," or "doublespeak." For instance, the Committee on Public Doublespeak of the National Council of Teachers of English reports that the U.S. military described a pencil as a "portable hand-held communications inscriber."[11] If such terminology is simply awkward and is not intended to mislead, the result is not necessarily unethical, although it is certainly unclear. On the other hand, if someone in the military is trying to conceal from government auditors that a ridiculous price was paid for pencils (such as specifying on the purchase order, "portable hand-held communications inscribers, $24.00 doz."), both ethics and clarity suffer.

The Committee on Public Doublespeak also reports that some witnesses in congressional hearings have used evasive, abstract language to avoid admitting that they had lied about the issue in question. During a 1987 foreign policy controversy, for example, one witness said that his "input was radically different from the truth"; however, he insisted that he had not lied. During the same hearings, a second witness said that his testimony was truthful, although he had "withheld" information and had "misled" the committee.[12] In your own speaking, you can avoid doublespeak of this sort by choosing concrete words that are at once clear and ethical.

In addition to choosing individual words carefully, you can help make your speeches concrete by *defining* your terms, and by *giving examples* of what you are talking about. For instance, a speaker discussing financial "assets" could say: "By 'assets' I mean anything you own that has some exchange value. For example, your VCR is an asset, because you can sell it, or trade it for something. On the other hand, your old socks are not assets, for they are not worth anything to other people."

In review, you can improve the overall clarity of your speeches by using language that is simple, familiar, and concrete. We are now ready to examine how you can make your speeches more interesting and persuasive by using vivid language.

Vividness

Speaking in a vivid style means that you use language that is colorful, fresh, and lively. Such language stirs the senses, causing the listener to form striking mental images that intensify interest and quicken the imagination. For example, instead of saying "before long, Bill wasted his money," a speaker could express the same idea this way: "Within a few short months, Bill foolishly squandered his inheritance." Similarly, compare these two ways of saying the same thing: "After losing four games in a row, we finally won one"; and, "After four consecutive weekends of drinking from the bitter cup of defeat, we now celebrate by drinking from the sweet cup of victory."

Vivid language is useful in gaining and holding interest in both informative and persuasive speaking. It is especially important in persuasion, for in persuasion you often need to go beyond holding interest to paint colorful word pictures that energize your appeals for decision and action. Research supports the view that the sensible use of lively, colorful language strengthens persuasive speaking.[13]

You can add vividness to your speeches by choosing your words carefully, and by arranging them creatively in your sentences and paragraphs. For example, contrast the following pairs of words and short phrases for dullness versus liveliness: "large" vs. "enormous"; "nice looking" vs. "stunningly beautiful"; "I was scared" vs. "I was terrorized"; and "it was a weak decision" vs. "it was a gutless compromise." You can use your dictionary or thesaurus to discover similar examples of striking and picturesque words and phrases that can be substituted for ordinary ones.

Use Figures of Speech

Figures of speech are also useful in adding vividness to your speaking. Those figures of speech that are employed often by public speakers include *similes and metaphors, repetition*, and *antithesis*. Let us examine these three stylistic devices in more detail.

Simile and Metaphor

Similes and metaphors are both forms of figurative comparison that provide colorful word pictures to help make speech ideas impressive and memorable. A simile is a *direct* comparison that usually employs "like" or "as," such as "My girlfriend is like a beautiful flower," or "He stands as firm as the Rock of Gibraltar." A metaphor, on the other hand, makes an *indirect* comparison; that is, the comparison is implied rather than stated directly. For example, a military metaphor occurs in the sentence, "The streets of our cities have become combat zones in the war on drugs." And Abraham Lincoln, in his Second Inaugural Address, delivered near the end of the Civil War, used a metaphor comparing America to a wounded person when he urged, "let us...bind up the nation's wounds."

A good example of the use of simile occurred in April, 1951, when General Douglas MacArthur addressed the U.S. Congress in defense of his views concerning the Korean War. President Harry Truman had recently dismissed the general as Commander of the United Nations forces in Korea because of insubordination. In making his case, MacArthur, who wanted a clear-cut military victory rather than a truce, described American policy as "appeasement," then compared appeasement to blackmail. "History teaches," he said, "that appeasement but begets new and bloodier war....Like blackmail, it lays the basis for new and successively greater demands until, as in blackmail, violence becomes the only other alternative." Later, in the same paragraph, MacArthur again used simile, comparing the Soviet Union to a serpent: "Like a cobra, any new enemy [such as the Soviets] will more likely strike whenever it feels that the...military or other potential is in its favor on a worldwide basis."[14]

In addition to similes, metaphors are widely used by public speakers. For example, the metaphor of the free marketplace is often employed as an argument for maximum freedom of speech. A number of years ago, Supreme Court Justice Oliver Wendell Holmes used the marketplace figure to urge greater liberty of expression in the United States when he said, "...the ultimate good desired is better reached by free trade in ideas,—that is, the best test of truth is the power of the thought to get itself accepted in the competition of the market."[15]

Martin Luther King regularly used metaphors in his speaking, including a number of different ones in his famous "I Have a Dream" speech. (The complete text of King's "I Have a Dream" appears in the appendices.) Early in the speech, King spoke metaphorically when he compared the cry for racial equality to cashing a check drawn on the "promissory note" of guarantees in the Constitution. As King put it:

> It is obvious today that America has defaulted on this promissory note insofar as her citizens of color are concerned. Instead of honoring this sacred obligation, America has given the Negro people a bad check, a check which has come back marked "insufficient funds." But we refuse to believe that the bank of justice is bankrupt. We refuse to believe that there are insufficient funds in the great vaults of opportunity of this nation. So we've come to cash this check—a check that will give us upon demand the riches of freedom and the security of justice.

When you use metaphors, be sure to keep the imagery internally consistent by avoiding the "mixed metaphor." A mixed metaphor occurs when the speaker employs two or more metaphors in the same phrase that are illogical when combined. The result is an awkward and incongruous figure of speech, such as "the president put the ship of state firmly on its feet." For example, you employ a poker metaphor consistently if you say, "when the chips are down, he plays a skillful game." However, if you mix poker and fire metaphors by saying, "when the chips are down, he fights fire with fire," the result is ridiculous. Notice the inconsistent, strained imagery in these mixed metaphors: "The winds of change struck like lightning, drowning us in a raging sea"; or "The governor holds tightly to the reins, while playing cat and mouse with the legislature."

Painting word pictures with similes and metaphors derived from consistent imagery helps add vividness to the ideas of the speaker. Furthermore, research confirms that metaphors can help strengthen persuasion. For example, one study compared literal conclusions in a speech attacking government aid to students to metaphorical conclusions on the same subject (using a death metaphor, the speaker described students as "fatalities" of government programs, and said that government aid will "murder" our values). The experiment concluded that the use of metaphors not only produced more attitude change in the direction of the view being advocated but also increased speaker credibility.[16] The sensible use of similes and metaphors should enhance your speeches as well.

Repetition

Another way to add vividness to speaking is to repeat a sound, word, or phrase, or to use a series of sentences arranged in parallel structure and beginning with the same words. Repeating the same sound in a series of words is called *alliteration*. A speaker on the drug problem, for instance, employs alliteration when he says, "we must defend ourselves against the dangerous demon of drug dependency," or when he compares drug dealers to "warlocks of chemical warfare" who, in selling drugs, "work their wicked ways" on society.

Another form of repetition occurs when a speaker uses the same word or phrase in a series of sentences. For example, Robert G. Ingersoll, the noted nineteenth-century American lecturer, used repetition in his address on "The Liberty of Man, Woman, and Child," when he said:

I believe in the fireside. I believe in the democracy of home. I believe in the republicanism of the family. I believe in liberty, equality and love.[17]

You can even combine alliteration and phrase repetition at times in public speaking. For example, a speaker celebrating the First Amendment to the U.S. Constitution could urge strong support for freedom of speech with these four points: "It protects the politician," "It protects the preacher," "It protects the press," and "It protects the public."

President Franklin Roosevelt used the repetition of parallel sentences for dramatic impact in his "Declaration of War Address," delivered on December 8, 1941 (the complete text appears in the appendices). After his opening remarks, and a summary of facts concerning the bombing of Pearl Harbor, Roosevelt spoke as follows:

> Yesterday the Japanese government also launched an attack against Malaya.
> Last night Japanese forces attacked Hong Kong.
> Last night Japanese forces attacked Guam.
> Last night Japanese forces attacked the Philippine Islands.
> Last night the Japanese attacked Wake Island.
> And this morning the Japanese attacked Midway island.

Antithesis

The use of antithesis is a third method of adding vividness to your speeches. Antithesis means presenting contrasts or opposites within the same sentence, or in adjoining sentences. Patrick Henry's famous line, "Give me liberty or give me death" is a good example of this stylistic device. To illustrate further, a person could use antithesis in a speech supporting jobs programs by saying, "we need work, not welfare...we need jobs, not handouts." Likewise, in arguing against one proposal and in favor of another, a speaker could use antithesis in this manner: "His solution is expensive; mine is modest in cost. His solution is for the short term; mine is permanent. And most important of all, his solution is repressive; mine sustains individual privacy and freedom."

President John F. Kennedy used antithesis effectively on a number of occasions. Perhaps the best known example is from his Inaugural Address, when he spoke as follows (the entire speech appears in the appendices).

> And so, my fellow Americans, ask not what your country can do for you, ask what you can do for your country. My fellow citizens of the world, ask not what America will do for you, but what together we can do for the freedom of man.

Other Figures of Speech

Although simile, metaphor, repetition, and antithesis are the figures of speech that you will probably use most often, there are a number of others that can be used to add color to a speech. To illustrate the possibilities, let us look briefly at two: irony and personification. *Irony* is a form of indirect ridicule or sarcasm in which the speaker says one thing, but means the opposite—such as saying in reference to an ugly, run-down building, "Isn't *that* a beautiful sight!" A person speaking in favor of racial harmony, for example, could use irony to criticize the Ku Klux Klan by saying: "*Of course* the Klan members love their neighbors; *of course* they believe in justice and equality; *of course* their cross burnings are little more than picnics or neighborhood social outings.''

Personification is a figure of speech that attributes the characteristics of life to inanimate things or ideas. To illustrate, in opening a speech on ''How to Shop for a New Car,'' a speaker could say, ''My old car gasped, coughed, and died last week. I had it hauled into the dealer's lot for burial—and in the process of shopping for a new car, learned some things that everyone should know.'' The person who says ''the trees put on their finest clothing in the fall,'' is using personification, as is the person who comments, ''for my entire life, I have had a love affair with Lady Liberty.''

Learning to Use Vivid Language

As you develop your ability to use vivid language, be alert to the problems of triteness and verbal excess. You can combat *triteness* by working to eliminate clichés from your speaking. A *cliché* is an expression that is so common, so overused, that it lacks rhetorical impact. For example, ''we hit the nail on the head,'' is a cliché; you can avoid it by substituting such language as, ''we were accurate in our analysis of the problem, and we solved it at once.'' You can find substitute language for other clichés as well. Here are some examples: instead of ''we are at a crossroads of history,'' say ''we must now make a decision on this issue''; instead of ''beyond a shadow of a doubt,'' say ''we were certain that we were doing it correctly''; instead of ''I've been busy as a bee,'' say ''I have worked hard, and have now finished the project''; and so forth.

Also, be careful to avoid *verbal excess* when speaking. That is, do not use language that is so extreme that it distracts your listeners, causing them to focus primarily on your style rather than on your ideas. Research confirms, for example, that vivid language should be used in moderation, for contemporary audiences will likely be repelled by stylistic excess. Specifically, an experiment was conducted in which speeches using low-intensity language were contrasted with speeches using high-intensity language. Examples of low- versus high-intensity words included these: ''unbecoming'' was contrasted with ''monstrous,'' ''large'' was contrasted with ''monumental,'' ''susceptible'' was contrasted with ''gullible,'' and ''free'' was contrasted with ''licentious.'' The experimenter concluded that the overuse of the intense words had a ''boomerang effect,'' causing the speaker to lose credibility, and reducing the effectiveness of the speech.[18]

Finally, you can establish for yourself a program of language improvement to help you speak with vividness that is appropriate to the audience and occasion. Such a program should include at least three points. First, use your dictionary and thesaurus regularly to find words that, while clear, add stylistic strength to your sentences. As a part of this idea, try writing out key sections of your speeches, using your dictionary and thesaurus to improve language quality. During rehearsal, practice from the written sections; then, either from notes or from memory, carry over the ''enriched style'' to the actual delivery of the speech. Second, study great speeches and use them as models. By reading the works of effective public speakers, such as Abraham Lincoln, Franklin Roosevelt, Winston Churchill, John F. Kennedy, and Martin Luther King, Jr., you can get ideas for improving your own speaking style. Third, speak often, paying close attention to your language during preparation and delivery.

This Chapter in Brief

In speechmaking, your language serves two key functions: the semantic function, concerning how words work, and the stylistic function, concerning your choice and arrangement of words for maximum clarity and persuasiveness. *Semantics* explains that words are symbols, meaning that they stand for something, but are not the same as what they stand for. The "something" that a word stands for is called the referent. Words, therefore, serve as "substitute stimuli." For example, the words "white rabbit" are symbols for a rabbit, but should not be confused with a real rabbit. Because they are symbols, words do not literally transfer meaning from the mind of the speaker to the audience. Rather, the function of words is to stir up meaning that is already present in the mind of the listener. Because you cannot literally *transfer* meaning from your mind to the mind of another person, you should be careful to use words that come as close as possible to stirring up your intended meaning. Careful audience analysis will help you choose the vocabulary level, and the specific words and phrases, that will best stimulate the meaning that you are thinking about and are trying to communicate to others.

Style concerns the words you choose, and the way you put those words together to communicate your ideas effectively to others. Three elements of style are of special concern to public speakers: appropriateness, clarity, and vividness. Appropriateness means that you should choose language for your speeches that is natural for you, and that fits the audience and the occasion. Clarity means that your language should be easy for the audience to understand, incorporating the qualities of simplicity, familiarity, and concreteness. Vividness means that your language should hold interest and help move the audience to commitment and action by being colorful and lively. Figures of speech, such as similes, metaphors, repetition, and antithesis, help make your speeches vivid.

The importance of language to effective communication is summarized well by George Campbell, the outstanding English teacher of public speaking, who wrote in the *Philosophy of Rhetoric* (1776):

> Eloquence hath always been considered...as having a particular connexion with language. It is the intention of eloquence to convey our sentiments into the minds of others, in order to produce a certain effect upon them. Language is the only vehicle by which this conveyance can be made. The art of speaking, then, is not less necessary to the orator than the art of thinking. Without the latter, the former could not have existed. Without the former, the latter would be ineffective.[19]

EXERCISES

1. Using the model speeches in the appendices, study the style of Franklin Roosevelt's "Declaration of War Address," John F. Kennedy's Inaugural Address, and Martin Luther King's "I Have a Dream." Note in particular the use of figures of speech, including simile, metaphor, repetition, and antithesis. In the future, and for appropriate audiences and occasions, employ some of the stylistic techniques of these great speakers in your own speeches.

2. While preparing your next persuasive speech, select a key argument or an important section (such as the conclusion) for special stylistic enhancement. Write out the section in full, then revise what you have written, focusing on making it more colorful and lively with vivid words and figures of speech. Incorporate your work into the rehearsal and delivery of the speech. Over time, keep working on your speaking style until you begin to feel that clarity and vividness are becoming a more natural part of your preparation and delivery.

SELECTED READINGS

Blankenship, Jane. *A Sense of Style: An Introduction to Style for the Public Speaker.* Belmont, Calif.: Dickenson Publishing Co., 1968. This brief text focuses on the use of language in public speaking, with chapters on word choice and rhetorically effective sentences. Chapter 6, ''Activities That Improve Style,'' provides a number of practical suggestions for your use in improving the use of language.

Harte, Thomas B.; Keefe, Carolyn; and Derryberry, Bob R. *The Complete Book of Speechwriting for Students and Professionals.* 2d ed. Edina, Minn.: Bellwether Press, 1988. This handbook on preparing the manuscript speech includes two chapters on style: Chapter 9, ''The Crafting of Ideas into Words,'' and Chapter 10, ''How to Create Memorable Phrases.'' The chapters include numerous examples of speech style ''in action.''

Hayakawa, S. I. *Language in Thought and Action.* 4th ed. New York: Harcourt Brace Jovanovich, 1978. This standard text in semantics focuses on how words work in both informative and persuasive situations. In this highly readable study, the student will encounter ideas on how to communicate more clearly, how to speak more responsibly, and how to become a better ''consumer of ideas'' in today's mass media society.

Lee, Irving J. *Language Habits in Human Affairs: An Introduction to General Semantics.* New York: Harper & Row, 1941. This little classic—which includes a Foreword by Alfred Korzybski, the ''father'' of general semantics—is one of the best explanations of general semantics ever written. The author, who was a teacher of speech at Northwestern University, has managed to make the theory of general semantics clear and useful.

Rogge, Edward, and Ching, James C. *Advanced Public Speaking.* New York: Holt, Rinehart and Winston, 1966. The authors discuss speaking style in two well-illustrated chapters. Chapter 6, ''Language,'' focuses on words and how they work, and Chapter 7, ''Style,'' elaborates by explaining a wide variety of stylistic techniques and figures of speech.

Thonssen, Lester; Baird, A. Craig; and Braden, Waldo W. *Speech Criticism.* 2d ed. New York: The Ronald Press, 1970. Chapter 16, ''The Style of Public Address,'' discusses the qualities of style that a public speech should achieve—such as correctness, clarity, appropriateness, and embellishment. A wide variety of figures of speech are presented and illustrated.

ENDNOTES

1. Thomas Wilson, *The Art of Rhetorique* (London: 1567). In Lester Thonssen, ed., *Selected Readings in Rhetoric and Public Speaking* (New York: H. W. Wilson,

1942), p. 175. Wilson was first published in 1553; Thonssen, however, quotes from the 1567 edition.

2. Alfred Korzybski, the father of modern general semantics, is credited with the map-territory metaphor for teaching that the word is not the thing. See Alfred Korzybski, *Science and Sanity: An Introduction to Non-Aristotelian Systems and General Semantics* (Lancaster, Pa.: The Science Press, 1933), p. 58. For a more recent discussion of the concept, see S. I. Hayakawa, *Language in Thought and Action*, 4th ed. (New York: Harcourt Brace Jovanovich, 1978), pp. 24–28.

3. For a discussion of these concepts, see Hayakawa, ibid., pp. 22–23.

4. Ibid., p. 280.

5. For a more complete discussion of the need to base speech upon reality, see Irving J. Lee, "Four Ways of Looking at a Speech, *Quarterly Journal of Speech* 28 (April 1942): 148–155.

6. Jane Blankenship, *A Sense of Style: An Introduction to Style for the Public Speaker* (Belmont, Calif.: Dickenson Publishing Co., 1968), p. 2.

7. For an excellent essay on sexist language, see Susan Mura and Beth Waggenspack, "Linguistic Sexism: A Rhetorical Perspective," in James Golden, Goodwin Berquist, and William Coleman, *The Rhetoric of Western Thought*, 3d ed. (Dubuque, Ia.: Kendall/Hunt, 1983), pp. 251–259. Note: this essay appears only in the third edition of this text.

8. Aristotle, *The Rhetoric*, trans. Lane Cooper (New York: Appleton-Century, 1932), p. 185.

9. Tamara Carbone, "Stylistic Variables as Related to Source Credibility: A Content Analysis Approach," *Speech Monographs* 42 (June 1975): 99–106, at p. 106.

10. Ben D. Zevin, ed., *Nothing to Fear: The Selected Addresses of Franklin D. Roosevelt, 1932–1945* (New York: World Publishing, 1946), p. 105.

11. "Stamp Out 'Doublespeak,'" *Parade Magazine*, January 10, 1988, p. 16.

12. Ibid.

13. For example, see John Waite Bowers, "Some Correlates of Language Intensity," *Quarterly Journal of Speech* 50 (December 1964): 415–420. Also, John Waite Bowers and Michael M. Osborn, "Attitudinal Effects of Selected Types of Concluding Metaphors in Persuasive Speeches," *Speech Monographs* 33 (June 1966): 147–155.

14. Douglas MacArthur, "Address Before Congress," delivered April 19, 1951, in John Graham, ed., *Great American Speeches* (New York: Appleton-Century-Crofts, 1970), p. 94.

15. Holmes's marketplace metaphor is from his dissent in the case, *Abrams v. United States*, 250 U.S. 616 (1919).

16. Bowers and Osborn, op. cit., pp. 151 and 155.

17. Robert G. Ingersoll's "The Liberty of Man, Woman, and Child" was first delivered about 1877. The quotation is from W. Maxfield Parrish and Marie Hochmuth, *American Speeches* (New York: Longmans, Green, 1954), p. 432.

18. John Waite Bowers, "Language Intensity, Social Introversion, and Attitude Change," *Speech Monographs* 30 (November 1963): 345–352.

19. George Campbell, *The Philosophy of Rhetoric*, II:1, in James L. Golden and Edward P. J. Corbett, *The Rhetoric of Blair, Campbell, and Whately* (New York: Holt, Rinehart and Winston, 1968), pp. 260–261.

Let your manner [of delivery]...be your own; neither imitated from another, nor assumed upon some imaginary model, which is unnatural to you.

—Hugh Blair,
Lectures on Rhetoric and Belles Lettres (1783)[1]

Chapter 13

DELIVERING THE SPEECH

I magine for a moment that a person has an important message that he or she wants to communicate to others. This individual has researched the subject and has prepared a well-organized and logically sound speech about it. When it is time to speak, however, the individual talks in a thin, weak voice that cannot be heard past the first few rows, mumbles words, stares at the floor, and rarely moves or gestures. How effective do you think such a presentation would be? You would probably agree that no matter how sound the content, much of the impact of the speech would be lost if it was poorly delivered.

You can think about your speeches as consisting of two inseparable components: what you have to say—that is, *content*; and how you say it—that is, *delivery*. Take away either component and you do not have a speech, for delivery without content is pointless, and content without delivery remains uncommunicated, and thus undisclosed, to the audience. To help you with the crucial component of delivery, this chapter addresses five areas of concern: types of speech presentation, characteristics of good delivery, vocal aspects of delivery, physical aspects of delivery, and practicing your speech.

I. Types of Speech Presentation

There are four basic types of speech presentation: *extemporaneous* (prepared but not memorized or read), *manuscript* (read word for word), *memorized*, and *impromptu* (spur of the moment). Let us examine each type in more detail.

Extemporaneous Speaking

An extemporaneous speech is one that is carefully prepared in advance, but is neither memorized nor read from a manuscript. Typically, the extemporaneous speech is outlined, rehearsed, and delivered from notes. Many speakers prefer extemporaneous speaking over other methods of delivery because it combines thorough preparation with flexibility in adapting to the audience and occasion, and because it facilitates direct, lively delivery. For these reasons, extemporaneous delivery is the type taught most often in public speaking courses; also, for prepared speeches, it is the type of delivery used most often by college graduates in their business and professional careers.[2]

After you have researched your speech topic and gathered your supporting materials, there are three major steps to preparing an extemporaneous speech. First, prepare a thorough outline. Second, prepare a "key word" note card based on the outline. Finally, rehearse your speech several times using the note card. Going to the first point, the outline is the place for you to clarify your thinking, arrange ideas in a logical sequence, and eliminate irrelevant content. Each point you intend to make, and each item of support you intend to use, should be stated briefly in the outline. For more information about outlining, see Chapters 9, 10, and 11.

The second step is to prepare the key-word note card. Your notes should follow the sentence outline in abbreviated form, with the introduction, body, and conclusion clearly marked. *For illustrations, see the model note cards, together with outlines and speeches, in Appendix II.* Here are some specific suggestions for note card preparation.

Use words economically. If one word is adequate to remind you of a point, let that one word do. If you need two or three words, then use them, keeping things as brief as you can.

Write out statistics and quotations in full. The exception to the rule of brevity occurs when you have complex statistics or direct quotations that must be said "exactly right." In such instances, write out the statistics or the quotation on the card, then read the item at the appropriate time in the speech.

Abbreviate your citations when qualifying a source. When you need to mention a source, put essential information on the note card to help you maintain accuracy. For example, if your source is the *Wall Street Journal* for March 29, 1988, you can jot down: "*Wall St. J.*, Mar. 29/88."

Mark the note card to suit you. Underlining important words, or highlighting points with colored markers, might help you keep your place and emphasize important ideas. The note card is for *your* convenience, so mark it to fit your needs.

Use more than one note card if necessary. Although you should avoid having a large number of note cards covering the speech in excessive detail, it is not unusual for a speaker to have two or three note cards. This is especially true when the speech includes several direct quotations. By using cards that are at least 4 by 6 inches or 5 by 8 inches in size, you can cover the essentials while keeping the number of cards to a minimum.

The third step is to rehearse the speech several times, using the notes that you have prepared. When rehearsing, glance at the note card, mentally picking up the next point from the key words that summarize that point, then look back at your imaginary audience. Develop the point extemporaneously (that is, in words that come to you at the time without further reference to your notes). By sticking to your notes, you can cover essential information, avoid irrelevant discussion, and finish the speech within the time limits.

Manuscript Speaking

A manuscript speech is one that is carefully prepared in advance, written out in full, and read word-for-word at the time of delivery. An advantage of this type of speech is that it permits the speaker to express ideas in precise, thoughtful language that is chosen for maximum accuracy, persuasiveness, and tact. This makes manuscript speaking useful for those in business and government who need to be careful about how a policy or complex proposal is set forth, for certain speeches of introduction, nomination, or presentation (when the the words spoken need to be "just right"), or for occasions when time limits are strict (such as a radio or television address).

The disadvantage of this type of presentation is that it often causes the speaker to focus on the manuscript rather than on the audience. Consequently, delivery becomes stilted and monotonous, lacking in visual directness and communicative body movement and gesture. In other words, manuscript delivery is often mechanical and *dull*. With practice, however, manuscript speaking can be effective. Here are some suggestions.

Outline the speech first. In other words, don't try to compose the manuscript until you have first organized your content. After this has been done, write the speech, using the outline as a guide.

Employ oral style. This means using clear, simple words, short sentences, and smooth transitions, just as you would when speaking extemporaneously.

Make the manuscript easy to use. Consider printing or typing the manuscript in large letters, and using double or triple spacing. Mark the pages to suit you (such as underscoring important words or phrases). Placing the manuscript in a looseleaf notebook helps hold things together as you move from page to page while speaking.

Rehearse several times. Use a tape recorder if one is available. Become thoroughly acquainted with the manuscript so that you are not tied to it.

When speaking, keep your focus on the audience. Use the technique of glancing at the manuscript to pick up the next sentence or two, then looking back at your listeners as you speak. Don't let the manuscript become a barrier between you and your audience.

Speaking from Memory

Memorized speaking means writing the speech out in full, memorizing it word for word, then delivering it without notes or a manuscript. This form of presentation has the same advantages as manuscript speaking in that you can choose your words carefully in advance. Also, visual directness is facilitated because you are not glancing at notes or a manuscript. However, the disadvantages are major. They include the danger of forgetting the speech (or portions of it), and being so afraid of forgetting that delivery is tense and unnatural rather than relaxed and conversational. Also, memorized speaking, like manuscript speaking, reduces the speaker's flexibility in adapting to the immediate circumstances of the occasion.

For the reasons just stated, and because today's audiences do not expect speeches to be memorized, most speakers use extemporaneous or manuscript delivery rather than memorized. On the other hand, those who can speak effectively from memory might find memorized delivery particularly useful for special occasions, such as commemoration speeches, or speeches of introduction, nomination, or presentation.

Impromptu Speaking

An impromptu speech is one that is delivered on the "spur of the moment," without any prior preparation by the speaker. For example, if you attend a campus meeting where an interesting topic is being debated, and you decide suddenly—without any specific preparation—to participate in the debate, your remarks would be impromptu.

Here are some suggestions for speaking on short notice. In the moments prior to your speech, decide on the key points you want to make, and if possible, jot them down in outline form on a note pad or piece of scratch paper. Use this rough outline to keep yourself on track so that you will not omit something important. (If no pencil and paper are available, concentrate on one or two key ideas for a moment so that you can recall them from memory while speaking.)

Open with a brief remark on why you are speaking, state your central idea, then use your outline (quickly written, or mental) to develop the body of the talk. After you have covered the essential points, pull things together with a summary, then appeal for agreement with your point of view. Keep your delivery direct and animated, just as you would on more formal occasions. By doing these things you can present your point of view in a clear, organized manner, thus enhancing the possibility that your speech—even though it is prepared quickly—is effective in changing attitudes and behavior.

II. Characteristics of Effective Delivery

Delivery Should Be Natural

The quotation from Hugh Blair at the beginning of this chapter spotlights a fundamental principle of effective speaking, namely, that one's delivery should be natural to the speaker. Although you can get ideas and inspiration for improving your delivery by observing the speaking of others, you should adapt what you learn to your own personality and style of speaking. For example, you might admire an effective public speaker on your campus or in your community, noting that he or she is direct and animated. As a result, you might decide on a program to improve your own eye contact and communicative bodily movement. In the process, however, continue to be yourself—you need not imitate the person who inspired you in the first place.

Delivery Should Support Content

Effective delivery supports speech content. Your voice, facial expression, bodily movement, and gestures should not call attention to themselves; rather, they should help you interpret and communicate your message to the audience. For example, if you are speaking to a group of fifteen or twenty fellow students in a typical college classroom, and you shout your remarks while pounding on the lectern and gesturing broadly as if you were in a coliseum, your audience would probably pay more attention to your delivery than to what you were saying. A more controlled delivery is called for—one that is appropriate to the occasion, and one that supports your message without distracting from it.

Delivery Should Be Conversational

A third trait of effective delivery is that it should be conversational—that is, it should be alert yet relaxed, and should be marked by vocal and physical variety without being too intense. Research informs us that the contemporary listener prefers a natural, conversational style of delivery, granting to speakers who speak this way a higher credibility that those who are excessively "dynamic."[3]

Delivery Should Be Direct and Lively

Finally, you should be direct and lively while you are speaking. Research confirms that audiences respond positively to visual directness. As one report concludes, "eye contact is an important delivery characteristic in establishing speaker credibility."[4] When you are speaking, therefore, look at your audience, moving the visual contact from section to section so that everyone present feels included. In addition to direct delivery, audiences like variety in gesture and bodily movement. Do not stand in the same position, or keep your hands in your pockets or clasped behind you, for long periods during a speech. Instead, move appropriately (such as stepping to the side of the lectern, or moving to the blackboard to jot down a key idea), and gesture in keeping with the points you are making (such as emphasizing an idea with an up-and-down motion of the hand or hands). Let us now explore further the subject of delivery, first by looking at the use of the voice, then by examining physical appearance and the use of the body.

III. Vocal Aspects of Delivery

When John F. Kennedy began his campaign for the presidency in 1960, those in his audiences, including reporters, often noted that his delivery was awkward, his voice tense and unpleasant, and his rate of speaking so rapid that he was difficult to understand. Because he did not take care of his voice, he developed a distracting hoarseness. And his rapid speaking rate was once "clocked at 240 words per minute, approximately 100 words a minute faster than normal speaking rates." One reporter described his delivery as resembling that of "a carnival barker," another said it was "hypnotically singsong," and a third characterized it as simply "deplorable." Recognizing that he had a problem, Kennedy sought the help of speech professionals, soon overcoming the negative characteristics of his delivery.[5]

John F. Kennedy is not the only famous speaker to have difficulty with the vocal aspects of delivery. Abraham Lincoln had a nasal quality to his voice, and he often mispronounced words; Winston Churchill had difficulty making a clear "s" sound; and early in her public career, Eleanor Roosevelt spoke in a thin, high-pitched voice that detracted from her effectiveness (with coaching, she developed a more pleasant vocal quality, but her voice was never rich and expressive). However, as Kennedy, Eleanor Roosevelt, and others have discovered, with professional advice, distracting vocal traits often can be significantly improved, and in some cases completely overcome. To assist you in your own speaking, the two sections immediately following examine key aspects of voice and diction.

There are four characteristics of the voice that you should be aware of, and should use for maximum effectiveness in public speaking: *quality, loudness, rate*, and *pitch*. Let us examine each of these elements of the human voice.

Voice Quality

The term "voice quality" describes those vocal characteristics that are unique to an individual, making a person's voice recognizable to others. This includes the pleasantness or unpleasantness of the voice. For example, we are referring to voice quality when we say "she has a nice speaking voice," or "his voice is harsh and tense." Desirable characteristics of the voice are often described with such terms as "rich," "pleasant," "soothing," or "deep and resonant." Undesirable characteristics are often described by such terms as "thin," "breathy," "nasal," "hoarse," "strident," or "muffled."

Many public speakers have no significant problems with voice quality, for their voices are pleasant to the ear and adequate for most speaking situations. On the other hand, research tells us that some unpleasant vocal qualities influence audiences to such an extent that they need attention.[6] This is particularly true if the voice is nasal, breathy, thin, or flat. As one important study concludes: a *nasal* voice in either males or females is associated with "a wide array of socially undesirable characteristics"; *breathiness* and *thinness* in the female voice communicate "shallowness" and "immaturity"; and a *flat* male or female voice often causes listeners to think of the speaker as sluggish, cold, and withdrawn.[7] If you have a problem with one of these undesirable characteristics (or with others, such as persistent hoarseness), seek your instructor's advice. Perhaps a self-help program can be designed that will enable you to improve your vocal quality. In serious cases, you might need the assistance of a voice and diction teacher, a speech pathologist, or a medical specialist.

Loudness

Loudness is that element of voice that enables you to be heard by all persons in the audience. For small groups, your approach can be to speak in an "amplified conversational mode" so that you are easily heard by everyone present. For large audiences, loudspeaker systems are generally available so that you can speak in your natural manner and still be heard by all. In addition, whether using a microphone or not, employ variety of loudness in order to hold audience interest. For example, you can say some words and phrases softly, others moderately loud, and others even louder when you need to emphasize a point. Keep loudness controlled, however, remembering that you can be forceful and persuasive without being shrill.

President Franklin D. Roosevelt is a good example of a speaker who knew how to vary the loudness of the voice for emphasis during a speech. For instance, in his First Inaugural Address, delivered March 4, 1933, Roosevelt used vocal emphasis—that is, loudness—to stress key ideas as he encouraged his listeners to join him in fighting the economic depression that afflicted the country. Early in the speech, Roosevelt built to an important point, saying it as follows (vocal emphasis noted in capital letters): "This nation is asking for ACTION, and action NOW." Later, in the same speech, he stressed the need for the regulation of certain financial institutions by saying, "There must be an END to speculation with OTHER PEOPLE'S MONEY."[8] The same technique was used effectively throughout the speech (and throughout his entire speaking career).

When you speak to large audiences over a loudspeaker system, as did President Roosevelt in the situation just mentioned, use the microphone effectively by following some simple rules. First, make sure the microphone is adjusted to suit your height, then stand back from it about twelve to fifteen inches. Properly installed amplification systems do not require you to talk with your mouth next to the microphone. Second, stay physically close to the microphone, yet be animated in your delivery. If the microphone is a "clip-on" type (that is, one attached to your clothing or otherwise worn by the speaker), your movement around the platform is less inhibited than if the microphone is fixed to the floor or to the lectern. If the microphone is fixed, you will need to depend mainly on gesture and head and torso movement for lively bodily communication. Third, keep your hands off the microphone, and avoid pounding on the lectern or shuffling papers that might create distracting noises. Finally, because the microphone carries your voice to the back of the room, you do not have to project with strong vocal force in order to be heard. This means that your voice can be highly communicative while remaining relaxed and conversational.

Rate

Your rate, meaning simply the speed at which you talk, can be measured by the number of words spoken per minute. The normal speech rate ranges from about 125 to 175 words per minute, with 150 words per minute being a rough "average." You can estimate your own rate by listening to two or three minutes of a tape recording of a speech you have delivered, counting the number of words in the sample chosen, then dividing the result by the number of minutes listened to. If your rate is about 100 words per minute or less, you will probably be perceived by your listeners as talking too slowly; if it exceeds 200 words per minute, you will probably be perceived as talking too fast.

There are three basic points concerning speaking rate that you should consider: talking fast enough; avoiding excessive speed; and variety. First, you should be aware that audiences generally dislike a slow, "drawling" rate of speaking, preferring a moderately rapid rate instead. As one study reports, the "preponderance of research shows that faster speaking enhances competence-related perceptions such as intelligence, objectivity, and knowledgeability." However, credibility is not harmed if a speaker slows down for a good reason, such as explaining an "unfamiliar or difficult topic."[9]

Second, avoid speaking too fast. As mentioned earlier concerning John F. Kennedy's rapid-fire delivery in the 1960 campaign, extremely fast speech interferes with audience comprehension of the message. Also, it can cause errors of articulation and pronunciation. If your rate is too fast, work with a tape recorder during your rehearsals to slow things down to about 150 words per minute. With practice, you can change the bad habit of overly rapid speech into the good habit of speech that is "moderately fast."

Finally, your speaking rate should be varied to help give vocal interpretation to your sentences and paragraphs. You can avoid a monotonous rate by slowing down at times, such as when you are explaining something or stressing an important point, and by speeding up occasionally, such as when you are reaching the climax of a key argument. Also, the *pause*—a brief interval of complete vocal silence—is useful both for variety and for emphasis. However, you should not vocalize (such as saying "uhhhh," "ahhhh," or "mmmmm") during the pause. Research shows that speakers who regularly use vocalized pauses are perceived by their listeners as lacking in competence and dynamism.[10] As a general rule, therefore, make appropriate use of the *silent* pause in your speaking, but avoid the vocalized one.

Pitch

Vocal pitch means the highness or lowness of the voice as measured on a musical scale. As a rule, the pitch of the male voice is lower than that of the female voice because the vocal folds of the male are usually longer and heavier than those of the female. (The longer and heavier the vibrating object, whether violin string or vocal folds, the slower the vibration; and the slower the vibration, the lower the pitch.) The pitch at which your voice functions best—that is, the level most natural for you—is called your *optimum* pitch. If you feel that you have a serious pitch problem (such as a pitch level that is too high), talk to your instructor about how to get a professional evaluation from a voice and diction teacher or a speech pathologist.

You should vary your pitch in public speaking for at least two important reasons: to avoid monotony, and to give interpretation to your ideas. First, variety in pitch helps hold attention and interest with your listeners. Research shows that variety in pitch is important, particularly in persuasive speaking, for a monotone pitch contributes to audience evaluation of the speaker as apathetic or weak in commitment to the opinions being expressed.[11]

In addition, you should alter the pitch appropriately to give interpretation and emphasis to your words and sentences. For example, questions are often spoken with a rising pitch (called an "inflection") at the end. To illustrate, say "Where have you *been*?" with a rising pitch and increased loudness on "been." Also, you can use a slightly higher pitch to orally distinguish between paragraphs or sections of your speech. You can do this by employing a higher pitch when you first state a main point or open a new paragraph, then dropping back to optimal pitch in the development or discussion of the point or paragraph. You will also need to vary the pitch (in conjunction with variation of loudness and rate) to "interpret" your supporting materials, such as illustrations and quotations.

Your Articulation and Pronunciation

Articulation and pronunciation are not the same thing, although they do interact and influence one another. *Articulation*, the narrower of the two terms, refers to how distinctly or indistinctly you utter the individual sounds of speech, such as making the "s" in "sit," or the "r" in "rabbit." *Pronunciation*, the broader term, includes articulating the individual sounds of a word, plus syllabic stress. Syllabic stress, a pronunciation factor in words of two or more syllables, means that one syllable is said *louder* than the other syllable or syllables. For example, in the word "accident," you should stress the first syllable, thus saying "AC-cident." If you stress the last syllable, saying "acci-DENT," the result is a "substandard" pronunciation. In a nutshell, we articulate individual speech sounds; we pronounce entire words.

Articulation

"Normal" articulation means uttering speech sounds sharply and distinctly; "faulty" articulation means failure either to utter a sound at all (such as omitting the final "t" in "test," thus saying "tess"), or uttering a sound in an indistinct or distorted way (such as saying "Go wimme" instead of "Go with me," or "thing a thong" for "sing a song"). Many persons employ "lazy" or relaxed articulation in everyday conversation with friends (examples: "lesseet" for "let's eat," or "gimmeuh break" for "give me a break"). No great harm is done by this, provided it is kept to a minimum, and does not overcome one's efforts to speak distinctly in more formal circumstances.

Making a public speech is one of those "more formal circumstances" that call for sharp articulation. Although you should form your sounds correctly and utter them distinctly during a speech, you should not "overdo it." Keep your articulation natural, yet clear, so that the audience perceives your speech as normal and unaffected. In the more formal setting of the speaking occasion, listeners expect—and deserve—to hear full and clear articulation of speech sounds. This expectation is supported by a research report that concludes that indistinct articulation in a public speech seriously erodes the audience's perception of speaker credibility.[12]

Pronunciation

Pronunciation standards are determined, not by majority rule, but by the usage of the educated, cultured leaders of a society. Thus, "chic" is pronounced "sheek" (not "chick"), and "gesture" is pronounced "jesschur" (not "guesschur"), because that is how the educated leaders of our society say them. Because pronunciation norms are determined by current usage, not by some unchanging rule or law, we should avoid describing pronunciation as "correct" and "incorrect." Instead, we should talk about pronunciation according to what is "standard" (current usage) and what is "nonstandard." In thinking of your own speaking, therefore, your goal should be to use *standard* pronunciation.

Most pronunciation problems result from one of these four mistakes: misplaced accent (that is, stressing the wrong syllable); adding unnecessary sounds; omitting needed sounds; and substituting or reversing sounds in a word. You can use these four categories in evaluating your own pronunciation habits. Here are some examples to help get you started (in each word below, the *standard* pronunciation is given first; additional examples of words often mispronounced are in the exercises at the end of this chapter).

Misplaced accent: *comparable* should be "COMparable," not "comPAREable"; *Detroit* should be "deTROIT," not "DEEtroit"; *impotent* should be "IMpuhtunt," not "imPOtent"; *equator* should be "eQUAtor," not "EEquator"; and *infamous* should be "INfumus," not "inFAMEus."

Unnecessary sounds: *almond* should be "ahmund," not "allmund" (the "l" is silent); *Illinois* should be "Illuhnoy," not "Illuhnoise" (the "s" is silent); *athlete* should be "athleet," not "athuhleet"; *integration* should be "integration," not "innergration"; and *statistics* should be "stetistiks," not "stustistiks."

Omission of sounds: *accessory* should be "aksessory," not "assessory"; *accurate* should be "akyourut," not "akkarut"; *company* should be "kumpenee," not "kumpnee"; *library* should be "liebrary," not "lieberry"; and *picture* should be "pikchure," not "pitcher."

Substitutions and reversals: *aggravate* should be "aggruvait," not "aggervait"; *diphtheria* should be "difftheria," not "diptheria"; *height* should be "hait," not "haith"; *length* should be "lenkth," not "linth"; and *irrelevant* should be "irrelavunt," not "irrevuhlunt."

You should take your pronunciation seriously, using an acceptable standard both in daily conversation and in public speaking. A part of the impression we make upon others, whether on a date, in a job interview, or delivering a speech, is shaped by our use of the language—including our pronunciation. Here are three suggestions. First, try to use standard pronunciation at all times, thus making polished pronunciation a "good habit." If you do this, you will make fewer pronunciation mistakes while delivering a speech. Second, listen to and learn from the pronunciation of educated speakers, such as television personalities, political leaders, ministers, and teachers. Finally, use a good, recent dictionary regularly to check on your pronunciation.

Vocal Aspects of Delivery in Summary

As we have seen, the vocal aspects of delivery include voice, articulation, and pronunciation. Your speaking voice should be pleasant and "expressive" (that is, your voice should have variety of loudness, rate, and pitch). Furthermore, your articulation of sounds should be distinct, and your pronunciation of words should be standard (that is, according to current usage). We are now ready to turn our attention to the physical aspects of delivery.

IV. Physical Aspects of Delivery

From the moment you start to walk to the speaker's stand to deliver your speech, the audience begins to form an opinion about you based upon your physical appearance and the way you "carry yourself." During your speech, listeners are also influenced by your facial expression, visual directness, posture, and communicative movements including gesture. Let us examine these elements of nonverbal communication, beginning with your physical appearance.

Listeners may be influenced by a speaker's physical appearance and behavior. (Joel Gordon)

Your Physical Appearance

Imagine for a moment that you are attending a graduation exercise at your college. Following preliminary activities, the main speaker steps to the podium wearing a pair of dirty jeans, a torn sweatshirt, and scruffy tennis shoes. In addition, you notice that he has not shaved for a day or so, and that his hair is rumpled and uncombed. No matter how wise the content of his speech, the speaker's odd physical appearance would likely dominate your response. As you can see from this example, and as research in nonverbal communication confirms, our physical appearance is a factor in the impression we make upon others.[13] In public speaking situations, listeners mix this impression with other factors to assign speaker credibility. And, as you are aware, speaker credibility (*ethos*) greatly influences audience response to your message.

The basic principle of physical appearance for public speaking is that it should blend with the occasion so that the audience will focus on what you say rather than on how you look. In other words, your physical appearance should not call attention to itself. (The exception is when a speaker's appearance serves as a visual aid, such as wearing an ethnic costume for a speech on a culture illustrated by the costume.) Research tells us that a positive appearance is particularly important in persuasion, for people are more likely to be influenced by persons who are neat, clean, and attractively dressed than by those whose appearance is unattractive.[14] For informal situations—such as talking to a group of campers, or speaking at a pep rally—an informal appearance might be acceptable. For other occasions, attention to grooming and dress should be included in your overall speech planning. The result can range from a decision to wear a neat campus style for a talk to your speech class, to wearing your "Sunday best" for a talk to a civic group or to a convention of a state organization.

Your Facial Expression and Visual Directness

Your facial expression and your eye contact are important forms of nonverbal communication during public speaking. In summarizing some key findings of modern research, one authority in nonverbal theory reports that your face communicates "interest or disinterest in other people," your intensity or "degree of involvement" in a situation, and even the "intellectual factor" of whether or not you understand what you are talking about.[15] In particular, your facial expression is highly important in communicating your sincerity and good will to your listeners. Thus, both common sense and empirical research tell you to begin your speech with a smile, keep an overall pleasant and positive facial expression throughout the speech, thereby "saying" to your audience, "I like you, I'm glad to be here, I know what I am talking about, and I am sincere."

Visual directness combines with facial expression to comprise your "facial means" of communication. Researchers tell us that the eyes are "the primary center of visual attention" because our "visual inspection" of others focuses on the eyes 43 percent of the time (the closest any other area gets is the mouth, which we focus on about 12 percent of the time during visual inspection).[16] When we are speaking, our eye contact helps us gain and hold audience attention, communicate the intensity of our feelings and emotions, and influence attitude change. As several authorities report, the greater the amount of eye contact, the greater our credibility and overall effectiveness in persuasion.[17]

Because visual directness is so important to effective public speaking, you should work on eye contact until you master it. This means to develop the *habit* of visual directness so that it is natural and easy for you. When the audience is small, as in a public speaking class, you should look from person to person while speaking, showing an interest in everyone present. When the audience is large, however, you need not try to look directly at each individual; rather, see persons in groups, or sections, moving your visual attention from section to section so that you cover all parts of the room. Avoid staring at any one person or group of persons. Also, do not stare at the floor, at the lectern (or your notes or manuscript on the lectern), at the ceiling, or at the wall in the back of the room. Instead, communicate eye to eye with your listeners, for this is what people like and expect.

Your Posture, Movement, and Gesture

Posture, movement, and gesture serve the dual function of helping to emphasize and interpret the content of the speech, and helping to establish a positive speaker image. You add meaning to speech content when you move and gesture in harmony with the ideas being presented, and when that movement and gesture help to communicate the meaning that you intend. For example, the first-hand observations of those who heard Abraham Lincoln speak confirm that he used movement and gesture effectively to interpret ideas and emphasize points. One observer recalled that, in a speech attacking the extension of slavery, Lincoln underscored a key point with a sweeping gesture in which he "raised his right arm to the right, bringing it down almost to his feet." Another listener noted that "to dot the ideas in the minds of his hearers," he extended "the long...index finger of his right hand." Yet another remarked that when Lincoln wanted to show that he detested an idea, "he would throw both arms upward, with fists clenched in determination."[18]

With appropriate adaptation to audience and occasion, the principles of movement and gesture used so well by Lincoln (and by other great speakers as well) should be employed by contemporary speakers. For instance, a student speaker who is advocating the addition of more officers to the campus police force might shake a clenched fist while saying, "We have got to put a stop to this crime wave of robberies and assaults on our campus!" Or, a citizen of the local community, when asking for a financial pledge to a good cause, might step toward the audience, with arms extended and palms open, while appealing for action ("we need your help; sign the pledge card tonight").

The second function of posture, movement, and gesture is to enhance speaker credibility. Research confirms that your body language is important in saying to your audience, "I like you, and I am confident and sincere about what I am saying."[19] To communicate good will and confidence, your posture should be alert, yet relaxed. Positive head movements, such as nodding, are helpful, as is leaning *toward* the audience rather than away from it. Also, you can communicate an attitude of friendship with body language that is "open" rather than "closed." In other words, speaker credibility is enhanced by extended and open arms and hands, as contrasted with a negative or "closed" position (such as folding the arms across the chest).

Here are some specific suggestions that can help you interpret content and establish good will at the time of the speech. To begin with, walk confidently to the front of the room as if to say, "I have something to say that I really want to say, and I am glad to be here." If you have notes or a manuscript, position them quickly on the lectern. Stand erect, with your weight balanced evenly on both feet; avoid nervous shifting from side to side. Do not apologize or make comments critical of yourself, such as, "I'm not a very good public speaker, so just bear with me while I talk." Keep the speech lively with purposeful, controlled movement and gesture. If you are using a speaker's stand, move from one side to the other occasionally, so you will not become "frozen" in one spot. If you are employing a visual aid, stand to one side of it so that the audience can see well; be sure to keep talking to your audience (that is, don't start talking to your visual aid). When you have completed your speech, walk confidently back to your seat without making negative remarks, such as "Whew! Am I glad that's over." In other words, keep communicating a positive image, even while returning to your seat.

Physical Aspects of Delivery in Summary

In summary, the physical aspects of delivery include your appearance, facial expression, visual directness, posture, movement, and gesture. Neatness and appropriate dress help keep the audience's focus on the ideas of the speech, thus strengthening communication. A friendly smile and a pleasant facial expression communicate good will; and direct eye contact helps say that you are interested in your listeners, and that you are confident and sincere. Erect posture, and "open," natural movement and gesture help interpret the ideas of the speech as well as enhance speaker credibility.

V. Practicing Your Delivery

Practicing your speech several times should strengthen your self-confidence and add to your effectiveness at the time of actual delivery. Here are some suggestions for your rehearsals.

Timing. Using a rough draft of your speech outline or manuscript, time your remarks by talking through the speech while keeping an eye on the clock. If the speech is too short or too long, revise the outline or manuscript appropriately. After you have the length just right, prepare the final, polished version of your outline or manuscript.

Note Cards or Manuscript. For an extemporaneous speech, prepare a note card based on the final sentence outline. To do this, reduce the points you need to remember to key words or short topics that will jog your memory when you glance at the note card. For a manuscript speech, consider marking the final draft to help direct your visual attention to words and phrases that you wish to emphasize.

Visual Aids. Prepare your visual aids, if any, in final form so that you can work with them during rehearsal. Practice how you will put them up, use them, and take them down.

Rehearsal. Practice the speech several times, standing as if you were before the audience, and using the actual note cards or manuscript that you will employ during delivery. If you are using note cards, hold them in the palm of one hand or place them on a "homemade" lectern (such as a stack of books) to match the facilities that you will have in the place of delivery. (Do the same for rehearsal with a manuscript.) As you speak, vary the voice for emphasis and interpretation, be visually "direct" with your imaginary audience, and use appropriate movement and gesture. Include in your rehearsal "hands on" practice with any visual aids that you plan to use. Try to have two or three practice sessions, spread over a day or two, rather than one long session. (For a speech class, perhaps you can rehearse a time or two in the classroom where you will actually deliver the speech.) You should now be ready to speak to your audience with confidence, for you know what you are going to say, and how you are going to say it. In a word, you are *prepared*.

This Chapter in Brief

There are four types of speech presentation: extemporaneous, manuscript, memorized, and impromptu. Extemporaneous delivery is based on careful preparation, but is neither memorized nor read word-for-word from a manuscript. As a general rule, the extemporaneous speech is delivered from notes which the speaker uses to stay "on track." *(For examples of speaker note cards, see Appendix II.)* The manuscript speech is written out in full, and read word-for-word by the speaker. The speaker should know the manuscript thoroughly in order to maintain eye contact and employ appropriate movement and gesture during the speech. Memorized delivery means writing out and memorizing a manuscript, then speaking entirely from memory. Because modern audiences do not expect speeches to be memorized, and because of the obvious difficulty of getting through the speech without forgetting part of it, most speakers today prefer extemporaneous or manuscript delivery for their prepared speeches. Finally, impromptu speaking is "spur of the moment," without any special preparation.

The delivery of your speech is the culmination of your speech preparation. For maximum effectiveness, your delivery should be natural, conversational, direct, and lively. Good delivery does not call attention to itself; rather, it is subordinate to and supporting of the content of the speech.

Delivery is composed of a number of vocal and physical aspects interacting with each other at the time of speech presentation. The vocal aspects of delivery include voice, articulation, and pronunciation. Your speaking voice should have a pleasant quality, be loud enough to be easily heard by all in the room, and have "expressive variety" of rate and pitch that serve to interpret the ideas of the speech to your audience. Also, articulate your speech sounds distinctly so that listeners will understand what you are saying, and pronounce your words according to current, acceptable standards of usage.

The physical aspects of delivery include your appearance, facial expression, visual directness, posture, movement, and gesture. You should be neat in appearance, and dress appropriately for the occasion. A pleasant facial expression, direct eye contact, erect posture, and controlled, meaningful movement and gesture not only strengthen the communication of your content but also help you build credibility (*ethos*) with the audience.

Practice your speech several times before actual delivery. During your rehearsals, use the same note cards or manuscript that you plan to employ on the day of the speech. Also, if you are using visual aids, include them in your rehearsals. If possible, rehearse a time or two in the room where the speech will be delivered.

EXERCISES

1. Prepare a list of words that you have difficulty pronouncing, then look up each one in a good, current dictionary, practicing the standard pronunciation until you master it. Keep adding to the list during the school year as other words occur to you. To help you get started, here are several words that are often mispronounced, arranged according to the four major pronunciation problems discussed in this chapter.

Misplaced accent: abdomen, affluent, bravado, finance, superfluous.
Unnecessary sounds: accompanist, column, corps, disastrous, grievous.
Omission of sounds: accessory, Arctic, environment, medieval, particularly.
Substitutions and reversals: Baptist, cavalry, cello, clique, disheveled.

2. Rehearse your next speech using a tape recorder. Begin by deliberately speaking a portion of the speech with a dull, unexpressive voice. Then start over, speaking the entire speech with an expressive voice—that is, giving emphasis and interpretation to the content with variations of loudness, rate, and pitch. Compare the two types of vocal technique during playback.

3. If you have access to a video camcorder, use it for a speech rehearsal. During video playback, pay close attention to your facial expressions, visual directness, posture, overall body movement, and gestures.

SELECTED READINGS

Bradley, Bert. *Speech Performance.* Dubuque, Ia.: Wm. C. Brown, 1967. This entire book concerns delivery, including eye contact, bodily movement and gesture, use of a microphone, and the four types of presentation: impromptu, extemporaneous, manuscript, and memorized.

Glenn, Ethel C.; Glenn, Phillip J.; and Forman, Sandra H. *Your Voice and Articulation.* 2d ed. Englewood Cliffs, N.J.: Prentice-Hall, 1989. This practical guide to improvement in voice, articulation, and pronunciation is filled with excellent explanations, illustrations, and exercises.

Harte, Thomas B.; Keefe, Carolyn; and Derryberry, Bob R. *The Complete Book of Speechwriting for Students and Professionals.* 2d ed. Edina, Minn.: Bellwether Press, 1988. This text covers speech preparation and delivery, with an emphasis on the manuscript speech.

Leathers, Dale G. *Successful Nonverbal Communication: Principles and Applications.* New York: Macmillan, 1986. This introductory text is clearly written, and is nicely organized for those seeking practical advice on the subject of nonverbal communication. Leathers covers a wide range of topics useful to the public speaker, including facial expressions, eye behaviors, bodily communication, personal appearance, and vocalic communication.

Mehrabian, Albert. *Silent Messages.* Belmont, Calif.: Wadsworth Publishing, 1971. Mehrabian was one of the first to integrate research in nonverbal theory, and apply it to a variety of communication situations. In particular, the public speaker should study the practical advice summarized in Chapter 7, "Perspective and Application."

Tarver, Jerry. *Professional Speech Writing.* Richmond, Va.: Effective Speech Writing Institute, 1982. As the title indicates, Tarver's book is about preparing and presenting the manuscript speech. Chapter 8 is on how to effectively deliver a speech from a manuscript.

ENDNOTES

1. The quotation from Blair's *Lectures on Rhetoric and Belles Lettres* is from Lester Thonssen, ed., *Selected Readings in Rhetoric and Public Speaking* (New York: H. W. Wilson, 1942), p. 261.
2. John R. Johnson and Nancy Szczupakiewicz, "The Public Speaking Course: Is It Preparing Students with Work Related Public Speaking Skills?" *Communication*

Education 36 (April 1987): 131–137. This study reports that 98 percent of college public speaking faculty teach extemporaneous delivery in classes; also, that alumni employ all four forms of speech delivery in the workplace (92 percent had used impromptu; 85 percent had used extemporaneous; 70 percent had used manuscript; and 54 percent had used memorized).

3. W. Barnett Pearce and Bernard J. Brommel, "Vocalic Communication in Persuasion," *Quarterly Journal of Speech* 58 (October 1972): 298–306.

4. Steven A. Beebe, "Eye Contact: A Nonverbal Determinant of Speaker Credibility," *The Speech Teacher* 23 (January 1974): 21–25, at p. 25.

5. James G. Powell, "Reactions to John F. Kennedy's Delivery Skills During the 1960 Campaign," *Western Speech* 32 (Winter 1968): 59–68.

6. See generally Dale G. Leathers, *Successful Nonverbal Communication: Principles and Applications* (New York: Macmillan, 1986), pp. 114–129. On p. 117, Leathers observes, "The dominant *quality* of a person's voice strongly affects the impression that person makes."

7. David W. Addington, "The Relationship of Selected Vocal Characteristics to Personality Perception," *Speech Monographs* 35 (November 1968): 492–503, at p. 502.

8. The quotations from Roosevelt's First Inaugural Address are from a voice recording in the possession of the author.

9. Judee K. Burgoon, David B. Buller, and W. Gill Woodall, *Nonverbal Communication: The Unspoken Dialogue* (New York: Harper & Row, 1989), pp. 247–249.

10. Kenneth K. Sereno and Cary J. Hawkins, "The Effects of Variations in Speakers' Nonfluency upon Audience Ratings of Attitude Toward the Speech Topic and Speakers' Credibility," *Speech Monographs* 34 (March 1967): 58–64.

11. See Leathers, op. cit., p. 116.

12. David W. Addington, "The Effect of Vocal Variations on Ratings of Source Credibility," *Speech Monographs* 38 (August 1971): 242–247, at p. 247.

13. For a review of the research in personal appearance, see Leathers, op. cit., pp. 89–113; and Burgoon, Buller, and Woodall, op. cit., pp. 51–62, and pp. 442–444.

14. Burgoon, Buller, and Woodall, ibid., p. 442.

15. Leathers, op. cit., p. 25.

16. Ibid., p. 42.

17. Beebee, op. cit., pp. 24–25; Burgoon, Buller, and Woodall, op. cit., pp. 433–436; and Leathers, op. cit., pp. 42–46.

18. Mildred F. Berry, "Abraham Lincoln: His Development in the Skills of the Platform," in William Norwood Brigance, ed., *A History and Criticism of American Public Address*, vol. 2 (New York: McGraw-Hill, 1943), p. 848.

19. The recommendations concerning posture, movement, and gesture are based upon research reported in Albert Mehrabian, *Silent Messages* (Belmont, Calif.: Wadsworth, 1971), pp. 111–136; Leathers, op. cit., pp. 50–68; and Burgoon, Buller, and Woodall, op. cit., pp. 424–459.

PART IV
Types and Forms of Public Speaking

66

> *The improvement of the understanding*
> *is for two ends: first, for our own*
> *increase of knowledge; secondly, to*
> *enable us to deliver and make out that*
> *knowledge to others.*

99

—John Locke[1]
(1823)

Chapter 14

SPEAKING TO INFORM

*S*everal years ago, social critic Alvin Toffler reminded us in *Future Shock* that the rate of increase in human knowledge has been "spiraling upward" for centuries, and has now reached unprecedented proportions. Toffler points out, for example, that about 1000 books were published in Europe during the entire year of 1500, but that today, on a world scale (Europe included), approximately 1000 books *per day* pour off modern, high-speed presses. Furthermore, he reports, the number of scientific journals doubles every fifteen years to accommodate the more than sixty million pages of scientific and technical literature published annually around the globe.[2]

Simply put, the rapid expansion of knowledge in the twentieth century means that we have more information to communicate than ever before in human history. Consequently, the study of public speaking, which in centuries past has been concerned almost exclusively with a rhetoric of persuasion, has begun to meet the challenge of the information explosion by expanding to include a rhetoric of information—that is, the theory and practice of effective informative speaking.

We can define *informative speaking* as *spoken discourse that is limited in intent to the communication of knowledge; its basic goal is to explain a subject to an audience so that those who listen achieve understanding*. Informative discourse differs from persuasion whose purpose is to change beliefs, values, and attitudes in directions intended by the speaker. In other words, persuasion is deliberately slanted and one-sided. Informative discourse, on the other hand, presents a subject in a more objective, neutral, and multisided way. For instance, a football coach making a speech to an audience of fellow coaches on why rule "X" of college football should be changed is speaking to persuade, for he is trying to change minds. That same coach explaining rule "X" to the team so that the players will comprehend it and follow it while playing is speaking to inform; here the goal is not to change minds, but to achieve understanding.

Also, note that even though an informative speech might have a persuasive effect on one or more persons in the audience, such an effect is not the goal of the speech to inform. For example, an objective lecture on the Battle of Gettysburg might create such an interest in the event that some in the audience might decide to visit the site of the battle. Nevertheless, we classify the lecture as "informative" because its *intent* is to achieve an understanding of a historical occurrence, not to motivate the action of journeying to Gettysburg.[3]

The purpose of this chapter is to help you improve your oral teaching skills by presenting the basics of a "rhetoric of informative speaking." It is assumed that you have studied the points concerning informative speaking in earlier chapters, for what follows is built upon the theoretical foundation established by those chapters. In particular, you will find it helpful to relate the material below to that of Chapter 5 on audience analysis, Chapter 6 on subjects and purposes, and the specific recommendations for organizing the speech to inform explained in Chapters 9, 10, and 11. We will now focus on informative speaking according to three key topics: the importance of informative communication to a free society; types of subjects for informative speeches; and objectives of informative speaking.

I. Informative Speaking in a Free Society

James Madison, our fourth president, wrote in 1822: "A popular government without popular information or the means of acquiring it, is but a Prologue to a Farce or a Tragedy; or, perhaps both. Knowledge will forever govern ignorance: And a people who mean to be their own Governors, must arm themselves with the power which knowledge gives."[4] In more recent times, Alexander Meiklejohn, one of America's leading free speech theorists, restated Madison's view by observing that the right to communicate is essential in a democracy because the voters "must be made as wise as possible. The welfare of the community requires that those who decide issues shall understand them."[5]

In a broad sense, the knowledge that each of us needs in order to participate fully in a democratic society is composed of a mixture of facts and opinions communicated to us through informative and persuasive discourse. Thus, we can say that both informative and persuasive speaking have their place in a free society, not only to provide us with the knowledge required for being good citizens, but also to guide our understanding of (and, in some cases, our participation in) a variety of institutions and groups that compose our society. Because the focus in this chapter is upon exposition, let us look at some typical uses of informative speaking.

In *institutions of government*, informative speaking is needed for teaching new members of the legislature or of the Congress the rules and procedures under which they will work; explaining to government employees (such as those who administer the Social Security program) the workings of the office and the laws that must be followed; explaining basic duties to members of a jury in a court of law; teaching election supervisors how to conduct an election; or giving the public factual information (such as on a foreign policy development) in a press briefing.

In *voluntary associations*, such as churches, student clubs, hobby organizations, and self-improvement groups, informative speeches are delivered on matters such as explaining the constitution and bylaws by which the group is governed, describing a plan for the renovation of a building, explaining how to properly use a piece of equipment (such as a loudspeaker system), or teaching members basic parliamentary procedure for conducting business meetings.

In *business and professional work*, informative speaking is needed to explain organizational rules and regulations, corporate organizational charts, policies and procedures for dealing with customers or clients, the way a new product works, and the reporting of profit or loss figures (or other types of information) to boards of directors.

And in *educational institutions*, informative speaking occurs in classroom lectures on subjects ranging from the philosophical ("Plato's views on the ethics of persuasion") to the practical ("How to edit a videotape"). Explanation is also called for when detailing safety procedures in a chemistry lab, teaching students how to properly document a research paper, reporting the results of a scientific survey, or explaining the student honor code to an assembly of incoming freshmen. Of course, informative speeches are also delivered in public speaking classes in order to help students improve their teaching skills.

258

*Part IV
Types and
Forms of
Public
Speaking*

II. Types of Subjects for Informative Speaking

There are a number of ways of classifying informative speeches. In the discussion above, for example, we classified informative speeches according to situation or context. Another method would be to group potential topics according to difficulty in teaching them to a specific audience (that is, subjects could be described as easy, moderately difficult, or very difficult to explain). A third method, and the one followed here, is to classify according to types of subject matter. This method is used below because it is clear and easy to follow, and because it provides a convenient system for illustrating a wide variety of ideas for informative speech topics. As a rule, your speeches to inform will concern one of five types of subjects: speeches about people, events, definitions and concepts, processes and procedures, and tangible objects. Let us look further at these five, including some specific examples of each.

Speeches About People

When you make a speech presenting objective knowledge about the life of a person, your talk can be classified as an informative speech "about people." Note that for the speech to fit the definition of "informative," it should avoid being biased; that is, it should present biographical facts—admirable and not so admirable—in a neutral way. Here are some examples of subjects for this type of speech.

Eleanor Roosevelt's Struggle to Become an Effective Speaker

John Quincy Adams: The Rhetorician and the President

Gen. Douglas MacArthur: The Authoritarian and the Democrat

Who Was Benedict Arnold?

Albert Schweitzer: Missionary and Physician

"I Love Lucy": The Story of Lucille Ball

John Doe: Founder of our College

As a rule, the important events of a person's life can be organized according to a chronological pattern, with the main points covering a sequence such as early, middle, and final years. A second method is to use a topical pattern, with each main point being a topical trait or characteristic of the individual you are discussing. The speech on General MacArthur, for example, could be organized around the two topics listed in the title above, namely, MacArthur the *authoritarian* and MacArthur the *democrat*. For an example of a speech organized according to a chronological plan, let us develop the subject concerning Eleanor Roosevelt.

Specific Purpose: To inform my audience of how Eleanor Roosevelt learned to be an effective public speaker.
Central Idea: Eleanor Roosevelt overcame her fear of public speaking by determination and practice.

I.   In her early life, Eleanor developed an inferiority complex.

II. After her marriage to Franklin Roosevelt, Eleanor determined to overcome her fear of speaking.

III. In her later years, Eleanor was known worldwide as an effective public speaker.

Speeches About Events

Speeches concerning events tell about things that have happened in the past. Subjects can range from one's vacation to a famous historical occurrence. Here are some examples of subjects about events.

The Struggle of American Women for the Right to Vote

The Golden Age of Greece

Exploring Mammoth Cave

How the Steam Engine Won the West

My Trip to the Soviet Union

"The Great American Pastime": The Story of Baseball

As with speeches about people, speeches about events are usually organized by either topical or chronological patterns. For instance, a speech on the Golden Age of Greece could be presented according to the three topics of *achievements in politics, achievements in philosophy and learning,* and *achievements in the fine arts*. On the other hand, here is an example organized according to a chronological pattern.

Specific Purpose: To inform my audience of the three major periods in the struggle for women's suffrage in America.
Central Idea: There are three major historical periods in the struggle of American women for the right to vote.

I.   The women's suffrage movement was born before the Civil War.

II. The women's suffrage movement matured and grew between 1865 and 1900.

III. The women's suffrage movement achieved its goal in the first two decades of the twentieth century.

260

Part IV
Types and
Forms of
Public
Speaking

A speech concerning definitions or concepts explains the meaning of a term or concept so that the audience will understand it. Here are some subjects that fit this type of informative speech.

The Fundamentals of Zen Buddhism

What Is Meant by "Common Law?"

"Semantics" and "General Semantics": How Do They Differ?

Linguistic Determinism: The Sapir-Whorf Hypothesis

The Concept of a "Liberal Education"

Einstein's Theory of Relativity

The "Prime Rate" and What It Means to You

Speeches about definitions or concepts are usually organized according either to chronological or to topical patterns. For example, a speech explaining the common law could be built around main points arranged chronologically, such as: *origins* of the concept of common law; *development* of the concept of common law; and *present meaning* of common law. Topical patterns are also useful for outlining this type of speech, as the following example from a student speech illustrates.

Specific Purpose: To inform the audience of what every college student should know about the "prime rate" of interest.
Central Idea: Today I want to explain the meaning of "prime rate," including its effect on you when you try to borrow money.

  I.   First, we need to understand what is meant by the term "prime rate."

 II.   Second, we need to understand how the prime rate is determined.

III.   Finally, we need to understand the effect of the prime rate on our borrowing.

Speeches About Processes and Procedures

Informative speeches concerning processes or procedures explain how something is done, how a thing is made, how something works, how a game is played, and so forth. Here are some examples of subjects for this type of speech.

Amending a Motion During a Business Meeting

How Your Vocal Mechanism Works

The Heimlich Maneuver: First Aid for Choking Victims

The Basics of Piano Tuning

How Molasses Is Made

Some informative speeches are about processes or procedures. They may explain how something is done, how something is made, how something works, and so on. (Russell Abraham/Stock, Boston)

Rules for Playing Soccer

Repairing a Leaky Faucet

Nature at Work: The Forming of Niagara Falls

As a general rule, processes and procedures are outlined according to a chronological pattern because this pattern naturally fits the steps for making or doing something, or for explaining a process. However, other plans are sometimes useful. Here, for example, is an informative outline on how to amend a motion organized topically by types of amendments.

Specific Purpose: To inform the audience about how motions are amended in parliamentary procedure.
Central Idea: There are three basic ways of amending a motion in parliamentary procedure.

I. The first way is to strike out a word or a phrase in the original motion.

II. The second way is to add a word or a phrase to the original motion.

III. The third way is to both strike out and add words or phrases to the original motion.

Speeches About Objects and Geographical Areas

Speeches about objects and geographical areas explain tangible things, such as a device (the parts of a personal computer), a building (the design of the White

House), or a geographical area (the layout of your campus). Here are some subjects that fit this classification.

262

*Part IV
Types and
Forms of
Public
Speaking*

Your VCR and How It Works

Monticello: Home of Thomas Jefferson

The Wankel Engine

The Rock of Gibraltar

The Golden Gate Bridge

Washington's Design of the Mount Vernon Estate

The Human Heart

Speeches concerning objects or areas fit well in either a chronological or a physical components pattern. A chronological plan could be employed, for example, if the speech emphasized how a design or layout had evolved over time (such as a speech on the plan of your campus, beginning with the early years when the school was small, through stages of expansion to the present layout of the grounds). A physical components pattern, on the other hand, explains each piece or section of the subject, one major component at a time. Here is an example of a speech outlined according to physical components (in this case, the four floors of a famous house).

Specific Purpose: To inform my audience of the floor plan of Thomas Jefferson's home at Monticello.
Central Idea: Thomas Jefferson's home at Monticello is composed of four floors, each with its own unique features.

I. The basement has several interesting features.

II. The first floor has several interesting features.

III. The second floor has several interesting features.

IV. The third floor has several interesting features.

In review, informative speeches can be classified according to five types of subjects, namely, speeches about people, events, definitions and concepts, processes and procedures, and tangible things (objects and geographical areas). We are now ready to consider some specific objectives of informative speaking—objectives that you need to have clearly in mind as you develop the subject you have chosen.

III. Objectives of Informative Speaking

Earlier in the chapter we defined informative speaking as spoken discourse intended to communicate knowledge. Also, we noted that the central goal of informative speaking is for the listener to achieve understanding. In order to accomplish this goal, you should prepare your informative speeches with three subordinate goals, or objectives, in mind: to *motivate* your listeners, to *clarify* the content, and to help your listeners remember—that is, *retain*—what you have said.[6]

Motivation

Motivation is what the speaker does to cause the listeners to want to learn the content of the speech. Several modern researchers, for example, report that *speaker credibility* is a significant factor in motivating listeners to learn.[7] Also, studies by psychologists have reported for many years that both *positive and negative incentives* (that is, both reward and penalty) are important in motivating learning.[8] Let us examine these means of motivation in more detail.

Establish Speaker Credibility

Since the days of Aristotle, teachers of public speaking have believed that establishing speaker credibility, or *ethos*, is an important part of persuasive speaking. Until recently, however, the study of whether or not *ethos* plays a significant role in informative speaking—that is, in the motivation of learning—has been neglected. Gradually, however, this oversight is being corrected. For instance, several contemporary researchers have reported that the motivation to learn is strengthened when listeners find the speaker likable, when they have confidence in the speaker's intelligence, and when they believe the speaker is knowledgeable on the subject. Stated briefly, research is confirming that listeners will learn more from your speaking if they perceive you as a person of good will and competence.[9]

You should communicate your good will from the outset by approaching the audience in a direct, friendly way. You can, according to one study, strengthen the bond of good will between you and your audience by smiling and establishing eye contact as you speak.[10] Also, you can comment positively about your topic. To illustrate, the speaker who begins by saying "I am pleased to speak to you on one of my favorite subjects," will be more attractive to the audience than one who says something negative, such as, "I really don't know why I decided to talk on this subject; but I had to talk about something, and this is all I could think of."

In addition to showing good will, you need to communicate to the audience that you know what you are talking about. As a rule, this is done in the introduction of the speech by tactfully mentioning your experience with the subject, or the extent of your research on it. For example, a speaker who is explaining how to clean the disc drive of a computer might say, "I am putting myself through school by repairing computers for a local electronics firm. One of the first things I had to learn was how to clean a disc drive. In the last two years I've performed this operation dozens of times." Similarly, if your talk is based more on research than on personal experience, briefly tell the audience about your research, including some of the major sources you used in developing your speech content. You can continue to reinforce your competence throughout the speech by being well-organized, by using language that is clear to the audience, and by maintaining high standards of pronunciation and grammar.

264

*Part IV
Types and
Forms of
Public
Speaking*

Employ Incentives

Generally speaking, incentives can be classified as either positive or negative. A *positive incentive* is one that offers to satisfy curiosity or to reward the listener with information that is relevant to his or her life. A *negative incentive* is one that threatens listeners with a penalty or punishment if they do not learn the information to be presented. Let us look further at both types.

Positive Incentives

Positive incentives, such as offering reward for learning and achievement, are preferable to negative ones. As one researcher reports, to reward "is more effective than to punish failure to achieve the expected level of performance."[11] At least two forms of positive incentives should be considered by the informative speaker: the satisfaction of curiosity, and relevant reward.

One way to motivate learning is to appeal to the natural curiosity of human beings. In public speaking, this is usually done in the introduction by asking questions that arouse the curiosity of the listeners, then promising to answer the questions as the speech progresses. Examples of questions that arouse curiosity are: "Have you ever wondered why the sky looks blue?" "What does digital mean?" "How do bees convert nectar to honey?" "How is it possible for bats to fly in the dark?" "How does aspirin relieve a headache?"

A second means of positive motivation is to promise a reward for learning the information you are about to present. The more relevant the reward to the lives of the listeners, the stronger the motivation. If you are speaking to college students, for example, a speech explaining a systematic method of note taking could offer a reward of improved examination scores, and higher course grades. Other examples would be a speech explaining how a person who falls into the water can stay afloat until rescued (the reward: saving one's own life); or how to prepare a professional job-search résumé (reward: improved chances of getting a good job). Additional rewards that could be used are: you will be more attractive to the opposite sex; you will achieve financial success; or you will be healthier.

Negative Incentives

Another means of motivating learning is to employ a negative incentive, such as penalty or punishment, for failure to learn. To illustrate, a penalty that all college students are familiar with is the threat of flunking an examination if the content of a lecture is not mastered.[12] Here are some additional examples of the use of penalty that might give you some ideas for your speaking in class and elsewhere. A speech on how to care for a VCR, including proper cleaning of the recording mechanism, could stress the penalty of a malfunction and an expensive repair bill if correct procedures are not followed. Or a speech on how to wire an electric lamp could stress proper steps and safety precautions, otherwise a person might get a painful electric shock or cause an electrical fire. Other penalties that might be employed: you will be less attractive to others;

you will disappoint parents and friends; you will lose money; you will endanger your health; or you will be the object of ridicule.

In brief, we have examined some ways of motivating listeners to learn from an expository presentation. These include establishing yourself as a friendly and knowledgeable speaker, and using both positive and negative incentives to encourage learning. Let us now turn our attention to a second objective of information speaking: being clear.

Clarification

Motivating an audience to learn does little good if the information they need to know is presented in a disorganized and complicated manner. Here are three suggestions for clarifying the content of informative speeches: make your purpose and main headings clear as you speak; explain the unfamiliar in terms of the familiar; and use visual aids.

Make Your Purpose and Main Points Clear As You Speak

At the outset, let us consider the results of three studies that relate to audience understanding of speech content. The first report concludes that a *statement of purpose announced early* in a speech considerably improves listener comprehension of the information that follows.[13] The second study reports that including a *preview of the main points* in the introduction produces "significantly greater amounts" of listener understanding than do speeches without previews.[14] The third study concludes that listeners learn more from a speech that is *well-organized* than from one that is disorganized.[15] Let us assume that you heed the advice of these research reports by preparing an outline that includes an early statement of purpose (central idea), a preview of main points, and a body organized according to a clear, logical set of main headings. How do you orally communicate this *written* preparation to your listeners? At least three techniques can be employed.

First, be sure to announce your central idea in a clear, firm voice near the end of your introduction. A speaker who is explaining the steps in the refining of sugar, for example, should look directly at the audience, and with distinct articulation and adequate loudness say, "Today I want to explain the four steps of sugar refining."

Second, employ oral signposts to call attention to each of the main points of the body of the speech. This is done by giving a preview of the main points at the end of the introduction, then by orally emphasizing each main point when you get to it. Continuing our example of a speech on sugar refining, after an announcement of purpose, the speaker could say: "The four steps that I am going to cover in my speech are, first, crushing the sugar cane; second, clarifying the juice; third, concentrating the purified juice; and, finally, forming sugar crystals." This could be followed by an oral signpost that points to the first main heading: "Let's begin with the crushing of the sugar cane." After explaining this process, the speaker would use an oral signpost to announce the next step by saying, "Now that the sugar cane is crushed, we are ready for

266

*Part IV
Types and
Forms of
Public
Speaking*

the second step, clarification, which concerns the removal of impurities from the juice." The same technique is used to announce steps three and four.

Third, make use of vocal emphasis and gesture. You employ vocal emphasis by varying your speaking rate (such as by talking slower, or pausing), or by saying a word or phrase louder than usual in order to call attention to it. Also, you can use gesture to help the audience keep up with a series of points. This simple but effective technique means holding up one finger for the first point, two fingers for the second point, and so on for each main heading of the talk.

Explain the Unfamiliar in Terms of the Familiar

How many times have you heard an informative presentation, such as a class-room lecture, that included unfamiliar technical terms or concepts that confused you because the speaker failed to make the technical language clear? You can help avoid this in your speaking by reducing the number of complex or technical terms to a minimum, and explaining those that are essential by presenting unfamiliar concepts in terms of the familiar. A teacher of word processing, for instance, can employ technical jargon (such as discussing "kilobytes of data") to explain the storage capacity of a disk drive; however, the jargon can be made meaningful by using word and page comparisons with which the students are familiar, such as: "this means that each disk will hold about 110 pages of standard double-spaced manuscript." Let us look at a more detailed example.

Suppose a speaker is trying to explain why radio and television stations must have a permit (called a "broadcasting license") from the government in order to operate. If the speaker says "the reason that a permit is required is because the electromagnetic spectrum limits the number of frequencies available for use," many listeners will not understand. Terms such as "electromagnetic spectrum" and "frequencies" are too unfamiliar to mean much. However, if the speaker employs familiar concepts while keeping the technical jargon to a minimum, the idea can be made clear. This might be done by explaining that nature has provided a limited number of electronic *highways*, or "frequencies," in the atmosphere that are suitable for radio and television signals to travel upon. The speaker could then say: "Once these highways, or 'frequencies,' are full, there are no more. If two or more broadcasters try to use the same electronic highway, the sound or picture your set receives will be scrambled. For this reason, the highways, or frequencies, must be rationed. And the ration ticket, issued by the Federal Communications Commission, is called a broadcasting license, or permit."

Use Visual Aids

Research on visual aids confirms that the use of charts, graphs, maps, models, and similar types of visual support increases the listener's comprehension of the information being communicated.[16] For example, an investigation of methods for improving an audience's understanding of statistical information found that visual supports in the form of simplified charts, graphs, and numerical tables are effective—and often *essential*—in making statistics understandable.[17]

In brief, research gives strong backing to the common-sense assumption that learning is greatly facilitated by easy-to-follow pictures, charts, or demonstrations; and that this is especially true if the information being presented is complex. Knowing this, you should give serious consideration to the use of visual aids as a means of making your informative speeches clear. For details on the preparation and use of visual supports, complete with illustrations of several forms, see Chapter 7 on "Supporting Materials for Public Speeches."

Retention

The third objective of informative speaking is retention, that is, presenting the content in a way that helps the listener remember what was said. To begin with, most of the suggestions made above concerning motivation and clarification also support retention, for a listener who is motivated to learn, and who clearly understands the purpose and main points of a speech, is more likely to remember important information than one who is not motivated or who hears a disorganized speech. Let us now examine two additional means of aiding listener memory and recall, namely, using concrete language, and stating a clear summary of important points near the end of the speech.

Use Concrete Language

Your listeners will better retain and recall what you say if you *employ concrete words and examples* rather than abstract language that is weak in specific details.[18] To illustrate, the abstract term "great literature" will likely not be remembered as well as concrete examples, such as mentioning "Plato's *Republic*," or "Shakespeare's *Hamlet*." Similarly, to say that "Mr. Jones was driving a large car" is not as specific or vivid as saying "Mr. Jones was driving in his Cadillac Seville." Other examples: instead of saying "study what the Founding Fathers said," be more exact by saying "study the writings of Thomas Jefferson and James Madison"; and instead of the abstract statement "a lot of Americans don't vote," point out the specific statistics on voting from the last national election.

Summarize Clearly

In addition, you can strengthen listener retention and recall by including a *clear summary of important points* in the conclusion of the speech.[19] This is not difficult to do; however, you ought to include the summary in your speech outline, and practice it during rehearsal, to make sure that you remember to do it as you move to end the speech. For instance, in concluding an informative talk on the four steps of sugar refining, the speaker could say: "Now that I have covered the final phase of sugar refining, let me go over all four steps again in order to pull things together. The first step is crushing the sugar cane; the second step is clarifying impurities from the juice; third is concentrating the juice; and fourth is the forming of sugar crystals."

This Chapter in Brief

268

*Part IV
Types and
Forms of
Public
Speaking*

Skill in communicating knowledge, which was neglected by the ancients, has become more and more important in contemporary times because of the information explosion. As citizens of a free society, we need to be thoroughly and accurately informed if we are to deal intelligently with the challenges of the day.

Informative speaking can be defined as spoken discourse that is limited in intent to the communication of knowledge. Unlike persuasive speaking, which attempts to change attitudes and behavior, informative speaking stresses explanation; its goal is to achieve *understanding*.

As a rule, an informative speech is about one of five general types of subjects: speeches about people, events, definitions and concepts, processes and procedures, and objects and geographical areas. There are three major objectives to informative speaking: motivation, clarification, and retention. You help *motivate* learning by establishing your credibility with the audience, and by providing incentives, such as reward or penalty. *Clarification* is enhanced by making your purpose and main points clear to the audience, explaining the unfamiliar in terms of the familiar, and using visual aids. *Retention* and recall are improved if you use specific rather than abstract language, and if you summarize well at the end of the speech.

EXERCISES

1. Think for a moment about the best teacher you have had, either in high school or in college. Make a list of the most effective teaching techniques used by this teacher. In particular, account for how the teacher motivated learning, made the material clear, and helped students remember what was covered. Make an effort to apply the items on your list to your own speaking.

2. Over the next several days, listen carefully to each of your instructors as they lecture on the subject matter of the course. Do any of them begin with a statement of purpose? How many give you a preview of the main points to be covered? Can you follow the main points easily? Does the instructor conclude with a clear summary? Make a note of those teaching techniques that you find helpful, and try to apply them to your own communication. Likewise, note those things that distract or confuse you, and try to avoid them when you speak.

SELECTED READINGS

Lucas, Stephen E. *The Art of Public Speaking.* 3d ed. New York: Random House, 1989. In Chapter 13, ''Speaking to Inform,'' Lucas makes some excellent recommendations for preparing the speech to inform, illustrating the discussion with a model informative speech.

Olbricht, Thomas H. *Informative Speaking.* Glenview, Ill.: Scott, Foresman, 1968. In this brief text, Olbricht focuses exclusively on informative speaking. His chapters on audience analysis, organization, and language are particularly helpful.

Rogge, Edward, and Ching, James C. *Advanced Public Speaking.* New York: Holt, Rinehart and Winston, 1966. Chapter 3 discusses "explaining" from a theoretical perspective, and Chapters 12, 13, and 14 define and illustrate various forms of informative speaking.

Walter, Otis M. *Speaking to Inform and Persuade.* 2d ed. New York: Macmillan, 1982. In Chapters 2, 3, and 4, Walter explains how to prepare an informative speech according to basic speech units, the use of various types of supporting materials to aid clarity, and the development of main points according to an overall "strategy of exposition."

ENDNOTES

1. John Locke, "Some Thoughts Concerning Reading and Study for a Gentleman," *The Works of John Locke*, Vol. III (London: Thomas Tegg, 1823; reprinted in Germany: Scientia Verlag Aalen, 1963), p. 293.
2. Alvin Toffler, *Future Shock* (New York: Random House, 1970), pp. 30–31.
3. For a discussion of the view that persuasive elements are present in expository discourse, see David K. Berlo, *The Process of Communication* (New York: Holt, Rinehart and Winston, 1960), p. 9; also, Thomas H. Olbricht, *Informative Speaking* (Glenview, Ill.: Scott, Foresman, 1968), pp. 14–16.
4. James Madison, letter to W. T. Barry, August 4, 1822. In Gaillard Hunt, ed., *Writings of James Madison*, vol. 9 (New York: Putnam's, 1900–1910), p. 103.
5. Alexander Meiklejohn, *Free Speech and Its Relation to Self-Government* (1948), collected with other Meiklejohn writings in *Political Freedom: The Constitutional Powers of the People* (New York: Oxford University Press, 1965), p. 26.
6. See Frank R. Hartman, "A Behavioristic Approach to Communication: A Selective Review of Learning Theory and a Derivation of Postulates," *AV Communication Review* 11 (September–October 1963): 155–190. Hartman reports that chief among things that interfere with communication and learning are failure to motivate, failure to be clear, and inadequate effort to prepare the listener to retain information in the face of distractions and competing messages.
7. Research on the relationship of source credibility to learning motivation is summarized in Kenneth D. Frandsen and Donald A. Clement, "The Functions of Human Communication in Informing: Communicating and Processing Information," in Carroll C. Arnold and John Waite Bowers, eds., *Handbook of Rhetorical and Communication Theory* (Boston: Allyn and Bacon, 1984), pp. 345–348.
8. For a review of the psychological literature on reward and penalty in motivating learning, see generally Stephen B. Klein, *Learning: Principles and Applications* (New York: McGraw-Hill, 1987).
9. Frandsen and Clement, ibid., pp. 346–347.
10. Derek H. Kelley and Joan Gorham, "Effects of Immediacy on Recall of Information," *Communication Education* 37 (July 1988): 198–207.
11. Stanford C. Ericksen, *Motivation for Learning: A Guide for the Teacher and the Young Adult* (Ann Arbor: University of Michigan Press, 1974), p. 77.
12. A number of studies report that students learn more thoroughly if they know they will be tested on the material being explained. See Frandsen and Clement, op. cit., p. 346.
13. Charles T. Brown, "Studies in Listening Comprehension," *Speech Monographs* 26 (November 1959): 288–294.
14. John E. Baird, Jr., "The Effects of Speech Summaries upon Audience Comprehension of Expository Speeches of Varying Quality and Complexity," *Central States Speech Journal* 25 (Summer 1974): 119–127, at 124.

15. Christopher Spicer and Ronald E. Bassett, "The Effect of Organization on Learning from an Informative Message," *Southern Speech Communication Journal* 41 (Spring 1976): 290–299.

16. Frandsen and Clement, op. cit., p. 344.

17. Gloria Feliciano, Richard Powers, and Bryant Kearl, "The Presentation of Statistical Information," *AV Communication Review* 11 (May-June 1963): 32–39; especially p. 38.

18. G. Wayne Shamo and John R. Bittner, "Recall as a Function of Language Style," *Southern Speech Communication Journal* 38 (Winter 1972): 181–187.

19. Baird, op. cit., pp. 124–125. Also, James Hartley and Mark Trueman, "The Effects of Summaries on the Recall of Information from Prose: Five Experimental Studies," *Human Learning* 1 (January-March 1982): 63–82.

" *So let Rhetoric be defined as the faculty of discovering in the particular case what are the available means of persuasion.* "

—Aristotle
The Rhetoric[1] (330 B.C.)

Chapter 15

THE MEANS OF PERSUASION

As we saw in Chapter 1, the ancient Greeks and Romans found that the art of persuasion was essential to the processes of democracy. Its use included debates in the assembly concerning government policies, legal arguments in the courts, public discussions concerning science, philosophy, and the arts, and speaking on ceremonial occasions. Today, as in centuries past, the art of persuasion remains indispensable to democracy and human liberty. Recognizing this, one modern teacher of public speaking has defined rhetoric as the study of persons persuading other persons "to make free choices."[2] Let us review some contemporary situations that call for persuasive speaking.

In *institutions of government*, persuasive speaking is important to political campaigns, policy debates in legislative bodies, courtroom arguments, and speeches by government officials who wish to communicate with the general public. In *voluntary associations*, such as clubs and churches, speaking includes talks in community programs, debates over policy during business meetings, and sermons. In *business and professional organizations*, persuasion is used in motivational programs, policy discussions, and public relations work. And in *educational institutions*, persuasion is the tool of the campus forum, student and faculty legislative bodies, various committees, and public relations activity promoting the school to the community.

Although we are constantly involved in the give-and-take of persuasive speaking in our lives, most of us spend little time considering how it works. Yet, an understanding of how we persuade one another is important to the citizens of a free society for at least two major reasons: such knowledge helps us to be more effective, ethical advocates of what we believe is right; and it educates us in how to be thoughtful consumers of the many persuasive messages that others aim at us. In this chapter, therefore, we turn our attention to an analysis of the means of persuasion. (In the chapter that follows we will apply our understanding to various types of persuasive speeches.)

As we approach our study of the means of persuasion, recall that this text defines *persuasive speaking* as *spoken discourse that is planned so as to modify the beliefs, values, attitudes, and behavior of others in directions intended by the speaker*. Three key terms of this definition need amplification at this point: "others" reminds us that persuasion is directed toward an audience; "in directions intended by the speaker" tells us that persuasion has a specific purpose, or goal; and discourse planned "so as to modify . . . beliefs, values, attitudes, and behavior" means that we must do more than inform—we must also prove our point to the satisfaction of those who listen. Let us look first at "others," meaning the audience.

The audience. Persuasive speeches should be based upon thorough audience analysis. This includes everything from the choice of a subject to the determination of the best arguments and evidence to use. Audience analysis also teaches us that we are speaking to human beings and must tailor speech content to human nature. Among other things, this means that we must *gain and hold the attention* of our listeners, and we must *be clear* when presenting our point of view. In other words, we are not going to persuade persons who do not listen or who do not understand what we are talking about. Therefore, as you study this chapter, keep in mind that effective advocacy requires that you apply not only the means of persuasion discussed below, but also the principles of interest and clarity developed in earlier chapters (in particular, see Chapters 5, 6, 7, and 14).

The speech purpose. The definition also emphasizes that *a persuasive speech should have a specific, realistic goal.* This means that you should have a definite change of attitude or behavior in mind, and that the change is practical for your audience. In short, your specific purpose should state a goal that you can reasonably expect to accomplish. For instance, you are unlikely to change republicans into democrats or democrats into republicans in a single speech (and perhaps not in a dozen speeches). However, you might achieve a more limited objective, such as persuading the voters of one political party to support a certain candidate of the other party in a given election ("Our candidate is better qualified than any other; don't let party loyalty cause you to vote for an incompetent person"). For more on speech goals and how to use them in organization and outlining, review Chapters 6, 9, and 10.

Proving your case. Assuming that you have analyzed your audience, chosen a realistic goal, and developed content that is interesting and clear, what remains for you to do? As the definition emphasizes, you have a responsibility when persuading that you do not have when informing, namely, *to prove your case.* For instance, a speaker who believes that gambling should be a matter of personal choice could propose: "Gambling should be legal for consenting adults." Aristotle observed that there are three "available means of persuasion"—that is, forms of support, or proof—by which speakers can persuade audiences to agree to such statements of opinion. These are: *logos*, or logical proof, consisting of evidence and reasoning; *ethos*, or ethical proof, meaning speaker credibility; and *pathos*, or emotional proof, consisting of appeals to human emotions, needs, and values.

Aristotle's three-part classification of rhetorical proofs remains useful, even today. After supplementing each part with modern research, we will follow Aristotle's system in this chapter. However, as you study *logos, ethos,* and *pathos,* keep in mind that, to the listener, the three forms of proof interact, overlap, and merge into a single persuasive stimulus. In other words, at any given moment in a speech, all three are present to some degree (for instance, when emphasizing logical reasoning, you cannot help but present speaker image—that is, *ethos;* and you will also include psychological elements, if only to a small degree). For purposes of clarity, however, each is presented separately in the discussion that follows.

I. Logos: *Logical Support*

The late A. Craig Baird, for many years professor of rhetoric and public address at the University of Iowa, once observed that rhetoric "is primarily logical, rather than non-intellectual, communication." The "intellectual content," he added, is central to the core of communication activity.[3] Research lends support to Baird's observations, for a number of modern studies emphasize the importance of sound reasoning and evidence in persuasive speaking, particularly when the audience strongly disagrees with the speaker's point of view.[4] Let us now look at how evidence and reasoning function as means of persuasion.

276

*Part IV
Types and
Forms of
Public
Speaking*

Evidence in Persuasive Speaking

Evidence (also called "supporting material") consists of the specific examples, comparisons and contrasts, statistics, and statements from authority used to make the general points of the speech persuasive. A point that is not backed up with evidence lacks substance and is weak in persuasive force. For example, a speaker who is urging listeners to pledge financial support to a local charity might state two reasons for giving: first, the charity assists people in need who are not helped by other community programs; and second, the charity spends all donations honestly. If the speaker simply states these two points, then sits down, few pledges of support would be forthcoming. However, if the speaker continues by backing the points with evidence—such as examples of people who are being helped, factual information on how funds are used, and favorable testimony from respected community leaders—the two general statements are made concrete, and are, therefore, more persuasive.

The evidence you select to support the points of a speech should meet three basic standards: it should be *accurate*; it should be *clear* to the audience; and it should be *relevant* to the purpose of your speech. In addition, you will often need to tell the audience the source of your evidence in order to strengthen its persuasiveness. This is called "qualifying your source," and its fundamental purpose is to give credibility to the examples, statistics, and authoritative statements that you employ. However, research shows that a simple statement of the source is not enough; for maximum persuasive effect, you should include a brief explanation of *why* the source is qualified.[5] Here is a hypothetical illustration.

Weak in persuasiveness (source's qualifications not given): "According to Dr. John Doe, a professor at a large state university, 60 percent of the nation's drinking water is dangerously polluted."

Strong in persuasiveness (source's qualifications given): "Following a three-year study of the drinking water used by Americans—a study commissioned by the federal Environmental Protection Agency and published only three months ago—Dr. John Doe, professor of chemistry at Great Northern State University, concluded that 60 percent of the nation's drinking water is dangerously polluted."

This text's primary discussion of evidence is found in Chapter 7 on "Supporting Materials for Public Speeches." At this point you might wish to review that chapter, paying special attention to the specific examples provided. Also, note that Chapter 8 concerning research will help in locating evidence for your speeches.

Reasoning in Persuasive Speaking

Reasoning is the mental process by which humans reach conclusions concerning what to believe, or what course of action to follow. When we reason by rational methods, basing our thinking on sound evidence and premises, we call the result "logical." However, when we jump to conclusions without checking the facts or without following rational methods, the result often deserves to be called "irrational" or "fallacious." In short, we can reason wisely or foolishly (or, as is often the case, somewhere in-between). We use reasoning in persuasive speaking in two important ways: first, during preparation, as we work our way through the issues that relate to the topic; and then, during the speech, to demonstrate to the audience the logical strength of the conclusions we have reached.

Most human reasoning can be explained according to the inductive and deductive methods of thought. This includes the two major variations, namely, reasoning by cause-to-effect (a form of induction), and reasoning by parallel case (which has elements of both induction and deduction). Our discussion of the forms of reasoning below includes attention to the ways in which inductive, deductive, causal, and parallel case thinking overlap and interact as we use them in our daily lives, and in our speaking.

Reasoning by Induction

Simply stated, induction is the process of reasoning from specific instances. We use induction when we examine several instances of a class of things, then reach a general conclusion about some common characteristic of that class of things. For example, suppose you have five pairs of Brand X shoes, and all of them fall apart when worn in wet weather. You check with friends, locating five more pairs of Brand X shoes; these, too, have fallen apart in wet weather. From these ten instances of the same class (all are Brand X shoes), and with a focus on a common characteristic (they fall apart in wet weather), you might reach the general conclusion that "all (or most) Brand X shoes are poorly made and will fall apart when wet." The process is illustrated by Figure 15.1. If you show the evidence (the ten ruined pairs of shoes) to other students and explain what happened, you would probably influence them to avoid buying that brand of shoe. Thus, by the process of induction (reasoning from the few to the many) you would have formed an opinion; and, in turn, by explaining how you arrived at that opinion, you would have influenced others.

You can put inductive reasoning to work in your speeches in at least two ways: by employing evidence derived from induction, and by developing inductive arguments of your own. Evidence based on inductive reasoning includes survey research such as public opinion polls and scholarly experiments that are repeated a number of times under controlled conditions to see if general conclusions are warranted. Thus, any time you cite the results of a Gallup or similar poll in a speech, you are using evidence derived from induction (polling is inductive because it moves from interviews with a small number of persons to announce general conclusions about a large number of persons).

Another use of induction in public speaking occurs when you creatively construct arguments based on reasoning from the specific to the general. For example, let us assume that you are planning a speech in favor of a national health insurance program in the United States. Your research turns up a number of successful programs in other industrialized societies, including Canada, England, France, and West Germany. With a focus on these four, your induc-

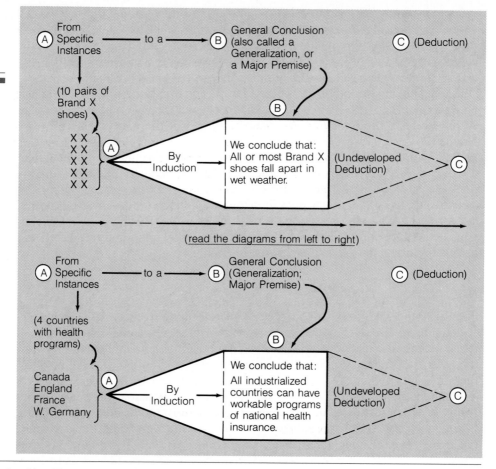

FIGURE 15.1

The Process of Induction. *The two examples above, as discussed in the text,*
illustrate the process of inductive reasoning. On the left, the narrow point (A)
represents the specific; *in the center, the broad section (B) represents the* general.
On the right, point C represents the deductive reasoning that can flow from B, but
which is undeveloped at this time. Both examples illustrate the definition of induction
as the process of reasoning from specific instances.

tive argument would go like this: Canada, England, France, and West Germany (typical instances of industrialized countries) have workable systems of tax-supported health insurance; we can conclude, therefore, that what works for them will work for industrialized countries in general (see Figure 15.1). You could present the argument in a speech by saying, "Proof that national health insurance programs do work comes from four currently in effect—the programs of Canada, England, France, and West Germany." You would then summarize essential details of each, and conclude by saying: "It should be clear, therefore, that industrialized countries can deliver quality health care to their citizens through national health insurance programs."

Testing Induction

To check the logical soundness of inductive evidence and arguments, you should apply at least two basic tests. *First, there must be an adequate number of instances to support the conclusion.* Basing a general conclusion on too few cases is called the fallacy of the "hasty generalization." To illustrate, if a pollster interviewed only five students from a student body of eight thousand, then announced that the views of those five represented the views of the entire campus, the pollster would be guilty of a hasty generalization. Obviously, a much larger number of student interviews would be needed for the conclusion to be dependable.

Second, the instances chosen must be typical (that is, they must be representative of the group as a whole). The use of nontypical instances results in faulty induction, for such instances do not fairly represent the group in general. For example, suppose that most Brand X shoes are well-made, and stand up well in wet weather; however, you choose to study a group of factory rejects that was shipped by mistake, concluding from this group that most Brand X shoes are inferior. Your conclusion in this case would be fallacious, of course, because the instances were not typical.

Reasoning by Deduction

We use deduction when we reason that what is true of an entire class of things applies to a specific member of that class. For instance, if we speak of humans as a class by saying, "all humans are mortal," we can reason about a specific member of that class by adding, "John is human, therefore, John is mortal." Because deduction begins with a generalization, such as "all humans are mortal," it is often described as reasoning from the general to the specific.

We can improve our understanding of logical reasoning by thinking of deduction as *complementary* to induction rather than antagonistic to it. Through deduction we can apply to a specific case the general rule that was reached inductively. Looked at in this manner, induction and deduction are viewed as logical methods that interact and support one another. More precisely, *deduction is seen as a continuation of the reasoning process that began with induction.*

The manner in which induction and deduction complement one another can be clarified with an illustration. In our earlier example of Brand X shoes, we reasoned inductively from ten pairs (instances), to conclude that all or most Brand X shoes were poorly made. Now, by deduction, we can *apply* that conclusion to other shoes. Suppose we are shopping for shoes, and spot a pair of Brand X in the shoe store window. We shake our head and walk by—no more Brand X shoes for us! In making that decision about the shoes in the window, we have reasoned deductively by applying to them the general conclusion reached earlier by induction. In a formal structure (called a syllogism), our thinking can be outlined as shown below. Also, note that the generalization, "Brand X shoes are poorly made, and will fall apart in wet weather," is *common* to both the inductive and deductive processes (see Figure 15.2).

Major Premise (generalization reached by induction): All (or most) Brand X shoes are poorly made, and will fall apart in wet weather.
Minor Premise (a member of the class): That pair of shoes in the window is Brand X.
Specific Conclusion: Therefore, the shoes in the window are poorly made, and will fall apart in wet weather.

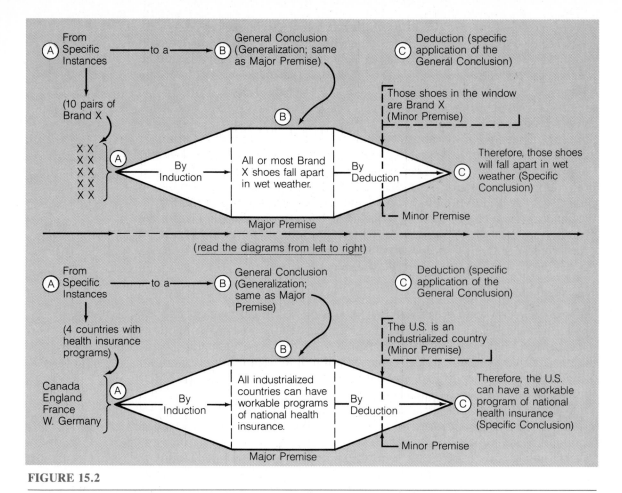

FIGURE 15.2

The Conclusion of Induction Is the Beginning of Deduction. *The examples above continue the reasoning process shown by Figure 15.1. Section B, center, is* common *to both induction and deduction. That is, the general conclusion of induction becomes the major premise of deduction. By adding the minor premise in C, right, you can reach a specific conclusion by deductive reasoning (also called "syllogistic reasoning").*

A syllogism is a deductive argument stated in a complete and formal way. As the example above illustrates, a syllogism consists of three parts: (1) a major premise, (2) a minor premise, and (3) a specific conclusion. The major premise is a general statement about a class of things; the minor premise names a member of that class of things; and the specific conclusion states that what is true of the class in general is true of the specific member. We can illustrate further using the topic of national health insurance, discussed above. The conclusion reached inductively was that "industrialized countries can deliver quality health care to their citizens through national health insurance programs." This generalization becomes the major premise of a deductive argument if you apply it to another industrialized country, such as the United States (see Figure 15.2). The resulting syllogism is as follows.

Major Premise: All industrialized countries can deliver quality health care to their citizens through national health insurance programs.
Minor Premise: The United States is an industrialized country.
Conclusion: Therefore, the United States can deliver quality health care to its citizens through a national health insurance program.

Occasionally, a deductive argument begins with a major premise that is so widely believed and accepted that it requires little, if any, supporting evidence. Such statements are sometimes called "truisms." For example, a truism of our democratic system is that "all persons are equal before the law." Another is that "all persons accused of a crime deserve a fair trial." When you employ an argument based upon such a premise, you will not need to spend much time supporting it; rather, you can move quickly to state and support your minor premise, which in truism-based arguments is often the point of disagreement, thus requiring strong support. To illustrate, let us assume that you are aware of voting fraud in campus elections, and that you are urging a student audience to support close supervision of future elections. You could begin with a truism, then argue your case primarily at the level of the minor premise. The deductive argument, adapted to speechmaking, would go something like this.

Major Premise (truism, usually accepted without debate): Election fraud should be prevented.
Minor Premise (strong support needed): The last two campus elections have involved election fraud.
Conclusion: On our campus, therefore, we need a plan to stop election fraud.

Testing Deduction

To confirm the logical soundness of deductive arguments, at least two tests should be applied. *First, check to see that the premises are proved.* If either the major premise or the minor premise is false (or is not adequately proved, and thus is not believed by the audience), the argument cannot stand. For example, if you assert that "all adult Americans vote, Jack is an adult American, therefore Jack votes," you reach a faulty conclusion because the major premise, "all Americans vote," is not true. On the other hand, if the major premise were true, but Jack was only six years old, the conclusion "Jack votes" would not follow because of the faulty minor premise.

Second, be sure that the specific conclusion flows logically from the premises. For example, suppose you know that all graduates of State College must take a computer course, and that Bill Jones is a State College graduate. If you conclude, "therefore, Bill Jones would make a great computer *salesperson*," you have reached an illogical conclusion, for neither of the premises mentions salesmanship. A logical conclusion would be limited to the following: "Therefore, we can assume that Bill Jones has had at least one computer course."

Reasoning by Causal Relation

Causal reasoning is a variation of induction in which two or more events are shown to be related to one another, with one causing the other. We use causal

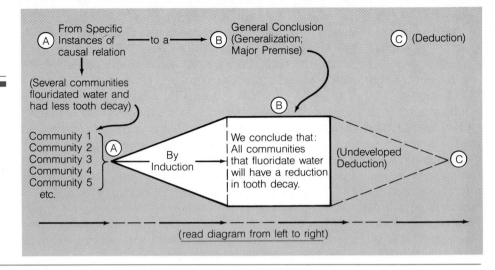

FIGURE 15.3

Causal Reasoning Is a Variation of Induction. *We reason by causal relation when two or more related events occur, and we conclude that one causes the other. Causal reasoning is a variation of induction, for the specific instances of causal relation (point A) form the basis for reasoning to a general conclusion (point B) about those instances. If twenty communities fluoridate their water (cause), and all have less tooth decay (effect), you can reason inductively that all communities that do the same thing will have less tooth decay.*

reasoning regularly in our daily lives, primarily in two sequences: from cause to effect, and from effect to cause. *Cause-to-effect reasoning* means that we begin with the cause, then consider its effect. An example would be: eating spoiled beef (cause) will make us sick (effect). On the other hand, if we start with the effect and reason back to the cause, we call the process *effect-to-cause reasoning*. To illustrate, if you make a perfect score on an exam (effect), and explain to a friend that you did well because you studied hard for two days (cause), your sequence is effect-to-cause.

We employ causal reasoning in a variety of ways in public speaking, such as when we argue that something that creates a harm must be controlled or stopped—e.g., the polluting emissions from smokestack industries (cause) must be reduced, or the forests will continue to die from acid rain (effect). Also, from a positive point of view, we employ causal reasoning when we urge keeping a program or activity that produces a desirable effect—e.g., continuing to fund a "meals on wheels" program for shut-ins because it helps those who are served to be healthier and happier.

Causal reasoning is usually described as a form of induction, for it moves from specific instances of causal relationship to a general conclusion about those instances. For example, if the fluoridation of your community's water supply (cause) results in a dramatic reduction in tooth decay (effect), and you learned that several other communities have had the same result, you could generalize that "fluoridation of the water supply reduces tooth decay." The inductive process at work here is illustrated by Figure 15.3.

Testing Causal Reasoning

To check the logical strength of arguments based upon causal relation, at least three tests should be rigorously applied. *First, there should be a genuine connection between the cause and the alleged effect.* Just because something happens following another event does not mean that the first event caused the second. To think this way without proof of a causal link is known as the "after which, therefore because of which fallacy." For example, suppose the police learned that an arsonist had eaten scrambled eggs for breakfast each morning before he set fires in the community; and, upon learning this, the town council banned scrambled eggs on the grounds that eating them caused one to burn buildings. If the only support for this action is the sequence of events—eggs first, arson second—town officials who decided on the ban are guilty of the "after which" fallacy.

Second, determine if there is a single cause, or a number of causes for an effect; and when several causes are at work, determine which ones are the most significant. Causal reasoning on social problems is sometimes simplistic because a complicated problem, such as crime, poverty, or juvenile delinquency, is attributed to a single cause when, in fact, the causes are many and complex. For example, the speaker who claims that juvenile delinquency is caused by divorce, or by poverty, overlooks the fact that some delinquents come from the homes of happily married and well-to-do parents. When speaking on complex issues where a variety of causes create the problem you are addressing, be careful to avoid the fallacy of the single or insignificant cause.

Finally, determine whether or not the alleged cause is strong enough to produce the effect attributed to it. For instance, the soldier who claims that the defeat of Nazi Germany in World War II was due to the heroism of his infantry squad is attributing too much power to one, small military unit. Likewise, the person who claims recovery from a serious illness because he took a vitamin pill while the doctor was not looking is giving too much credit to the medical efficacy of a single vitamin pill.

Reasoning by Parallel Case

Reasoning by parallel case—also called literal analogy or comparison—is to argue that what happened in one situation will happen in a similar situation. For instance, if a neighbor installs a high-efficiency furnace and reduces his fuel bill by half, and you decide to do the same in order to reduce your fuel bill, you are reasoning from one furnace installation to another—that is, by parallel case. When you purchase food of a certain brand, are impressed with the quality, and buy that brand again, you are using parallel case ("those Summer Maid canned peaches were delicious, so I'll buy another can"). Public speakers often argue by parallel case, such as when they compare the programs of one city or state to those of another city or state, or when they reason that what worked well for one organization or institution will work well for a similar organization or institution.

Reasoning by parallel case can be thought of as a "logical shortcut" that is grounded in the overall inductive-deductive process, but that leaves out most of the formal steps of that process. Specifically, parallel case opens with the

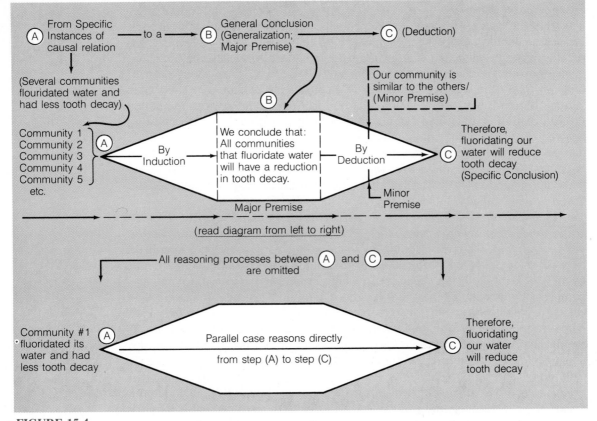

FIGURE 15.4

Reasoning by Parallel Case. *Reasoning by parallel case is a logical shortcut that omits most of the steps of the inductive-deductive process. The diagram at top shows the inductive-deductive process with all steps from A to B to C completed. The diagram at the bottom shows parallel case reasoning reaching the same conclusion (at point C) as the diagram at the top; it does this by moving directly from A to C. Reasoning by parallel case is also called* literal analogy, *or* comparison.

first step of induction (a specific case), then applies it directly to the final step of deduction (another specific case), omitting all steps in-between. The nature of this logical shortcut is illustrated by Figure 15.4.

Testing Parallel Case Reasoning

To check the logical strength of parallel case reasoning, two basic tests should be applied. *First, make sure that the information concerning the cases is accurate.* For instance, if a speaker urges a student club to "raise lots of money by selling candy, just as the Drama Society did," only to learn that the Drama Society actually lost money on the deal, the argument will collapse because the speaker neglected to check the facts.

Second, make sure that the cases being compared are alike in essential details. The more alike the cases are, the stronger the logical strength of the argument. For example, a speaker who urges the governing board of a rural community to adopt a certain program because it worked well in New York City and Chicago is on shaky logical ground, for large cities are different from rural areas in many respects. It would be better for that speaker to reason from one rural community to another rural community, with attention to similarities in such matters as economics, geography, and cultural history.

Now that we have considered the use of sound evidence and logical reasoning (specifically, reasoning by induction, deduction, causality, and parallel case), let us examine a second means of persuasion: the influence of the message source upon the audience.

II. Ethos: *Speaker Credibility*

Several years ago an experiment was conducted at Northwestern University in which a persuasive speech on the subject of national health insurance was recorded, and the recording was played to three different audiences. One audience was told that the speech was by the Surgeon General of the United States; another audience was told that it was by the Secretary General of the Communist Party of America; and the third was informed that the speech was by a college sophomore. Shift-of-opinion ballots marked by listeners before and after the recorded speech was played revealed that, although each group heard the same recording, those who attributed it to the most prestigious speaker, namely, the Surgeon General, registered the greatest change of attitude. In short, the source perceived by the audience to have the strongest credibility was the most persuasive.[6] Similar results have been reported by a number of other experimenters.[7]

These studies confirm a means of persuasion known to rhetoricians since the days of the ancient Greeks, namely, source credibility, for we are influenced more by speakers whom we like, respect, and trust than by those who arouse our hostility and suspicion. As Aristotle observed in the *Rhetoric*, "The character of the speaker is a cause of persuasion when the speech is so uttered as to make him worthy of belief."[8] Aristotle called this form of influence *ethos*, or "ethical proof." Let us examine the elements of ethical proof, then look at some specific ways by which it is established with the audience.

The Elements of Ethos

Source credibility, or *ethos*, can be defined as *a set of attitudes that the audience holds concerning the speaker*. The three key attitudinal elements of this set, as identified by Aristotle and sustained by modern research, are good character, competence, and good will.[9] Put in terms of your own persuasive speaking, you will be more effective if your listeners perceive you as a person who is trustworthy (good character), intelligent and knowledgeable on the subject (competent), and possessing good intentions and a friendly disposition (good will).

Information for evaluating your credibility reaches the audience by two routes: your reputation, or prior *ethos*, meaning what the audience knows about you before the speech begins; and demonstrated *ethos*, what you say and do while delivering the speech. The problem you face concerns how to communicate effectively your qualifications and good intentions to the audience. Let us examine some specific recommendations.

Prior Ethos

Credibility begins with what listeners know about the speaker in advance. We earn a positive reputation by education and experience that qualifies us to speak on the subject, and by being known as a fair, honest, and thoughtful individual. In your public speaking class, you gain prior *ethos* with your classmates by your general campus reputation (nice person, friendly, intelligent, etc.), and by your first speeches of the course. If you begin the course by speaking intelligently on topics that you are informed about, you will enhance your image with your audience. The attitude that you should work to build might be reflected by comments such as the following from your classmates: "I like to hear him speak—he's always well-prepared and worth listening to."

Demonstrated Ethos

At the time of the speech, your prior *ethos* is enhanced, sustained, or diminished by what is said about you (if you are introduced by another person), by your physical appearance and delivery, and by your speech content. If you are to be formally introduced, provide accurate information about yourself to the program chairperson prior to the speech. On the day of the speech, you might wish to check with the person doing the introduction to see if he or she seeks additional details concerning your qualifications. Remember that a positive introduction gets you off to a good start, making it easier to win a friendly hearing for your ideas.

Once you begin to speak, your *ethos* is demonstrated in at least three interacting dimensions: quality of content, skill in delivery, and fluency in use of the language. Evaluating the *content of your speech* is one of the primary ways that an audience assigns credibility. The content of your introduction, for instance, can include a reference to your qualifications to speak, whether from research or from personal experience. If your speech is based on research, include information in the introduction about the key sources you have used. On the other hand, if your speech is based on personal experience, explain the nature of that experience briefly and tactfully. For example, in the introduction of a persuasive speech in support of fraternities and sororities, a sorority member could mention her personal experience this way.

> My discussion today of the positive role that fraternities and sororities play on our campus is not as an outsider. Three years ago I became a member of a sorority, and have lived in the sorority house since that time. Last year I was the sorority's secretary, and this year I am serving as vice-president— a job that includes planning a variety of fund-raising projects for community charities.

After you have mentioned your qualifications in the introduction, be sure to "follow through" with an informed analysis, clear organization, sound ar-

Both classicial and contemporary theory emphasize the need to motivate an audience, not only with logical arguments but also with appeals to human emotions, needs, and values. (Beryl Goldberg/Monkmeyer Press)

guments, and strong evidence in support of your central idea. In this way you impress the audience as a speaker of intelligence and expertise whose ideas deserve serious consideration. Furthermore, by your content—especially in the introduction—you can establish common ground with your listeners, identifying your background and interests with theirs, thereby strengthening listener perceptions of your trustworthiness, credibility, and good will.[10] (For examples and suggestions on establishing common ground, see the discussion on the use of audience and occasion information in Chapter 5.)

In addition to content, your *delivery* and your *linguistic skills* influence your *ethos*. The speaker who looks directly at the audience and begins in a confident, friendly manner will gain audience respect and good will better than one who frowns, hems and haws, and stares at note cards or at the speaker's stand. Concerning the importance of eye contact, for instance, one experimental study concluded that "an increase in the amount of eye contact" by a public speaker "enhances the listener's perception of the speaker's credibility."[11] In addition, fluency in the use of language (including a good vocabulary, correct grammar, clear articulation, and accurate pronunciation) helps build and sustain audience confidence.[12] This is so because your use of language influences the audience's evaluation of your knowledge and intelligence—key elements of source credibility.

Thus far we have considered two means of persuasion: *logos*, or the logical strength of speech content, including reasoning and evidence; and *ethos*, or the attitude of the audience toward the speaker, including perceptions of the speaker's good character, competence, and good will. We now turn our attention to the third "available means of persuasion": appeals to audience psychology, or *pathos*.

288

Part IV
Types and
Forms of
Public
Speaking

III. Pathos: *Appeals to Audience Psychology*

As you know from your own experience as a listener, some speeches that are thoughtful in content are ineffective in persuading the members of the audience to change their attitudes or behavior. Often this is because the content, while clear and logical, is unimaginative and dull. Such speeches ignore the human desire for reasoned discourse to be presented in an interesting and moving way so that the audience is energized and motivated to decision and action. Aristotle recognized this psychological fact of life by teaching that speakers not only should argue logically, but also should stir the audience with appeals to *pathos*—that is, to human emotions, such as fear, anger, and pity.

Contemporary research informs us that understanding psychological appeals requires us to consider more than the emotions. In particular, the persuasive speaker should be aware of human needs and human values. Therefore, we can define psychological appeals to include those elements of speech content that motivate the audience by appealing to human *emotions, needs*, and *values*. Although the three overlap and interact with one another, we will consider them singly for purposes of clarity and emphasis.

Appeals to Emotions

Early in the *Rhetoric*, Aristotle remarks: "Persuasion is effected through the audience, when they are brought by the speech into a state of emotion." Later, he stated that by emotions he meant "those states which are attended by pain and pleasure, and which, as they change, make a difference in our judgments; for example: anger, pity, fear, and all the like, and also their opposites." In *De Oratore*, the Roman rhetorician Cicero explains emotional appeals as "the feelings on which we have to work" in the minds of listeners; his list of "feelings" included *love, hatred, anger, envy, pity, hope, joy, fear*, and *anxiety*. Similar lists can be found in numerous public speaking texts, both ancient and modern.[13]

Although lists of emotions provide an incomplete picture of the psychological appeals available to the public speaker, they do have some practical value. The value is not in a speaker's use of an extreme, mindless emotionalism that produces an uncritical response; rather, the rhetorical value is in the sensible and appropriate use of *pathos* to add persuasive strength to ideas that are grounded in reason, but which also touch on human feelings. An example would be the Independence Day speaker who employs moving examples of bravery from the period of the American Revolution, thereby stirring feelings of love of country. There is nothing wrong with this, provided it is not done to excess. Here are some emotions to which you could appeal in a responsible manner, together with some typical situations that might be fitting for such appeals.

Positive (pleasurable) emotions: *joy, relief, elation, happiness, patriotism.* Ceremonial occasions such as graduation exercises, patriotic celebrations, and inauguration addresses; talks of religious inspiration; political campaign speeches.

Negative (painful) emotions: *fear, anger, sympathy, pity, sorrow, shame.* Speeches concerning crime prevention, or national defense; talks on social problems such as aiding the sick and homeless, or dealing with the AIDS crisis; eulogies.

You can add sensible emotional appeals to your speeches in two ways: by careful choice of language, and by the type of supporting materials you use (for instance, examples and quotations lend themselves well to the communication of *pathos*). To illustrate, a student speaker who was a volunteer in the local Muscular Dystrophy Association (MDA) delivered an actuating speech to his public speaking class, urging his classmates to give time and financial support to the MDA. Along with other forms of support, he effectively appealed to the emotions of pity and sympathy with a true story of a birthday party for one of the children in the MDA program. While the child "watched and laughed," the speaker said in a direct, sincere delivery, "others had to push the buttons and turn the cranks" on the toys he had received, because the handicapped child was unable to perform such tasks for himself. The speaker then urged: "You, too, can help make a child happy by giving some of your time to our local MDA chapter."[14] In a discussion following the talk, several members of the class expressed an interest in working with the MDA program, primarily because they were moved by the specific examples in the speech.

Keeping the rhetorical value of appeals to human emotions in mind, let us now turn our attention to a related area of psychology—appeals based upon human needs.

Appeals to Needs

All human beings have needs, wants, desires—those life forces operating within us that motivate decision and action. Our needs range from the specific and easy-to-understand, such as the necessity for food and water, to the more abstract, complex, "psychological" needs, such as the desire to love and be loved, or the desire to accomplish something worthwhile in life. Knowledge of needs will help you adapt speech content to your audience, for by demonstrating how your proposal satisfies human wants and desires, you can better motivate listeners to change their attitudes and behavior.

Among the various explanations of human needs by social psychologists, that of A. S. Maslow stands out because of its clarity and practicality. Maslow employs a hierarchy of five levels, beginning with the predominant physiological and safety needs that must be satisfied before we begin to concentrate on other things (see Figure 15.5). When our physical and safety needs are met, we are able to focus upon "higher" wants and desires, such as the social, professional, and life-fulfilling ones. Maslow recognizes that we are more likely to dream of success in our jobs, discuss philosophy, or compose poetry when our stomachs are full, when we are in good health, and when we feel secure from harm.[15] Let us look at needs in more detail.

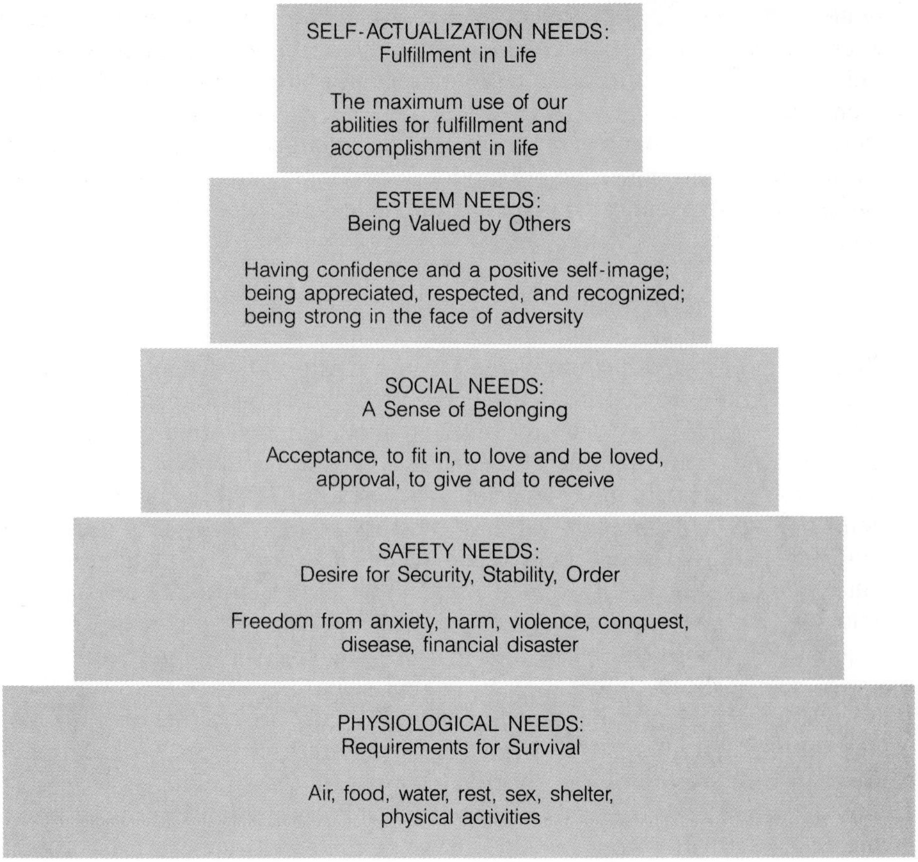

SELF-ACTUALIZATION NEEDS:
Fulfillment in Life

The maximum use of our
abilities for fulfillment and
accomplishment in life

ESTEEM NEEDS:
Being Valued by Others

Having confidence and a positive self-image;
being appreciated, respected, and recognized;
being strong in the face of adversity

SOCIAL NEEDS:
A Sense of Belonging

Acceptance, to fit in, to love and be loved,
approval, to give and to receive

SAFETY NEEDS:
Desire for Security, Stability, Order

Freedom from anxiety, harm, violence, conquest,
disease, financial disaster

PHYSIOLOGICAL NEEDS:
Requirements for Survival

Air, food, water, rest, sex, shelter,
physical activities

FIGURE 15.5

Maslow's Hierarchy of Needs. *According to psychologist A. H. Maslow, human needs emerge in a hierarchy, beginning with physical and safety needs, then ranging to social, esteem, and self-actualization needs. Only after basic needs are met do we turn our attention to the satisfaction of higher needs, such as belonging, being appreciated, and eventually achieving fulfillment and accomplishment in life.*

Physiological Needs: Requirements for Survival

Our physical needs take precedence over all others because they are essential to life and well-being. Specifically, these include air, food, water, rest, sex, shelter, and physical activity. Appeals to physiological needs are appropriate on topics such as health inspection of food products, clean air and water, rest and relaxation, sexual attraction, comfortable housing, sensible exercise, and so forth. For example, a speech supporting a bond issue for building a modern water system in your community could include an appeal to physical needs.

Safety Needs: Security, Stability, and Order

As our physiological needs are met, we turn our attention to our desire for safety. More specifically, we want to be free from anxiety, harm, violence, conquest, disease, and financial disaster. Instead, we prefer security, stability, and order. Persuasive appeals derived from our safety needs include proposals to join with others for purposes of protection from harm, patriotic concerns for national security, maintaining healthy bodies, having an adequate income and savings, having medical insurance, and so forth. Safety appeals could be employed in persuasive speeches on topics such as opposition to nuclear power, wearing seat belts while driving, joining an anticrime neighborhood watch program, or starting a campus escort service to prevent sexual assaults.

Social Needs: A Sense of Belonging

When physiological and safety needs are met, we turn our attention to the social needs. These include the desire to be accepted, to belong, to fit into a group; to love and be loved by family and friends; to be approved by those around us; and to give to others and receive from others. You could appeal to the social needs in persuasive speeches on a variety of topics, such as: urging listeners to join a social group (such as a fraternity or sorority, drama club, or hiking club); attending a get-acquainted party or dance; taking part in a program on how to work well with other people; purchasing a certain gift for a friend or loved one; or giving money to a worthwhile cause.

Esteem Needs: Being Valued by Others

Esteem needs go beyond "belonging" to reach the higher desire of being valued by others. This includes possessing a positive self-image and a sense of confidence; being appreciated and respected; having a good reputation; achieving, and having achievement recognized; being strong in the face of difficulty, while avoiding feelings of inferiority, weakness, or failure. Appeals to esteem needs could be employed on topics such as: getting a good education; taking a special training course (to better succeed in one's career); learning to communicate effectively; taking action that will facilitate financial independence; purchasing certain clothing or accessories ("dress for success"); and buying a prestigious automobile or home.

Self-Actualization Needs: Fulfillment in Life

Maslow explains self-actualization as "the full use and exploitation of talents, capacities, [and] potentialities...." Self-actualized people, he adds, are those who are "fulfilling themselves" and who are "developed or developing to the full stature of which they are capable."[16] In brief, self-actualization can be described as a maximum use of our abilities for fulfillment and accomplishment in life. This includes an acceptance of self, others, nature, and "reality"; a confident, scientific approach to living that avoids irrationality and superstition; a strong personal system of ethics; a healthy sense of humor; independence of thought; and an appreciation for civilizing values. Appeals to our desire for self-actualization could be employed in speeches with such themes as: doing something for the satisfaction of accomplishment ("Dare to Be Different: Read the Great Books of the Western World"); rethinking a point of view because of "the facts" in the case ("Reconsidering the Drug Problem: Let's

Do Something That Works''); choosing what is right, even if you are in the minority (''Defending the Rights of Minorities: Why It Must Be Done''); or doing something because it is democratic and humane (''You Should Join Amnesty International'').

292

Part IV
Types and
Forms of
Public
Speaking

Appeals to Values

Values can be defined as *''enduring beliefs'' that specific modes of conduct (such as honesty) and specific goals of existence (such as a world at peace) are preferable to opposite modes of conduct or goals of existence (honesty is preferable to dishonesty, and peace is preferable to war).*[17] Values grow out of our basic needs and are influenced by society, culture, and personal experience. For instance, we learn from our culture and from direct experience that, as a rule, courtesy is preferable to rudeness, cleanliness is preferable to filth, and knowledge is preferable to ignorance.

Psychologist Milton Rokeach, a leading authority on human values, reports a number of key findings about values that are helpful to the public speaker. Rokeach recognizes that value appeals are useful in persuasion, observing that values help us decide what is ''worth trying to influence or to change.''[18] The high value our culture places on human freedom, for example, can influence us to oppose various forms of government control over our lives. Thus, a persuasive speech urging the audience to fight censorship by joining an anticensorship organization, such as People For the American Way, could include a strong appeal to our preference for freedom.

Rokeach identifies two types of values: the *instrumental*, meaning specific behaviors of which we approve (such as tolerance); and the *terminal*, meaning our preferred end-states of existence, or ultimate goals (such as happiness). Rokeach recognizes that some values are more important than others. Based upon survey research of Americans, and starting with the highest or most important value, here is his ranking of the top ten values for both types.[19]

Instrumental Values   (behaviors that we prefer); being: (1) *honest* (truthful, sincere); (2) *responsible* (reliable); (3) *ambitious* (hard-working); (4) *forgiving* (willing to pardon others); (5) *open-minded*; (6) *courageous* (stand up for your beliefs); (7) *helpful* (concern for others); (8) *loving* (affectionate); (9) *capable* (competent); and (10) *clean* (neat).

Terminal Values   (ultimate goals); we should try to achieve: (1) *world peace*; (2) *family security* (provide for loved ones); (3) *freedom* (independence; free choice); (4) *equality* (brotherhood, equal opportunity for all); (5) *self-respect* (self-esteem); (6) *happiness* (contentedness); (7) *wisdom* (maturity, understanding life); (8) *national security* (protection from attack); (9) *salvation* (saved, eternal life); and (10) *true friendship*.

Additional values shared by Americans upon which you could base persuasive appeals include *good physical health, kindness, generosity, intelligence, respect for science, a sense of humor, a comfortable life, a fair and just society, patriotism, and a reverence for the Constitution.*[20] On those occasions when you argue that something should be done because it is the *honest, ethical* thing to do, that the audience should act on its *convictions* (*courage*), or that listeners should *take on a hard job and accomplish it* (*ambition*), you are using appeals derived from instrumental values. Also, when you argue that your proposal will help achieve such things as *personal freedom, social equality, family security,* or *happiness*, you are using appeals derived from terminal values.

This Chapter in Brief

The "available means of persuasion" consist of three major forms of support, or proof: *logos*, or logical proof, meaning evidence and reasoning; *ethos*, or ethical proof, meaning speaker credibility; and *pathos*, or emotional proof, meaning appeals to audience psychology (specifically, to human emotions, needs, and values). Logical proof consists of strong evidence (such as examples, statistics, and statements from authority), and sound reasoning (inductive, deductive, causal, and parallel case). Although evidence and reasoning should form the foundation of all of your persuasive efforts, it is particularly important to emphasize *logos* when the audience disagrees with your point of view.

Ethos, or ethical proof, consists of audience attitudes concerning the speaker's good character, competence, and good will. Often described as "speaker credibility," ethical proof in practice means that speakers who are perceived as trustworthy, knowledgeable, and friendly will be more effective than those perceived as immoral, incompetent, or hostile. You achieve credibility with your audience in two ways: by the reputation that precedes you (prior *ethos*), and by what you say and do during the speech itself (demonstrated *ethos*). Your reputation is enhanced by your education and experience on the subject (competence), and by being known as a person who is honest, fair, friendly, and thoughtful. You demonstrate your credibility at the time of the speech with content that is logical and well-organized, by delivery that is direct and lively, and by fluency (using good vocabulary, grammar, and pronunciation).

Pathos, or emotional proof, is the third means of persuasion available to the speaker. Emotional proof (also described as "appeals to audience psychology") refers to those elements of the speech that motivate listeners by stimulating human emotions, needs, and values. Appeals to emotions include speech materials that stir "positive" feelings such as joy, happiness, or elation, and "negative" feelings such as fear, anger, or pity. Appeals to needs include those identified by psychologist A. H. Maslow, namely, our physiological, safety, social, esteem, and self-actualization needs. Appeals to values include those identified by psychologist Milton Rokeach, namely, "instrumental values" (specific behaviors that we prefer) such as honesty, reliability, ambition, and courage; and "terminal values" (ultimate goals of existence), such as a world at peace, family security, personal freedom, equality, and wisdom.

Having surveyed the available means of persuasion, we turn our attention in the chapter that follows to the application of those means to specific types of persuasive speeches.

EXERCISES

294

*Part IV
Types and
Forms of
Public
Speaking*

1. While listening to speeches in various campus and community settings, make notes on those characteristics of speakers that help establish credibility, as well as those that diminish credibility. Compare your findings with the discussion of *ethos* in this chapter, then apply your conclusions to your own speaking. What specific things should *you* do to better achieve strong credibility with your audiences?

2. Study Martin Luther King's "I Have a Dream" speech (in Appendix III), paying particular attention to King's use of *pathos*. Using the discussion of *pathos* in this chapter as a guide, write down as many appeals to specific emotions, needs, and values as you can find in this famous speech.

SELECTED READINGS

Bradley, Bert E. *Fundamentals of Speech Communication: The Credibility of Ideas.* 5th ed. Dubuque, Ia.: Wm. C. Brown, 1988. In particular, see Chapter 6, "Creating Credibility," in which Bradley discusses how to establish *ethos* with your audiences.

Campbell, Karlyn K. *The Rhetorical Act.* Belmont, Calif.: Wadsworth, 1981. Campbell explains and illustrates the problems of communicating *ethos* in Chapter 6, "Obstacles to Source Credibility."

Huber, Robert B. *Influencing Through Argument.* New York: David McKay, 1963. Huber emphasizes the use of sound reasoning and evidence as a means of persuasion. His explanations are illustrated with numerous examples.

Larson, Charles U. *Persuasion: Reception and Responsibility.* 4th ed. Belmont, Calif.: Wadsworth, 1986. Chapter 4, "The Tools of Motivation," discusses psychological appeals, and Chapter 5 discusses logical appeals in persuasion.

Ross, Raymond S., and Ross, Mark G. *Understanding Persuasion.* Englewood Cliffs, N.J.: Prentice-Hall, 1981. Recommended as a brief, readable presentation of modern research in persuasion. In particular, see the discussion of ethical and emotional appeals in Chapter 2, "Springboards of Motivation."

ENDNOTES

1. Aristotle, *The Rhetoric*, trans. Lane Cooper (New York: Appleton-Century, 1932), p. 7.
2. Everett Lee Hunt, "Rhetoric as a Humane Study," *Quarterly Journal of Speech* 41 (April 1955): 114–117, at p. 114.
3. A Craig Baird, *Rhetoric: A Philosophical Inquiry* (New York: Ronald Press, 1965), p. 51.
4. For a study supporting the centrality of logical proofs in persuasion, see Richard E. Petty and John T. Cacioppo, "The Effects of Involvement on Responses to Argument Quantity and Quality: Central and Peripheral Routes to Persuasion," *Journal of Personality and Social Psychology* 46 (January 1984): 69–81. Concerning the importance of evidence, see James C. McCroskey, "A Summary of Experimental Research on the Effects of Evidence in Persuasive Communication,"

in R.

ers of

f Hu-
5.

971,''
omes

. 215–
ed by
ricans
ccom-
alues
March/

of Speech 55 (April 1969): 169–176; also, Robert N. Bostrom
Tucker, ''Evidence, Personality, and Attitude Change,'' *Speech*
1arch 1969): 22–27.

er, ibid., p. 27.

an, ''An Experimental Study of the Effects of Ethos in Public
h *Monographs* 16 (September 1949): 190–202. This report is
n's doctoral dissertation, Northwestern University, 1948.

Carl I. Hovland and Walter Weiss, ''The Influence of Source
munication Effectiveness,'' *Public Opinion Quarterly* 15 (Win-
50. Also, W. F. Strong and John A. Cook, *Persuasion: A Prac-
ctive Persuasive Speech* (Dubuque, Ia.: Kendall/Hunt, 1987),

toric, trans. Lane Cooper (New York: Appleton-Century,

ey and Thomas J. Young, ''Ethos and Credibility: The Con-
irement After Three Decades,'' *Central States Speech Journal*
–34. McCroskey and Young in their 1981 survey of the litera-
ude that modern research supports the classical elements of
npetence, and good will, with particular importance placed
competence. Also, see James L. Golden, Goodwin F. Ber-
E. Coleman, *The Rhetoric of Western Thought*, 4th ed. (Du-
/Hunt, 1989), pp. 523–534. To Aristotle's three elements of
uist, and Coleman add *charisma*—''the power dimension.''
ontent that establishes both the speaker's intelligence (exper-
identification with the audience (common ground) is recog-
etoricians but also by social psychologists. For a summary of
ogists on the matter, see R. Glen Hass, ''Effects of Source
ognitive Responses and Persuasion,'' in Richard E. Petty et
esponses in Persuasion* (Hillsdale, N.J.: Lawrence Erlbaum,

Eye Contact: A Nonverbal Determinant of Speaker Credibil-
r 23 (January 1974): 21–25.

e positive effects of verbal fluency upon the speaker's cred-
d R. Miller and Murray A. Hewgill, ''The Effect of Variations
idience Ratings of Source Credibility,'' *Quarterly Journal of*
1964): 36–44; Kenneth K. Sereno and Gary J. Hawkins,
ations in Speakers' Nonfluency upon Audience Ratings of
Speech Topic and Speaker's Credibility,'' *Speech Mono-*
57): 58–64; and David W. Addington, ''The Effect of Vocal
s of Source Credibility,'' *Speech Monographs* 38 (August

es are to Aristotle, *The Rhetoric*, op. cit., pp. 9 and 92; and
l Orators*, trans. J. S. Watson (Carbondale: Southern Illinois
)). For a modern discussion of emotional proof, see Wayne
f Persuasion*, 2d ed. (Boston: Houghton Mifflin, 1968), pp.

ophy Association,'' persuasive speech to actuate delivered
lass in advanced public speaking, University of North Caro-
ctober, 1987.

eory of Human Motivation,'' *Psychological Review* 50 (July
ee generally A. H. Maslow, *Motivation and Personality*, 2d
r & Row, 1970).

296

Part IV
Types and
Forms of
Public
Speaking

16. A. H. Maslow, "Self-Actualizing People: A Study of Psychological Health," J. Lowry, ed., *Dominance, Self-Esteem, Self-Actualization: Germinal Pap A. H. Maslow* (Monterey, Calif.: Brooks/Cole, 1973), p. 178.

17. The definition of values is paraphrased from Milton Rokeach, *The Nature man Values* (New York: The Free Press, 1973), pp. 1–25; see especially p

18. Ibid., p. 13.

19. Milton Rokeach, "Change and Stability in American Value Systems, 1968– *Public Opinion Quarterly* 38 (Summer 1974): 222–238. The list provided from the 1971 survey, pp. 226–227.

20. For a summary of several value systems, see Wayne C. Minnick, op. cit., p 220. A 1989 Gallup Poll confirmed some of the main needs and values identi Maslow and Rokeach, ranking the top five social values identified by Am as a good family life, a good self-image, being healthy, having a sense of plishment, and working for a better America. See "Social Values: Public Intangible Assets More Than Material Possessions," *The Gallup Report* (April, 1989): pp. 35–44.

> *Since the function of oratory is in fact to influence men's souls, the intending orator must know what types of soul there are….Hence a certain type of hearer will be easy to persuade by a certain type of speech to take such-and-such action for such-and-such reason, while another type will be hard to persuade. All this the orator must fully understand….*

—Plato,
Phaedrus (ca. 370 B.C.)[1]

Chapter 16

SPEAKING TO PERSUADE

*T*here are at least three methods by which human beings try to get other human beings to change their behavior: coercion, bribery, and persuasion. Coercion means the use of threats or force, such as telling a person that punishment of some sort will follow if he or she does not do what is demanded ("stop criticizing the government, or we will put you in jail"). Bribery means to offer money or some other form of payment to get a person to do what one wants done ("vote for my candidate and I will give you $50.00"). Although in some circumstances, coercion and bribery can be temporarily effective in changing behavior, neither is a means for a voluntary and genuine change in beliefs, values, or attitudes. (Here we can recall the wisdom of the proverb, "A man convinced against his will is of the same opinion still.") For voluntary, genuine change in the thinking of our fellow citizens, we look to persuasion—a method that provides for alternative arguments, free choice, and majority rule, thus making it compatible with democratic values. Our emphasis, of course, is upon persuasion by means of public speaking.

As you study this chapter on speaking to persuade, remember that the specific details of speech preparation and delivery have been explained earlier in the text. In particular, keep in mind the principles of audience analysis, as discussed in Chapter 5, and the methods of organizing and outlining the persuasive speech, as explained in Chapters 9, 10, and 11. If you have not yet done so, study carefully the content of the preceding chapter on the "Means of Persuasion." We are now ready to examine two important topics that round out our discussion of the speech to persuade, namely, types of persuasive speeches and several research-based approaches to persuasion.

I. Types of Persuasive Speeches

Although persuasive speeches can be classified in different ways, the method used here is one based upon the attitude of the audience toward the subject of the speech. A major advantage of this approach is that it helps focus your thoughts during speech preparation on those for whom the speech is planned—your listeners. In Chapter 5 we defined an *attitude* as *the predisposition of an individual (or an audience) to evaluate an issue, action, object, symbol, person, or situation in an unfavorable or favorable way*. Thus, the attitude of your audience on your topic determines what type of persuasive speech you need to prepare; that is, whether the speech is to convince, to actuate, or to reinforce. When your audience has an unfavorable or neutral attitude toward your topic, you should prepare a *convincing speech*; when an audience has a favorable attitude on a subject, but is doing little about it, you should prepare an *actuating speech*; and when the audience has a favorable attitude toward your topic, but needs to have that attitude strengthened, you should prepare a *reinforcing speech*.

Recall from Chapter 6 the three general purposes of public speaking, namely, to entertain, to inform, and to persuade. When your general purpose is to persuade, it is now appropriate for you to note in your written outline

These need a speech <u>to convince</u>

STRONGLY	MODERATELY	NEUTRAL	MODERATELY	STRONGLY
most difficult	difficult	least difficult		
unfavorable oppose disagree	unfavorable oppose disagree	undecided	favorable support agree	favorable support agree

FIGURE 16.1

Attitude Scale and the Speech to Convince. *An audience that is in disagreement with the speech purpose, or is neutral toward it, needs to hear a speech* to convince *(that is, to change attitudes). Note that the stronger the unfavorable attitude, the more difficult the task of convincing. There is little use in trying to move an audience to action until it is first convinced.*

which type of persuasion you have in mind. This is easy to do, for you simply substitute for "to persuade" the infinitive phrase that specifies which of the three types of persuasion you are planning, namely, whether "to convince," "to actuate," or "to reinforce." Here are some examples.

To convince.   Instead of saying "*to persuade* my audience that...," say: "*To convince* my audience that the president of the United States should be elected by direct vote of the people instead of by the electoral college."

To actuate.   Instead of saying "*to persuade* the members of my audience...," say: "*To actuate* the members of my audience to register to vote."

To reinforce.   Instead of saying "*to persuade*," say: "*To reinforce* my audience's belief in the Bill of Rights."

Let us now examine each type in more detail.

The Speech to Convince

The speech to convince is directed to those who disagree with, or who have no opinion on, the point of view you plan to present. As Figure 16.1 illustrates, audience attitudes on the subject range from strongly unfavorable to moderately unfavorable to neutral. This includes the audience that is extremely unfavorable—even hostile—to your opinion. However, not all audiences that need convincing are hostile. In fact, those who are moderately unfavorable to neutral may be friendly toward the speaker and harbor no intense objections to the speaker's view. (This occurs often in public speaking classes.) Such listeners are willing to listen, but they are reserving judgment until convinced that a change of attitude is justified. Also, notice that there is no point in making a speech to convince to an audience that agrees with you from the outset, for, as is obvious, such an audience is already convinced.

The response you seek in a speech to convince is *mental* (or "covert," meaning that it is within the mind, and therefore, not observable). You do not urge action (which is "overt," meaning that it is observable); rather, you ask for a change of thinking toward the subject under discussion. Even though, in theory, most persuasion implies some type of future action, the speech to convince does not call for specific action. Furthermore, contemporary research teaches us that when your goal is to convince, you should emphasize logical proof (*logos*) as the primary means of persuasion so that listeners will have an intellectual foundation upon which to base their change of attitude.[2] Without such a foundation, attitude change is likely to be minimal, weak, and lacking in permanence. This does not mean that you should spend all of your speaking time on logical support, to the neglect of *ethos* and *pathos*. However, it does mean that no matter how credible you are as a speaker and how extensive your appeals to emotions, needs, and values, you should be certain that the logical basis of your case is communicated to the audience clearly and persuasively.

To illustrate, a speaker should prepare a speech to convince if he or she decided to advocate handgun control to an audience of National Rifle Association (NRA) members. The specific purpose might be stated this way: "To convince the members of my audience that strict handgun control is in their best interest, and in the best interest of American society." Here are some additional examples of specific purposes for speeches to convince (assuming in each case that the audience is neutral or disagrees with the proposal).

To convince my audience that we should stop subsidizing college sports.
To convince my audience that all advertising of alcoholic beverages should be prohibited.
To convince my audience that the speech of all political groups, including undemocratic ones such as the KKK or the Nazi Party, is protected by the First Amendment.
To convince my audience that random drug testing violates the right of privacy.

An example of an important speech to convince occurred during the presidential campaign of 1960 when candidate John F. Kennedy, a Catholic, decided to answer the anti-Catholic arguments that were directed against him. The central theme of these arguments was that Kennedy, if elected, would use his political authority to favor the Catholic religion over others, thus violating the First Amendment. Kennedy secured a platform for addressing the religion issue by accepting a speaking invitation from the Greater Houston Ministerial Association.

On September 12, 1960, Kennedy spoke to the Houston ministers in what his friend and adviser Theodore Sorensen has called "the best speech of his campaign and one of the most important in his life."[3] Why so important? Because Kennedy and his campaign staff knew that the candidate must convince the voting public of his commitment to separation of church and state, or he might lose votes in what the polls showed would be a close election. Therefore, the audience for the speech was broader than the group of ministers who sat before him; it included all American voters who had reservations about having a Catholic president, or who were neutral on the issue.

Kennedy built his speech to convince around a clear, logical statement of principle—his belief in church-state separation. He then backed that assertion

302

*Part IV
Types and
Forms of
Public
Speaking*

with additional statements of belief on several key subissues (such as his opposition to tax support for church schools), supporting each in turn with references to his public record as a member of the U.S. Congress. He strengthened the persuasiveness of his *logos* with the skillful use of psychological supports, such as appeals to patriotism and religious tolerance. Kennedy's central argument was delivered in language clear and unequivocal early in the address.

> I believe in an America where the separation of church and state is absolute—where no Catholic prelate would tell the President (should he be a Catholic) how to act and no Protestant minister would tell his parishioners for whom to vote—where no church or church school is granted any public funds or political preference—and where no man is denied public office merely because his religion differs from the President who might appoint him or the people who might elect him.[4]

Further amplifying his position, Kennedy mentioned three specific examples of public positions he had taken on church-state matters before becoming a candidate for president: "I ask you...to judge me on the basis of fourteen years in the Congress—on my declared stands against an ambassador to the Vatican, against unconstitutional aid to parochial schools, and against any boycott of the public schools (which I attended myself)...." Kennedy then dramatized his commitment to church-state separation with an unusual promise that served as a climax for the speech.

> Whatever issue may come before me as President, if I should be elected—on birth control, divorce, censorship, gambling, or any other subject—I will make my decision in accordance with these views, in accordance with what my conscience tells me to be in the national interest, and without regard to outside religious pressure or dictate. And no power or threat of punishment could cause me to decide otherwise.
>
> But if the time should ever come—and I do not concede any conflict to be remotely possible—when my office would require me to either violate my conscience, or violate the national interest, then I would resign the office, and I hope any other conscientious public servant would do likewise.

The speech accomplished its goal. Americans in general were convinced that Kennedy, if elected, would support the doctrine of separation of church and state. As Theodore Sorensen, who helped Kennedy prepare the speech, later observed, the speech did not eliminate the religious issue completely; however, it "made unnecessary any further full-scale answer from the candidate" on the subject.[5]

The Speech to Actuate

In theory, you can deliver a speech to actuate to any audience, even one that has strong differences with you from the outset. In practice, it is difficult to actuate an audience successfully if you must first overcome a moderate-to-strong unfavorable attitude. In other words, if your audience disagrees with the underlying attitude upon which the recommended action is based, you are probably unwise to try to change that attitude and move to the action phase,

	These must first be convinced before being moved to action			These are ready for a speech to <u>actuate</u>	
	STRONGLY	MODERATELY	NEUTRAL	MODERATELY	STRONGLY
	unfavorable oppose disagree	unfavorable oppose disagree	undecided	favorable support agree	favorable support agree

Attitude Scale and the Speech to Actuate. *An audience that is in attitudinal agreement with the speaker at the outset is ready for a speech* to actuate, *based on that agreement. However, those who are neutral or opposed are not ready for such action unless they are first* convinced.

all in one speech. As Figure 16.2 illustrates, such an audience is more appropriately viewed as one for a speech to convince. In short, convince first, actuate second; and if this is too much for one speech, limit your general purpose to convincing.

On the other hand, an audience that holds a favorable attitude toward your subject at the outset is "ready" to respond positively to an appeal for action. You can even include those neutrals who first can be moved into the camp of moderate support for your view (although they will require some convincing before they are willing to act). For short speeches to actuate, such as those usually assigned in a public speaking class, this means that you should carefully choose a subject on which your audience already agrees with you, but is doing nothing about, and try to move that audience to act upon that existing, agreeable attitude.

The response you seek in a speech to actuate is more than mental—it is *overt and observable*. It includes such actions as voting, signing a petition, donating money, joining an organization, starting a self-help program (for instance, a plan of daily exercise), going to a professional for help (such as seeing a doctor about a persistent pain), buying a product or a service, and so on. An example would be a speech to a group of people who agreed from the start that medical insurance was a good thing, but who had none. The purpose of the speech would be something like this: "To actuate my listeners to sign up for a basic medical insurance program." Here are some additional examples of specific purposes for speeches to actuate.

To actuate my audience to sign a petition urging Bill Jones to run for student body president.
To actuate my audience to join the National Wildlife Association.
To actuate my audience to stop smoking.
To actuate the members of my class to sign up for a free workshop on how to prepare credentials for a job search.

As noted earlier, the speech to convince usually demands a primary emphasis upon logical proof as the means of persuasion; the speech to actuate, however, calls for a more balanced approach in which you give "equal time" to both logical and psychological proofs. This is especially true when your audience agrees with you from the start about the underlying attitude, but needs

A speech to convince usually demands strong use of logical proof. A speech to influence action, however, may call for a balance of logical and psychological appeals. (Billy Barnes/Stock, Boston)

to be motivated to act upon that attitude. Your logical appeals should be mixed in approximate equal amounts with those psychological appeals that motivate commitment by stirring audience emotions, needs, and values. Speech supports that tend to have a useful mix of the logical and the psychological include examples from real life, vivid comparisons and contrasts, and moving testimony from persons who are admired by the audience. For instance, if you are urging classmates to join the annual "Toys for Tots" campaign, the use of true stories of families and individual children who have been helped, and the testimony of past participants about the satisfaction of helping others, would be powerful motivational supports.

An example of an important speech to actuate occurred early in 1933 when newly inaugurated President Franklin D. Roosevelt delivered the first of his popular radio talks—known as "fireside chats"—to the American people. In the weeks before the inauguration, hundreds of American banks had failed and, as a result, thousands of ordinary people had lost their life savings. A general panic ensued as people rushed to withdraw their funds from those banks still open. The entire banking system of the United States faced imminent collapse.

President Roosevelt wasted no time in addressing the crisis. On the evening of inauguration day, he and his advisers began work on a plan to save the banks. While the plan was developed and appropriate legislation was approved by Congress, Roosevelt ordered all banks closed. For a week, the banking system was completely shut down. Then, on Sunday evening, March 12, 1933, only eight days after he was sworn in, Roosevelt spoke to the nation. His radio listeners were friendly and sympathetic—yet, on the matter of trusting the banks, they needed reassurance based upon facts before acting to redeposit their money (or, for those who had not yet withdrawn their funds, before deciding to leave their money in the bank).

306

*Part IV
Types and
Forms of
Public
Speaking*

Roosevelt began the speech with a clear statement of goals, as follows.

I want to talk for a few minutes with the people of the United States about banking—with the comparatively few who understand the mechanics of banking but more particularly with the overwhelming majority who use banks for the making of deposits and the drawing of checks. I want to tell you what has been done in the last few days, why it was done, and what the next steps are going to be. I recognize that the many proclamations from State capitols and from Washington, the legislation, the Treasury regulations, etc., couched for the most part in banking and legal terms, ought to be explained for the benefit of the average citizen. I owe this in particular because of the fortitude and good temper with which everybody has accepted the inconvenience and hardships of the banking holiday. I know that when you understand what we in Washington have been about I shall continue to have your cooperation as fully as I have had your sympathy and your help during the past week.[6]

Employing a problem-solution plan, Roosevelt explained why the bank problem had occurred, then summarized the steps his administration would follow to correct the situation. Obviously, the solution had to be presented clearly and persuasively if the speech was to be effective in persuading people to start using the banking system again. After explaining that the process of reopening would be carefully supervised by the government, Roosevelt presented the heart of his appeal for trust in the system. Here are some key selections from that appeal.

As a result, we start tomorrow, Monday, with the opening of banks in the twelve Federal Reserve Bank cities—those banks which on first examination by the Treasury have already been found to be all right. That will be followed on Tuesday by the resumption of all their functions by banks already found to be sound in cities where there are recognized clearing houses. That means about 250 cities of the United States....

On Wednesday and succeeding days banks in smaller places all through the country will resume business, subject, of course, to the Government's ability to complete its survey. It is necessary that the reopening of banks be extended over a period in order to permit the banks to make applications for the necessary loans, to obtain currency needed to meet their requirements and to enable the Government to make common sense checkups.

...It needs no prophet to tell you that when the people find that they can get their money—that they can get it when they want it for all legitimate purposes—the phantom of fear will soon be laid. People will again be glad to have their money where it will be safely taken care of and where they can use it conveniently at any time. I can assure you, my friends, that it is safer to keep your money in a reopened bank than it is to keep it under the mattress.

Roosevelt then moved to his conclusion by urging public support for the plan. Having laid the logical foundation for a restoration of confidence in the

These are ready for
a speech to reinforce

STRONGLY	MODERATELY	NEUTRAL	MODERATELY	STRONGLY
unfavorable oppose disagree	unfavorable oppose disagree	undecided	favorable support agree	favorable support agree

Attitude Scale and the Speech to Reinforce. *When the speaker and the audience are in firm agreement from the start, and the speaker is not trying to initiate action, a speech* to reinforce *is appropriate. Such a speech seeks to* strengthen *an existing attitude or action; it does not attempt to change attitudes or initiate new action.*

banks, he now expanded his use of psychological supports, including appeals to patriotism and to the rejection of fear. "It has been wonderful to me to catch the note of confidence from all over the country," Roosevelt said, finishing the speech as follows.

After all, there is an element in the readjustment of our financial system more important than currency, more important than gold, and that is the confidence of the people themselves. Confidence and courage are the essentials of success in carrying out our plan. You people must have faith; you must not be stampeded by rumors or guesses. Let us unite in banishing fear. We have provided the machinery to restore our financial system; it is up to you to support and make it work.

It is your problem, my friends, no less than it is mine. Together we cannot fail.

James MacGregor Burns, Roosevelt's biographer, observes that this speech was a "brilliant success."[7] The facts support Burns's assessment, for citizens responded in large numbers to Roosevelt's call for action by redepositing hoarded funds, and by starting to use the banking system again.[8]

The Speech to Reinforce

The speech to reinforce is also described in the literature of persuasion as speaking "to strengthen," "to stimulate," or "to inspire."[9] No matter what label is used, the principle behind the name is this: the speech to reinforce neither attempts to shift attitudes (as, for example, from unfavorable to favorable), nor does it try to initiate action; rather, its purpose is *to strengthen existing attitudes or actions*. As Figure 16.3 illustrates, the general purpose "to reinforce" fits those occasions when speaker and audience are in agreement from the beginning. A good example is the pep rally, where the communicators (cheerleaders) and audience (students) are on the same side from the outset. Other examples are graduation speeches, commemorative addresses (such as speeches on national holidays), eulogies for admired persons, and motivational talks to salesmen during a sales campaign.

The speech to reinforce can seek either a mental (covert) response or an observable (overt) response, because some occasions call for a speech to re-

308

Part IV
Types and
Forms of
Public
Speaking

inforce attitudes (mental response), and other occasions call for a speech to reinforce actions (observable response). An example of an occasion for reinforcing an attitude would be a campus Founders' Day celebration, during which a speaker might talk about what the school has meant to its students and to the community over the years. There is no disagreement between speaker and audience, thus, no forceful argumentation is called for. Rather, the purpose would be something like this: "To reinforce the dedication of my listeners to their alma mater" (or, using similar language, "To inspire in my listeners a deeper devotion to our alma mater").

An example of a speech to strengthen an action would be a pep talk by a candidate for student office to a group of supporters halfway through a campaign. The campaign workers already believe and have acted—however, they need to do more because the candidate is behind in the polls. The purpose of such a talk might be: "To reinforce the actions of my supporters so that they will put forth an extra effort in the final days of the campaign." Here are some additional examples of occasions for speeches to reinforce.

An inspirational speech to the leaders of a political party would be an occasion to strengthen an attitude (covert response): "To reinforce my audience's belief in the principles of our party."

An inspirational speech on the life of a person whom the audience admires is a time for strengthening an attitude (covert response): "To reinforce my audience's appreciation for the contributions of Thomas Jefferson to our political liberties."

A motivational talk a few days before final exams to a group of students in a program for academic underachievers, complimenting their success to date, then urging an extra measure of work (overt response): "To reinforce the willingness of the students in the program to put forth a strong study effort during the period of final exams."

The available means of persuasion for speeches to reinforce consists primarily of psychological proof, that is, appeals to emotions, needs, and values (see the discussion of *pathos* in the preceding chapter). This is so because the speaker and the audience are in basic agreement from the start; therefore, it is unnecessary to try to change attitudes by emphasizing logical argument and evidence. For instance, appeals to emotions such as joy, elation, and patriotism would be fitting for a pep talk to volunteers in a political campaign when polls predicted victory, and the speaker is urging a "final big push to hold the lead." Similarly, appeals to the social need of giving to others, combined with the value we place on being helpful to people less fortunate than ourselves, could form the basis for a speech to reinforce action in a fund-raising campaign for a worthwhile cause, such as Easter Seals. Speech materials useful for reinforcing include moving examples (true stories in particular), comparison and contrast, and testimony (especially quotations from history and statements from persons admired by the audience).

Abraham Lincoln's "Gettysburg Address" is an excellent example of the speech to reinforce. Delivered on November 19, 1863, at the dedication of the Gettysburg National Cemetery, the speech commemorated those who died in the battle of early June of that year. Lincoln recognized that he and his audience would be in agreement from the beginning, and consequently, that the occasion called for a speech to inspire. As you read the speech, notice that its rhetorical effect is achieved not by logical argument and evidence, but by Lincoln's brilliant use of language that stirs human emotions and values, thereby strengthening shared attitudes.

> Fourscore and seven years ago our fathers brought forth on this continent a new nation, conceived in liberty, and dedicated to the proposition that all men are created equal.
>
> Now we are engaged in a great civil war, testing whether that nation, or any nation so conceived and so dedicated, can long endure. We are met on a great battlefield of that war. We have come to dedicate a portion of that field as a final resting place for those who here gave their lives that that nation might live. It is altogether fitting and proper that we should do this.
>
> But, in a larger sense, we cannot dedicate—we cannot consecrate—we cannot hallow—this ground. The brave men, living and dead, who struggled here, have consecrated it far above our poor power to add or detract. The world will little note nor long remember what we say here, but it can never forget what they did here. It is for us, the living, rather, to be dedicated here to the unfinished work which they who fought here have thus far so nobly advanced. It is rather for us to be here dedicated to the great task remaining before us—that from these honored dead we take increased devotion to that cause for which they gave the last full measure of devotion; that we here highly resolve that these dead shall not have died in vain; that this nation, under God, shall have a new birth of freedom; and that government of the people, by the people, for the people, shall not perish from the earth.[10]

Types of Persuasive Speeches in Summary

In review, early in the process of preparing a persuasive speech, determine the attitude of the audience (whether unfavorable, neutral, or favorable) toward your proposal. Then, based upon this determination, decide whether the speech should be to convince, to actuate, or to reinforce. Plan a speech *to convince* when the audience attitude is unfavorable or neutral; support your points with logical argument and sound evidence. Plan a speech *to actuate* when the audience is in general agreement on the underlying attitude, but is doing little about it; support your points with a balance of logical and psychological proofs. Finally, plan a speech *to reinforce* when your audience agrees with you from the outset concerning the attitude or action you are advocating; support your points with effective psychological proofs (appeals to emotions, needs, and values). For an overview of the ideas presented in this summary, see Figure 16.4.

II. Research-Based Approaches to Persuasive Speaking

After you have analyzed audience attitudes on your subject, and—based on that analysis—have determined whether your general purpose is to convince, to actuate, or to reinforce, consider developing an overall approach to the

310

*Part IV
Types and
Forms of
Public
Speaking*

TYPES OF PERSUASIVE SPEECHES	AUDIENCE ATTITUDE TOWARD SPEECH PURPOSE	MEANS OF PERSUASION TO EMPHASIZE	GOAL AND RESPONSE SOUGHT
To Convince	Opposed (or neutral)	Logical (sound reasoning and evidence)	Mental agreement (a covert, nonobservable response)
To Actuate	In favor, but doing little about it	Balance between logical and psychological	Action (an overt, observable response)
To Reinforce	In favor, but can be strengthened: a. Intensify an existing attitude b. Intensify an existing action	Psychological (appeals to emotions, needs, and values)	a. A stronger attitude (covert) or b. Improved action (overt)

FIGURE 16.4

Key Factors of Each Type of Persuasive Speech. *This chart will help you to understand how the key factors of audience attitude, means of persuasion, and speech goal vary for the three types of persuasive speeches. By reading from left to right, for example, you can see that the speech* to convince *is appropriate for an audience* opposed *to your purpose, that you should stress* logical proof *in the content of the speech, and that the goal you seek is* mental agreement *by those who listen.*

speech that is based on recent research. The discussion below will assist you in developing such an overview by summarizing four research-based approaches to persuasion, namely: the logical argument approach, the argument/ counter-argument approach, the cognitive consistency approach, and the reward/penalty approach. The four were chosen because they meet the standards of *significance* (each is the subject of important research), *practicality* (each is readily adaptable to the public speaking situation), and *communication ethics* (each harmonizes with the recommendations in Chapter 3 that the members of your audience be considered persons of dignity, worth, and critical capacity).

The Logical Argument Approach

In his lectures on effective speaking and writing, published in 1783, English rhetorician Hugh Blair stated: "...let every orator remember, that the impression made by fine and artful speaking is momentary; that made by argument and good sense, is solid and lasting."[11] Happily for those who have faith in human reason, Blair's "argument and good sense" remains an effective means of persuasion, as the research reported below will attest. You make use of this traditional approach when you emphasize *logos* (sound reasoning and evidence) as your primary means of persuasion.

The logical argument approach is particularly appropriate for the speech to convince, and for the speech to actuate when the audience first needs to be convinced to change its underlying attitude before action is recommended. This observation is based upon experimental studies, reported by both social psychologists and communication scholars, which conclude that a logic-based approach is needed in either of two circumstances: first, *when the audience is opposed to your proposal*; and, second, *when the audience perceives your topic to be vital to its interests.*[12] The studies revealed that in either circumstance, *logos* was essential for genuine change to occur (or, put differently, without a strong logical foundation, *ethos* and *pathos* were inadequate to effectively change minds). One can infer from this finding that the stronger the opposition, and the more vital the perceived interest, the more effective should be your use of logical proof.

Your use of evidence (such as examples, comparisons and contrasts, statistics, and statements from authority) is critical to the effectiveness of the logical argument approach. Several contemporary studies report that speeches backed by strong evidence produce more change in audience attitudes than those without evidence.[13] In addition, we learn that the use of good evidence significantly increases sustained attitude change while, at the same time, it enhances the persuader's credibility (the higher the quality of evidence used, the higher the *ethos* assigned by the audience to the communication source).[14]

Furthermore, for significant change in attitudes to occur in a persuasive speech, research instructs us that the evidence you use should be perceived by your listeners as having *all three* of the following characteristics:[15]

Novelty. The evidence should be fresh and new. Old information, such as examples and statistics that the audience has heard before, is not as persuasive as new information.

Importance. The evidence should be important to the audience. The more it touches on vital interests, the more persuasive it will be.

Plausibility. The evidence should be believable. This is established by your *ethos*, and by the skill with which you establish the credibility of the sources you are using (for instance, telling where you got the material, and explaining why the source is qualified).

To be effective, your evidence must be explained well to the audience. Research supports the recommendation that you should present evidence so that your listeners understand it and see its relationship to the argument that it supports.[16] In other words, the audience might miss the point you are making and remain unconvinced unless you explain clearly how the evidence supports your argument. During your rehearsal of the speech, you can work to achieve both of these standards by practicing the presentation of the evidence in terms that are easily grasped (pay close attention to clarity and simplicity in language; avoid complex statistics and long, complicated quotations; use visual aids where needed; and so on), and by being careful to relate the materials to the argument under discussion.

The Argument/Counter-Argument Approach

This second approach is a variation of the logical argument method discussed above. Argument/counter-argument means that after you state your position and support it with strong reasoning and evidence, you then *answer the main objections to your point of view*. In other words, build your case, then demolish the opposing case. Research shows that refuting opposing views adds to the persuasiveness of your message in the following circumstances:[17]

312

*Part IV
Types and
Forms of
Public
Speaking*

■ *When the audience attitude at the beginning of the speech is opposed to your point of view*. As with the one-sided argument approach discussed above, this finding suggests that the use of counter-argument is appropriate for speeches *to convince*.

■ *When the audience is well-educated*. This conclusion suggests that the better educated the audience, the more you need to consider presenting an answer to opposing arguments as a part of your strategy of persuasion.

■ *When the audience will later be subjected to counterpersuasion*. This result suggests that in speaking situations where the audience will hear arguments on two or more sides of an issue, or in campaigns where a variety of views are communicated to the public, the use of counter-argument helps to strengthen a persuasive proposal against counterpersuasion.

In addition, at least two studies confirm that you will be more effective in the use of counter-argument if you *present your case first, and answer opposing views second*, rather than the other way around.[18] You can work argument and counter-argument into the outline in a number of ways, including using them as subordinate points under a main point, or as main points within themselves. For example, if you divide the body of the speech into two major units, with your constructive argument forming the first unit, and your answer to opposing arguments forming the second unit, you have organized your speech around argument/counter-argument. In skeleton form, such a two-point outline would look like this:

Central Idea: Statement of your proposal for solving a problem (such as, "We need strict controls on the sale of handguns in the United States").

I.   There are two main reasons why my proposal should be adopted.
  A.   State your first reason, and support it with evidence.
  B.   State your second reason, and support it with evidence (and so forth if additional reasons are given).

II.   The two main objections to my proposal are illogical and not supported by the facts.
  A.   The first objection is logically weak (answer the objection with counter-argument and evidence).
  B.   The second objection is logically weak (answer the objection with counter-argument and evidence, and so forth).

The Cognitive Consistency Approach

Another approach is to base your speech planning on a theory of modern psychology known as "cognitive consistency."[19] *A cognition is any belief, value, or attitude held by an individual*. For example, a person might hold a positive, supporting attitude toward programs designed to help the needy; this attitude of support can be classified as a "cognition." *By "consistency" is meant that one's beliefs, values, attitudes, and behaviors, are in harmony with each other—that is, they are not inconsistent.* For instance, the person who has a positive attitude toward programs for the needy, but who donates nothing to charity, is behaving in a manner inconsistent with his or her cognitions. To be consistent, that individual needs to change either the attitude or the behavior.

There are three basic propositions about human thought and conduct that emerge from the research on cognitive consistency. Taken together, these propositions form the theoretical basis for an approach to persuasion.[20]

1 People prefer a state of consistency among their beliefs, values, attitudes, and behaviors.

2 Persons who are inconsistent in their cognitions and behaviors are uncomfortable; this discomfort motivates change that will restore consistency.

3 Therefore, persuasive speeches that identify inconsistencies in audience beliefs, values, attitudes, or behaviors, and that propose changes that will restore harmony and balance, have a strong advantage toward effectiveness.

When planning a speech using the cognitive consistency approach, you should be aware that research shows that once discomfort is created in the listener, *the listener often tries to avoid the argument you are making* (the listener can refuse to listen; ignore you; walk out; and so forth).[21] On the other hand, your goal is get members of the audience to listen carefully and consider making the change in attitude or behavior that you propose. To help achieve this, plan your introduction carefully so that listeners will be attracted to you and to the content of the speech, and will want to listen to your remarks (see Chapter 11 for suggestions on preparing effective introductions). In a nutshell, gaining interest and winning a friendly hearing early in the speech is especially important when your argument is based upon cognitive consistency.

The cognitive consistency approach can be employed in persuasive speeches to convince or to actuate. For speeches *to convince*, you would need to demonstrate that the attitude you are trying to change is out of harmony with some other belief, value, or attitude held by the listener. For example, assume that you are planning to speak in favor of racial tolerance to an audience that is racially intolerant. You are aware that most of those in the audience attend church, and are members of patriotic societies. You could build your case for tolerance on the inconsistency between principles of both religion and patriotism (emphasizing such values as brotherly love, democratic respect for each individual, and so forth), and racial prejudice. You could then propose a way to achieve consistency, namely, cultivate an attitude of tolerance to replace racial prejudice.

For speeches *to actuate*, you would need to demonstrate that the listener's current behavior is inconsistent with important cognitions, and that the course of action you are proposing will bring the listener's attitudes and behavior into harmony with each other. For instance, a speech advocating safe driving could be planned around the value listeners place upon being law-abiding citizens; you would emphasize that driving safely, including observing the speed limit, is consistent with being a law-abiding person. Similarly, a speech to actuate listeners to sign a petition opposing nuclear power could be based upon an audience attitude supporting a safe environment. Thus, you could stress that signing the petition harmonizes with the attitude in favor of environmental safety.

314

*Part IV
Types and
Forms of
Public
Speaking*

You can work the cognitive consistency approach into your outline in a variety of ways. For instance, in a problem-solution speech *to actuate*, you could explain the problem as an inconsistency between what the audience believes and how the audience behaves. Your solution could propose an action that fits with the belief, thereby restoring consistency. Or you could develop a speech *to convince* by first reviewing and confirming a fundamental principle the audience accepts, and second, by demonstrating how the audience attitude that you are trying to change is inconsistent with the more general, fundamental principle. An example, based on the inconsistency between the tenets of democracy and the practice of censorship, could be outlined as follows.

I. A basic principle of our free, democratic society is that each person is trusted to make moral and political choices for himself or herself. (State the fundamental principle accepted by the audience; develop it convincingly with subarguments and evidence.)

II. Censorship by the government violates the principle that we trust the individual to make decisions for himself or herself. (State the attitude that you are trying to change; with subarguments and evidence, show how it is inconsistent with point I above.)

Central Idea   (the conclusion that restores consistency): Therefore, to be true to your belief in freedom and democracy, you should support the elimination of censorship for adults in the United States.

The Reward/Penalty Approach

As the label suggests, the reward/penalty approach means that you support your central idea in a persuasive speech by emphasizing the desirable things (rewards) that will happen if your view is adopted, then strengthen the argument by pointing out the undesirable things (penalties) that will occur if your proposal is rejected. In the literature of persuasion, this approach is also described by labels such as "honey and vinegar," "carrot and stick," "positive and negative," and "hope vs. fear." Numerous research reports conclude that both reward and penalty are highly motivating to human beings, and are, therefore, effective approaches to persuasion.[22]

You have three options in the use of reward and penalty in public speaking: you can build on *reward only* ("start saving now for a happy retirement"); you can build on *penalty only* ("stop smoking, for it can kill you"); or, as is recommended here, you can *include both reward and penalty in the same speech*. Rewards can include the tangible (win a color television), achieving a goal (earn a job promotion), or an internal satisfaction (feeling good because you donated to charity). Penalties reflect the opposite of rewards, namely, losing something tangible, the disappointment of failing to achieve a goal, having a negative self-image, catching a dreaded disease, and so forth.

The appeal based upon fear is one common form of negative motivation that we encounter regularly. For instance, the slogan "just say no to drugs" is usually accompanied with penalty appeals based upon fear of the destructive consequences of drug use; the AIDS epidemic has sparked a campaign for "safe sex practices" that makes maximum use of the fear of catching a painful, incurable disease; and insurance companies urge us to purchase liability insurance for our cars and our homes so that we will not worry about the penalty of financial ruin in case we are at fault in an accident. Additional subjects for which fear appeals might be appropriate include establishing a campus escort service to protect students from assault, having regular medical checkups to avoid cancer and other diseases, and wearing one's seat belt to help protect from severe injury or death in case of an automobile accident. If you plan to use fear-based penalty as a motivating factor in a persuasive speech, consider these findings from recent research reports:[23]

■ *Fear appeals that are not believable, or that are too vivid and frightening, are counterproductive.* Listeners reject or "tune out" fear appeals they do not believe, or that they find overly vivid and revolting. (In other words, employ believable appeals, and do not overdramatize them.)
■ *The issue should be made relevant to the listener, and the speaker should make clear how the course of action being proposed will avoid the undesirable consequences being discussed.*
■ *Although fear is a psychological appeal* (see Maslow's hierarchy of human needs, discussed in Chapter 15), *it must be backed with strong evidence if it is to have a lasting impact upon the listener.*
■ *Fear appeals are strengthened if they include other persons, such as a spouse or children, valued by the listener.* (For example, a speech to a group of concerned neighbors opposing the approval of a nearby hazardous waste disposal facility could emphasize the danger to everyone in the area, including the family members of those in attendance.)

Although the reward/penalty approach can be applied to persuasive messages in a number of ways, it is particularly useful in a problem-solution speech *to actuate* in which you (1) explain the problem, (2) propose a workable solution to the problem (action), then (3) vigorously support your analysis by setting out the good things that will happen if your solution is adopted (reward), and the bad things if it is not (penalty). In skeleton outline form, the body of such a speech would look like this:

I. *Problem.* Explain the problem; in subpoints, using strong evidence, prove that it is serious; show how it concerns your audience.

II. *Solution.* Explain your proposed solution to the problem; in subpoints, set out a plan of action.

III. *Reward/Penalty.*
   A. (Reward) Explain the positive things that will result if your solution is adopted; support with evidence.
   B. (Penalty) Explain the negative things that will result if your solution is rejected (can include fear appeals); support with evidence.

316

*Part IV
Types and
Forms of
Public
Speaking*

As was explained earlier, the four approaches discussed above—the logical argument approach, the argument/counter-argument approach, the cognitive consistency approach, and the reward/penalty approach—were chosen because of the strong research base upon which each rests. If none of them fits your needs for a particular speech, simply "file them for future reference." Perhaps next time one of them will be helpful. Also, you can apply part of an approach, or combine elements of two or more approaches, without using any one of them in its entirety. Other approaches that you can consider include building a persuasive appeal around *a basic human need*, planning a speech around *a value (or set of values)* that is important to the audience (see the discussion of both needs and values in Chapter 15), or developing a creative approach of your own that adapts your knowledge of persuasion to the subject, audience, and occasion.

This Chapter in Brief

In a free society, persuasive speaking is an essential tool of civilized decision making, serving as a substitute for bribery or force. Persuasive speeches can be classified according to three types—convincing, actuating, and reinforcing—depending upon the attitude of the audience toward the topic. The speech *to convince* is called for when the audience is opposed to the topic; the speaker's goal is to change audience attitude. The speech *to actuate* is appropriate when the audience is in basic agreement with the speaker's attitude, but is not doing anything about it; the speaker's goal is to initiate action. The speech *to reinforce* is called for when the audience agrees with the speaker from the outset, and the speaker's goal is to intensify and strengthen that agreement.

Four research-based approaches to planning a persuasive speech are discussed, namely, the logical argument approach, the argument/counter-argument approach, the cognitive consistency approach, and the reward/penalty approach. Having examined the principles of informative and persuasive speaking in some detail in this chapter, and in the two that precede it, we are now ready to consider speeches that do not neatly fit the molds labeled "to inform" or "to persuade." Thus, we turn our attention in the chapter that follows to special forms of public speaking, and speeches for special occasions.

EXERCISES

1. Before your next persuasive speech in your public speaking course, conduct a poll of the attitudes of your classmates on the topic of your speech (you will find suggestions for doing this in Chapter 5). Use the results of your poll to determine your general persuasive purpose, that is, whether your speech is to convince, to actuate, or to reinforce.

2. After studying the cognitive consistency approach to persuasion as explained in this chapter, make a list of student attitudes and/or actions that you believe are inconsistent with each other (this attitude and that attitude or behavior don't go together). Use the list to plan a speech to your class (or other student group) based upon the cognitive consistency approach to persuasion.

SELECTED READINGS

Dickens, Milton. *Speech: Dynamic Communication.* 3d ed. New York: Harcourt Brace Jovanovich, 1974. Dickens includes a chapter on each of the three attitude-based purposes of persuasive speaking: Chapter 14 concerns the speech to reinforce, Chapter 15 the speech to convince, and Chapter 16 the speech to actuate.

Hunt, Gary T. *Public Speaking.* 2d ed. Englewood Cliffs, N.J.: Prentice-Hall, 1987. Hunt places a strong emphasis upon the theory and practice of persuasive speaking in Chapters 13, 14, and 15. Topics discussed include the place of persuasion in American society, forms of proof, the use of evidence, and basic strategies and tactics of persuasion.

Ross, Raymond S., and Ross, Mark G. *Understanding Persuasion.* Englewood Cliffs, N.J.: Prentice-Hall, 1981. Chapter 3 on "Theories of Persuasion" includes an excellent discussion of consistency theories that would help broaden the student's understanding of cognitive consistency.

Strong, W. F., and Cook, John A. *Persuasion: A Practical Guide to Effective Persuasive Speech.* Dubuque, Ia.: Kendall/Hunt, 1987. This entire text is about persuasive speaking, with a special emphasis on how the public speaker can use the cognitive consistency approach to persuasion.

Verderber, Rudolph F. *The Challenge of Effective Speaking.* 6th ed. Belmont, Calif.: Wadsworth, 1985. In Part IV, Verderber discusses persuasive speaking in four practical, readable chapters. Of special interest are Chapter 14 on the speech to convince, and Chapter 15 on the speech to actuate.

ENDNOTES

1. Plato, *Phaedrus*, trans. R. Hackforth (Indianapolis, Ind.: Bobbs-Merrill, 1952), p. 148.
2. For example, see James C. McCroskey, "A Summary of Experimental Research on the Effects of Evidence in Persuasive Communication," *Quarterly Journal of Speech* 55 (April 1969): 169–176; and Richard E. Petty and John T. Cacioppo, "The Effects of Involvement on Responses to Argument Quantity and Quality: Central and Peripheral Routes to Persuasion," *Journal of Personality and Social Psychology* 46 (January 1984): 69–81.
3. Theodore C. Sorensen, *Kennedy* (New York: Harper & Row, 1965), p. 215.
4. The selections from Kennedy's speech of September 12, 1960, to the Houston Ministerial Association are from a voice recording in the possession of the author.
5. Sorensen, op. cit., pp. 217–218.
6. All quotations are from Samuel I Rosenman, comp., *The Public Papers and Addresses of Franklin D. Roosevelt* (New York: Random House, 1938), vol. 2,

318

Part IV
Types and
Forms of
Public
Speaking

pp. 61–65. The Rosenman text has been corrected by the author, using a voice recording of the speech, to include Roosevelt's interpolations made during actual delivery.

7. James MacGregor Burns, *Roosevelt: The Lion and the Fox* (New York: Harcourt, Brace & World, 1956), p. 168.

8. For statistics on the return of money to the banking system following FDR's first fireside chat, see Rosenman, op. cit., "Note," pp. 65–66.

9. See, for example, Giles W. Gray and Waldo W. Braden, *Public Speaking: Principles and Practice*, 2d ed. (New York: Harper & Row, 1963), pp. 379–396, where the speech to reinforce is called a speech to "stimulate." Also, Milton Dickens, *Speech: Dynamic Communication*, 3d ed. (New York: Harcourt Brace Jovanovich, 1974), pp. 263–275, where the term "reinforce" is used.

10. The text of the "Gettysburg Address" is from John G. Nicolay and John Hay, eds., *Abraham Lincoln: Complete Works* (New York: The Century Company, 1920), vol. 2, p. 439.

11. Hugh Blair, *Lectures on Rhetoric and Belles Lettres* (1783), in James L. Golden and Edward P. J. Corbett, *The Rhetoric of Blair, Campbell, and Whately* (New York: Holt, Rinehart and Winston, 1968), p. 106.

12. For a study by psychologists, see Richard E. Petty and John T. Cacioppo, op. cit.; for a study by a communication scholar, see William L. Benoit, "Argumentation and Credibility Appeals in Persuasion," *Southern Speech Communication Journal* 52 (Winter 1987): 181–197.

13. James C. McCroskey, op. cit.; Robert N. Bostrom and Raymond K. Tucker, "Evidence, Personality, and Attitude Change," *Speech Monographs* 36 (March 1969): 22–27; and John A. Kline, "Interaction of Evidence and Readers' Intelligence on the Effects of Short Messages," *Quarterly Journal of Speech* 55 (December 1969): 407–412.

14. McCroskey, op. cit., p. 175; also, Kline, ibid., p. 412.

15. Donald D. Morley and Kim B. Walker, "The Role of Importance, Novelty, and Plausibility in Producing Belief Change," *Communication Monographs* 54 (December 1987): 436–442.

16. Michael Burgoon and Judee K. Burgoon, "Message Strategies in Influence Attempts," in G. J. Hanneman and W. J. McEwen, *Communication and Behavior* (Reading, Mass.: Addison, Wesley, 1975), pp. 151–153.

17. Carl I. Hovland, Irving L. Janis, and Harold H. Kelley, *Communication and Persuasion: Psychological Studies of Opinion Change* (New Haven, Conn.: Yale University Press, 1953), pp. 105–111. For a summary of additional research on the use of counter-argument, see Raymond S. Ross and Mark G. Ross, *Understanding Persuasion* (Englewood Cliffs, N.J.: Prentice-Hall, 1981), pp. 140–147.

18. Loren J. Anderson, "A Summary of Research on Order Effects in Communication," in Jimmie D. Trent, Judith S. Trent, and Daniel J. O'Neill, eds., *Concepts in Communication* (Boston: Allyn and Bacon, 1973), pp. 128–134.

19. The overlapping family of consistency theories, known variously as balance theory (Heider), congruity theory (Osgood and Tannenbaum), and dissonance theory (Festinger), is usually traced to F. Heider's "Attitudes and Cognitive Organization," *Journal of Psychology* 21 (1946): 107–112. See also Charles E. Osgood and Percy H. Tannenbaum, "The Principle of Congruity in the Prediction of Attitude Change," *Psychological Review* 62 (1955): 42–55; and Leon Festinger, *A Theory of Cognitive Dissonance* (Palo Alto, Calif.: Stanford University Press, 1957).

20. The three points are adapted from Gerald R. Miller, Michael Burgoon, and Judee K. Burgoon, "The Functions of Human Communication in Changing Attitudes and Gaining Compliance," in Carroll C. Arnold and John Waite Bowers, eds.,

Handbook of Rhetorical and Communication Theory (Boston: Allyn and Bacon, 1984), pp. 430–441.

21. For a discussion of avoidance as a response to consistency arguments, see Ross and Ross, op. cit., pp. 103–106.

22. For a review of research on reward and penalty see: Erwin P. Bettinghaus and Michael J. Cody, *Persuasive Communication*, 4th ed. (New York: Holt, Rinehart and Winston, 1987), pp. 153–160; Michael Burgoon and Judee K. Burgoon, "Message Strategies in Influence Attempts," op. cit., pp. 160–161; Gerald R. Miller, "Persuasion," in Charles R. Berger and Steven H. Chaffee, *Handbook of Communication Science* (Newbury Park, Calif.: Sage Publications, 1987), pp. 468–474; Gerald R. Miller, Michael Burgoon, and Judee K. Burgoon, "The Functions of Human Communication in Changing Attitudes and Gaining Compliance," op. cit., pp. 423–424; and Mary John Smith, *Persuasion and Human Action* (Belmont, Calif.: Wadsworth, 1982), pp. 230–232.

23. Concerning fear appeals, see Bettinghaus and Cody, op. cit., pp. 159–160; and Burgoon and Burgoon, "Message Strategies in Influence Attempts," op. cit., pp. 160–161.

"

There are a number of occasions on which speechmaking is traditional and expected and for which speechmaking is a central part of the ceremony itself....[These include] memorial services, testimonial dinners, anniversaries, and dedications, for example.

"

—Robert G. King,
Forms of Public Address (1969)[1]

Chapter 17

SPECIAL FORMS AND OCCASIONS

*I*n your speaking on campus and in the community you will encounter a variety of special situations that are not appropriate for the usual informative or persuasive speech. Rather, these occasions call for a special form of public speaking; for instance, the graduation exercise calls for a commencement address, the awards ceremony calls for appropriate "presentation remarks," and the after-dinner occasion often calls for an entertaining speech. Of course, the rhetorical principles that apply to speaking in general also apply to these and other special forms. However, there are some practical suggestions, specific to the type of speech and occasion, that you should consider when preparing the specialized talk. In order to cover these suggestions in an organized manner, this chapter considers the following three topics: special forms of persuasive speaking; speeches of courtesy; and the speech to entertain.

I. Persuasive Speeches: Special Forms

Three special forms of persuasion deserve our attention at this point, namely, the speech of inspiration, the speech of nomination, and the speech of good will. The inspirational speech is a variation of the speech to reinforce, the speech of nomination is a special type of the speech to actuate, and the speech of good will, depending upon audience attitudes, can be either to convince or to reinforce. Let us look first at the speech of inspiration.

Speeches of Inspiration

The inspirational speech can be defined as a persuasive speech to reinforce that is delivered on a special occasion of commemoration or celebration. Here, the term "to inspire" is a synonymn for the term "to reinforce," as explained in the preceding chapter on persuasive speaking. In other words, inspirational speeches are appropriate when the speaker and the audience are in agreement from the outset, and the goal of the speech is to strengthen an attitude held by both speaker and listener. Such speeches do not address controversial issues; rather, they seek to stir shared feelings and to deepen appreciation. They should be prepared with the following points in mind.

1. *The central idea should state a positive thought that is easy to agree with.* For instance, a talk honoring the life of Dr. Martin Luther King, Jr., delivered to an audience of his admirers, could have as the central idea: "Dr. King's struggle for freedom is an inspiration to all humankind."

2. *The main points of the body should be stated in a smooth and subtle manner.* The points need not stand out in bold relief, as they often do for speeches that emphasize logical arguments and evidence. Instead of saying "My first point is...," say something more indirect, such as "An important part of Dr. King's philosophy was a belief in the dignity of each individual"; and instead of saying, "Now let us look at my second point," say "But human dignity was not the only thing important to Dr. King—he also believed in social justice"; and so forth.

3. *Use supporting materials that focus upon emotions and values.* There is little, if any, need for "hard evidence," such as statistics and expert testimony, in an inspirational speech. Instead, emphasize psychological appeals by using moving examples, comparisons and contrasts, and literary and historical quotations and allusions.

4. *Employ dignified language and delivery.* For tributes, commemorations, and celebrations, the language should be polished and the delivery dignified. This does not mean to use "flowery" words or somber voice; however, it does suggest that the language, voice, and bodily communication should be appropriate to the occasion.

5. *Finally, inspirational talks should be brief.* As a rule, audiences will not respond well to a "long-winded oration," whether on the Fourth of July, or for a commencement ceremony. (You can probably confirm this from personal experience.) Keep in mind that Lincoln's "Gettysburg Address," one of the outstanding ceremonial speeches of all time, was very brief, consisting of only 267 words.

Two important forms of the speech to inspire are the eulogy and the speech of commemoration or celebration. Let us consider each in turn.

The Eulogy

The eulogy can be defined as a speech in honor of a deceased person in which the speaker praises that person's life, character, and achievements. An example would be the funeral address commending the life of a recently deceased person. Eulogies are not limited to funeral addresses, however; they also include speeches honoring any deceased individual—such as inspirational talks about famous persons from history. Examples would be speeches celebrating the lives of Thomas Jefferson, Abraham Lincoln, Eleanor Roosevelt, or Martin Luther King, Jr.

When preparing a eulogy you should avoid listing in detail the events of a person's life or career, such as all schools attended, all degrees earned, all jobs held, and so forth. Such detail is boring and lifeless. Instead, follow the advice of Aristotle who observed in the *Rhetoric* that the "eulogist necessarily draws his materials from the noble deeds, actual or reputed," of the person being praised.[2] In other words, select a few significant and positive events, qualities, and achievements from the individual's life, formulate them into main headings, and illustrate each heading with specific details from the life of the person about whom you are speaking.

As a general rule, the main points of the eulogy are organized according to either a chronological pattern emphasizing periods of achievement in the person's life, or according to a topical pattern with each topic stating an outstanding trait or accomplishment. For example, a eulogy on the life of Lou Gehrig, the famous baseball player, could be organized chronologically, according to (1) Gehrig's youthful accomplishments, (2) Gehrig's outstanding career in baseball, and (3) Gehrig's valiant struggle against a fatal disease. On the other hand, here is an outline of a eulogy organized according to a topical plan (each main point is an admirable trait stated as a topic).

324

*Part IV
Types and
Forms of
Public
Speaking*

Specific Purpose: To inspire in my audience an appreciation for the qualities of greatness in the life of Clarence Darrow.

Central Idea: Clarence Darrow was a great man whose life is worthy of our admiration.

I. Clarence Darrow, the intellectual, was a thoughtful social critic. (Supporting material: include quotations by Darrow and statements about Darrow made by others.)

II. Clarence Darrow, the attorney, was a defender of the outcast and the weak. (Supporting material: include examples from Darrow's legal career.)

III. Clarence Darrow, the fighter for social justice, was a man of courage. (Supporting material: include examples of Darrow's activities on behalf of social justice.)

The Speech of Commemoration or Celebration

Speeches of commemoration and celebration are similar in that both are delivered during ceremonies that celebrate an event or some type of accomplishment. The difference is that *the speech of commemoration concerns past events or accomplishments, whereas the speech of celebration focuses upon current matters.* For instance, the speech of commemoration is appropriate for patriotic and historical occasions (Independence Day, Memorial Day), programs honoring the origins of an institution (University Founders' Day), and organizational and institutional anniversaries ("Fifty Years of Progress with First National Bank"). On the other hand, occasions for speeches of celebration include graduations, and dedications of buildings, places, or facilities (such as the opening of a new state park).

Two common complaints concerning commemorative or celebratory speeches are that they are too long and that they are trite. If you are to deliver a speech of either type, you can prevent the first problem by keeping your remarks brief (this can range from two or three minutes for presenting an award, to twelve-to-fifteen minutes for a commencement speech). You can eliminate the second complaint by making a special effort to include innovative supporting materials (and by avoiding trite expressions, old jokes, and illustrations that listeners have heard numerous times before).

As a rule, speeches of commemoration and celebration can be organized according to a chronological pattern or a topical pattern. To illustrate, a commemorative address celebrating an organization's first twenty-five years could be planned according to the chronological system of (1) origins of the group, (2) years of growth and development, and (3) recent achievements. Or, a speech in honor of the retirement of an outstanding teacher could be built around topics, such as the following.

Specific Purpose: To inspire in my audience an appreciation for the teaching career of Dr. Jane Doe.

Central Idea: Dr. Jane Doe has been a positive influence on our lives during her thirty years at State University.

I. She taught us to think for ourselves.

II. She taught us to appreciate the fine arts.

III. She taught us the importance of good character.

The Speech of Nomination

The nominating speech can be defined as a persuasive speech to actuate in which the speaker urges the audience to vote for a certain candidate for an office or to bestow an honor of some type. Nominating speeches are delivered to large and small groups, ranging from national political conventions to business meetings of campus and community organizations. Such speeches should focus on the specific requirements and standards of the office or honor at stake.

The central idea of the nominating speech is usually stated in a direct way, such as, "I am pleased to nominate Joe Jones for our club's annual Service Award," or "Mary Smith is highly qualified to be chairperson of our party, and I am happy to nominate her for that office." The main points, which state the reasons why the listener should vote for the speaker's candidate, should be few in number (two or three at most). As a rule, these points are organized according to a problem-solution plan (our organization has problems, and my candidate has a program that will solve them), or a topical plan (with each topic representing a trait that qualifies the nominee for the office or honor).

For example, you could organize a short nominating speech around two trait-centered topics: (1) My candidate is *experienced*; and (2) My candidate is *capable*. Both of these points should be backed with concrete supporting materials, such as examples of the nominee's qualifying experience, and statements from persons respected by the audience concerning the nominee's capabilities. Finally, the nominating speech should be delivered in a direct and enthusiastic manner that communicates to the audience the speaker's sincerity in making the nomination.

The Speech of Good Will

The speech of good will is persuasive in nature, having as its goal the creation or strengthening of a positive, friendly attitude toward an organization, business, profession, institution, or cause. Examples would be talks designed to win friends for the labor movement, the Heart Association, a chain of department stores, the medical profession, a student organization, or a college or university. Those who work in the field of public relations often communicate messages of good will, both in spoken and written form. Note that the immediate focus of the good-will speech is winning friends—not action; however, the long-range effect of a successful speech might involve action of some type—such as joining an organization, donating money to a cause, or attending a certain college.

As a general rule, the speech of good will attempts to strengthen favorable attitudes that the audience has toward the subject of the speech. For instance, when the president of your college speaks to community groups about institutional planning, he or she often delivers a speech of good will that seeks to

326

*Part IV
Types and
Forms of
Public
Speaking*

affirm and nourish the audience's existing support for your school. On the other hand, there are some occasions that call for a good-will speech of a more convincing nature, such as when the audience is uninformed on the subject, or holds negative attitudes toward it. Let us assume, for instance, that a manufacturing company has been falsely accused of causing a serious pollution problem in the community. An officer of the company planning a good-will speech would need to overcome the erroneous charge with factual data (that is, try to remove the negative attitude) before moving on to discuss other topics, such as ways in which the company serves the community. Thus, careful audience analysis is called for when planning the speech of good will so that you will know whether your general purpose should be to convince (remove a negative attitude and substitute a positive one), or to reinforce (strengthen an existing positive attitude).

The speech of good will should open with a friendly introduction that helps establish your *ethos*, and that relates the subject of the speech to audience interests. Then, state your central idea in a congenial manner. For example, the college president speaking to the Rotary Club might phrase the central idea this way: "Today I would like to sketch for you some of the plans we have for greater service to our community and state." Or a fraternity officer speaking to a student audience on behalf of Greek organizations might say: "Let me tell you about some of the 'good neighbor' programs that are sponsored by the fraternities and sororities on our campus."

Patterns for organizing the main points of the body of a good-will speech can vary. At times a chronological pattern will fit (the organization has served the community in the past, it serves in the present, and we intend to improve our service in the future); or a pattern based on geographical areas can be employed (our profession provides services to the city, to the surrounding area, and to the state); also, a topical plan is often useful (fraternities and sororities serve the university community by teaching academic responsibility, financial responsibility, and social responsibility).

The content of the good-will speech should be both informative and interesting. Supporting materials should be carefully selected to explain and illustrate each point in a way that appeals to audience attitudes and interests. Concrete examples are particularly effective. A good-will speech on behalf of fraternities, for instance, might illustrate programs of social responsibility with examples of fraternity fund-raising and service activities for local charities. The conclusion of the good-will speech should review the major points made, and appeal to the audience for continued understanding and support. An appropriate quotation, brief illustration, or touch of humor can be used to effectively "wrap up" the speech.

Here is an abbreviated outline of the body of a good-will speech delivered to a public speaking class by a student who was familiar with the company she spoke about (a close relative was an executive officer of the firm).[3] Notice that the body of the speech is organized according to two key topics: product quality, and community contributions.

Specific Purpose: To reinforce the audience's attitude of good will toward the Southern Elevator Company.

Central Idea: Today I want to tell you about the product and the contributions of Greensboro's own maker of elevators—the Southern Elevator Company.

I. The Southern Elevator Company makes a quality product. (This point is supported with historical information on the founder's concerns for quality and safety, and specific explanations of how the elevators are designed, installed, and tested for dependability and safety.)

II. The Southern Elevator Company contributes to the local community in many ways. (This point is supported with specific examples of contributions to local educational, artistic, and charitable organizations, and with statistics on how the firm helps the local economy through the number of people employed and its payroll.)

II. Speeches of Courtesy

Speeches of courtesy are called for on a variety of occasions, ranging from a small group assembled to hear a speaker (a speech of introduction is needed), to elaborate ceremonial occasions where distinguished guests are recognized and honors are announced. You will need to prepare a speech of courtesy if you are asked to introduce a speaker or a guest, extend a welcome to a new member or a visitor, present an award, or respond to a welcome or presentation of some type. Generally, the speech of courtesy conforms to the following three standards.

1. *As a rule, the speech of courtesy is not tightly organized.* Such speeches need not be presented with clear-cut main points and subpoints, such as you would use for a persuasive speech to convince or to actuate. Rather, the remarks are blended together so that the appropriate sentiment is expressed without the usual attention to logical argument and organization.

2. *Speeches of courtesy are positive and pleasant in tone.* They do not argue controversial views, or advocate change; instead, they reinforce the affirmative aspects of an occasion. The speaker should communicate his or her sincerity with a direct and friendly delivery. A touch of humor is usually appropriate for this type of talk.

3. *Speeches of courtesy are short.* Rarely should they exceed four to five minutes in length, and often they are only one to two minutes long.

Keeping these points in mind, let us examine four common forms of the speech of courtesy, namely, introductions, welcomes, presentations, and responses.

The Speech of Introduction

An introduction can be defined as a speech in which a guest speaker is presented to an audience. Your goal in a speech of introduction is to put the audience in a receptive state of mind for the speaker and the subject of the speech. Remember that what you say can greatly help or hurt the audience's

Many campus and community situations call for special forms of speaking rather than informative or persuasive speeches. (Jaye R. Phillips/The Picture Cube)

perception of speaker credibility (*ethos*); therefore, you should take your assignment seriously. Here are three fundamental recommendations.

Remember that you are not the main speaker. In other words, focus upon building up the other person; do not attempt to steal the show. A key element in doing this is to keep *your* comments short (usually, an introduction of about one minute to one-and-a-half minutes will do).

Prepare your remarks carefully. Secure information about the speaker in advance, selecting from it those details the audience needs to know in order to appreciate that person's qualifications. This usually includes brief mention of significant educational and professional experience, as well as why this individual is a good choice to speak on this subject to this particular audience. Also, be sure the speaker's name (and the pronunciation of it), and position or title, are correct. Talk with the speaker before the program begins to confirm the accuracy of what you plan to say. You can use a note card for listing the informational points you intend to make, occasionally glancing at your notes to "stay on track" during your presentation. A direct, extemporaneous delivery is better than reading your introduction word-for-word.

Avoid trite and awkward remarks. Introductions are often hackneyed or embarrassingly lavish. You can avoid these problems by creative planning which should include the elimination of stale expressions and excessive praise from your speech. For instance, steer clear of such time-worn expressions as

"Our speaker today needs no introduction," and extravagant language, such as, "I have known our remarkable speaker for many years, and believe me, my friends, there is no person anywhere in the world better qualified, more distinguished, more eminent, or more eloquent to talk to us on this important subject."

To illustrate, assume that the program chairperson of the University Pre-Law Society has arranged for a local attorney to speak to the group. The chairperson has secured a copy of the guest's personal résumé, and has talked with that person by phone on several occasions to confirm meeting details and the accuracy of the introductory remarks. The guest might then be presented as follows.

Good evening, fellow Society members. Fifteen years ago our speaker was, like yourself, a prelaw student in our school. His intense interest in the law, even as a student, led him during his senior year to work with other prelaw students in founding our Society. In fact, he was more than a "Founding Father"—he was our group's "George Washington," for he was elected the first president of the University PreLaw Society after he helped to organize it.

Following graduation, and after completing law school at Northwestern University, he returned home to pass the bar, and to join the local law firm then known as Smith and Davis. He has been with this firm ever since. Although his specialty is corporation law, he has maintained a keen interest in the criminal justice system—particularly in how well that system serves the indigent and the poor. Because of this interest, he was recently made chair of the county bar association's legal aid committee.

In keeping with his interest in the quality of justice for all citizens, he will talk to us tonight on the subject, "With Liberty and Justice for All—Maintaining Our Ideals After Passing the Bar." I am happy to present to you one of our own graduates, and now a partner in the firm of Smith, Davis,...and *Brown*—attorney John W. Brown.

The Speech of Welcome

The speech of welcome can be defined as a talk that attempts to make an individual or a group of guests or visitors feel accepted and appreciated by the host organization or community. The goal is congeniality between the parties involved. Such speeches are appropriate when clubs recognize guests, businesses recognize visitors (such as greeting those about to tour a plant), educational institutions welcome groups to the campus, and officials of local government offer the "key to the city" to those attending a conference or convention.

When preparing a speech of welcome, secure the correct names of the individuals or groups involved and be familiar with where they are from, whose guests they are, the purpose of their group, why they are visiting, and so forth. Adapting this information to the audience and the occasion, you can greet the person or group, comment on why they are present, extend the good will of your organization to them, and mention areas of mutual interest that they should anticipate and enjoy during their visit.

330

*Part IV
Types and
Forms of
Public
Speaking*

The Speech of Presentation

The presentation can be defined as a speech recognizing the contributions and achievements of an individual or a group by the giving of an award of some type, such as a gift, prize, plaque, or certificate. Occasions for speeches of presentation include retirement dinners, school honors convocations, a club's annual awards ceremony, the recognition by a business of an outstanding employee or group of employees, and national and international events such as awarding a Pulitzer or a Nobel prize. The goal of the speech is to communicate to all present (and, in some cases, to the public at large) the nature of the award and the good feelings of the sponsoring group toward those being honored.

In some cases, the speaker knows the recipient of the award well, as is true when a co-worker presents a gift to a retiree, or a debate coach announces the coaching staff's choice for outstanding team of the year. In such instances, the names and circumstances will be common knowledge to the speaker. However, if you are to present an award to someone with whom you are unfamiliar, be sure to get names, titles, and other information correct, and consult with others to confirm the accuracy of what you intend to say. In a nutshell, the speech of presentation should communicate essential information plus the respectful congratulations of the sponsors of the event.

The Speech of Response

The speech of response can be defined as a reply to a speech of courtesy, such as a welcome or a presentation. Quite often, the response is impromptu, and consists of only a few words. For example, if you are welcomed as a guest to a meeting of an organization, you might respond with a simple "Thank you— I'm delighted to be with you today." Or, if you are surprised with an award of some type, you might respond by saying "Thank you for this honor—I am flattered by it, and accept it with a feeling of deep appreciation."

Occasionally, however, the speaker knows in advance that a more formal response is expected. In such instances, your remarks should be planned according to the nature of the occasion, and should include acknowledgment of the welcome or presentation, a statement of appreciation on behalf of yourself or of the group you represent, and appropriate compliments to those who extended the welcome or made the presentation.

III. The Speech to Entertain

The speech to entertain can be defined as a talk designed to delight and to please. It can be described as "rhetorical recreation," for its goal is to produce feelings of enjoyment and amusement in the audience. The entertaining speech should not be confused with the informative or persuasive speech that makes extensive use of highly interesting supporting materials, such as humorous stories, but which retains the primary purpose of informing or persuading. Strictly speaking, a speech "to entertain" is limited to that which diverts, amuses, and pleases the audience.

The entertaining speech is often delivered in an after-dinner context. It is especially appropriate when fun and relaxation are desired rather than something more serious. However, after-dinner talks can be light-hearted and still have a serious informative or persuasive point to them, thereby going beyond the limited goal of entertainment. If, for example, in an after-dinner context, your purpose is to communicate information, and you do so in an interesting manner, your speech should be classified as one to inform (albeit an informative speech that is extremely interesting). Likewise, if you present an amusing persuasive speech in an after-dinner context, your speech should be classified as one to persuade (that is, a persuasive speech that uses much entertaining material for support). However, if your primary goal is to delight and please, not to inform or to persuade, your speech should be classified as one to entertain. It is the general purpose, not the after-dinner or other context, that makes the difference.

The speech to entertain should be brief, with a maximum length of about twelve to fifteen minutes in most "real life" circumstances. It should be prepared according to the same basic procedures that you follow for your other speeches, as adapted to the goal of entertaining. Here are some suggestions concerning subjects, organization and content, and delivery.

1. *The subject for the entertaining speech should be appropriate to speaker, audience, and occasion.* The speech to entertain should not be a collection of unrelated jokes, stories, and quotations. As with other speeches, it should be unified around a subject and a central theme. Your own knowledge and interests, as well as the nature of the audience and occasion, can provide you with ideas for subjects. For example, an experienced salesperson speaking at a sales convention could develop a humorous speech on "How to Lose a Sale." The specific purpose might be: "To entertain my audience with a humorous presentation, based upon personal experience, of various ways to lose a sale." Or a drama teacher delivering an entertaining speech at a theater awards banquet might talk on "Great Snafus of the Stage," with this specific purpose: "To entertain my audience with true stories of humorous mistakes made by actors and technical crews during live theater productions."

Entertaining speeches do not have to be funny, although most do employ humorous materials to some degree. Subjects based upon travel, adventure, and unusual experiences can be entertaining, holding audience interest with content that depends upon the elements of novelty, suspense, and mystery. For instance, a student whose hobby is parachuting might prepare a speech with this specific purpose: "To entertain my audience with accounts of my three close calls with disaster in my hobby of parachuting."

2. *The structure and content of the entertaining speech are not highly logical.* Because your primary goal is to gain and hold audience interest, not to instruct or to persuade, you need not be concerned with organization and content based on logical reasoning and evidence. Overall, your talk can be structured around an introduction, body, and conclusion, as is standard in speech planning. The content of these divisions is what makes the talk entertaining, as the following points suggest.

332

*Part IV
Types and
Forms of
Public
Speaking*

The *introduction* should open with a story or quotation that catches attention and leads smoothly into the theme of the talk. At an appropriate place in the introduction, state the central idea in a relaxed, informal way.

The *body* of the speech should be loosely structured around main points that give unity and movement to your central idea. All plans or patterns of organization are "fair game" for the speech to entertain, provided they are adapted sensibly to the goal of the speech. Each point should be supported with entertaining examples, comparisons and contrasts, literary allusions, and quotations; even simple statistics, if novel or humorous, are appropriate.

The *conclusion* should sustain the light-hearted spirit of the speech while pulling things together by focusing on the theme of the talk. Close the speech with an appropriate joke, example, short poem, proverb, or quotation that relates to the subject and effectively "wraps things up."

For example, assume that a teacher is asked to deliver a humorous after-dinner speech to an audience of fellow teachers attending a convention. The speaker decides to build the talk around a collection of amusing answers to examination questions. A skeleton outline of the talk (the introduction and conclusion are implied, but not stated), using a topical pattern for the main points of the body, is given below. In this outline, each main point of the body is developed with three or four examples of funny answers to exam questions from the speaker's files.

Specific Purpose: To entertain my audience with humorous answers students have given to examination questions.

Central Idea: Tonight I would like to tell you about some of the unusual answers to examination questions that I have collected from colleagues, and from my own classes, over the years.

I. First, let us consider some unusual answers from students in the fine arts.

II. Second, let us consider some unusual answers from students in the social sciences.

III. Finally, let us consider some unusual answers from students in the hard sciences.

3. *The delivery of the entertaining speech should be direct and relaxed.* As a rule, you should not read this type of speech from a manuscript. Instead, know the content well, and deliver it extemporaneously, emphasizing a natural, conversational approach. In other words, although you are thoroughly prepared, the delivery should seem almost impromptu, creating the impression that you are giving the talk "out of your head" for the first time.

This Chapter in Brief

There are a number of special types of public speaking that, as a rule, are derived from the unique nature of the occasion. These include special forms of persuasion, speeches of courtesy, and the speech to entertain.

Special forms of persuasion include speeches to inspire, the speech of nomination, and the speech of good will. Speeches to inspire, such as the eulogy or the speech of commemoration or celebration, are not controversial in nature, but are delivered to audiences that, from the outset, share a common attitude on the subject with the speaker. Inspirational speeches are appropriate for occasions such as remembering the life of a great person (for example, a speech on the life of Abraham Lincoln), commemorating a significant event from the past (such as the founding of an organization), or celebrating a current event (such as dedicating a new building).

The speech of nomination is a short persuasive speech in which the speaker urges the members of the audience to vote for a certain candidate for office. And the speech of good will is a persuasive speech designed to create a friendly and positive attitude toward the subject of the speech (such as an organization, business, profession, institution, or cause).

Speeches of courtesy include introductions, welcomes, presentations, and responses. These speeches are usually brief and are a part of some larger event or program. They may be loosely organized provided there is coherence and movement in what is said. When preparing a speech of courtesy, the speaker should be careful to get names, job titles, and similar data correct (including pronunciations).

The speech to entertain is one with the limited purpose of delighting and pleasing the audience. The entertainment can be based on humor or on other things such as travel or adventure. Although entertaining speeches need to be carefully prepared, they need not be highly logical in content. This is because the goal of the speech to entertain is enjoyment, not changing audience attitudes or behavior.

EXERCISES

1. Assume that you are to nominate a student acquaintance for class president, or for some other campus office. Interview that person, then prepare a short speech of nomination for the office you have chosen.

2. Select a company, organization, or cause that you like and support. Outline a speech of good will for your choice, assuming that your audience will be a local civic club (such as Rotary, or the Junior Chamber of Commerce).

3. During the next several weeks or months, listen carefully to the speeches of introduction you hear on campus and in the community. Evaluate the effectiveness of each introduction, and adapt what you learn to your own speaking.

4. Assume that you are to introduce a classmate to your speech class. After an interview, prepare a one-minute introduction that would be suitable for that person's next classroom speech.

SELECTED READINGS

King, Robert G. *Forms of Public Address.* Indianapolis, Ind.: Bobbs-Merrill, 1969. King gives instructions for preparing various types of inspirational talks, and for the entertaining speech. He illustrates his recommendations with model speeches.

334

*Part IV
Types and
Forms of
Public
Speaking*

Lucas, Stephen E. *The Art of Public Speaking*. 3d ed. New York: Random House, 1989. In Chapter 15, "Speaking on Special Occasions," Lucas explains and gives examples of various types of occasional speeches, including introductions, presentations and acceptances, and the after-dinner speech.

Lyle, Guy R., and Guinagh, Kevin, comps. *I Am Happy to Present*. New York: H. W. Wilson, 1953. Lyle and Guinagh have collected a variety of introductions from real life, and have arranged them according to the profession of the person being introduced (business people, educators, journalists, and so forth). They include a short essay on preparing "The Artful Introduction."

Rogge, Edward, and Ching, James C. *Advanced Public Speaking*. New York: Holt, Rinehart and Winston, 1966. All of Chapter 11 is devoted to "The Speech of Entertainment." The authors discuss how to prepare and deliver the speech to entertain, and how to make the best use of such factors of attention and interest as humor, suspense, exaggeration, and wordplay.

Yeager, Willard H. *Effective Speaking for Every Occasion*. 2d ed. New York: Prentice-Hall, 1951. Yeager explains and provides models of a variety of special forms of public address, including the good-will speech, the eulogy, the speech of celebration, and the entertaining speech.

ENDNOTES

1. Robert G. King, *Forms of Public Address* (Indianapolis, Ind.: Bobbs-Merrill, 1969), pp. 58–59.
2. Aristotle, *The Rhetoric*, trans. Lane Cooper (New York: Appleton-Century, 1932), p. 156.
3. Adapted from a speech by June Jarman, delivered to the advanced public speaking class, University of North Carolina at Greensboro, October, 1984.

Appendix I

SPEECH CRITICISM: ANALYZING AND EVALUATING PUBLIC SPEECHES

"Certainly a principal aim of the study of public discourse is to enable us to participate fully in the communicative process, both as clear, effective persuaders, and as intelligent, hard-headed receivers of persuasion."

—James R. Andrews, *A Choice of Worlds: The Practice and Criticism of Public Discourse* (1973)[1]

Making decisions about informative and persuasive messages is an important part of your life. You regularly receive a wide variety of messages that others direct toward you, including classroom lectures, student speeches, television news and documentaries, newspaper and magazine articles, discussions with friends on a wide range of social issues, various forms of advertising, religious appeals, and speeches of candidates for public office. Although the primary emphasis of this text is on explaining how you can become a more effective public speaker, an important subtheme concerns how you can become a more thoughtful consumer of the messages you receive—especially those received from public speeches.

Your ability to think critically about the speeches you hear is important for at least three reasons: it helps you, it helps others, and it benefits society in general. First, your rational analysis and evaluation of speeches helps you become a more logical consumer of messages. In other words, the habits of critical thinking inherent in good speech criticism can be applied to the evaluation of political campaigns, various types of advertising, newspaper editorials, and so forth. Also, by listening carefully to others you get ideas for improving your own speaking.

Second, by being a careful listener, you can help other speakers. Your opportunities for helping range from making constructive suggestions to fellow students in your public speaking class to assisting a friend or professional colleague prepare and rehearse a speech.

Finally, your thoughtful response to speaking helps improve the overall quality of democratic debate, for it pressures public communicators to speak wisely and responsibly. With these thoughts in mind, let us examine some basic principles of speech criticism, then see how you can apply those principles to the speeches you hear.

I. The Principles of Speech Criticism

Speech criticism can be defined as *informed, fair-minded analysis and evaluation of a speech.* Although there are variations in how speech criticism is defined and approached, this definition serves the beginning critic well.[2] As a method of *analysis,* speech criticism explains what is going on, and why it works or does not work. As a method of *evaluation,* speech criticism makes informed judgments on the effectiveness, artistic quality, and social worth of a speech.[3] The term "criticism" as used here does not mean partisan attack, negativism, or mindless faultfinding. To the contrary, speech criticism should be constructive, pointing out both the strong and weak points of the speech. Also, it should be balanced in assessing the effectiveness, eloquence, and social value of the speech.

As defined above, speech criticism includes both analysis and evaluation. Although these processes interact and overlap with one another in practice, we will separate them here for purposes of discussion. In the material that follows, therefore, we will first examine speech analysis, then consider speech evaluation.

Speech Analysis

Speech analysis means the activity of explaining in rhetorical terms what is going on as a speech is being delivered. It employs rhetorical theory to make clear why the speech works or does not work, and it offers suggestions for improvement when something in a speech is not working well. For example, the listener who notes that the introduction to a speech is dull and that its content is generally unrelated to the subject is acting as a speech critic. Something is not working well, and the listener knows it. When that listener-critic goes further to explain what is wrong, and to suggest specific ways of correcting the problem (such as "open the speech with relevant interest materials"), he or she continues to use speech analysis. You do this each time that you weigh the strengths and weaknesses of the speeches you hear in class and elsewhere.

The important point is that speech analysis is neither impractical nor overly complex. To the contrary, it is something you do regularly. For instance, if a speaker claims that something is true, but presents no evidence to support the claim, you are analyzing the speech when you ask, "Where is your evidence?" You continue your analysis when you note how well a speech is organized, how clear and persuasive it is, and how effectively it is delivered.

You can use the chapters of this public speaking text as a convenient starting place for locating specific rhetorical principles for speech analysis. For example, Chapter 5 discusses the principles of audience and occasion analysis; Chapter 6 explains how to choose a subject and purpose; and so forth to the end of the book. A brief summary of these principles appears on most criticism forms used in public speaking classes. Such a summary appears in this appendix in Figure I.1, the Public Speaking Comments Form.

Speech criticism without evaluation is incomplete. Although speech analysis helps us understand what is going on during the speech, it does not draw conclusions concerning the broad human, aesthetic, and social issues involved. To complete the process of speech criticism, therefore, the critic needs to stand back from the details in order to consider the speech as a whole, including the context in which it was delivered. The resulting evaluation should assess the *effectiveness, artistic quality,* and *social worth* of the speech. Let us look at these three areas more closely.

Effectiveness

Speeches are prepared and delivered in order to create a certain effect on an audience. The speech to inform seeks to achieve understanding; the speech to persuade endeavors to change audience attitudes or behavior. In the case of a persuasive speech, for example, the speech would be considered effective if it moved the audience to change its attitudes or behavior in directions intended by the speaker. However, if attitudinal and behavioral change do not occur as intended by the speaker, the speech would be judged ineffective. To make these judgments, the critic must know at least two things: the speaker's goal and the audience's response to it.

Determining the *goal* of a speech is not always an easy task. For example, the critic can determine the goal without much difficulty when a speaker states the central idea clearly and keeps the speech moving logically toward the announced goal. This is the case for most speeches delivered in public speaking classes. On the other hand, the critic will have difficulty when the central idea is not announced and the content is poorly presented (as sometimes occurs with untrained speakers). Also, the critic must be alert for deception, for occasionally a speaker deliberately conceals the goal from the audience. For example, a person might make a speech on ''Clean Up Toxic Waste,'' with a stated goal of securing public support for strict environmental legislation. However, if the speech consists primarily of an attack on how a specific county commissioner voted on environmental issues, and the speaker is planning to run against that commissioner in the next election, the primary goal might be to gain votes for the speaker rather than support for environmental legislation. In any case, the critic should make the best possible judgment about what the speaker is trying to achieve.

After the goal of the speech is determined, the critic then evaluates effectiveness in terms of *audience response to that goal.* Gathering information on audience response is sometimes easy, and at other times difficult. For classroom speeches, for instance, you can judge the reaction of those around you, and even ask questions of audience members when class is over. Even then, not all shades of response will be known to you. In other situations, such as speeches reported in the mass media, you can secure helpful information from reading news reports and editorials, listening to television commentators, and studying public opinion polls on the topic. After weighing all the evidence, you need to make an informed judgment about whether or not the audience responded as the speaker intended.

One interesting factor in evaluating effectiveness is whether the response to the speech is immediate or delayed. In some instances, effectiveness can be assessed by observing the immediate response to a speech, as when a candidate for student government urges "vote for me," and the next day wins the election. This was certainly true of President Franklin Roosevelt's Declaration of War Address, delivered to Congress on December 8, 1941, one day following the Japanese attack on Pearl Harbor. Roosevelt called for a declaration of war, and Congress complied (with only one dissenting vote).

At other times, the result is not immediately clear. For instance, Lincoln's Gettysburg Address was not well received by the audience at Gettysburg. However, in the months following, many who read the address sensed its greatness. As the years went by, Lincoln's remarks at Gettysburg were recognized as a rhetorical classic. Thus, the wise critic considers both immediate and long-range success, realizing that what seems effective at the moment might prove temporary, and what seems ineffective at the moment might prove permanent.

Artistic Quality

Another area of concern for the rhetorical critic is the artistic quality of the speech. Artistic quality means the aesthetic element of speechmaking, including excellence in form, content, language, and delivery. Let us look briefly at these four components.

Form. The speech should be well organized, with a balance among introduction, body, and conclusion. The speech should flow smoothly from idea to idea, and from section to section. At the conclusion, the listener should have a sense of completeness.

Content. The content of the speech should not only be clear and logically sound but also it should be literate. Supporting materials should be of the highest quality, as demonstrated by the use of outstanding examples, comparisons and contrasts, and quotations from history and literature.

Language. The language of the speech should be clear, appropriate, and vivid. It should also be correct in grammar, superior in its vocabulary, and refined in its phrasing of sentences and paragraphs.

Delivery. The delivery of the speech should be marked by high standards of pronunciation, effective application of the voice for emphasis and interpretation, and polished use of bodily communication to enhance meaning.

To complete your evaluation of artistic quality, consider whether or not the speech has earned—or has the potential for earning—a place of honor and permanence in the annals of speechmaking. Examples of speeches that merit such an honor include Lincoln's Gettysburg Address and Second Inaugural Address, Franklin D. Roosevelt's First Inaugural Address and Declaration of War Address, John F. Kennedy's Inaugural Address, and Martin Luther King's "I Have a Dream" speech.

Social Worth

The social worth of a speech refers to its moral dimension and human consequences. A speech can be effective and eloquent, yet be dishonest in its content and socially harmful in its results. The speeches of Adolph Hitler to the people of Germany in the 1930s are examples of such rhetoric. Therefore, to complete the task of evaluation, the speech critic should go beyond effectiveness and artistic quality to assess the ethics and the social consequences of the speech.

Ethics

When evaluating the ethics of a speech, consider whether or not the speech represents what the speaker believes, demonstrates respect for the audience, and presents content that is accurate and rational. Let us look closer at each of these standards.

To begin with, ethical speeches emerge from beliefs that are genuinely held by the speaker. The speaker should not ask an audience to accept a viewpoint that he or she does not believe. In evaluating this factor, listen closely for speaker sincerity at the time of delivery. Then, research the matter by talking about the speaker's views with those who know the speaker well. Also, you can compare and contrast the proposals of the speech with public stands taken by the speaker in the past, and with the purposes and goals of the organizations with which the speaker is affiliated.

Second, the ethical speech is based on respect for the critical capacity of the audience. When evaluating this factor, observe whether or not the speaker genuinely respects the ability of people to think for themselves. A speech based on respect for persons encourages the audience to weigh all sides of the issue, consider the case on its merits, and make rational decisions. Such a speech does not mislead the audience about the speaker's purpose, or build its case by deliberate appeal to fallacy or mindless emotion.

Finally, the ethical speech is sound in content. Such a speech is based on the speaker's in-depth knowledge of the subject. The speech should define terms carefully, employ sound reasoning and evidence, and set out the arguments clearly and honestly so that the audience can think rationally about them. Also, supporting materials should be accurate, clear, and relevant to the subject.

Social Consequences

To complete your evaluation of the social worth of a speech, consider its consequences, not only for those in the immediate audience, but also for society at large. This means doing at least two things: determining who benefits most if the proposals of the speech are adopted, and considering whether or not the speech supports the principles of a free society. Concerning the first point, if the chief beneficiary is the speaker (or the clients of the speaker) rather than the listeners and society in general, the rhetorical critic should take note. By calling attention to self-serving rhetoric, and soundly condemning it, the critic fulfills an important social responsibility. Second, the worthwhile speech in a free society honors and supports the fundamental democratic value of respect for individuals, and the assumptions that flow from this value. These assumptions include a preference for persuasion over force, the practice of freedom of expression so that all views can be heard, rule by majority vote after full and free debate, and respect for the civil liberties of all.

Let us now examine how you can apply these ideas to the speeches you hear.

II. The Practice of Speech Criticism

The principles of speech criticism are applied below according to two rhetorical contexts, namely, the context of the public speaking classroom that includes both an educational and a rhetorical function, and the general context of society at large.

Criticizing Classroom Speeches

The criticism of classroom speeches should take into consideration the educational purpose of the situation. Because the classroom speech has both an educational and a rhetorical function, the critic should be particularly careful to be constructive when analyzing and evaluating student speeches. Among other things, the critic should remember that the speeches are made within the limits set by the goals of the course. These limits sometimes include specific instructions as to the type of speech (whether informative or persuasive), the length of presentation ("deliver a five-minute speech on..."), the nature of the content ("deliver a speech explaining a process or a procedure"), and even the organizational pattern to be followed ("for this speech, use Monroe's motivated sequence").

As a practical matter, you can organize your criticism of classroom speeches around the four essential elements of any public speaking situation: the *speaker,* the *speech,* the *audience,* and the *occasion* (including the broad social context in which the speech is given). These four elements can be arranged in an order that generally follows your thought processes during listening. For example, as the speaker begins, you naturally start to respond to the content of the speech. While listening to content, you assess speaker credibility and make a judgment about how well the speaker has adapted to the audience and occasion. Finally, you assess the overall effectiveness, ethics, and social consequences of the speech.

The Public Speaking Comments Form, shown in Figure I.1, is an instrument for speech criticism that covers both analysis and evaluation, and that is derived from the four elements of public speaking mentioned above. Although the various topics of criticism mix together at the time of delivery, the form permits you to separate the critical process into convenient parts so that you can record your thinking in an organized manner. Notice that points 1–7 focus on the *speech* (subject, content, and delivery); point 8 focuses on the *speaker*; and points 1 and 9 concern *audience* analysis. Finally, points 1 and 10 address the *occasion, ethics, and social consequences.* Let us examine the form in more detail, including basic cross-referencing to chapters in this text where you can find more information about the points on the form.

The Speech: Subject and Content (points 1–4). Early in the speech make a judgment concerning the appropriateness of the subject to the speaker, audience, and occasion. Evaluate the speaker's expertise on the subject, how well the subject fits the concerns of the student audience, and the suitability of the topic to the classroom situation (including how closely it follows the instructions for the specific assignment). While listening to the introduction, consider how well the speaker captures audience attention, orients the class to the topic, motivates interest, and states the central idea. When evaluating the body, pay particular attention to clarity of organization and the persuasiveness of the arguments and evidence used. In the conclusion, listen for a clear summary of key ideas and an effective appeal for decision and action. For more details, see Chapters 5, 6, 7, 10, and 11.

Speech Presentation (points 5–7). When evaluating speech presentation, consider language, voice and diction, and bodily communication. The language should be clear, and it should stir the senses and create vivid mental images. Evaluate the use of vocal variety to interpret and give emphasis to the ideas of the speech, and listen for distinct articulation of speech sounds and the use of standard pronunciation. When judging bodily communication, look for eye contact that is direct and friendly, posture that is erect and alert, and movement and gesture that are supportive of speech content. For more on presentation, see Chapters 12 and 13.

Speaker Credibility (point 8). The evaluation of credibility, or *ethos,* includes your perception of the speaker's good will, good moral character, and intelligence. When assessing good will, consider the speaker's sincerity, friendly attitude, and the respect shown for the worth and critical capacity of the listeners. When judging good character, consider such things as the trustworthiness and integrity of the speaker, including the speaker's use of reasoning and evidence (the trustworthy speaker does not deliberately mislead the audience with fallacious reasoning and false or distorted evidence). Finally, evaluate intelligence and expertise, with special attention to how well-informed the speaker is on the subject of the speech. For a discussion of *ethos,* see Chapter 15.

Analysis of Audience by the Speaker (point 9). Audience response to a speech is a key test of rhetorical effectiveness. Therefore, you need to determine how well the speaker has analyzed the audience, and how wisely the results have been used to adapt content to audience attitudes, knowledge, and interests. Also, consider the appropriateness of the presentation to the audience, including such things as physical appearance, language, grammar, and pronunciation. See Chapter 5 for more details concerning audience analysis.

Artistic Quality (points 2 through 7). Your evaluation of artistic quality occurs throughout the speech. You should keep quality in mind when you comment on the overall organization, the content of the introduction, body, and conclusion, the language used, standards of pronunciation, and delivery. Artistic quality is discussed in several parts of this text; see especially Chapters 7, 10, and 11 on organization and content, and Chapters 12 and 13 on language and delivery.

Effectiveness, Ethics, and Social Consequences (point 10). Finally, make a general assessment of the speech. For informative speeches, evaluate the degree to which the audience understood what was said. For persuasion, evaluate the effectiveness of the speech in presenting content clearly, and in changing attitudes and behavior. Then, consider the ethics and social consequences of the speech by judging whether or not the speaker sincerely believed in the point of view being advocated, used argument and evidence honestly, and

PUBLIC SPEAKING COMMENTS FORM

Speaker: _____ Topic: _____ Date: _____

To the listener: judge each of the 10 items below by encircling a number on the three-point scale.

    1 = below average (needs improvement)
    2 = average (good, but can be better)
    3 = above average (well-done)

In the comments sections, jot down as many helpful suggestions as you have time for. Unless your instructor asks that your evaluation remain anonymous, sign your form before giving it to the speaker.

_____
(signed)

THE SPEECH: Comments

1. CHOICE OF SUBJECT   1   2   3
   Appropriate to speaker
   Appropriate to audience
   Appropriate to occasion

2. DEVELOPMENT OF INTRODUCTION   1   2   3
   Gain attention
   Orient to topic
   Clear central idea

3. DEVELOPMENT OF BODY   1   2   3
   Identifiable main points
   Clear content
   Sound reasoning
   Sound evidence
   Holds interest

4. DEVELOPMENT OF CONCLUSION   1   2   3
   Summary of key ideas
   Clarity
   Persuasiveness
   Originality

SPEECH PRESENTATION: Comments

5. LANGUAGE   1   2   3
   Appropriate
   Clear
   Vivid

6. VOICE, ARTICULATION, PRONUNCIATION   1   2   3
   Vocal variety
   Distinct articulation
   Standard pronunciation

FIGURE I.1

7. BODILY COMMUNICATION   1   2   3
Visual directness
Posture
Movement and gesture

THE SPEAKER (ethos): Comments

8. SPEAKER CREDIBILITY   1   2   3
Good will, respect for audience
Good character
Expertise and good judgment

AUDIENCE ANALYSIS: Comments

9. ANALYSIS OF AUDIENCE BY SPEAKER   1   2   3
Attitudes
Knowledge
Interests

OVERALL EVALUATION: Comments

10. EFFECTIVENESS; ETHICS AND SOCIAL CONSEQUENCES   1   2   3
Clarity
Persuasiveness
Holding interest
Ethics and social consequences

OTHER COMMENTS

What did you like best about this speech?

What are your major recommendations for improvement?

spoke for the benefit of the audience and society at large. For more on effectiveness, see Chapters 14, 15, and 16; and for a discussion of ethics, see Chapter 3.

The topics discussed above can help you develop an organized method of analyzing and evaluating speeches. At times, your criticism will be mental only—that is, you will keep your thoughts to yourself without writing them down or filling out a form. On other occasions, you might wish to use the form (or be asked to do so by your instructor). Here are some suggestions for using the form in your class.

1 Keep your focus on the speaker, not on the form. Look at the speaker as much as possible. During the speech, write your comments in a nondistracting manner.

2 To begin, fill in speaker, topic, and date, then listen carefully to the introduction before writing more. Start filling out the form as the speaker finishes the introduction, judging points 1 and 2 (choice of subject and development of introduction). As the speech moves along, fill in the other points when you are ready, completing all rankings during the conclusion.

3 Try to encircle the 1-2-3 rankings (on the right-hand side of the form) for each of the ten points. However, do not feel obligated to write additional comments in all sections of the form. Two or three thoughtful suggestions are preferable to a dozen that are hastily done.

4 Be *constructive* in your remarks, using tactful language throughout, especially when commenting on weak points. (If your instructor asks you for an oral critique, begin by talking about the strong points of the speech, then gradually work your way to the points that need improvement.) Think of the evaluation as a positive, persuasive message you are sending the speaker; then, use your communication skills to make your suggestions palatable.

5 At the end of the speech, fill out the "other comments" section at the bottom by jotting down what you liked best, and what you think most needs improvement.

Finally, be sure to develop a positive, receptive approach to the critiques of *your* speeches done by the instructor and your classmates. As your listeners make suggestions to you, communicate to them your willingness to learn and improve. You can do this by asking questions, being pleasant in discussing the criticism, and thanking them for their ideas. This approach will encourage listeners to help you identify and overcome rhetorical weaknesses—otherwise, they might be reluctant to mention something that you ought to be aware of. When you feel a comment is without merit, do not be defensive. Instead, seek clarification, discuss the matter with the critic, then mull it over before making a judgment about it. For example, you might conclude that the suggestion is not very helpful, and that you will simply ignore it. On the other hand, you might decide that it had merit after all.

Let us now turn our attention to how these principles can be extended to speech criticism in society at large.

Criticizing Speeches in Society at Large

The criticism of speeches in society at large can follow a pattern similar to the one explained above. However, because speaking situations outside the classroom are much more diverse than the classroom provides, you will need to give extra attention to the historical and situational context for such speeches. Placing the speech in this larger context means determining the general historical and social setting, then focusing on the specific situation from which the speech emerged.

History and Social Setting

Speeches are not delivered in a vacuum. They flow from the persons, events, and issues of the period in which they occur. The first step of intelligent criticism, then, is to become informed about the historical forces that gave birth to the speech, and to study the life of the speaker. Your research should include histories, biographies, and accounts in newspapers, news magazines, magazine articles, and the like concerning the historical period, the speaker, and the audience and occasion for the speech. Having done this research, you are better able to place the speech in context. Also, by being familiar with the background of the speaker you can better understand why he or she, and not some other person, delivered the speech. You should then consider the specific speaking situation.

The Specific Situation

The speaking situation occurs within the general historical context discussed above. Here, however, you focus narrowly to consider the *reason* for the speech as determined by the situation. The situation that calls forth the speech can be either problem-centered or tradition-bound. Let us look first at the problem-centered reason.

One of the fundamental reasons for public speaking is to address a problem, the solution of which is important to the audience. In his widely acclaimed essay on "The Rhetorical Situation," Lloyd Bitzer describes this as an *exigence,* meaning "an imperfection marked by urgency," a need to be met, or a defect to be corrected.[4] For example, Patrick Henry's "Give Me Liberty or Give Me Death" speech was made in response to the exigence of the American Revolution; many of Abraham Lincoln's speeches were delivered in response to the exigence of the Civil War; and Martin Luther King's "I Have a Dream" speech was made in response to the exigence of racism in American society. In these and similar cases, the appropriate human response is a speech that analyzes the exigence and proposes a practicable solution to it. In preparing to criticize such speeches, your research needs to explain the exigence so that you can intelligently evaluate the effectiveness and worth of the speech.

The second reason for a speech is to comply with tradition. Speeches given for this reason do not necessarily address a problem. Rather, they are appropriate elements of such traditional activities as graduations (the commencement speech), awards ceremonies (speeches of presentation and acceptance), and conventions (keynote speeches). When the speech you are criticizing is of this type, rather than a response to an exigence, you need to gather information on the history and purposes of the institution or organization involved. For instance, when criticizing a commencement address, you need to know about the school where it was delivered; or when criticizing a convention keynote address, you should be familiar with the convention's sponsors and the theme of the convention.

After you have carefully studied the general historical and the specific situational contexts for the speech, you should proceed with your analysis and evaluation according to the standards explained earlier. In summary form, these standards are as follows.

Speech Criticism in Brief

Speech criticism consists of informed, fair-minded analysis and evaluation of public speaking. *Speech analysis* means using the principles of rhetoric to explain what is going on during speechmaking, including a discussion of what works well and why, and what does not work well and why. Fair-minded analysis covers both the merits and the faults of the speech. *Speech evaluation* means interpreting the speech as a whole, and in context, according to its effectiveness, artistic quality, and social worth.

In practice, speech criticism analyzes the organization and content of the speech, including its use of reasoning and evidence. It also explains the strong and weak points of speech presentation, how skillfully the speaker analyzed the audience, and how well the speaker established his or her credibility.

The evaluation of effectiveness considers how much the audience learned from the speech, and whether or not attitudes and behavior were changed as intended by the speaker. The evaluation of quality considers aesthetic excellence in form, content, language, and delivery. The evaluation of worth considers ethics and social consequences, including whether or not the speaker believed in what he or she said, used argument and evidence honestly, and spoke for the general benefit of the audience and society at large.

As you practice the art of speech criticism, keep in mind a thought from Lester Thonssen, A. Craig Baird, and Waldo W. Braden, three of America's distinguished rhetorical scholars. In *Speech Criticism,* a standard work in the field of rhetoric, they state: "The rhetorical critic...must make judgments based upon interpretative analyses [and]...must arrive at certain conclusions despite the fact that a totality of information cannot be secured. But the careful critic bases...value judgments upon reliable data, meticulously tested and checked. In other words, [the speech critic]...strives for responsibility of statement."[5]

EXERCISES

1. Make a photocopy of the Public Speaking Comments Form. Attend a campus or community event that features a public speaker, and fill out the form as you listen. If the speaker were to ask you for a brief critique, what specific recommendations would you make for improving content and delivery?

2. Choose one of the student speeches from Appendix II or Appendix III for analysis and evaluation. Focus your criticism on the elements of organization, reasoning, and evidence. List specific strong and weak points for each of these elements. As

a result of this exercise, what ideas do you get for improving the organization, reasoning, and evidence of your own speeches?

3. When you are listening to a speech, you usually give at least some attention to a variety of rhetorical elements (as illustrated by items 1 through 10 of the comments form). However, you can do speech criticism that is limited to just *one* rhetorical element, such as speech organization, the use of evidence, or how well the speaker analyzed the audience. Here are some suggestions for speech criticism focused on one element.

   a Criticize the *delivery* of a campus speech. Be thorough, covering general physical appearance, visual directness, bodily movement and gesture, and voice, articulation, and pronunciation. For ideas, see Chapter 13 of this text.

   b Criticize the *language* of a great speech from American history (such as one in Appendix III). Include the standards of clarity, appropriateness, and vividness. For other ideas on language, see Chapter 12 of this text.

   c From a campus or community speech, criticize *one* of the following rhetorical elements: use of logical reasoning; holding audience interest; achieving clarity; effectiveness of introduction and conclusion; building speaker *ethos*; ethics and social consequences.

SELECTED READINGS

Andrews, James R. *The Practice of Rhetorical Criticism.* 2d ed. White Plains, N.Y.: Longman, 1990. This text is an excellent resource for the student critic. In addition to defining and explaining the practice of speech criticism, Andrews provides a number of good examples of critical essays written by leading rhetorical scholars.

Arnold, Carroll C. *The Criticism of Oral Rhetoric.* Columbus, Ohio: Charles E. Merrill, 1974. Arnold begins with two simple questions: "What happened when A spoke seriously to B?" And, "Did A achieve as much as was possible in rhetorical relationship with B?" Building upon these questions, Arnold explains how to analyze and evaluate the content, structure, language, and delivery of a speech.

Bitzer, Lloyd F. "The Rhetorical Situation." *Philosophy and Rhetoric* 1 (Winter 1968): 1–14. Bitzer's essay on the situational nature of rhetoric is a modern classic that deserves study by all serious students of public address. Bitzer helps the student understand that rhetoric is an appropriate human response to a situation consisting of an exigence, an audience, and constraints.

Cathcart, Robert. *Post Communication: Rhetorical Analysis and Evaluation.* 2d ed. Indianapolis, Ind.: Bobbs-Merrill, 1981. Cathcart's introduction to rhetorical criticism, written for the beginner, presents basic principles of criticism in connection with a variety of contemporary examples.

Foss, Sonja K. *Rhetorical Criticism: Exploration and Practice.* Prospect Heights, Ill.: Waveland Press, 1989. Foss explains and illustrates a variety of approaches to rhetorical criticism.

Thonssen, Lester; Baird, A. Craig; and Braden, Waldo W. *Speech Criticism.* 2d ed. New York: Ronald Press, 1970. This standard work on rhetorical criticism emphasizes classical principles but with modern applications. It surveys the history and development of rhetorical theory from the days of Aristotle to the twentieth century. An excellent reference work for the public speaker.

1. James R. Andrews, *A Choice of Worlds: The Practice and Criticism of Public Discourse* (New York: Harper & Row, 1973), p. 5.

2. For examples of a variety of approaches to rhetorical criticism, see Sonja K. Foss, *Rhetorical Criticism: Exploration and Practice* (Prospect Heights, Ill.: Waveland Press, 1989).

3. For a discussion of analysis and evaluation as the essentials of speech criticism, see James R. Andrews, "'Wise Skepticism': On the Education of a Young Critic," *Communication Education* 38 (July 1989): 178–183. For a discussion of effectiveness, quality, and worth as the key elements of evaluation, see Robert Cathcart, *Post Communication: Rhetorical Analysis and Evaluation,* 2d ed. (Indianapolis, Ind.: Bobbs-Merrill, 1981), pp. 105–124.

4. Lloyd F. Bitzer, "The Rhetorical Situation," *Philosophy and Rhetoric* 1 (Winter 1968): 1–14.

5. Lester Thonssen, A. Craig Baird, and Waldo W. Braden, *Speech Criticism,* 2d ed. (New York: Ronald Press, 1970), p. 25.

Appendix II

EXTEMPORANEOUS SPEAKING: MODEL OUTLINES, NOTE CARDS, AND SPEECHES

An extemporaneous speech is carefully prepared, but it is not memorized or read from a manuscript. As a rule, the speaker outlines the speech in detail, then prepares a set of "key word" note cards based on the outline. During delivery, the speaker glances at the note card when necessary to jog the memory, expressing each point in language that emerges naturally at the moment. In Chapter 13 on delivery, you will find a discussion of how to prepare your note cards. In abbreviated form, the recommendations include the following.

1 Keep the wording on the card as brief as possible.
2 However, to aid accuracy, write out direct quotations and statistics as fully as needed.
3 Abbreviate your sources on the card as a reminder to state them during the speech.
4 Mark the note card to suit your needs.

Let us now look at two student speeches, one informative and the other persuasive, each with a model outline and sample note cards based upon the outline.[1] (For another example of an informative speech outline, see the model on "The 'Fair Use' of Copyrighted Material" near the end of Chapter 10.) The texts of the delivered speeches are supplemented with commentary that calls attention to the application of specific rhetorical principles.

A Model Informative Speech
Rob Craig[2]

Title: Now You See It, Now You Don't: The Technology of the Stealth Bomber
Specific Purpose: To inform the audience about the technology that enables the Stealth B-2 Bomber to evade conventional radar.
Pattern for Main Points of Body: Component parts

INTRODUCTION

I. Imagine hearing a loud noise in the sky, looking up, and seeing an aircraft that looks like a bloated boomerang.
    A. It has wings, but no fuselage or tail.
    B. It is colored in a sinister charcoal black.

II. You would be looking at a Stealth B-2 Bomber which is designed to be "invisible" to conventional radar.
    A. The Stealth is a cousin to an earlier "flying wing," the Northrop YB-49, which was not fully developed because it was unstable in flight.
    B. Stealth has overcome the stability problems of the older version of the "flying wing."
        1. Stealth has successfully passed its first flight tests.
        2. Stealth has a top speed of 600 miles per hour.

Central Idea: Modern technology makes the Stealth Bomber "invisible" to conventional radar.

III. I will explain this technology in two points.
    A. First, I will explain those factors of *external* design that help make the plane "invisible."
    B. Second, I will explain those factors of *internal* design that help make the plane "invisible."

BODY

I. The Stealth Bomber employs several features of *external* design that help it evade radar.
    A. The first exterior antiradar feature is the "flying wing" shape.
        1. The sweeping curves help diffuse and deflect radar beams.
        2. The absence of a fuselage and a tail helps it hide from radar beams.
    B. The second exterior antiradar feature is the nonmetallic honeycomb coating.
        1. The ceramiclike coating helps absorb radar beams.
        2. In addition, the coating has a honeycomb design that further absorbs radar beams.
            a. The radar beams enter the honeycomb where they are "trapped" rather than reflected.
            b. The honeycomb design has been compared to a roach trap—or "roach motel"—that allows roaches in, but will not let them out.
    C. The third exterior antiradar feature is the special coating on the cockpit windows.
        1. The coating is transparent, allowing the pilot to see out.
        2. The special coating traps radar beams.

II. The Stealth Bomber employs several features of *internal* design that help it evade radar.
  A. The airframe is constructed of nonmetallic materials that help absorb radar beams.
    1. These special materials include strong human-made compounds such as polymers.
    2. These special materials include Fibaloy, a synthetic fiber reinforced with glass.
  B. The engines are designed to help frustrate enemy radar.
    1. The engines have a low "radar profile" because they are buried within the flying wing.
    2. The engines are coated with radar-absorbing materials.
    3. The engines have a special exhaust system that helps make the craft "invisible" to detection devices.
      a. Exhaust gasses are mixed with cool air before exiting the craft, thus helping evade heat detection.
      b. Exhaust gasses exit at the *top* of the craft, not at the rear, to further frustrate heat-detection systems.

CONCLUSION

I. I hope that I have helped you to understand how advanced technology helps to hide the Stealth Bomber from radar detection.
  A. This technology includes three key features of *external* design.
    1. The first is the "flying wing" shape.
    2. The second is the nonmetallic honeycomb coating.
    3. The third is the nonreflective coating on the cockpit windows.
  B. This technology includes two key features of *internal* design.
    1. The first is the construction of the airframe with nonmetallic materials.
    2. The second is the design of the engines.

II. Perhaps my talk, entitled "Now You See It, Now You Don't," should be called instead "Now *You* See It, Now *They* Don't."
  A. It is true that you can see the black "flying wing" if it flies overhead.
  B. But to enemy radar, the Stealth is a technological marvel of "now *they* don't."

Now You See It, Now You Don't:
The Technology of the Stealth Bomber

(Before reading the speech as delivered, study the outline above. Then, notice how the speaker follows the outlined sequence of points, yet expresses himself extemporaneously during delivery. In other words, the speaker uses language that comes to him naturally at the moment, without slavishly adhering to the exact wording of the outline.)

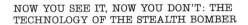

NOW YOU SEE IT, NOW YOU DON'T: THE
TECHNOLOGY OF THE STEALTH BOMBER

①

<u>Introduction</u>

I. Look up/loud noise/bloated boomerang.
    A. Big wing, no fuselage or tail.
    B. Sinister black.
II. Stealth B-2, "invisible" to radar.
    A. Cousin of Northrop YB-49
       "wing."
    B. B-2 more stable, has passed tests.

<u>Central Idea</u>: Explain technology that makes
Stealth "invisible" to radar.

III. Preview, 2 points:
    A. <u>External</u> design.
    B. <u>Internal</u> design.

Body

I. <u>External</u> design.
    A. Shape: wing, curves, no fuselage
       or tail.
    B. Coating: nonmetallic, honeycomb
       (absorbs radar).
    C. Cockpit windows, special surface
       (absorbs radar).

②

(<u>Body</u>, contd.)

II. <u>Internal</u> design.
    A. Airframe, nonmetallic
       (synthetic fibers—polymers,
       Fibaloy with glass).
    B. Engine design.
       1. Buried in wing.
       2. Antiradar coating.
       3. Exhaust system (cools,
          out the <u>top</u>).

Conclusion

I. Summary:
    A. <u>External</u> design: flying wing
       shape, honeycomb coat, cockpit
       windows.
    B. <u>Internal</u> design: nonmetallic
       airframe, engine buried in wing,
       exhaust cool and out the top.

II. Recall my title: "Now You See It,
    Now You Don't."

    But to enemy radar, Stealth is...

    "Now <u>You</u> See It, Now <u>They</u> Don't."

FIGURE II.1

Speaker's Note Cards for "Now You See It, Now You Don't." A thorough key-word
note card follows the outline carefully, but in very brief form. Here, the speaker
includes just enough information to "jog the memory" for the next point. The note
cards shown here utilize the front and back of *one* 4″ × 6″ note card. The number in
the upper right-hand corner helps the speaker keep the note cards in sequence, a
procedure that is even more useful for long speeches that require several note cards.

**The speech opens with a
hypothetical example that
catches audience attention and
focuses on the subject.**

Imagine for a moment that, while walking across
the campus, you hear a loud noise in the sky.
You look up and see an aircraft that reminds you
of a bloated boomerang, or flying wing. It is a sin-
ister plane, charcoal black in color. What I am
describing is not from some science fiction
movie—rather, it is a real aircraft that is the result
of years of secret research and development. It is
the Stealth B-2 Bomber, an American aircraft that
is virtually invisible to radar.

**This brief bit of background
information helps the audience
understand how the plane was
developed.**

The Stealth Bomber is actually a cousin to the
post-World War II experimental plane, the
Northrop YB-49, nicknamed the "Flying Wing."

The YB-49 was so unstable in flight that it did not get beyond the experimental stage of development. However, the Stealth, which has a top speed of 600 miles per hour, has passed its first flight tests.

The speaker states the *Central Idea.*

The Central Idea is followed by a preview of the main points of the Body.

In this speech, I will explain the technology of the Stealth Bomber that makes the aircraft "invisible" to conventional radar. To do this, I will first explain the technology as applied to the exterior of the plane, then I will discuss interior elements of design.

The *Body* of the speech begins with the statement of the first main heading.

"This design begins" introduces the first subpoint under the main heading.

The Stealth Bomber employs a superior external design to help it evade conventional radar. This design begins with the streamlined shape and the sweeping curves that diffuse and deflect radar beams. Because this streamlined "flying wing" has no regular fuselage, and no tail, it presents a lower "profile" to radar.

The second supporting point is identified with an "oral signpost" when the speaker says "second."

For clarity, the "honeycomb design" is compared to a roach trap.

Second, the entire aircraft is coated with a non-metallic, ceramiclike material that absorbs radar beams. The surface of this material is formed in an elaborate honeycombed pattern. This honeycomb "traps" radar beams so that they cannot be reflected, thus breaking the electronic cycle essential for detection. The honeycomb design is sometimes called a "roach motel," meaning that it works like a roach trap that lets the insects in but won't let them out.

The third supporting point under the first main heading is identified with an "oral signpost."

The third exterior feature is the special coating on the windows of the cockpit. This coating is transparent so that the crew can see out. However, it is made of a special material that absorbs radar beams. This, combined with the honeycombed surface of the flying wing, means that the entire surface is nonreflective to radar. Now that we have looked at the key elements of exterior design, let us turn our attention to the interior.

The speaker uses a transition sentence to move smoothly to the second main heading.

The second main heading is stated; in the sentence the speaker informs the audience that this heading will be covered in two subpoints. An "oral signpost" identifies the first subpoint.

The function of the airframe is clarified by comparing it to the chassis of a car.

There are two key elements of interior design that help the Stealth Bomber evade radar. The first of these is the plane's airframe, which is similar to the chassis of an automobile. Instead of being made of metal, which is the standard practice, the airframe of the Stealth is constructed from strong, nonmetallic materials that help absorb radar beams. These materials are human-made compounds such as polymers, or synthetic fibers such as Fibaloy, which is reinforced with glass.

The "oral signpost" method is used again to mark the second subpoint under main heading II.

The second internal factor concerns the engines. To begin with, the engines are not located on the surface of the plane, but are "buried" within the flying wing to enhance the low radar profile. Also, the engines are coated with radar-absorbing materials. Finally, the engines have a unique exhaust system that mixes cool air with the hot exhaust gasses before they are thrust from the aircraft. The cooled gasses then exit from the top of the plane rather than out the rear. This has the effect of further concealing the Stealth from electronic detection.

The speaker smoothly moves into the *Conclusion* of the speech.

A summary of key points is stated to the audience.

I hope that I have helped you understand some of the key elements of technology that make the Stealth B-2 Bomber "invisible" to conventional radar. As I have explained, this technology is applied both externally and internally. The external factors include the "flying wing" shape, the nonmetallic honeycomb surface, and the nonreflective coating on the cockpit windows. The internal factors include an airframe constructed of nonmetallic materials, and special designs applied to the engine.

The speaker then plays on the words of the title of the speech in order to provide a "creative touch" to the ending. This helps wrap things up in a satisfying manner.

Remember that the title of my talk is "Now You See It, Now You Don't." Perhaps I should reword that to "Now *You* See It, Now *They* Don't." Indeed, if the Stealth flew over our campus today, you could see the black "flying wing" as it passed. However, if, from a distance, an enemy radar were trying to detect this technological marvel, you can now understand why the second part of my title might be changed to "Now *They* Don't." That's Stealth, America's "invisible" airplane.

A Model Persuasive Speech
by Susan Minielli[3]

(Notice the use of specific forms of evidence—especially examples, statistics, and statements from authority—in this speech. A direct, convenient method of recording the source of evidence in the outline is to put source information in parentheses at the end of the sentence where it is used. This simple method is illustrated below.)

> **Title:** Campus Crime
> **Specific Purpose:** To actuate the audience to become directly involved in combating campus crime.
> **Pattern for Main Points:** Problem-solution

INTRODUCTION

I. Last November, Anne Marie, a University of Kentucky freshman, was accosted on her way home from the library.
   A. Three men tried to force her into a car.
   B. An officer and three students witnessed the attack, but did nothing to help.
      1. Finally the officer intervened, telling the men that their "fun was over."
      2. The officer then walked Anne Marie to her room.
   C. Anne Marie's attackers were not arrested.
      1. This illustrates the growing problem of campus crime.
      2. It also illustrates the indifference that many show toward the problem.

II. The focus in this speech is on two major types of crime: property crime and violence.
   A. The FBI defines both types (*Crime in the United States,* 1986).
      1. Property crimes include such things as burglary, larceny-theft, automobile-theft, and arson.
      2. Crimes of violence include such things as murder, non-negligent manslaughter, rape, robbery, and aggravated assault.
   B. Our campuses are experiencing both types of crimes.
      1. One report says that 96 percent of crimes reported on college campuses concern thefts and burglaries (*The Police Chief,* June 1987).
      2. However, crimes of violence, such as rape, are on the increase.
         a. A recent study by Indiana State Senator Joseph Corcoran revealed that "between 15 and 20 percent of college women will be raped in a residence hall before they graduate or leave school."
         b. The study added: "Another 20 to 25 percent will be the victims of attempted rape or sexual assault."

Central Idea: Campus crime is a serious issue, demanding a program of action.

III. Now that we have examined some of its parameters, let us look at campus crime in more detail.
   A. First, we will examine the problem and some of its causes.
   B. Second, we will examine some steps for dealing with the problem.

BODY

I. Awareness of the seriousness of campus crime is necessary if we are to combat it successfully.
   A. Campus crime creates serious difficulties for the universities and the students.
      1. The universities suffer losses of both finances and prestige.

a. The University of California system has suffered losses.
    (1) Financial losses for theft exceed $250,000 at the Los Angeles and Davis campuses, and over one million dollars statewide (*Marin Independent Journal,* October 25, 1986).
    (2) Prestige loss from the high crime rate keeps some top scholars and athletes from attending certain schools, such as the University of California, Berkeley.
b. Other universities, such as Michigan State, Ohio State, Colorado, and Indiana, have been plagued by high crime rates.
    (1) In early March, Indiana University police received three reports of sexual attacks.
    (2) At the University of Utah, a student reported the theft of artwork and personal property amounting to $25,000, creating much negative publicity for the school.

2. The student victims suffer personal losses.
a. Students suffer financially from theft and other property crimes.
    (1) Students lose directly, such as theft of wallets, stereos, and cars.
    (2) Students also lose by having to pay higher tuition to help cover the losses to the university.
b. Students often suffer emotionally from crimes of violence.
    (1) A female student at the University of Louisville who was the victim of gang rape suffers emotionally.
        (a) Her grades have dropped drastically.
        (b) She has become a recluse and suicidal.

B. Some of the causes of campus crime are inexcusable.
1. Apathy and the failure to prosecute is an inexcusable element of campus crime.
a. In the case of the University of Louisville student who was gang-raped, the university took no action against the men involved (*Louisville Courier-Journal,* March 31, 1986).
    (1) Four of the five rapists pled guilty in a court hearing, yet the university said nothing.
    (2) The victim responded: "It looks like the university doesn't care."
b. Unfortunately, such apathy can be found nationwide.
    (1) Bernice Sandler, Executive Director for the Association of American Colleges Project for the Status and Education of Women, says that "most campus authorities are still turning their backs on the problem."
    (2) Such leniency helps create an insecure environment and a reluctance of victims to report crime.
2. Carelessness and a lack of concern by students aggravate the problem.
a. A female student at Ball State University failed to lock her door, thus allowing an attacker to enter her room.
b. Many students leave belongings unprotected while they eat or relax in a lounge.

    c. Some students invite trouble by walking alone at night.

    d. Others become intoxicated, and are unable to take care of their safety needs.

II. A program of action can help combat campus crime.

    A. The first step is to become aware of the problem.

        1. Specific information, such as FBI statistics on campus crime, must be secured.

        2. This information must be publicized in campus publications and on bulletin boards.

    B. The second step is for the school administration to act on campus safety.

        1. The Ohio State University has reduced campus crime by improving lighting, increasing police visibility, and working with Columbus police (*Columbus Dispatch*, October 27, 1986).

        2. The University of Michigan has implemented a program to combat campus crime.

            a. The program includes an emergency telephone system and a "Nite Owl" transportation system.

            b. Leo Heatley, Safety Director of the University of Michigan, states, "The combination will make the campus a safer place."

    C. The third step is for the students to cooperate in combating campus crime.

        1. Students should keep their doors locked.

        2. Students should not walk alone at night, but should develop and use a "Walking Buddy" system.

        3. Students should avoid excessive amounts of alcohol and other substances that lessen their defenses.

        4. Students should keep their belongings with them at all times.

CONCLUSION

I. In this speech, we have examined campus crime.

    A. We have looked at the problem, including its financial and emotional costs.

    B. We have looked at a solution that calls for awareness by all, action by the administration, and cooperation by the students.

II. At the beginning I told you about Anne Marie from the University of Kentucky, who was attacked by three men.

    A. Fortunately, she was not permanently hurt.

    B. However, two weeks after they attacked Anne Marie, the same three men raped a campus sophomore.

        1. The sophomore dropped out of school and is still undergoing counseling.

        2. This example illustrates the vicious cycle of campus crime.

III. We must act to end this cycle, for, like Anne Marie and the unnamed sophomore, we all remain potential victims.

①

CAMPUS CRIME

Introduction

I. Anne Marie, U. Ky. freshman.
   A. Accosted by 3 men.
   B. Officer, students watched before helping.
II. Two types of crime: property, violence.
   A. FBI defines:
      1. Property: burglary, larceny, auto, arson, etc.
      2. Violence: murder, manslaughter, rape, robbery, assault, etc.
   B. Both occur on our campuses.
      1. 96% are thefts (says Police Chief, June/87).
      2. But violence increasing. Ind. State Sen. Joseph Corcoran: 15%–20% col. women will be assaulted in dorms; attempts on 20% to 25% more.

Central Idea: Campus crime is a serious issue, demanding a program of action.

III. Preview:
   A. Examine problem and some causes.
   B. Examine solution.

②

Body

I. Problem—we must take matter seriously.
   A. Hurts both schools and students.
      1. Schools (money, prestige).
         a. U. Calif. system, theft: Los Angeles, Davis, over $250,000; million statewide (Marin Ind. J., Oct. 25/86).

            Prestige loss, U. of Calif, Berkeley, top scholars, athletes.

         b. Other schools: Mich., Ohio, Colo., Ind. (Ind. U. 3 sex attacks March; Utah theft of art, property $25,000).
      2. Students, too, are victims.
         a. Financial: wallets, stereos, cars; pay higher tuition too.
         b. Violence (U. of Louisville female, assaulted, dropped out, suicidal).
   B. Some causes inexcusable.
      1. Apathy, failure to prosecute.
         a. Case, U. of Louisville took no action (L. Courier-J., March 31/86), though 4 of 5 men pled guilty. Victim: "IT LOOKS LIKE THE UNIVERSITY DOESN'T CARE."

FIGURE II.2

Speaker's Note Cards for "Campus Crime." With careful planning, and by using both sides of the cards, the complete key-word outline for this speech will go on two 4" × 6" note cards. Notice that sources are stated in abbreviated form. Also, all direct quotations are done in capital letters for easy reading.

Campus Crime

(As you read the speech, notice how effectively the speaker uses concrete evidence to illustrate and support her ideas. Also, the speech serves as an excellent model of how to state one's sources in a smooth, persuasive way during actual delivery.)

The speech begins with an interesting example that grabs the attention of the listener.

Anne Marie, a University of Kentucky freshman, was accosted on her way home from the library last November. Three men grabbed her and tried to force her into a car. A campus security officer and three students were witnesses to the attack. Only after repeated yells for help did the officer approach. He told the boys that their "fun was over" and they should go home. He then walked

(causes, apathy contd.)

    b. Apathy, nationwide.
    Bernice Sandler, Exec. Dir.
    Assoc. Am. Col. Project for
    Status & Ed. of Women:
    "MOST CAMPUS AUTHORITIES
    ARE STILL TURNING THEIR
    BACKS ON THE PROBLEM."

    Result: insecure environment

  2. Also, students are careless.
    a. Ball State female, assaulted,
      had not locked door.
    b. Belongings unprotected.
    c. Walk alone at night.
    d. Intoxicated.

II. <u>Solution</u>: program of action needed.
  A. <u>Awareness</u> (secure info such as FBI,
    publicize).
  B. <u>Administration</u> act.
    1. Ohio State, lights, police
      coop., reduced crime (<u>Columbus</u>
      <u>Dispatch</u>, Oct. 27/86).
    2. Mich., "Nite Owl" transport, &
      telephone system. Mich. Safety
      Director Leo Heatley: "THE
      COMBINATION WILL MAKE THE
      CAMPUS A SAFER PLACE."
  C. <u>Students</u>: lock doors, groups at
    night, sober, watch belongings.

Conclusion

I. Summary:
  A. Problem includes <u>financial</u> and
    <u>emotional</u> costs.
  B. Solution includes:
    1. <u>Awareness</u>.
    2. <u>Administrative</u> action.
    3. <u>Student</u> cooperation.
II. From introd., story of Anne Marie,
  U. of Ky., was attacked by 3 men.
  A. She was not permanently hurt.
  B. But, 2 weeks later, same 3 men
    raped another student who <u>was</u>
    hurt; dropped out of school, now
    in counseling. <u>Vicious cycle</u>!

III. <u>ACT NOW</u> ON <u>YOUR</u> CAMPUS to combat
  campus crime.

  All of us, like Anne Marie and the
  others, are <u>potential</u> victims!

Anne Marie to her room. Anne Marie's attackers were not arrested, warned, or otherwise notified that their behavior was not only unacceptable, but also *illegal*. This is just one example of crime on college campuses. And the indifference toward this crime has allowed the problem to escalate.

My focus in discussing this campus problem is on major types of crime. The 1986 FBI Uniform Crime Report, *Crime in the United States,* included statistics on both property and violent crimes. Property crimes include burglary, larceny-theft, automobile-theft, and arson. Violent crimes are murder and non-negligent manslaughter, rape, robbery, and aggravated assault. A study in a June, 1987, article of *The Police Chief* indicated that 96 percent of crimes reported on a college campus were thefts and burglaries, while less than 1 percent were forcible rapes. However, recent studies cited by Indiana State Senator Joseph

The speaker defines the type of crime that she will discuss, using FBI material to give credibility to her definition.

The speaker smoothly cites her source. The statistics are given in round numbers that are easy to remember.

The source is given, and the quotation is kept short for maximum impact on the audience.

Corcoran show that "between 15 and 20 percent of college women will be raped in a residence hall before they graduate or leave school. Another 10 to 25 percent will be the victims of attempted rape or sexual assault."

The speaker states the *Central Idea* of the speech.

A preview of the problem-solution division of the body of the speech is stated.

As you can see, campus crime is a serious issue, demanding a program of action. We have seen some of the parameters of campus crime, but now we need to look at the matter in more detail. First, we will examine the problem and some of its causes, then we will look at some practical steps for dealing with the problem.

The *Body* begins here with a statement of the problem.

The source for the statistics is given, and the numbers are reported in round figures.

Campus crime creates serious difficulties for the universities, and for the students. The universities suffer losses of both finances and prestige. According to San Rafael, California's *Marin Independent Journal,* October 25, 1986, schools such as the University of California, Los Angeles and Davis, suffered from thefts and missing equipment that amounted to $250,000, leading to state losses well over one million dollars.

This paragraph includes a number of short, specific examples.

The University of California, Berkeley, has one of the highest crime rates in the nation. Campus Police Chief Derry Bowles believes that the FBI's released figures are keeping top scholars, athletes, and other prospective students away from Berkeley. Other universities such as Michigan State University, the Ohio State University, the University of Colorado, and Indiana University have also been plagued by high crime rates. For example, during the first two weeks of March, Indiana University police received three reports of sexual attacks. And the University of Utah suffered from negative publicity when a student reported losses of $25,000 when campus thieves stole or damaged original artwork and personal belongings. Financial losses due to thefts of equipment, and negative publicity due to other crimes on campus, have ultimately caused tuitions to rise to cover the costs. In turn, this has caused enrollments to drop.

As done earlier, the statistics are reported in round figures to aid audience understanding.

Transition from university harm to student harm.

Specific examples that students can easily identify with.

But the most obvious as well as the most serious problem is that faced by students who are victims of campus crimes. Students suffer financially from stolen wallets, stereos, and cars which inevitably lead to increased insurance rates. Students are also the ones who pay for the university's losses through higher tuition.

Effective use of a moving
example.

Victims also suffer emotionally. A University of Louisville freshman who was the victim of gang rape in October, 1985, admitted, "I was paranoid. I was afraid to go anywhere by myself—day or night. Everything was chaotic, and I was crying all of the time." Her grades dropped drastically; she became a recluse and suicidal.

The problems created by campus crime are severe, and some of the causes are inexcusable. Universities have helped perpetuate the problem due to their lax attitude and their refusal to prosecute. According to the Louisville *Courier-Journal,* March 31, 1986, the university took no action against the men who raped the girl, even though four of the five pleaded guilty in a Jefferson County district court hearing. The rape victim summed up her feelings by saying, "It looks like the university doesn't care."

The source is worked into the
speech in a smooth manner.

Unfortunately, this lack of concern can be found across the nation. Bernice Sandler, Executive Director for the Association of American Colleges Project for the Status and Education of Women, affirms that "most campus authorities are still turning their backs on the problem." This leniency has helped to create an insecure environment in which crimes are more likely to occur and students are less likely to report them.

Again, the source is mentioned
in a brief but effective
manner.

The speaker continues to use
short quotations to add a
"punch" to the argument.

But students themselves often add to the insecure environments. A Ball State University student was attacked by a man with a hunting knife who was able to enter her room because she had failed to lock her door before leaving. Many students leave belongings unprotected while they eat dinner or relax in a lounge. Other students invite trouble by either walking alone at night, or becoming intoxicated at parties. All of these behaviors lead to an environment of easy accessibility for criminals.

Additional specific examples
that students can easily
understand and relate to.

Because campus crime is a serious problem for the university and students, it is necessary that actions be taken to help combat the causes. The following proposal may not eliminate crime completely, but it will create an environment less conducive to crime, and one in which students need not fear reporting crimes. I will first look at crime awareness, then focus on some actions that can be taken by the university and, finally, by the students.

Part II of the Body—the
solution step—begins here.

The speaker previews the
steps of her solution.

The speaker uses an "oral signpost" by saying the "first step."

The first step—crime awareness—is an essential prelude to the other solutions. The FBI has helped by publishing campus crime statistics, but the university and students must acknowledge that information, publicizing it in school newspapers and newsletters, and on bulletin boards. No problem can be solved until the parties involved admit to the problem and feel the need for a solution—much like an alcoholic, admitting the problem is half the battle.

The second step of the solution is presented.

Specific examples, backed with a statement of source, add weight to the argument.

Once the problem is accepted, the school administrations can take some necessary steps to create a safer environment. According to the October 27, 1986, *Columbus Dispatch,* the Ohio State University has reduced its crime rate over the past two years, in part by improving lighting on the campus, increasing police visibility, and gaining cooperation from Columbus police. The University of Michigan has implemented an emergency telephone system and a "Nite Owl" transportation system in an attempt to reduce crime. According to Leo Heatley, University of Michigan's Safety Director, "The combination will make the campus a safer place."

The source is qualified, and the quotation is kept short.

An "oral signpost" is used to identify the "third step."

But the university's actions will not succeed without the third step—student cooperation. Students can help in several simple ways. Lock your door at all times. Never walk alone at night. Students could join together to form "Walking Buddy" systems to create safety in numbers. Avoid excessive amounts of alcohol and other substances that lessen your defenses. Keep your belongings with you at all times. These steps, taken by both men and women, would help to decrease all types of campus crime.

The *Conclusion* begins with a transition sentence, and a brief summary of the key points presented above.

Now that you know the seriousness of campus crime, including its financial and emotional costs, you can begin to deal with the problem with the steps I have outlined. These include a sharpened awareness, action by the administration, and cooperation by the students.

This reference to the opening example gives a sense of "completeness" to the speech.

The first example is supported with a second one that strengthens the argument.

Remember Anne Marie, the University of Kentucky freshman I mentioned at the beginning? Fortunately, she was not permanently hurt by her attackers. However, two weeks after Anne Marie was attacked, the same three men raped a sophomore on campus. She dropped out of school, and is still undergoing counseling today.

**The speech ends with an
appeal for action.**

Unfortunately, this example is just one part of the vicious cycle of campus crime. And until we do something to end this cycle, we will all remain potential victims.

ENDNOTES

1. The model informative speech by Rob Craig included an outline and a manuscript. The model persuasive speech by Susan Minielli included only a manuscript; the outline was prepared by the author from the published manuscript. Also, the author is responsible for the sample note cards for both speeches.
2. The informative speech by Rob Craig was delivered in February, 1990, in a public speaking class at the University of North Carolina at Greensboro. It is used with the permission of Rob Craig.
3. The persuasive speech on campus crime was delivered by Susan Minielli in the 1988 speaking competition of the Interstate Oratorical Association. At the time of the contest, Minielli was a student at Ball State University. The speech appears in *Winning Orations: 1988,* and is used with the permission of the Interstate Oratorical Association.

Appendix III

SPEECHES FOR STUDY AND DISCUSSION

Declaration of War
Franklin D. Roosevelt

Franklin D. Roosevelt (1882–1945) was elected to the office of President of the United States in 1932. He was reelected in 1936, 1940, and 1944, thereby becoming the nation's only four-term president. He died in 1945, a few months after taking the oath of office for the fourth time. His years of public service were marked by excellence in public address.

The Declaration of War speech was delivered to a joint session of Congress—and to the American people via radio—on December 8, 1941, just one day following the surprise Japanese attack on the American fleet at Pearl Harbor. Notable for its brevity, the speech addresses the national crisis appropriately and eloquently.

In its original form, the first line of the speech read: "Yesterday, December 7th, 1941—a date which will live in world history...." *[Emphasis supplied.] Before the speech was delivered, Roosevelt, who had a fine ear for vivid oral language, changed "world history" to "infamy." The change was highly effective—so much so that the speech is often called the "Day of Infamy Address." This bit of rhetorical history can remind you that word choice* does *make a difference in your speaking.*

The text is from a voice recording of the speech.

1 Yesterday, December 7th, 1941—a date which will live in infamy—the United States of America was suddenly and deliberately attacked by naval and air forces of the Empire of Japan.

2 The United States was at peace with that nation and, at the solicitation of Japan, was still in conversation with its government and its Emperor, looking toward the maintenance of peace in the Pacific. Indeed, one hour after Japanese air squadrons had commenced bombing in the American island of Oahu, the Japanese Ambassador to the United States and his colleague delivered to our Secretary of State a formal reply to a recent American message. And while this reply stated that it seemed useless to continue the existing diplomatic negotiations, it contained no threat or hint of war or of armed attack.

3 It will be recorded that the distance of Hawaii from Japan makes it obvious that the attack was deliberately planned many days or even weeks ago. During the intervening time the Japanese government has deliberately sought to deceive the United States by false statements and expressions of hope for continued peace.

4 The attack yesterday on the Hawaiian Islands has caused severe damage to American naval and military forces. I regret to tell you that very many American lives have been lost. In addi-

tion, American ships have been reported torpedoed on the high seas between San Francisco and Honolulu.

5 Yesterday the Japanese government also launched an attack against Malaya.

6 Last night Japanese forces attacked Hong Kong.

7 Last night Japanese forces attacked Guam.

8 Last night Japanese forces attacked the Philippine Islands.

9 Last night the Japanese attacked Wake Island.

10 And this morning the Japanese attacked Midway Island.

11 Japan has, therefore, undertaken a surprise offensive extending throughout the Pacific area. The facts of yesterday and today speak for themselves. The people of the United States have already formed their opinions and well understand the implications to the very life and safety of our nation.

12 As Commander-in-Chief of the Army and Navy, I have directed that all measures be taken for our defense.

13 But always will our whole nation remember the character of the onslaught against us.

14 No matter how long it may take us to overcome this premeditated invasion, the American people in their righteous might will win through to absolute victory.

15 I believe that I interpret the will of the Congress and of the people when I assert that we will not only defend ourselves to the uttermost but will make it very certain that this form of treachery shall never again endanger us.

16 Hostilities exist. There is no blinking at the fact that our people, our territory, and our interests are in grave danger.

17 With confidence in our armed forces, with the unbounding determination of our people, we will gain the inevitable triumph—so help us God.

18 I ask that the Congress declare that since the unprovoked and dastardly attack by Japan on Sunday, December 7th, 1941, a state of war has existed between the United States and the Japanese Empire.

Inaugural Address
John F. Kennedy

John F. Kennedy (1917–1963) delivered his Inaugural Address before a large audience assembled in front of the U.S. Capitol Building on January 21, 1961. Typical of inaugural addresses, the speech sets out for the nation and the world a number of ideals and themes that mark the thinking of the new president (for Kennedy, these included world peace, support for human liberty, and concern for the poor and oppressed). The speech is memorable for its excellence in accomplishing this goal.

To give dignity and persuasive force to his ideals, Kennedy makes regular use of figures of speech and carefully crafted sentences. Metaphors abound ("the torch has been passed," "the trumpet summons us again"), as do examples of antithesis ("If a free society cannot help the many who are poor, it cannot save the few who are rich"). By presenting noble ideas with stylistic grace, Kennedy earned for this speech a permanent place in the history of great speechmaking.

The text is from a voice recording of the speech.

1 We observe today not a victory of party but a celebration of freedom, symbolizing an end as well as a beginning, signifying renewal as well as change, for I have sworn before you and Almighty God the same solemn oath our forebears prescribed nearly a century and three quarters ago. The world is very different now, for man holds in his mortal hands the power to abolish all forms of human poverty and all forms of human life. And yet the same revolutionary beliefs for which our forebears fought are still at issue around the globe—the belief that the rights of man come not from the generosity of the state but from the hand of God.

2 We dare not forget today that we are the heirs of that first revolution. Let the word go forth from this time and place to friend and foe alike that the torch has been passed to a new generation of Americans, born in this century, tempered by war, disciplined by a hard and bitter peace, proud of our ancient heritage, and unwilling to witness or permit the slow undoing of those human rights to which this nation has always been committed, and to which we are committed today, at home and around the world.

3 Let every nation know, whether it wishes us well or ill, that we shall pay any price, bear any burden, meet any hardship, support any friend, oppose any foe, to assure the survival and the success of liberty.

4 This much we pledge and more.

5 To those old allies whose cultural and spiritual origins we share, we pledge the loyalty of faithful friends. United, there is little we cannot do in a host of cooperative ventures. Divided, there is little we can do, for we dare not meet a powerful challenge at odds and split asunder.

6 To those new states whom we welcome to the ranks of the free, we pledge our word that one form of colonial control shall not have passed away merely to be replaced by a far more iron tyranny. We shall not always expect to find them supporting our view, but we shall always hope to find them strongly supporting their own freedom and to remember that, in the past, those who foolishly sought power by riding the back of the tiger ended up inside.

7 To those people in the huts and villages of half the globe struggling to break the bonds of mass misery, we pledge our best efforts to help them help themselves, for whatever period is required, not because the Communists may be doing it, not because we seek their votes, but because it is right. If a free society cannot help the many who are poor, it cannot save the few who are rich.

8 To our sister republics south of our border, we offer a special pledge to convert our good words into good deeds in a new alliance for progress to assist free men and free governments in casting off the chains of poverty. But this peaceful revolution of hope cannot become the prey of hostile powers. Let all our neighbors know that we shall join with them to oppose ag-

gression or subversion anywhere in the Americas, and let every other power know that this hemisphere intends to remain the master of its own house.

9 To that world assembly of sovereign states, the United Nations, our last best hope in an age where the instruments of war have far outpaced the instruments of peace, we renew our pledge of support to prevent it from becoming merely a forum for invective, to strengthen its shield of the new and the weak, and to enlarge the area in which its writ may run.

10 Finally, to those nations who would make themselves our adversary, we offer not a pledge but a request that both sides begin anew the quest for peace before the dark powers of destruction unleashed by science engulf all humanity in planned or accidental self-destruction. We dare not tempt them with weakness, for only when our arms are sufficient beyond doubt can we be certain beyond doubt that they will never be employed. But neither can two great and powerful groups of nations take comfort from our present course, both sides overburdened by the cost of modern weapons, both rightly alarmed by the steady spread of the deadly atom, yet both racing to alter that uncertain balance of terror that stays the hand of mankind's final war.

11 So let us begin anew, remembering on both sides that civility is not a sign of weakness and sincerity is always subject to proof. Let us never negotiate out of fear, but let us never fear to negotiate. Let both sides explore what problems unite us instead of belaboring those problems which divide us. Let both sides, for the first time, formulate serious and precise proposals for the inspection and control of arms and bring the absolute power to destroy other nations under the absolute control of all nations. Let both sides seek to invoke the wonders of science instead of its terrors. Together let us explore the stars, conquer the deserts, eradicate disease, tap the ocean depths, and encourage the arts and commerce. Let both sides unite to heed in all corners of the earth the command of Isaiah to ''undo the heavy burdens and let the oppressed go free.'' And if a beachhead of cooperation may push back the jungle of suspicion, let both sides join in creating a new endeavor, not a new balance of power but a new world of law, where the strong are just and the weak secure and the peace preserved.

12 All this will not be finished in the first one hundred days, nor will it be finished in the first one thousand days, nor in the life of this Administration, nor even perhaps in our lifetime on this planet, but let us begin.

13 In your hands, my fellow citizens, more than mine, will rest the final success or failure of our course. Since this country was founded, each generation of Americans has been summoned to give testimony to its national loyalty. The graves of young Americans who answered the call to service surround the globe. Now the trumpet summons us again, not as a call to bear arms, though arms we need, not as a call to battle, though embattled we are, but a call to bear the burden of a long twilight struggle, year in and year out, ''rejoicing in hope, patient in tribulation,'' a struggle against the common enemies of man: tyranny, poverty, disease, and war itself. Can we forge against these enemies a grand and global alliance, north and south, east and west, that can assure a more fruitful life for all mankind? Will you join in that historic effort?

14 In the long history of the world, only a few generations have been granted the role of defending freedom in its hour of maximum danger. I do

not shrink from this responsibility, I welcome it. I do not believe that any of us would exchange places with any other people or any other generation. The energy, the faith, the devotion which we bring to this endeavor will light our country and all who serve it, and the glow from that fire can truly light the world. And so, my fellow Americans, ask not what your country can do for you, ask what you can do for your country. My fellow citizens of the world, ask not what America will do for you, but what together we can do for the freedom of man.

15 Finally, whether you are citizens of America or citizens of the world, ask of us here the same high standards of strength and sacrifice which we ask of you. With a good conscience our only sure reward, with history the final judge of our deeds, let us go forth to lead the land we love, asking His blessing and His help, but knowing that here on earth God's work must truly be our own.

I Have a Dream
Martin Luther King, Jr.

On August 28, 1963, Martin Luther King, Jr. (1929–1968) delivered his "I Have a Dream" speech from the steps of the Lincoln Memorial in the nation's capital. His immediate audience consisted of more than 200,000 supporters who had come to Washington from all parts of the country to take part in a day of peaceful demonstration on behalf of civil rights. In addition, millions of Americans heard the speech on radio or watched it on national television.

King spoke in the afternoon of the hot, August day, after most of the scheduled events were completed. The crowd forgot its weariness, however, when King began to speak. In a clear, melodious voice, and using language that gave persuasive force to the concepts of human dignity and human freedom, King set out his dream. His use of figurative language is particularly effective, as is his ability to emphasize ideas with the stylistic devices of repetition and parallel structure. The result is one of the great speeches of American history.

The text is from a recording of the speech. It is reprinted here with the permission of Joan Daves (copyright by Martin Luther King, Jr., 1963).

1 I am happy to join with you today in what will go down in history as the greatest demonstration for freedom in the history of our nation.

2 Five score years ago, a great American, in whose symbolic shadow we stand today, signed the Emancipation Proclamation. This momentous decree came as a great beacon light of hope to millions of Negro slaves, who had been seared in the flames of withering injustice. It came as a joyous daybreak to end the long night of their captivity.

3 But one hundred years later, the Negro still is not free. One hundred years later, the life of the Negro is still sadly crippled by the manacles of segregation and the chains of discrimination. One hundred years later, the Negro lives on a lonely island of poverty in the midst of a vast ocean of ma-

terial prosperity. One hundred years later, the Negro is still languished in the corners of American society and finds himself an exile in his own land.

4 And so we've come here today to dramatize a shameful condition. In a sense we've come to our nation's Capitol to cash a check. When the architects of our republic wrote the magnificent words of the Constitution and the Declaration of Independence, they were signing a promissory note to which every American was to fall heir. This note was a promise that all men—yes, black men as well as white men—would be guaranteed the unalienable rights of life, liberty, and the pursuit of happiness.

5 It is obvious today that America has defaulted on this promissory note insofar as her citizens of color are concerned. Instead of honoring this sacred obligation, America has given the Negro people a bad check—a check which has come back marked "insufficient funds."

6 But we refuse to believe that the bank of justice is bankrupt. We refuse to believe that there are insufficient funds in the great vaults of opportunity of this nation. And so we've come to cash this check—a check that will give us upon demand the riches of freedom and the security of justice.

7 We have also come to this hallowed spot to remind America of the fierce urgency of now. This is no time to engage in the luxury of cooling off or to take the tranquillizing drug of gradualism. Now is the time to make real the promises of democracy. Now is the time to rise from the dark and desolate valley of segregation to the sunlit path of racial justice. Now is the time to lift our nation from the quicksands of racial injustice to the solid rock of brotherhood. Now is the time to make justice a reality for all of God's children.

8 It would be fatal for the nation to overlook the urgency of the moment. This sweltering summer of the Negro's legitimate discontent will not pass until there is an invigorating autumn of freedom and equality. Nineteen sixty-three is not an end, but a beginning. Those who hope that the Negro needed to blow off steam and will now be content will have a rude awakening if the nation returns to business as usual. There will be neither rest nor tranquillity in America until the Negro is granted his citizenship rights. The whirlwinds of revolt will continue to shake the foundations of our nation until the bright day of justice emerges.

9 But there is something that I must say to my people, who stand on the warm threshold which leads into the palace of justice. In the process of gaining our rightful place, we must not be guilty of wrongful deeds. Let us not seek to satisfy our thirst for freedom by drinking from the cup of bitterness and hatred.

10 We must forever conduct our struggle on the high plane of dignity and discipline. We must not allow our creative protest to degenerate into physical violence. Again and again we must rise to the majestic heights of meeting physical force with soul force.

11 The marvelous new militancy which has engulfed the Negro community must not lead us to a distrust of all white people. For many of our white brothers, as evidenced by their presence here today, have come to realize that their destiny is tied up with our destiny. They have come to realize that their freedom is inextricably bound to our freedom. We cannot walk alone.

12 As we walk, we must make the pledge that we shall always march ahead. We cannot turn back. There are those who are asking the devotees of civil

rights, "When will you be satisfied?" We can never be satisfied as long as the Negro is the victim of the unspeakable horrors of police brutality. We can never be satisfied as long as our bodies, heavy with the fatigue of travel, cannot gain lodging in the motels of the highways and the hotels of the cities. We cannot be satisfied as long as a Negro in Mississippi cannot vote and a Negro in New York believes he has nothing for which to vote. No, no, we are not satisfied, and we will not be satisfied until justice rolls down like waters, and righteousness like a mighty stream.

13 I am not unmindful that some of you have come here out of great trials and tribulations. Some of you have come fresh from narrow jail cells. Some of you have come from areas where your quest for freedom left you battered by the storms of persecution and staggered by the winds of police brutality. You have been the veterans of creative suffering. Continue to work with the faith that unearned suffering is redemptive.

14 Go back to Mississippi, go back to Alabama, go back to South Carolina, go back to Georgia, go back to Louisiana, go back to the slums and ghettos of our Northern cities, knowing that somehow this situation can and will be changed. Let us not wallow in the valley of despair.

15 I say to you today, my friends, so even though we face the difficulties of today and tomorrow, I still have a dream. It is a dream deeply rooted in the American dream.

16 I have a dream that one day this nation will rise up and live out the true meaning of its creed, "We hold these truths to be self-evident, that all men are created equal."

17 I have a dream that one day on the red hills of Georgia the sons of former slaves and the sons of former slaveowners will be able to sit down together at the table of brotherhood.

18 I have a dream that one day even the state of Mississippi, a state sweltering with the heat of injustice, sweltering with the heat of oppression, will be transformed into an oasis of freedom and justice.

19 I have a dream that my four little children will one day live in a nation where they will not be judged by the color of their skin but by the content of their character. I have a dream today.

20 I have a dream that one day, down in Alabama, with its vicious racists, with its governor having his lips dripping with the words of interposition and nullification, one day right there in Alabama little black boys and black girls will be able to join hands with the little white boys and white girls as sisters and brothers. I have a dream today.

21 I have a dream that one day every valley shall be exalted, every hill and mountain shall be made low, the rough places will be made plain and the crooked places will be made straight, and the glory of the Lord shall be revealed, and all flesh shall see it together.

22 This is our hope. This is the faith that I go back to the South with. With this faith we will be able to hew out of the mountain of despair a stone of hope. With this faith we will be able to transform the jangling discords of our nation into a beautiful symphony of brotherhood. With this faith we will be able to work together, to pray together, to struggle together, to go to jail together, to stand up for freedom together, knowing that we will be free one day.

23 This will be the day—this will be the day when all of God's children will be able to sing with new meaning, "My country 'tis of thee, sweet land of

liberty, of thee I sing. Land where my fathers died, land of the pilgrim's pride, from every mountainside, let freedom ring." And if America is to be a great nation, this must become true.

24 So let freedom ring from the prodigious hilltops of New Hampshire. Let freedom ring from the mighty mountains of New York. Let freedom ring from the heightening Alleghenies of Pennsylvania!

25 Let freedom ring from the snowcapped Rockies of Colorado! Let freedom ring from the curvaceous slopes of California!

26 But not only that. Let freedom ring from Stone Mountain of Georgia!

27 Let freedom ring from Lookout Mountain of Tennessee!

28 Let freedom ring from every hill and molehill of Mississippi. From every mountainside, let freedom ring.

29 And when this happens, when we allow freedom to ring—when we let it ring from every village and every hamlet, from every state and every city—we will be able to speed up that day when all of God's children, black men and white men, Jews and Gentiles, Protestants and Catholics, will be able to join hands and sing in the words of the old Negro spiritual, "Free at last! Free at last! Thank God almighty, we are free at last!"

Democratic Convention Keynote Address
Barbara C. Jordan

Barbara C. Jordan (1936–   ) delivered this keynote address to the Democratic National Convention in New York City on July 12, 1976. At the time the speech was delivered, Jordan, a black attorney from Texas, was a member of the U.S. House of Representatives from the Houston district. As she spoke, the audience, which had not responded with much enthusiasm to the speakers who preceded her, quieted, listened intently, and soon began to interrupt with applause. At the conclusion, Jordan was called back to the podium for a sustained ovation.

Jordan's keynote address is a superior example of the speech to reinforce. Indeed, the purpose of a keynote speech is to strengthen audience unity by reinforcing common attitudes. Jordan accomplished this with a combination of appropriate content and effective delivery. In content, she emphasized traditional American values such as patriotism, optimism about the future, trust in the common people, and individual liberty. She delivered her thoughts in a clear, forceful voice that was marked by the deliberate articulation of speech sounds. In this speech, Jordan achieved what is expected of a keynote speaker—she inspired the audience.

The text of the speech is reprinted with the permission of Vital Speeches of the Day *(as published in the issue of August 15, 1976, pp. 645–646).*

1 One hundred and forty-four years ago, members of the Democratic Party first met in convention to select a Presidential candidate. Since that time, Democrats have continued to convene once every four years and draft a party

platform and nominate a Presidential candidate. And our meeting this week is a continuation of that tradition.

2 But there is something different about tonight. There is something special about tonight. What is different? What is special? I, Barbara Jordan, am a keynote speaker.

3 A lot of years passed since 1832, and during that time it would have been most unusual for any national political party to ask that a Barbara Jordan deliver a keynote address...but tonight here I am. And I feel that notwithstanding the past that my presence here is one additional bit of evidence that the American Dream need not forever be deferred.

4 Now that I have this grand distinction what in the world am I supposed to say?

5 I could easily spend this time praising the accomplishments of this party and attacking the Republicans but I don't choose to do that.

6 I could list the many problems which Americans have. I could list the problems which cause people to feel cynical, angry, frustrated: problems which include lack of integrity in government; the feeling that the individual no longer counts; the reality of material and spiritual poverty; the feeling that the grand American experiment is failing or has failed. I could recite these problems and then I could sit down and offer no solutions. But I don't choose to do that either.

7 The citizens of America expect more. They deserve and they want more than a recital of problems.

8 We are a people in a quandary about the present. We are a people in search of our future. We are a people in search of a national community.

9 We are a people trying not only to solve the problems of the present—unemployment, inflation—but we are attempting on a larger scale to fulfill the promise of America. We are attempting to fulfill our national purpose; to create and sustain a society in which all of us are equal.

10 Throughout our history, when people have looked for new ways to solve their problems, and to uphold the principles of this nation, many times they have turned to political parties. They have often turned to the Democratic Party.

11 What is it, what is it about the Democratic Party that makes it the instrument that people use when they search for ways to shape their future? Well I believe the answer to that question lies in our concept of governing. Our concept of governing is derived from our view of people. It is a concept deeply rooted in a set of beliefs firmly etched in the national conscience of all of us.

12 Now what are these beliefs?

13 First, we believe in equality for all and privileges for none. This is a belief that each American regardless of background has equal standing in the public forum, all of us. Because we believe this idea so firmly, we are an inclusive rather than an exclusive party. Let everybody come.

14 I think it no accident that most of those emigrating to America in the 19th century identified with the Democratic Party. We are a heterogeneous party made up of Americans of diverse backgrounds.

15 We believe that the people are the source of all governmental power; that the authority of the people is to be extended, not restricted. This can be

accomplished only by providing each citizen with every opportunity to participate in the management of the government. They must have that.

16 We believe that the government which represents the authority of all the people, not just one interest group, but all the people, has an obligation to actively, underscore actively, seek to remove those obstacles which would block individual achievement...obstacles emanating from race, sex, economic condition. The government must seek to remove them.

17 We are a party of innovation. We do not reject our traditions, but we are willing to adapt to changing circumstances, when change we must. We are willing to suffer the discomfort of change in order to achieve a better future.

18 We have a positive vision of the future founded on the belief that the gap between the promise and reality of America can one day be finally closed. We believe that.

19 This my friends, is the bedrock of our concept of governing. This is a part of the reason why Americans have turned to the Democratic Party. These are the foundations upon which a national community can be built.

20 Let's all understand that these guiding principles cannot be discarded for short-term political gains. They represent what this country is all about. They are indigenous to the American idea. And these are principles which are not negotiable.

21 In other times, I could stand here and give this kind of exposition on the beliefs of the Democratic Party and that would be enough. But today that is not enough. People want more. That is not sufficient reason for the majority of the people of this country to vote Democratic. We have made mistakes. In our haste to do all things for all people, we did not foresee the full consequences of our actions. And when the people raised their voices, we didn't hear. But our deafness was only a temporary condition, and not an irreversible condition.

22 Even as I stand here and admit that we have made mistakes I still believe that as the people of America sit in judgment on each party, they will recognize that our mistakes were mistakes of the heart. They'll recognize that.

23 And now we must look to the future. Let us heed the voice of the people and recognize their common sense. If we do not, we not only blaspheme our political heritage, we ignore the common ties that bind all Americans.

24 Many fear the future. Many are distrustful of their leaders, and believe that their voices are never heard. Many seek only to satisfy their private work wants. To satisfy private interests.

25 But this is the great danger America faces. That we will cease to be one nation and become instead a collection of interest groups: city against suburb, region against region, individual against individual. Each seeking to satisfy private wants.

26 If that happens, who then will speak for America?

27 Who then will speak for the common good?

28 This is the question which must be answered in 1976.

29 Are we to be one people bound together by common spirit sharing in a common endeavor or will we become a divided nation?

30 For all of its uncertainty, we cannot flee the future. We must not become the new puritans and reject our society. We must address and master the

future together. It can be done if we restore the belief that we share a sense of national community, that we share a common national endeavor. It can be done.

31 There is no executive order; there is no law that can require the American people to form a national community. This we must do as individuals and if we do it as individuals, there is no President of the United States who can veto that decision.

32 As a first step, we must restore our belief in ourselves. We are a generous people so why can't we be generous with each other? We need to take to heart the words spoken by Thomas Jefferson:

33 "Let us restore to social intercourse that harmony and that affection without which liberty and even life are but dreary things."

34 A nation is formed by the willingness of each of us to share in the responsibility for upholding the common good.

35 A government is invigorated when each of us is willing to participate in shaping the future of this nation.

36 In this election year we must define the common good and begin again to shape a common future. Let each person do his or her part. If one citizen is unwilling to participate, all of us are going to suffer. For the American idea, though it is shared by all of us, is realized in each one of us.

37 And now, what are those of us who are elected public officials supposed to do? We call ourselves public servants but I'll tell you this: we as public servants must set an example for the rest of the nation. It is hypocritical for the public official to admonish and exhort the people to uphold the common good if we are derelict in upholding the common good. More is required of public officials than slogans and handshakes and press releases. More is required. We must hold ourselves strictly accountable. We must provide the people with a vision of the future.

38 If we promise as public officials, we must deliver. If we as public officials propose, we must produce. If we say to the American people it is time for you to be sacrificial; sacrifice. If the public official says that we (public officials) must be the first to give. We must be. And again, if we make mistakes, we must be willing to admit them. We have to do that. What we have to do is strike a balance between the idea that government should do everything and the idea, the belief, that government ought to do nothing. Strike a balance.

39 Let there be no illusions about the difficulty of forming this kind of a national community. It's tough, difficult, not easy. But a spirit of harmony will survive in America only if each of us remembers that we share a common destiny. If each of us remembers, when self-interest and bitterness seem to prevail, that we share a common destiny.

40 I have confidence that we can form this kind of national community.

41 I have confidence that the Democratic Party can lead the way. I have that confidence. We cannot improve on the system of government handed down to us by the founders of the Republic, there is no way to improve upon that. But what we can do is to find new ways to implement that system and realize our destiny.

42 Now, I began this speech by commenting to you on the uniqueness of a Barbara Jordan making the keynote address. Well I am going to close my

speech by quoting a Republican President and I ask you that as you listen to these words of Abraham Lincoln, relate them to the concept of a national community in which every last one of us participates: "As I would not be a slave, so I would not be a master. This expresses my idea of Democracy. Whatever differs from this, to the extent of the difference is no Democracy."

A Student Speech to Inform

Dust
Theresa Buescher

Theresa Buescher's speech about dust was the final-round winner in informative speaking in the 1987 National Championship Tournament in Individual Speaking Events. At the time of delivery, Buescher was a student at Illinois State University. The speech is a good example of how a common subject can be presented in a fresh and interesting manner. Notice that the transcript records audience laughter from time to time, thereby revealing that the audience responded positively to the speaker's use of humor.

The text of the speech is from 1987 Championship Debates and Speeches, *and is reprinted with the permission of the American Forensic Association.*

1 Forty-three million tons settle over the United States each year. Irving Addler says that we may inhale up to four hundred thousand million particles of this per day. No, it's not second-hand smoke. Irving Addler is the author of a book entitled *Dust.*

2 *Webster's New World Dictionary* defines "dust" as any finely powdered matter. Scientists who study dust define it more specifically as any particulate matter over one micron in size—and that's pretty small since the human eye is unable to detect anything under ten microns.

3 Dust is nothing to sneeze at. And to find out exactly why this is true, we need to examine some facts about dust that may very well surprise you. To do this, we will look at different types of dust, the microscopic world of dust, and how this world affects our world.

4 There are many, many different types of dust. The number one contributor to dust, as reported in the November, '86 issue of *Discover,* is soil. Salt is a close second, with three hundred million tons finding their way out of the ocean each year. Volcanic activity and forest fires, the third and fourth most common forms of naturally occurring dust, are generated by what scientists consider to be "dust events."

5 Now, in a good year for dust [laughter], forest fires can account for up to 7 percent of the world total. But volcanos make perhaps the greatest dust of all. When the Indonesian island of Krakatoa erupted on August 26th and 27th of 1883, it sent some four hundred cubic miles of earth into the atmo-

sphere, some of which made it up to an altitude of one hundred thirty thousand feet. Three months later the dust from this eruption reached Europe, where three days later the light was still much dimmer than normal.

6 Not all our dust, however, is naturally occurring. Don Aslet, the self-described Billy Graham of the Pine-Sol set, professional cleaner and author of *Clutter's Last Stand,* and *Should I Dust or Vacuum First,* tells us that rubber dust from car tires wearing down is a real problem in cities, towns, and near highways. The dust travels up and settles on our windows, but only to about the third floor. It completely cuts out at about the seventh floor, which is one reason why more important people have offices on higher floors, and also why we use one hundred and thirty-five thousand gallons of Windex per day.

7 We may not feel it necessary to concern ourselves with all these types of dust—because, perhaps, of the greatest interest to us is the dust that we find in our houses. Dust expert John Fergeson of the Cincinnati-based Drecket Company, makers of Endust, tells us that our houses contain matter from all over the world and even outer space. Comets and disintegrating meteorites increase the mass of the earth by ten thousand tons per year. Surprisingly enough, unless you live in a factory town like Stubenville, Ohio, the air inside your house is approximately twice as dusty as the air outside. So opening up the windows in this room and letting the breeze blow through would actually clean it.

8 The average six-room city or suburban dwelling can accumulate up to forty pounds of dust per year. In a single cubic inch of air there may be between eight hundred thousand and one million six hundred thousand tiny particles. And a single puff from a cigarette puts four million of these particles into the air.

9 Much of this dust is too small to ever settle. Scientists who study how fast dust falls—undoubtedly, very patient people [laughter]—tell us that a particle of, say, .25 microns will spend ten hours dropping just one foot in still air. Well, since the air in our house is seldom if ever still, much of this dust will never settle. And, since it is constantly with us, it is called "resident dust."

10 The dustiest room in the house is the kitchen. This is because dust there gets sticky from triglycerides which are released when fatty foods are cooked. This greasy dust then forms a velvety mat just like the one all of you probably have on the top of your refrigerators right now.

11 Dust may look alive, because it probably is. Interestingly enough, there is more than just inert matter in our dust. It is teeming with micro-organisms and their unborn children. [Laughter] Any number of insects along with molds, mildews, and—in extreme cases—small plants, may be living in your dust right now. Penny Ward-Moser, the author of *The Real Dirt on Dust,* had her household dust analyzed by the Maryland Medical Laboratories to find out just what was living in her house besides her, her husband, and her cat. She found a fungus, which is a noted cause of ear and respiratory infection, various colorful forms of penicillin, and a few less pleasant fungi. But, the real kicker came from the dust off her air conditioner intake and from her ceiling fan. They had gangrene. Micrologist Chris Coruthers explains

that this is not at all uncommon, because these types of bacteria will commonly enclose themselves in hard spores and let the wind carry them where it will.

12 Perhaps the most fascinating inhabitant of our dust is the *dermatophagoides farinae*—the house dust mite. These mites were discovered in 1965 and since then we have found that there are fifteen species in the world, all of which are so small that ten will fit inside a period. They have a life span of only forty-five to sixty days. They feed off the approximately fifty million skin scales that we shed every day, although, happily, they cannot live off living skin. Instead, they live in beds, stuffed furniture and, of course, dust balls. David Bodanis, in his book *The Secret House*, tells us that forty-two thousand of these mites may live on one ounce of mattress dust. That works out to an approximate two million on a double bed. Talk about strangers in the night. [Laughter]

13 Now that we have seen the inanimate and the animate worlds of dust, let's see how these worlds affect us. The two most apparent manifestations concern the atmosphere, and our health.

14 Once dust particles are caught up into the air, they usually float high into the sky where they become the nuclei for the formation of water droplets. If there were no dust, we would have no clouds. In addition to this, dust particles in the air, depending on their size, scatter light of different wavelengths. When the sun is high in the sky its rays do not pass through much dust, thus making it appear as yellow light. But, at sunset, when its angle is lower and its rays will pass through much more dust, the sun in the sky may appear a firey red.

15 This is because the smaller particles of dust—which are the ones usually in the air—scatter the shorter waves at the blue end of the light spectrum allowing the red light at the other end of the spectrum to reach our eyes. Now, if some dust event should occur, such as the great Chicago fire, which would put a lot of large particles into the air, the red light would be scattered making the sun appear cool and the moon blue. The conditions for this phenomenon very rarely happen, which is why, dust historians tell us, we have the phrase "once in a Blue Moon."

16 Dust can also affect our health. Many people hit with storms in the 1933 dust bowl event suffocated right where they stood. Others developed impacted bronchial tubes—an almost unheard-of condition under normal circumstances. Doctors would thump and massage patients until they could expand their lungs enough to cough up pencil-shaped columns of dust.

17 These dust storms are a very unusual occurrence, the likes of which we will probably never encounter in our lifetimes. But, according to the American Lung Association, the dust that we find in our houses and in our air can affect us in a variety of ways. Bacterial and fungus infections are caused by inhaling certain active organisms. Irritation of the nose and throat is caused by inhaling certain structurally scratchy particles of dust such as those from asbestos or insulation.

18 Internal tissue damage occurs when radioactive decay products cling to dust and are inhaled. Trapped in your lungs, these decay products will break down further, and by doing so, will release small bursts of energy which can damage lung tissue and lead to lung cancer.

19 All lung diseases caused by dust are called pneumoconiosis, a word of Greek derivation meaning "dusty lung." There are many different types of pneumoconiosis, all specific to the type of dust that causes it. Most of these diseases are associated with coal miners or stone workers who are exposed to these dusts over long periods of time. But, they are certainly not the only people who are affected with the diseases.

20 In addition to lung diseases, there are also systemic disorders which are caused by the blood absorbing toxic dusts and producing allergic reactions. Concerning allergic reactions, keep in mind that dust is made up of particles from many types of substances. So, a person might develop a reaction to certain materials in the dust. The reaction could then be triggered by inhalation of the dust containing these materials. Edward Baker, a scientist who studies mites for the Department of Agriculture, tells us that most people who believe themselves to be allergic to dust are actually allergic to the dust mite, or the approximately twenty fecal pellets these mites produce every day.

21 We have seen that there are a variety of types of dust, ranging from soil to rubber dust from our automobile tires. Also, we have examined the microscopic world of dust, noting that it includes such things as penicillin, fungi, and several types of dust mites. Finally, we have seen that dust affects our atmosphere and our health.

22 Dust is the dictionary of our lives, consisting of every imaginable material, hosting a metropolis of micro-organisms, and giving us beautiful sunsets as well as lung diseases. We can see that there is much more to dust than meets the eye, and that the study of such particulate matter has gone well beyond the vacuum cleaner. As hard as it may be to admit it, your mother was right—there *is* stuff growing under your bed. [Laughter, applause]

A Student Speech to Persuade

Donate Blood
Chris O'Keefe

Chris O'Keefe's persuasive speech to actuate was delivered at the 1987 public speaking competition of the Interstate Oratorical Association. At that time, speaker O'Keefe was a student at George Mason University, Fairfax, Virginia. Note that the action he recommends is realistic, for giving blood is something that the members of the audience can do in their local communities. Also, notice how carefully the speaker states and qualifies his sources, and how nicely he uses a moving, personal experience to open and close the speech.

The text of the speech is from Winning Orations: 1987, *and is published here with the permission of the Interstate Oratorical Association.*

1 On December 12, 1964, a "healthy" eight-pound baby boy was born at the George Washington Hospital in Washington, D.C. Although the child appeared healthy at first, the advanced medical technology of the age was able to determine that in fact, this was an illusion. Internal bleeding had begun and a blood transfusion was necessary. Although the child's blood type was a common one—O-positive—local blood banks and hospitals were depleted of this blood type at the time, and a transfer from out of state was necessary. However, Dr. Richard Melbourne assessed, "The time it would take to transfer blood from out of state would mean the child's life."

2 It was then that nurse Christine Miller stepped to the forefront to make the first blood donation of her life. Mrs. Miller had always been afraid of the needle, but now was able to see for the first time the invaluable contribution that donating blood makes. That it, literally, saves another's life. Mrs. Miller stated in a personal interview, "If more people had the type of experience I had, there would be more registered blood donors."

3 Unfortunately, most people don't appreciate the valuable contribution their donation of blood would make, and those who do understand may have irrational fears regarding contracting some disease, such as AIDS. To understand the ramifications of individuals like ourselves not donating blood, we need to understand the problem, including how and why this issue has returned to the forefront in the 1980s, and why people hesitate to donate blood. Also, we need to see what steps it takes to become a registered blood donor.

4 From the turn of the century, right through to the 1940s, there was not much need for blood drives or filled blood banks simply because medical science had not yet reached a stage where blood transfusions were common. Moving into the 50s and 60s, however, emergency surgeries were becoming more and more common, and copious amounts of stored blood were necessary. The American Medical Association joined with the Red Cross to mount far-reaching advertising campaigns designed to inform Americans of the need for blood and to encourage them to become registered blood donors. These efforts were so successful that the following decade saw this country's constant need for blood consistently assuaged.

5 But the 1980s have definitely been a different situation, with the first indications coming from New York City. The January 1, 1984 issue of the *New York Times* carried a strong plea for citizens to visit blood donating centers, but to no avail. The August 2, 1986 issue of the *New York Times* stated that blood supplies in New York had dropped to a three-year low. According to the Greater New York Blood Center, supplies are so low today that blood actually needs to be imported from Europe where there is a surplus. It is shocking to learn that with one donation equaling one unit, and each unit having a processing fee of over $100, that in 1986 the Greater New York Blood Center imported over 75,000 units of Euroblood.

6 The fact is, blood supplies had mysteriously and suddenly declined all over the nation. According to an American Association of Blood Banks report, published in January of 1986, every blood bank in this country contains, on the average, 13 percent less blood than is necessary for standard operation. The drastic drop-off point for this nation's blood supply can be traced back to the summer of 1982—the AIDS scare.

7 Acquired Immune Deficiency Syndrome is the disease caused by the HTLV III virus, and it is an irrational fear of receiving AIDS by donating blood that has prevented the donation by millions of Americans. As a direct consequence, thousands upon thousands needlessly die each year because of the lack of blood. It is common knowledge that AIDS is a disease of the blood, so many people are afraid that by donating blood they are putting themselves at risk. However, as long ago as November of 1985, the American Medical Association published a report stating clearly, "It is only when you *receive* blood through a transfusion that any risk is run. The blood donor is at *no risk whatsoever.*" Unfortunately, many Americans remain uneducated to this point. According to an ABC news poll published in the March 12, 1987 issue of the *Washington Post,* one out of every three Americans believes that they can receive AIDS by donating blood.

8 The Red Cross Association, blood supplier for half of America's blood, states that there is another major reason people do not donate: "They are simply not asked." A recent news story brings this issue to light. On January 4th of this year, an Amtrak passenger train collided with a Conrail freight train on the outskirts of Baltimore, Maryland. According to the January 5 *Washington Post,* the blood supplies from local blood centers and hospitals were depleted to aid those passengers who were critically injured. But still there was not enough blood. Local newscasters then made a plea to Baltimore residents urging them to visit blood centers immediately. Hundreds arrived to donate, and in interviews conducted afterward, almost all stated that they felt good about what they had done—that they had made a valuable contribution and had made a difference. We must remember that whether these disasters are brought to our attention or not, the silent need isn't any less significant.

9 Well, the solution is not to be found in a letter to Congress or in a speech on the mall—rather, it is found in ourselves. Becoming a registered blood donor is easy to do. Simply contact your local hospital or Red Cross center and ask, "When is the best time to come in and donate blood?" When you donate there also will be other benefits. For example, you will receive a free "mini-physical" that tests your blood for hepatitis, syphilis, and the HTLV III virus. Furthermore, many blood centers will give you credit points when you donate so that if *you* are ever in need of blood, it will be supplied at no cost.

10 Some of us may be in a situation where we simply *cannot* donate blood for health or other reasons. There is still a great deal to be done. If you work for a company, inform your employer that a company that sponsors a blood drive can have the wages of the employees who donate deducted as a contribution. If fifty employees who earn $20 an hour take one hour to donate blood, the United States government will pick up the $1,000 tab.

11 In order to sponsor a blood drive, Terry Goche, a public affairs representative at the Red Cross National Headquarters in Washington, D.C., states that you need only follow a simple, five-step process. First, call your local Red Cross chapter and ask to speak to a donor recruiter. Second, establish the place. If a room cannot be found, a bloodmobile can be sent. Third, establish the time the blood drive will take place. Fourth—advertise it. The Red Cross will not only supply posters stating the time and place, but in

many cases will supply volunteers to help put up the posters. And fifth—provide recognition, such as posting an office bulletin or a donor honor roll acknowledging those who donated. The Red Cross will visit any work area if there are at least thirty individuals who donate. The United Blood Services will visit if there are only ten.

12 In 1985, the J. Walter Thompson Advertising Agency spent $500,000 to create a slogan for the Red Cross to encourage people to donate blood. After all the testing and all the research, the result was one, simple word: "GIVE," with the "V" shaped like a heart. The word connoted that donating blood is a gift-giving, with blood itself as the gift. Now, I appreciate that "gift" more than most, for on December 12, 1964, I was the eight-pound baby boy who without Christine Miller's donation would not be here today to speak about donating blood.

13 As I've been told the story of Mrs. Miller's donation through the years, I've become increasingly aware of the fact that most people don't appreciate the valuable contribution their donation of blood would make. Hopefully, that appreciation exists now. So, if you can donate, do; if you can't, encourage others. But above all remember that what is at stake are human lives.

INDEX